NUCLEAR DESIGNS

D0081736

BRUCE D. LARKIN

NUCLEAR DESIGNS

Great Britain, France, & China in the Global Governance of Nuclear Arms

TRANSACTION PUBLISHERS
NEW BRUNSWICK (U.S.A.) AND LONDON (U.K.)

Copyright © 1996 by Transaction Publishers, New Brunswick, New Jersey 08903.

All rights reserved under International and Pan-American Copyright Conventions. No part of this book may be reproduced or transmitted in any form or by any means, electronic or mechanical, including photocopy, recording, or any information storage and retrieval system, without prior permission in writing from the publisher. All inquiries should be addressed to Transaction Publishers, Rutgers—The State University, New Brunswick, New Jersey 08903.

This book is printed on acid-free paper that meets the American National Standard for Permanence of Paper for Printed Library Materials.

Library of Congress Catalog Number: 95-23279
ISBN: 1-56000-239-5
Printed in the United States of America

Library of Congress Cataloging-in-Publication Data

Larkin, Bruce D., 1936-
Nuclear designs : Great Britain, France, and China in the global governance of nuclear arms / Bruce D. Larkin.
p. cm.
Includes bibliographical references and index.
ISBN 1-56000-239-5 (alk. paper)
1. Nuclear weapons--Government policy--Great Britain. 2. Nuclear weapons--Government policy--France. 3. Nuclear weapons--Government policy--China. 4. Nuclear arms control. 5. Nuclear nonproliferation. 6. World politics--1989- I. Title.
U264.5.G7L37 1995
327.1'74--dc20

95-23279
CIP

Contents

Appendices

Figures and Tables

Introduction

The Cold War has given way to new concerns for global security policy. Nationalism, authoritarianism, economic uncertainty, local wars, and puzzlement about collective action dominate the new agenda. Still, Cold War legacies persist. Among the most vexing are nuclear programs, stocks, and deployments.

We invoke here only as a memory the keen edge of fear associated with the nuclear Cold War. Nonetheless, the five declared nuclear weapon states—United States, Russia, Britain, France, and China—continue to modernize their forces and deploy them, ready for use. Others have followed suit, or aspire to do so. Few doubt that development continues in Israel, Pakistan, and India. The nuclear intentions of North Korea, Iraq, and Iran are subject to scrutiny.

There is, however, a new candor in US—Russian nuclear relations, which makes possible frank conversation about the utility and dangers of nuclear arms.

The Choices

At this unexpected conjuncture lies a choice among alternative nuclear futures. If the Cold War inoculated states against a return to runaway nuclear arming, the choices come down to three: the *status quo*, disengagement, or abolition. Measures of calculated disengagement—withdrawing tactical nuclear weapons, removing nuclear weapons from surface ships, shifting away from land-based strategic missiles with many warheads, force reductions—have already been carried out by Russia and the United States. More such measures are promised. These are welcome, but they take place in a context which confirms status quo nuclearism. Only if prompt use is rendered impossible—a "radical disengagement" including non-deployment—could nuclear weapon states insulate themselves against risks of use inherent in deployed forces. Arguments along these lines might appeal to those who reject status quo nuclearism but hesitate to abandon a "trump card" playable in some uncertain future. They might also appeal to those who anticipated that proposing multilateral abolition would open them to charges of naiveté and treason. But advocates of abolition argue that the surest, clearest, and most enforceable security against nuclear war lies at zero, not in half measures. This text does not attempt to resolve the issue between "radical disengagement" and abolition. Instead, observing the contradiction between the weapons states' nuclearism and the norm of non-proliferation, it argues that the claim that nuclear weapons in a few hands are safer than nuclear weapons in no hands should be subject to close and wide scrutiny. Stronger, it argues that nuclear weapon states have a compelling obligation to explore and consider alternatives to status quo nuclearism.

Our point of entrée into global nuclear issues lies through the nuclear weapons programs of Britain, France, and China. This text explores how their substantial capabilities and declared purposes bear on choices for a nuclear future, and shows how each of them justifies the status quo. Britain and France say their nuclear forces are key to their security in the present and in future worlds. China would not give up her force except as part of a comprehensive renunciation. The text introduces the arguments they offer for their weapons and sets out the nuclear establishments, political institutions, concerns, and public views which illuminate their belief that nuclear weapons serve their interests.

The conclusion we are compelled to draw is that the three "minipowers" not only reinforce nuclearism—in which nuclear war is held at bay by terror and uncertain self-restraint—but also by their example complicate the case against proliferation. If they should decide, instead, that abolition or agreed and safeguarded non-deployment would in fact enhance their security, they could make the case to Russia and the United States as no others could make it. It would become possible as a pragmatic matter to bring the two preeminent nuclear states into an abolition or non-deployment regime, and they could make a compelling case that others should renounce nuclear deployment and nuclear aspiration.

Nuclearism and the Nuclearist State

We define "nuclearism" as the belief that the state achieves net advantage from holding nuclear weapons. The *nuclearist state* would choose to maintain a nuclear force even if all other states declared they would not.

But does that actually characterize the five self-acknowledged nuclear weapon states? The first difficulty is that declaratory policy has taken quite the other position. In some statements, at least, each of the five has said its "long-term" objective is global denuclearization—while stressing the obstacles and preconditions which must be met. The second difficulty is that all explain their programs primarily as programs to deter (or "dissuade") other nuclear-armed states from nuclear threats or attack. As long as other states appear committed to keeping their forces deployed, nuclear weapon states have no need to explain clearly whether they are *nuclearists*—in our sense—or not.

Still, the five seem to be following a path in which the question of abandoning nuclear deployments is never posed. It is in this sense that we are on solid ground in describing them as servants of the status quo. Even their modest measures of disengagement protect their core strategic nuclear forces from political criticism. In this status quo world, some reductions in warheads would occur, especially as large forces obsolesce. Cuts could be recorded in agreements modeled on SALT and START and proliferation codified in adjustments to the NPT. Despite the appearance of "control" and "reduction," however, over the years—more slowly than predicted thirty years ago, but inexorably nonetheless—more states would succeed in arming themselves with nuclear weapons.

Why Consider Only Britain, China and France?

In addition to the five declared nuclear weapon states whose nuclear programs are known and formally acknowledged, other states have more ambiguous nuclear programs. India acknowledged testing a nuclear device; it has not admitted making nuclear weapons, but has a visible missile program, and analysts attribute to India a complementary weapons program as well. Israel declines to declare its nuclear weapons, despite widespread belief that it has an inventory of perhaps 200 warheads. Pakistan denies having nuclear weapons but "acknowledges" that others believe it has weapons ready-to-assemble; there seems no doubt that there is an active weapons program. Belarus, Kazakhstan, and Ukraine inherited Soviet weapons on their territory when the Soviet Union broke up, but do not have national nuclear programs. South Africa made a few nuclear weapons and then, by its account, disassembled them and abandoned the program. Iraq was cut short, its physical facilities destroyed, but its expertise intact. Four states which were positioned to pursue nuclear weapons have decided, in early stages, not to do so: Canada, Sweden, Brazil, and Argentina. The intentions of North Korea and Iran remain unclear. Several industrial states certainly have the technical capacity to move promptly into a nuclear weapons program if they chose to do so (including Switzerland, Germany, and Japan).

Why confine this study, for the most part, to Britain, France, and China, rather than some other choice of states?

Russian and US arms control measures are negotiated against a backdrop of British, French, and Chinese nuclear inventories. In asking whether cuts beyond START II would enhance their security, Russia and the United States would first, of course, query the bilateral stability of their own resultant force postures. But the next question—and more pressing as US and Russian warheads numbers declined—would be whether the resultant forces took adequate regard of British, French, and Chinese holdings. Could Russian or US "secure second-strike capability" be put at risk simply because launchers were fewer? Could strategic stability be suddenly upset by covert procurement and "breakout"? Could Britain, France, or China abandon their present commitment to non-proliferation?[1] And would stability withstand pooling weapons, or transfers among allies?[2]

1. Any nuclear weapon state could supply prospective proliferators with equipment, materials and expertise useful for a nuclear program and for nuclear delivery systems. The United States charges that Chinese and Russian assistance and sales to non-nuclear nations undermine non-proliferation. They reply that they are engaged only in permissible commercial transfers. France, now a committed advocate of non-proliferation, assisted nuclear research programs in

Of course, US and Russian weapons threaten second-tier states, as well. Second-tier *uncertainty* about Russian and US intentions can translate into stubborn resistance to any arms control concessions which Russia and the United States might seek from Britain, France, and China. Can China be confident that its deterrent remains viable, even after Washington and Moscow accept cuts, if Russian and US abilities to locate Chinese systems become increasingly acute? Because the United States and Russia have better satellite surveillance capabilities and the attack submarines to follow and threaten Chinese SSBNs, China could well insist on retaining greater numbers to offset the vulnerability of its forces.

Each of the Three identifies strongly as a "nuclear weapon state." It has, after all, spent heavily to acquire the industrial and military capabilities which constitute its nuclear status. Within government, and among those active in political affairs, the arguments on behalf of nuclear weapons have been vigorously made and repeatedly certified. Political capital invested in nuclearism may be even more significant than its economic cost. The momentum to retain both weapons in hand and the productive capability to fabricate new ones, therefore, runs deep and strong.

It follows that the Three—like the United States and Russia—must be significant players in moves to non-proliferation, management, reduction, or abolition of nuclear weapons, if such moves are to take place. Nuclear disengagement and disarmament can be achieved only by consent.

Given, then, that lesser nuclear weapon states have a significant role to play in the arms control debate, why have we chosen to focus only on Britain, France, and China? We used three criteria to select the states of interest.

First, the state had to have enough weapons and delivery capabilities to matter. Second, there had to be enough documentary material on the record to make analysis possible; in effect this required that the state have a *declared* program. Third, the program should have

---

Iraq and Israel; and the British government, like that of many other industrial states, permitted non-nuclear but weapons-related and systems-related transactions with Iraq in the 1980s while denying publicly that it was doing so.

2. Britain's Trident II (D-5) missiles are in fact pooled with US missiles.

been deliberate, from the decision to begin nuclear research to the decision to deploy nuclear weapons and delivery systems.

The first criterion excluded small and candidate programs, except as instances in a general discussion of proliferation dangers. The second criterion excluded India, Israel, and Pakistan, and the third Belarus, Kazakhstan, and Ukraine. The Israeli program, according to revelations by Mordechai Vanunu, may have achieved 200 nuclear weapons, deliverable by aircraft and missile—a substantial force which creates issues not only for the Middle East but for nuclear weapons control more generally. A case could have been made for Israel's inclusion in this study, but the rather slender public record tilted against doing so.

In the end, only Britain, France, and China maintain sufficient warhead inventories and production capabilities to have strong effects on how Russia and the United States view the adequacy of their own strategic capabilities. This could change. Israeli, Indian, or Pakistani capabilities could grow. Ukraine might seize and command the systems on her territory. But for now Britain, France, and China stand apart.

A Note on Methodology

The approach used here to identify significance and sift for reliability is that customary in narrative historical and political studies. At some junctures the reader may also notice three more deliberate methods. One is familiar *capabilities analysis*, the second *scriptic analysis*. The third is *focused comparison*.

Capabilities analysis establishes what weapons systems the state has procured and deployed, and its underlying productive capabilities. Merely knowing a state's capabilities does not permit conclusions about what that state's leaders actually plan to do. However, there is a compelling logic in the other direction: the state cannot perform acts for which it does not have the means, and its ability to create means (in some specified period of time) is limited if the precursors are not in place. Military and political analysts do, in fact, infer intentions from capabilities. Students of two countries' relations will therefore be alert to how each reads capabilities to discern intentions.

Under the rubric *scriptic analysis* we bring together several familiar questions asked by students of political decisions: How does the leadership interpret the world in which it must act? What strategic practices does it consider appropriate to this situation? What positive examples from its past political history does it draw upon as analogs to the present? And what negative examples is the leadership bound and determined to avoid in the future? What stories do they tell about prospective foes?

Political leaders, acting under uncertainty, compensate for incomplete knowledge by interpreting their historical experience as a carrier of "lessons." A leadership need not be iron-bound to an "operational code" to draw repeatedly on experience its members believe revelatory. The future is foreseen in stories of the past. Decision-makers employ accounts and *scripts*—generalized accounts centered on appropriate steps to take in a situation of a certain kind—when they debate just what kind of situation they confront, and then make key choices to procure, deploy, abandon, or brandish nuclear weapons.

Focused comparison turns on close study of likeness and dissimilarity between cases, highlighting characteristics associated with differences in salient outcomes. George and Smoke applied "focused comparison" to foreign relations episodes in which an opponent challenged US objectives in a "third area" and policy-makers responded by endeavoring to deter.[3]

---

3. Theirs is the classic work employing this technique in security studies: Alexander George and Richard Smoke, *Deterrence in American Foreign Policy. Theory and Practice* (New York: Columbia University Press, 1974), pp. 95-97. The method has some kinship to "statistical-correlational" approaches, they write, in that it "proceeds by asking a limited number of questions or testing a limited number of hypotheses," but is also kindred to the intensive case-study method, in that cases are examined in some depth. The method employs "a standardized set of questions or hypotheses" to ensure "comparability of results":

   "By specifying the differing circumstances or causes that led to different results in the various cases, the investigator can illuminate in an explicit, orderly fashion the complexity of deterrence phenomena and the variation in outcomes. Comparison of cases can thus lead to what might be termed 'contingent general-

Here, for example, we will note that in both Britain and France, tight budgets gave added reason to strip down the nuclear weapons program and commit to a minimum deterrent. However, the French stress on an autonomous program required maintaining missile-frame and missile engine capabilities which remained outside British consideration.

For the most part our use of these methods is implicit. Methods are sometimes used in conjunction with one another. The reader will recognize them in what we choose to treat and the arguments we make. In the concluding chapter, however, we will take up each approach in turn, identifying how it has shaped our analysis, and then discuss why these methods are well-suited to a study of nuclear futures.

The Path

The first and last chapters aside, this work is in three sections. The first is chapter 2, an overview of British, French, and Chinese nuclear programs. It sets out present inventories and statements of policy.

The second section—consisting of chapters 3 though 6—develops the arms control positions of Britain, France, and China, and explores subjects central to global nuclear arms control. Chapter 3, on proliferation, takes as its fulcra the Non-Proliferation Treaty and the proposed Comprehensive Test Ban. Chapter 4 addresses the somewhat different issue of reductions by nuclear weapon states. Under the rubric "coordinations" chapter 5 confronts the fact that the nuclear weapon states have engaged in many transactions among themselves, and continue to do so; they recognize common interests, and among those interests, many would argue, is safeguarding their nuclear eminence. Effective reassurance turns on verification: chapter 6 brings in

---

izations'—'if circumstances A then outcome O'—which can be an important part of theory and have important implications for practice.

". . . what the focused comparison method can offer in place of a high degree of formal verification may be something more valuable—potentially a significantly greater degree of relevance to real policy problems than is usually enjoyed by statistically validated generalizations (or, for that matter, the conclusions of a single case study)."

changing technologies, and states' commitments to them, which create new capacities to verify.

In the third section—chapters 7 through 9—we take up the *whys* and *why nots* of British, French, and Chinese commitments to nuclear weapons. Chapter 7 tours institutional and public engagement with nuclear forces. Chapter 8 asks what are the costs? what are the risks? And chapter 9 explores the reasons why—despite costs and risks—successive leadership generations, citing threats and evincing fears, have insisted that nuclear weapons make for greater security.

We began this Introduction by anticipating some of the conclusions of chapter 10. It may help in reading the text to appreciate that we take the evidence to require three important conclusions. One will be familiar to students of the non-proliferation regime: Britain, France, and China, by insisting on the value of nuclear weapons to their security, make the case that any state, if its leaders are concerned for its security, should acquire nuclear weapons. Those who follow French, Chinese, or British affairs will recognize the second: that among political leadership in each of the three states are strong advocates of continued deployment and development of nuclear weapons.

Our third important conclusion is that nuclearism's permanence should not be taken for granted: there should be express private and governmental initiatives to model and simulate non-nuclear practice. Since the position of each nuclear weapon state is different, however, what must be rigorously examined are not only global terms—institutions, verification methods, challenge practices, "societal verification"—but the express reassurances which each state must achieve if a given non-nuclear alternative is to pass the test of domestic political acceptability. Designing, testing and assessing alternatives should be done in the open, not only because that is the best protection against distortion and resistance, but because the stakes will require public assent. Alternatives certainly also require canvassing means to dampen the possibility of "conventional" war, given the perverse currency of the nondisconfirmable claim that nuclear weapons prevent war.

Finally, the reader might better appreciate how we have explored the quandary of nuclear weapons by bearing in mind the question to which this inquiry repeatedly returned: if the institutional and pragmatic skills exist to design and sustain the *management* of existing nuclear weapons without unauthorized use or nuclear war—as advocates of holding nuclear weapons insist—would it be any more difficult to design and sustain a regime in which nuclear weapons were prohibited?

• • •

Acknowledgments

I am especially grateful to the founders of the University of California Institute on Global Conflict and Cooperation—Herbert York and his associates James Skelly and Allen Greb—and to the present director, Susan Shirk, who have distinguished themselves by their encouragement of studies in this subject.

A number of students assisted me in managing materials, most helpfully Shana McGough, Deborah Jordan, Joshua Lieb, Jon Carnero, and—taking on also production issues as the text reached closure—Mirna Saab.

Bob Holmes, an accomplished science writer, commented extensively on draft and organization. I have sought to respect Jenn Pattee's insistence that text be direct and accessible. Jenny Pournelle contributed a decisive intervention. I am especially mindful of each of their contributions and of the help of Lisa Hunter and Marianna Alves.

Many kind people gave their time to discuss these issues with me, and of course I relieve them of any responsibility for the views expressed in this study, which at many points part from their own. A number of present and former officials clarified the positions of their respective governments. Colleagues generously offered their views and contacts: in France, especially Pascal Boniface, Jean-Paul Hébert, Jérôme Paolini, Alain Carton, François Thual, Venance Journé, and Bruno Barrillot; in Britain, Patricia Chilton, Lawrence Freedman, John Simpson, and Beatrice Heuser; and in China personnel of several centers, including the Institute of American Studies of the Chinese Academy of Social Sciences, Institute of Applied Physics and Computational Mathematics, Institute of Contemporary International Relations, and the Chinese Institute of International Strategic Studies.

Notes record my debts to the pioneering work of Stan Norris and his colleagues at the Natural Resources Defense Council, and John Lewis, Xue Litai and Hua Di of the Center for International Security and Arms Control at Stanford University.

Interviews and archival research were aided by funds from the United States Institute of Peace, University of California Institute on Global Conflict and Cooperation, and the Committee on Faculty Research of the University of California at Santa Cruz. The opinions, findings, and conclusions or recommendations expressed in this work are those of the author and do not necessarily reflect the views of the United States Institute of Peace. With respect to texts of British government documents, Crown copyright is reproduced with the permission of the Controller of HMSO. Roger Mortimore of MORI contributed selected opinion survey data.

This study is an element of ongoing work in the Adlai E. Stevenson Program on Global Security at the University of California at Santa Cruz; and we invite colleagues to bring errors, suggestions and new materials to our attention [china@cats.ucsc.edu]. A Web page on this study is maintained at [http://www.webcom.com/~larkin/]. Donors and the Stevenson Program are ritually absolved of responsibility for the views in this text.

My wife, Helen Kruse Larkin, must however accept responsibility for the support and encouragement she tendered during the unfolding of this study, and her remarkable patience at my absences and distractions.

Lehenagh, Lislevane, Co. Cork
1 July 1995

1

Nuclear Choices

Boutros Boutros-Ghali, opening the 1995 Nuclear Non-Proliferation Treaty Review and Extension Conference, called for an end to nuclear weapons: "No more testing. No more production. . . . Reduction and destruction of all nuclear weapons and the means to make them should be humanity's great common cause."

By contrast, on the day the conference opened *The New York Times* quoted a recent remark of the US ambassador to the Conference that calls for more rapid disarmament were "propaganda." "American officials," it reported, "say it is unrealistic to expect a nuclear-free world anytime soon."[1]

Abolish nuclear weapons? Or keep them for the indefinite future? Of course, these questions have been on the table since 1945. But they are posed with fresh significance in the 1990s. Russia and the United States have declared that they are not enemies, and Britain, France, and China also disavow having enemies among the nuclear powers. Either Russia or the United States, by itself, could prevent Boutros-Ghali's cause from achieving its goal. Despite that—or perhaps because of it—the question *what global nuclear policy best serves our interest* is posed to Beijing, Paris, and London, as well as to Moscow and Washington. The second-tier Three can act to sustain the status quo, strengthening those in the United States and Russia who identify nuclear weapons with their national interest. Or they can challenge the status quo, and challenge Russia and the United States to adopt a non-nuclear understanding of their national needs.

The first premise of this book is that Britain, France, and China, in an altered political world, must again consider what global nuclear policies best serve their interests. This chapter introduces the choices available to them. It does not address their forces or procurement plans or explore their technical capabilities. These are taken up later.

1. *The New York Times*, 17 April 1995.

Here we sketch the decision environment of leaderships and publics of the three "second-tier" nuclear powers, locating them in the political issues they must confront.

The second premise is that anyone considering nuclear futures must take the British, French, and Chinese forces into account. How Britain, France, and China respond to proposed nuclear futures must have enormous impact on what global future is chosen. Boutros-Ghali's cause would fail if Britain, France, or China were to refuse it adamantly.

Do nuclear weapons serve their holders' "national interests"? Are they useful? Weapons are a practical matter. They are designed and deployed for practical effects. It is not surprising, then, that there are many different answers to the question "are nuclear weapons useful?," since utility is a function of circumstance. A weapon to deter nuclear attack is ill-suited to protecting delivery of food and medicine.

Moreover, in the practical world "useful" steps have unwanted consequences, not easily weighed against intended purpose. Bearing such difficulties in mind, however, we find that the principal dispositions toward nuclear weapons turn heavily on people's answers to two questions: "are they useful?" and "are their inherent dangers tolerable?" Not surprisingly, those who are drawn to nuclear weapons' usefulness also imagine that states can manage them.

US and Soviet (Russian) arms control policies have changed radically since 1985. The changes can be summed up as reductions, revelations, consultations. What effects have these had on the Three? Like Russia and the United States, each of the Three has also been compelled to define its stance on nuclear proliferation more clearly—and more publicly. In the mid-1990s that has meant declaring positions on several dicey subjects: is the global non-proliferation regime adequate? how could Israel, Pakistan and India be induced to come in? should we abandon nuclear tests? if so, how much should we spend on simulations? and how can we use the Non-Proliferation Treaty to advance non-proliferation without endangering our own nuclear forces?

The NPT Review and Extension Conference itself has reshaped the debate. Non-nuclear weapon states are emboldened. Japan has found a new voice. Abolition is a topic for discussion as it was not before May 1995. The world has, in this respect, changed.

Nuclear Choices

Setting nuance aside, there are six distinct positions about the political and military use of nuclear weapons. Each reflects judgments of utility, danger, and the capacity of the State to manage nuclear weapons safely.

The nuclear status quo—in which Britain, France, and China take part—bridges three of the principal positions.

1. *Nuclear war-fighters* talk of how to use nuclear weapons, either because they are the best weapons for a hypothetical war, or because others will use them. States either deploy nuclear weapons or submit. Nuclear weapons are best understood as very powerful conventional weapons.

   No longer often voiced, this view circulated after World War II, expressing the script of arming and fighting which had grown up in the pre-nuclear era.

2. *Wielders* share with war-fighters the conviction that having nuclear weapons gives an advantage, but they recognize that thinking of nuclear weapons as "old bombs made large" will lead to fateful and irrecoverable disasters.

   On some points—that nuclear weapons will not go away, and that states which intend to remain free must have them—wielders and war-fighters work from similar premises. Wielders see in nuclear weapons a source of prestige, influence, and—to speak bluntly—power. They believe they can manage a nuclear capacity responsibly and exercise it for political advantage. In rare circumstances nuclear weapons might actually be used, with great care and discrimination. Most who hold this view, however, stop short of imagining their actual use: political gain is to be achieved by being *able* to detonate nuclear weapons, not by actually doing so. These are *nuclear wielders*.

3. *Holders* follow nuclear wielders in believing that nuclear weapons will not go away, that the state can manage nuclear weapons without losing control, and that the nuclear state receives prestige and influence. Their defining position, however, is that nuclear weapons are necessary for deterrence of other nuclear states, and

to meet contingencies which might arise beyond the horizon of foresight.

They do not expect ever to detonate a nuclear weapon against an enemy, and are quite explicit about it. They actively reassure other states that *barring nuclear attack, or a threat as grave* they have no intention of using or threatening to use their nuclear weapons.

4. *Arms controllers* center on management, control, and stabilization of nuclear forces. They are less optimistic that nuclear weapons can be safely maintained in inventory. Nuclear weapons imply risk. Since there are several nuclear states each must maintain a credible deterrent capability, but priority should be given to steps—typically multilateral steps—to reduce the dangers inherent in nuclear weapons. The only reason to have nuclear weapons is to deter nuclear attack, so other missions, such as deterring conventional attack and backing up assertive strategies, should be refused.

5. *Disengagers* depart from arms controllers in emphasizing the extraordinary destructive capacities of nuclear weapons. In its reformist version, this means deterrence can be achieved at low levels, subject to careful control; forces are *selectively* disengaged. In its radical version, it is deeply pessimistic about the long-term capacity of states to manage nuclear forces without using them. Existing forces should be subject to severe controls, put insofar as possible beyond ready access by military or civil authority.

6. *Abolitionists*, like disengagers, stress the destructiveness of nuclear weapons. They doubt that "disengagement"—even complete non-deployment—can adequately guard against use. In any case, they contend that abolition is politically easier to achieve, and technically easier to enforce, than any scheme which retains nuclear weapons under national, joint, or international control.

These six positions, then, range between two simply stated poles: one, that security lies in being ready to fight a nuclear war, and the other, that security lies in being unable to fight a nuclear war. In practice, of course, those committed to one position typically hold some dispositions and attitudes characteristic of adjoining positions. These views can be found among the military, political leadership, defense analysts, and public of all five declared nuclear weapon states.

FIGURE 1.1
Six Views of Nuclear Weapons

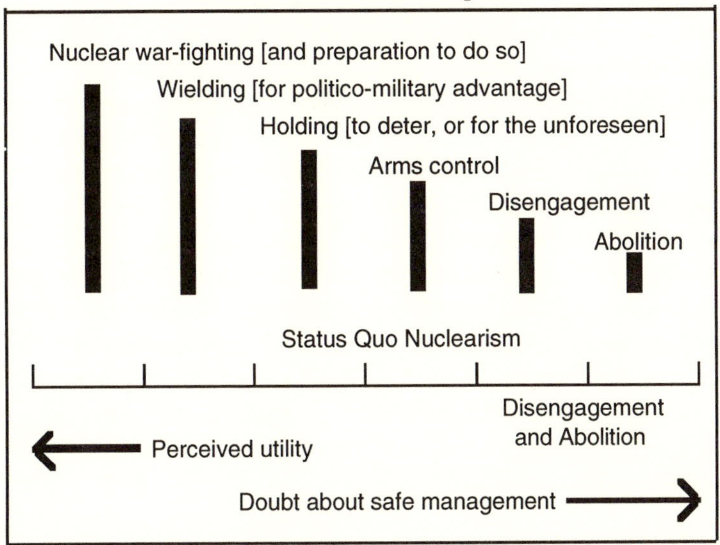

The consensual range *in all five declared nuclear weapon states* centers on holders, but includes wielders, arms controllers, and disengagers as well. (China's declaratory policy urges "complete prohibition and thorough destruction" of nuclear weapons, but its practical position—as long as others have nuclear weapons—is like that of other holders.) Internal arguments concern what capabilities to retain or create and how far toward disengagement and abolition the state should move. Where is the greatest security to be found?

Positions of the Three

Where does each of the Three stand on this spectrum? It may be useful to speak of the center of gravity of the consensus in a given country, provided we understand that it is a rough judgment.

French arguments in 1992 revealed sharp internal divisions.

Some officials and public figures argued vigorously that France required a nuclear capacity with which to threaten any "third-world dictator" who might in the future challenge French security; in citing Qadaffi of Libya or Sadaam Hussein of Iraq they showed themselves to be wielders, threatening some future nuclear proliferator or a state which might mount a non-nuclear assault on French interests. Others, mainstream holders, argued for the status quo. A third group were holders, but strongly interested in arms control. They wanted a capable and autonomous French deterrent, but a truly minimum one, in a world in which proliferation and Star Wars initiatives were restrained by international agreement. The *Livre Blanc sur la Défense* of early 1994, a compromise document embracing views of "holders" and "arms controllers," insists on the necessity of deterring threats to France but keeps "wielding" at arm's length.

Britain, by contrast, was deeply hunkered down to protect its special position as a nuclear state. Little public debate takes place. Wielding is not an issue. Onetime Labour Party calls for British unilateral nuclear disarmament are now almost completely silent.

Britain's fundamental position was set out succinctly by Malcolm Rifkind, secretary of state for defense, in a talk on 16 November 1993:

> Having achieved a stable and secure system of war-prevention in the Cold War context, we should be in no hurry to throw away the benefits. NATO strategy, and the United Kingdom nuclear contribution within it, is designed to preserve stability at a minimum level of deterrence . . .
>
> Our desire to preserve stability in Europe is matched by our equal determination to foster stability elsewhere, which means preventing the introduction of nuclear weapons . . . The aim must be to secure an international environment in which states are not motivated even to consider proliferation, and in which every possible measure is taken to ensure that the means of proliferation are not made available. . . .
>
> Nuclear weapons will continue to have a positive and constructive role within a particular frame work which has been developed, with difficulty, over decades. Beyond those limits there lie enormous dangers in the proliferation of nuclear weapons.[2]

---

2. House of Commons. Session 1993-94. Defence Committee. Second Report. *Progress of the Trident Programme*. 4 May 1994. Written Evidence. 5. "Excerpt from a speech made by the Secretary of State for Defence, entitled 'UK Defence Strategy: A Continuing Role for Nuclear Weapons?' (17 [*sic*] November

China's position reflects the fact that her deterrent remains incomplete. Beijing continues to voice abolition as declaratory policy—"complete prohibition and thorough destruction"—but simultaneously pursues a fully credible and robust deterrent. Far from urging that nuclear weapons be wielded, consensus focuses on *acquiring* and then *holding* nuclear weapons once acquired. The center is wary of specific nuclear arms control measures, fearing they could be used by Russia and the United States to prevent China's modernization and consolidate US and Russian superiority. So the Chinese consensual range is much narrower than in France or even Britain.

Is the relationship of second-tier states to these five positions distinct from that of Russia and the United States? Or are the five states more nearly similar? At an earlier time—for example, when Khrushchev was blustering with 100 MT weapons, or John Foster Dulles warned of "massive retaliation"—the superpowers acted as wielders to an extent unthinkable, given their small programs, for the second-tier states. With forty years' experience, however, views of large and small nuclear weapons holders have appreciably converged. All are more cautious, less given to displaying their weapons, more aware of the catastrophic effects of large-scale nuclear weapons use for all.

The Non-Use and Non-Proliferation Regimes

Since 1945 the nuclear weapon states have *in effect* maintained a *non-use regime*, but have brandished weapons and made muted threats to use them, both by the simple fact of their deployment and by specific statements, transfers, and changes of alert level at times of confrontation.

Measures against technology transfer were first practiced as unilateral steps to retain front-runner advantage. Later, this *non-proliferation regime* was codified in the Non-Proliferation Treaty (NPT). In addition to its provisions against acquisition of nuclear weapons by new states, the NPT requires good-faith negotiation of disarmament by existing nuclear-weapons states, eventually leading to the abandonment of nuclear weapons.

In that respect the NPT is one element of an *arms control regime*

1993)," p. 34.

or *management regime* posited on joint management of levels, types, deployment, disengagement, and decommissioning of nuclear warheads and delivery systems. Some see arms control as a preliminary to abolition (with interim stability objectives); others view arms control as a means to enhance stability of persistent nuclear forces (while also reassuring the public). The NPT also embraces a norm of *non-possession*, for all non-nuclear weapon states, and commits all adherents—subject to conditions—to realize an *abolition regime*.

"Regime" designates a body of rules and practices, sometimes set down in an agreed text, which clarifies expectations and regulates consensual permissions. These four regimes—non-use, non-proliferation, management, and non-possession—have their sole force from the acts and promises of authoritative officers of states. In some respects they support one another: non-use, for example, works against proliferation, while non-proliferation may support non-use. But pursuing the four regimes at once flirts with inconsistency, and can engender outright conflict. The management of nuclear weapons draws its *raison d'etre* from deterrence, which requires a readiness to use, even if that readiness is intended to serve non-use. Moreover, management implies possession, which contradicts a non-possession regime applied to all. The nuclear weapon states skirt these contradictions by several devices: they talk of the weapons in highly focused contexts—for example, as weapons potentially "in the hands of terrorists"—and they claim management and non-proliferation for the present but abolition for some indefinite future. They take their possession of nuclear weapons as an incontestable fact and right, and aspirations for possession as a criminal wrong.

French, British, and Chinese nuclear programs have implications for the four regimes of non-use, non-proliferation, management, and non-possession. One family of implications follows from the assumption that something akin to the status quo will persist indefinitely. Quite different implications follow if one assumes, instead, that further significant denuclearization measures will be placed on the table.

Nuclear Weapons Among Nuclear Weapon States

From the vantage of Britain, France, and China, there is good reason to study alternatives to the strategic nuclear status quo. New arrangements could actually endanger security, introducing greater risk. Alternatively, they could decrease the likelihood of nuclear war, or of unauthorized use, without offsetting harms.

START II

In January 1993 George Bush and Boris Yeltsin set their names to the START II Treaty. That agreement provides that by 2003 (or as early as 2000) Russia and the United States will each have 3500 or fewer strategic warheads, a reduction of roughly 70 per cent from the number deployed before START I and II were agreed. Its authors certainly took British, French, and Chinese programs into account, concluding that even after START II cuts mutual US-Russian deterrence, and their capacity to deter others, would remain secure.

Deeper Cuts

The best current estimate, least confident about China, is that Britain, France, and China will deploy about 900 strategic nuclear weapons in 2000, of which 600 will be aboard British and French submarines.[3] Thus, under START II the aggregate minipower strategic arsenal in the year 2000 might approach a third that of Russia.

If the United States and Russia cut even further than envisaged in START II, and the minipowers did not, the minipowers' share of the whole would grow still further. At some point Russia or the United States would certainly insist that no more cuts be made unless the minipowers also took part. Among the questions faced by the Three, not as a technical exercise in numbers but as a political and strategic issue, is whether they should *resist* yielding some of their nuclear capability at that juncture. To what ends have the minipowers built nuclear weapons, and what purposes do they now see them serving?

3. Norris et al. estimate deployed British warheads at 300 in 1991 and 292 in 2000 (of which 192 are submarine-borne), after dropping to 200 in the early 1990s as SSBNs were withdrawn before their replacements were operational. They take the French force in 1991 to be 538 and in 2000 464 (of which 402 will be submarine-borne). Acknowledging the greater uncertainties about the Chinese force, they estimate China has 300 deployed weapons and an additional 150 "tactical" nuclear weapons "which are available, but not deployed." Robert S. Norris, Andrew S. Burrows and Richard W. Fieldhouse, *Nuclear Weapons Databook*, volume V. *British, French, and Chinese Nuclear Weapons* (Boulder, Colorado: Westview, 1994) pp. 65, 214 and 358-359. Henceforth cited as Norris et al.

Issues of numbers arise with the question "wouldn't a smaller force serve as well?" So we must also understand how qualitative claims about purpose and the actual forces—size, composition, training—are connected.

Disengagement

The United States and Russia have taken modest steps to disengage. They signed the INF Treaty (1987) and have removed nuclear weapons from battlefield forces and surface ships. They have agreed to "detarget" one another. They are reducing the numbers of warheads and delivery vehicles.

During the Cold War the superpowers deterred one another by instant readiness to retaliate, the epitome of engagement. Disengagement measures—including *impediments* to the use, or the prompt use, of nuclear weapons—can be thought of as *functional approximations of reductions.* For example, warheads could be separated from their launchers and placed in monitored warehouses, from which they had to be removed and physically mounted before they could be used. They could not be used *quickly* or *secretly*. Therefore they could not be used *accidentally*, *impetuously*, or *by someone who was not authorized*.

If leaders had to announce their intention to make nuclear weapons ready, and could only resume possession of them after some days had passed, they would have the benefit of disengagement, but could resort to nuclear weapons in the event of "unforeseen" changes in security. They could sidestep the criticism of abolition that it gives up a capability which might be needed for survival. But as long as they did not invoke "necessity," the effect would have some similarity to abolition. A nuclear war *could* be fought—as it could not in an abolition world—but only after a period in which political forces could mobilize against it.

Disengagement and deeper cuts may be mixed. The INF Treaty contains just such provisions. Nuclear warheads were severed from missiles, which were crushed, and undertakings were exchanged not to build or deploy intermediate-range systems. The warheads themselves, however, were retained by their owners.

A further question for the Three, then, is how they might respond to—or press for—moves to disengage.

Abolition (Zero)

Abolition is reduction to zero. It implies prohibition. By definition, the minipowers must take part, whether jointly, or by responsive unilateral steps. Moreover, the same strict demands to avoid concealment, and to perform effective monitoring and verification, apply to each of the minipowers, as well as to Russia and the United States.

Given that no established nuclear weapon state can be compelled to denuclearize, abolition can be achieved only by consent of all. This veto would ensure a minipower one last chance to extract concessions from its nuclear capacity—another reason why disengagement, rather than abolition, might appear attractive.

A persuasive case can be made that abolition is easier to verify and sustain than any other outcome. However, in an abolition world every nook and cranny in which a nuclear weapon state might have hidden nuclear weapons has new salience; issues of access and verification that are less compelling when states are permitted several tens or hundreds of warheads become paramount at zero.

Relations of Nuclear and Non-Nuclear States: "Extended Deterrence" and Positive Assurances

Relations between states having nuclear weapons and those without raise different questions. Relations *among nuclear weapon states* are dominated by concepts of alliance, restraint, deterrence, and negotiated management. They concern shared political understandings, even when the parties are ostensible enemies. Relations *between states which are nuclear-armed and those which are not* turn on alliance, restraint, negative guarantees, positive assurances, asymmetric exposure, and subordination, recognized in part in the terms of the Non-Proliferation Treaty. These relations reflect weakness and deference, even when the parties are ostensible friends.

Could Britain, France, and China, before electing to "go nuclear," have chosen otherwise? They could have disregarded US and Soviet weapons. Ignoring nuclear weapons, they would have relied on the nuclear powers to forego nuclear attack (or serious and consequential threat of attack), whether out of good will or calculation. Or they could have sheltered behind one (or both) of the superpowers, relying on that state to make nuclear threats—deterrent threats—on their behalf. Sheltering is well-recognized in the "extended deterrence" offered to allies, and in "positive assurances" to non-nuclear states. States without nuclear weapons today have these same three choices: to arm, ally, or ignore.

Most practice a policy of disregard, bolstered by seeking generic "negative assurances" and "positive assurances."[4] Conscious of their remove from Eurasian centers of bloc confrontation, judging that they had no bond of history or blood by which to commit a nuclear weapon state to risk on their behalf, the state leaders of Africa, Latin America, and the smaller peripheral states of south and southeast Asia have taken it as their lot to accept exposure. If actively concerned with the issue, they have expressed that concern in UN organs and negotiations on the Non-Proliferation Treaty.

The remaining states have followed several distinct strategies. First, in a few cases leaders have decided, despite the costs, to develop nuclear weapons themselves. India, Israel, South Africa, and Pakistan have designed and built nuclear weapons. South Africa claims it has dismantled its weapons and abandoned the program.[5] Iraq, and pos-

---

4. "Negative assurances" or "negative guarantees" are commitments *not to use nuclear weapons*, in defined circumstances, against stipulated targets. For example, a state might give a "no first use" commitment that it would not be the first to use nuclear weapons in an episode. Or it might stipulate that it would not use nuclear weapons against a state not deploying them.

   "Positive assurances" or "positive guarantees" are commitments—often cast in indirect or ambiguous language—to assist a non-nuclear weapon state subject to nuclear attack or threats of attack from a nuclear power. However allusively the commitment may be written, it must be public, for otherwise it would have no deterrent effect.

5. India exploded a nuclear device in 1974; it has not displayed nuclear weapons. Israel is believed, confirmed by the Mordechai Vanunu affair, to have two hundred or more nuclear weapons and means of delivery. South Africa disclosed that it undertook a nuclear weapons program, fabricated six or seven warheads, never tested, and then destroyed the warheads, though the revelations may have been importantly incomplete. Pakistan has neither declared nor displayed nuclear weapons, but statements of former officials appear intended to tell of a well-advanced program. In 1994 former Prime Minister Nawaz Sharif said "I confirm Pakistan possesses the atomic bomb," prompting a Pakistani Foreign Ministry reply that "In the course of its development of a peaceful nuclear program, Pakistan has acquired the capability to acquire nuclear weapons, but we have made a sovereign decision not to produce them." *International Herald Tribune*, 25 August 1994. Analysts with access to intelligence data take it as a fact that Pakistan and India now have nuclear weapons, or can assemble them in a short time. On Sweden, see Martin Fehrm, "Sweden," in Josef Rotblat (ed),

sibly Iran and North Korea, aspire to nuclear status. Argentina and Brazil, once aspirants, have declared that they no longer are. (Sweden and Canada elected not to pursue bomb programs.) Ceausescu's Rumania reportedly flirted with a nuclear program.[6] Second, some states have sought and received guarantees within the framework of an alliance: NATO certainly implied an extension of US (and British) guarantees to the NATO allies.[7] Third, the nuclear weapon states have made unilateral declarations. China, for example, has forsworn first use. Fourth, non-nuclear weapon states have sought generic assurances *as a group*, and some assurances have been extended by nuclear weapon states. The 1968 British, Soviet, and US commitments acknowledged in Resolution 255 of the United Nations Security Council, undertaken as part of the negotiation with non-nuclear weapon states on the NPT, are the most comprehensive example of guarantees, even if they are also a study in avoidance of binding text. Fifth, in a few instances non-nuclear weapon states have sought explicit positive assurances from a nuclear weapon state, outside the "alliance" framework of the Cold War. India's 1964-65 contacts with Britain may have been of this kind.

A nation that builds robust nuclear weapons capabilities seeks stability through a deterrent force under national control. But in solving its own security problem it creates security problems for others, who perceive a new threat. This is the logic of proliferation. The builder creates an asymmetric and fundamentally threatening relationship to states without nuclear weapons. China may have resolved an issue of status and autonomy vis-à-vis the United States and the Soviet Union in 1964, but it created an issue for India and Japan. India

---

Non-proliferation: The why and the wherefore (London: Taylor and Francis, 1985), pp. 213-220; on Israel, see Seymour Hersh, *The Samson Option: Israel's Nuclear Arsenal and American Foreign Policy* (New York : Random House, 1991); on South Africa, see the forthcoming book by Renfrew Christie; David Albright, "South Africa and the Affordable Bomb," in *Bulletin of the Atomic Scientists*, July-August 1994, pp. 37-47; and David Albright, "South Africa's Secret Nuclear Weapons," in *ISIS Report*, May 1994 (Institute for Science and International Security).

6. "*Vremya*" (Moscow television), 19 April 1995.

7. NATO preparations assumed the possibility of nuclear attack against the alliance, and the possibility of the alliance introducing nuclear weapons against conventional attack. The North Atlantic Treaty itself, however, only commits each party to take "such actions as it deems necessary" to restore security.

created an issue for Pakistan, Israel for Iraq. The effect is to bolster the case of advocates of new nuclear programs.

The question which haunts this study is whether there is any *other* path than that taken by Britain, France and China by which a leadership can secure its people's future in a world with *some* nuclear states. The question clearly has two forks: do Britain, France and China secure their people's futures by deploying a nuclear deterrent? and was there—is there—any other path? We will introduce the notion of "positive assurances" here and then return to it, from time to time, throughout the text.

"Positive Assurances"

The most focused discussion of positive assurances took place around drafting and approval of the Non-Proliferation Treaty (1968). Neither negative nor positive assurances were written into the NPT, but three nuclear weapon states—the USSR, United Kingdom, and United States—drafted a joint text of qualified positive assurances which they submitted to the United Nations Security Council. It was then passed by the Security Council as Resolution 255 on 19 June 1968.[8] As the key sections of the text show, the resolution acknowledges unilateral undertakings of the three drafters and recognizes their freedom to act, but it makes no commitment to the non-nuclear-weapon states:

> The Security Council . . .
>
> 1. Recognizes that aggression with nuclear weapons or the threat of such aggression against a non-nuclear-weapon State would create a situation in which the Security Council, and above all its nuclear-weapon State permanent members, would have to act immediately in accordance with their obligations under the United Nations Charter;
>
> 2. Welcomes the intention expressed by certain States that they will provide or support immediate assistance, in accordance with the Charter, to any non-nuclear-weapon State Party to the Treaty on the Non-Proliferation of Nuclear Weapons that is a victim of an act or an object of a threat of aggression in which

---

8. The vote was 10 for, none against, and 5 abstaining. For: Canada, China, Denmark, Ethiopia, Hungary, Paraguay, Senegal, USSR, United Kingdom, and United States. Abstaining: Algeria, Brazil, France, India, and Pakistan. Mohamed I. Shaker, *The Nuclear Non-Proliferation Treaty: Origin and Implementation 1959-1979*, volume 2 (New York: Oceana, 1980), pp. 476-477.

nuclear weapons are used;

3. Reaffirms in particular the inherent right, recognized under Article 51 of the Charter, of individual and collective self-defence if an armed attack occurs against a member of the United Nations, until the Security Council has taken measures necessary to maintain international peace and security.

The joint text did not satisfy those non-nuclear states, including India, which sat in the Eighteen Nation Disarmament Conference, forerunner of today's Conference on Disarmament. As part of the *quid pro quo* for signing an NPT they had sought automatic assurances of aid. India was concerned by China's program.[9]

Beijing had not yet assumed China's seat on the Security Council. Its position at this time—in the early stages of weapons building, and only beginning to emerge from the Cultural Revolution—was that the decision to build nuclear weapons or not was an issue of sovereignty and "breaking the monopoly of the superpowers" a good thing. Beijing attacked the joint draft even before it had been formally submitted to the Security Council for discussion, framing it as part of a US-Soviet maneuver against China.[10]

Both the United States and Soviet Union suggested that France also take on commitments of the pledge. US negotiator William C. Foster said he hoped France would commit to immediate action to defend non-nuclear-weapon states which signed the proposed treaty.[11] But at that juncture France was not taking part in the Eighteen Nation Disarmament Conference in Geneva, and when Resolution 255 came before the Security Council she abstained. French representatives told the Security Council and General Assembly that French nuclear weapons were for defense only and were not intended to be used to threaten or attack.[12] Almost twenty-five years would pass before

---

9. *The New York Times*, 8 March 1968. Mohamed Shaker observes that positive guarantees became "entangled" in non-proliferation issues from China's first nuclear weapons test, which had a particular impact on India. There was "no doubt" the declarations and Resolution 255 "were mainly aimed at the People's Republic of China." Shaker, vol. 2, pp. 515, 520, 532.

10. Shaker, p. 534. *Renmin Ribao*, "A Grave Step in Forming a US-Soviet Counter-Revolutionary Nuclear-Military Alliance," *Peking Review*, vol. 11 no. 2, pp. 31-32.

11. *The New York Times*, 8 March 1968.

12. Shaker, p. 533, citing A/PV. 1672 (prov.), 12 June 1968, p. 7 and SCOR, 1430th meeting, 17 June 1968, paragraph 52.

France and China signed the NPT.

Resolution 255 accords nuclear-weapon states a special status. This raises two kinds of issues. One asks: if Japan or Germany were to become a permanent member of the Security Council, would it want to have nuclear weapons? The second speaks of the special responsibilities of UN Security Council permanent members in talking of the British or French or Chinese nuclear program. Should these be linked?

Paragraph 1 of Resolution 255 says that all UN members but *above all* the nuclear-armed permanent members must respond to nuclear aggression against a non-nuclear weapon state "in accordance with their obligations under the United Nations Charter." Still, the Charter was written and adopted before Hiroshima and says nothing about nuclear weapons. It records that Members "confer" on the Security Council—not on the permanent members—"primary responsibility for the maintenance of international peace and security."[13] The Security Council determines which members shall carry out its decisions "for the maintenance of international peace and security."[14] There is no special standing for permanent members, except that they must "concur" in the Security Council decision. Confounding "permanent member" status and "nuclear-armed" status complicates both the issue of UN commitment to maintain international peace and security and the issue of nuclear futures. They are obviously related, but in no simple way.

The Frailty of Assurances

The effort expended to obtain both negative and positive assurances shows that non-nuclear states wanted firm public commitments. They would get restraint ("negative") and deterrence ("positive") on the cheap. In return for nuclear weapon states' committing to negotiate nuclear disarmament, they would forego weapons programs themselves, programs most of them had neither intentions nor resources to undertake. If they later chose to, they could execute an escape clause in the NPT, allowing them to leave it.

Logically assurances are worth nothing. If "positive assurances"

13. United Nations Charter. Article 24.

14. *Ibid.*, Article 48.1.

would take the form of a nuclear response to an errant nuclear-weapon state, the enforcer would open itself to retaliation. Would an otherwise secure state run that risk? This logic had led France to conclude in the 1960s that US guarantees could not be relied upon.

Guarantees to non-nuclear states, however veiled and dependent on political will at the time they would be called, declare a script of retaliation. Their force lies, however, in an argument from interest: that no nuclear weapon state could allow another to gain commanding sway and resources by making nuclear threats. This fact made positive guarantees credible *enough*: that is, undismissible, and marking too great a risk to run.

Then Why Build Nuclear Weapons?

Why aren't non-nuclear states satisfied by assurances from their nuclear partners? In short: because assurances cannot resolve three ineradicable uncertainties.

First is that the guarantor, however sincere today, might turn aside at the crucial moment. For example, it could be paralyzed by domestic turbulence.

Second, even a committed guarantor might read a specific threat or incursion as tolerable, not serious enough to bring in nuclear arms. For example, a "regional" nuclear weapon state carefully modulating the diplomatic and grand-strategic use of its nuclear weapons could have important effects without provoking intercession by the nuclear-armed guarantor.

Third, a guarantor could change color and become the enemy.

In short, assurances persuasive *for any future contingency* are unavailable. Non-nuclear states, like the nuclear weapon states themselves, are dependent upon the restraint and prudence of those who have nuclear weapons. But their objective choices—at a decisive moment—are unmistakably fewer than those available to nuclear-armed states. If they judge that condition intolerable, they may embark on a nuclear weapon program of their own. Something like that was part of the calculus of Britain, of France, and of China. This fact sets the context for the three programs we will now examine.

2

Nuclear Programs

Every known nuclear weapon has been designed and assembled in a state program, through institutions funded by the state and subject to state authority. The resultant nuclear warheads remain—in principle—under the exclusive continuing control of the state which ordered them made. Those concerned—political figures, managers, designers, builders, and military deployers—have conducted an extended but shrouded discussion of the weapons' capabilities and utilities. In each nuclear weapons state, they have reached a consensual negotiated position that nuclear weapons are justified—indeed, necessary—despite their costs and risks. Generations of political leaders and civil servants have committed to that view. Any proposal to turn away from nuclear forces would require explaining why costly and consequential choices made in the past were no longer correct, or had been in some measure unsound when made.

"Threat assessments" aside, momentum sustaining nuclear forces comes from each country's nuclear consensus, forces in being, and plans for the future. In this chapter we address a few basic questions. When was the nuclear program begun? What were the key steps taken? What forces are now deployed? What new major systems are being built? And—exploring the purposes of nuclear tests and plans for their "simulation"—what future capabilities would nuclear weapons states want as the price for agreement to a Comprehensive Test Ban?

We begin by surveying present forces (1995) and those anticipated around the year 2000. The principal nuclear systems of Britain, France, and China are set out in table 2.1. The figures for the year 2000 are projections based on current knowledge. British and French procurement plans appear to be quite clear. Chinese plans, of course, are least accessible to public view, so that projections of Chinese forces are necessarily speculative.

TABLE 2.1

British, French and Chinese Nuclear Systems

Britain and France. Mid-1994.

Before *Vanguard*-Class SSBN and *Triomphant*-Class SNLE

	BASING	UNITS	WARHEADS # X YIELD EACH	TOTAL WAR-HEADS	RANGE (km)
BRITAIN	SSBN	45 A3TK	2 x 40 Kt	**90**	4700
	Aircraft:				
	Tornado	72GR1/1A	2 x 40 Kt	**90**	4700
FRANCE	SNLE	64 M4	6 x 150 Kt	**384**	6000
	Silo-based	18 S3D	1 x 1 Mt	**18**	3500
	Aircraft				
	Mirage	18 IVP ASMP	1 x 300 Kt	**18**	1570+
	Mirage	45 2000N ASMP	1 x 300 Kt	**42**	2750+

Britain and France. Early 2000s.

Projected Systems After Completion of New Classes

(This table also reflects expected abandonment of British airborne WE177 bombs carried by Tornado aircraft and 18 French silo-based missiles.)

	BASING	UNITS	WARHEADS # X YIELD EACH	TOTAL WAR-HEADS	RANGE (km)
BRITAIN	SSBN	48 Trident II (D-5)	4 X 100 Kt	**192**	7400-11,000[a]
FRANCE[b]	SNLE	64 M45	6 x 150 Kt	**384**	> 6000

Table 2.1 continued

	Aircraft:[c]				
	Mirage	18 IVP ASMP	1 x 300 Kt	**18**	1570+
	Mirage	45 2000N ASMP	1 x 300 Kt	**42**	2750+

China. Mid-1994.
Principal Nuclear Weapons Systems

	BASING	UNITS	WARHEADS # X YIELD EACH	TOTAL WAR-HEADS	RANGE (km)
CHINA[d]	SSBN	24 JL-1	1 x 200-300 Kt	**24**	1700
	Fixed	4 DF-5	1 x 4-5 Mt	**4**	13,000+
	Mobile	36 DF-21	1 x 200-300 Kt	**36**	1800
	Fixed	20 DF-4	1 x 3.3 Mt	**20**	4750
	Fixed	50 DF-3	1 x 3.3 Mt	**50**	2800

China. 2000.
Principal Systems Anticipated to Be Deployed in the Year 2000
(Not including DF-3 and DF-4 missiles which may still be deployed at that time.)

	BASING	UNITS	WARHEADS # X YIELD EACH	TOTAL WAR-HEADS	RANGE (km)
CHINA[e]	SSBN	24 JL-1	1 x 200-300 Kt	**24**	1700
	SSBN	~20 JL-2[f]	?	**~ 20**	~ 8000
	Fixed	4+ DF-5	1 x 4-5 Mt	**4+**	13 000+
	Mobile	36 DF-21	1 x 200-300 Kt	**36**	1800
	Mobile	[?] DF-31[g]	?	**?**	8000

Notes to Table 2.1:

"SSBN" and "SNLE" designate a ballistic-missile submarine. China's DF-3, DF-4, and DF-5 missiles are liquid-fueled. The mobile DF-21 and DF-31 are solid-fuel missiles. China issues no data on missile numbers; figures in table 2.1 are derived estimates.

a Norris et al. report a range of 7400 km at a full payload, and 11,000 at "reduced payload." *Nuclear Weapons Databook*, vol. 5, p. 169.

b France intends the first of a new *Triomphant*-class SNLE (SSBN) to enter service in 1996. Three others will follow. The total number of warheads is expected to remain at 384. Whether the M45 missile with which the first boats of the class will be equipped is followed by a longer-range M5 remains to be seen. Yield of 150 kt was attributed to planned French test by Jacques Baumel in September 1995.

c Ranges shown for aircraft carrying the ASMP standoff missile do not include the 90-350 km range of the missile itself.

d Chinese aircraft, thought to deploy about 150 bombs, are not shown. The principal aircraft are 120 H-6 (B-6) with a range of 3100 km carrying one to three bombs.

e See previous note.

f Lewis and Xue, *China's Strategic Seapower*, p. 121, speculating on Chinese intentions from cited sources and inferring range from its being called a "long-range" missile. China plans to deploy the new SSBN 09-04 with a new JL-2 8000 km warhead by the year 2000. Number of missiles on 09-04 "not confirmed."

g The DF-31 was first reported test-launched on 30 May 1995. We can only speculate that some units will be deployed by 2000.

Sources: Largely adapted from Norris et al., *Nuclear Weapons Databook*, vol. 5, *British, French, and Chinese Nuclear Weapons*, esp. pp. 9-11. Some older systems noted by Norris et al. are omitted. Estimates for JL-2 from Lewis and Xue, *China's Strategic Seapower*, p. 121 (see note f).

Table 2.1 shows the new destructive capabilities which Britain, France, and China intend to deploy within a few years. Procurement decisions distill the agreement present, amidst disagreement within the state, about how to position defense toward uncertainty. Weapons procured have a further effect, in that once constructed they persist, endowing successive governments with lethal capabilities they did not choose, and confronting those abroad with a material fact. The weapons program itself constitutes an example for nuclear aspirants.

We will introduce each of the three programs in turn, compare the weapons test programs of the three countries, and then consider some similarities and differences. Readers who wish detailed information about these programs, including weapons development, test, delivery systems, deployments, and the weapons themselves are encouraged to consult volume 5 of the *Nuclear Weapons Databook*.[1]

French Nuclear Weapons: An Overview

What Were the First French Steps Toward Nuclear Weapons?

Charles de Gaulle learned of the atomic bomb before Hiroshima; during a visit to Canada in July 1944 he was briefed by Bertrand Goldschmidt and other French participants in the Chalk River nuclear research group, a component of the British-Canadian-US cooperation to build the bomb.[2] On 18 October 1945 President de Gaulle created the Commissariat à l'Énergie Atomique (CEA), which was charged to perform both military and civilian nuclear research.[3]

In July 1952 the National Assembly approved a five-year plan which included building plutonium production reactors and an extraction plant, clear signs of an intention to build nuclear weapons. A meeting of Cabinet and other officials on 26 December 1954 led to official approval of a secret program to achieve the bomb. Norris et al. underscore the close group by which the nuclear weapons program was brought into being:[4]

> The manner by which France decided to actually build the bomb was not the result of a single decision, nor was it a "clear-cut long-range policy rationally planned and executed." The decision was taken without any public knowledge or Parliamentary debate on the potential military implications of atomic energy. As in the United States, the Soviet Union, and Great Britain, a small group of scientists, in collaboration with military and government officials, brought the bomb program to fruition. For many years the CEA and other agencies operated without clear-cut official sanctions to build the bomb, yet a small cadre relentlessly progressed toward the goal.

---

1. Norris, Robert S., Andrew S. Burrows and Richard W. Fieldhouse. *Nuclear Weapons Databook,* volume 5. *British, French, and Chinese Nuclear Weapons* (San Francisco: Westview Press, 1994). Natural Resources Defense Council. Earlier volumes review the US and Soviet programs.

2. Bertrand Goldschmidt, *The Atomic Adventure* (New York: Macmillan, 1964), p. 38.

3. 18 October 1945, by Ordinance N° 45-2563. Marcel Duval and Yves Le Baut, *L'arme nucléaire française: Pourquoi et comment?* (Paris: Kronos, 1992), pp. 22, 235, 250.

4. Norris et al., p. 183, citing Lawrence Scheinman, *Atomic Energy Policy in France Under the Fourth Republic* (Princeton: Princeton University Press, 1965), pp. 94, 210, 212.

France first tested on 13 February 1960 at Reggane, in the Sahara. Its first thermonuclear test took place on 24 August 1968 at Fangataufa, in the south Pacific.[5] The French nuclear delivery capacity evolved in the 1960s and 1970s centered on three systems. These mirrored the Soviet and US "triad": aircraft-borne systems, a land-based ballistic missile, and a submarine-launched ballistic missile. France also built, but has now set aside, a short-range battlefield capability. The SSBN (SNLE) fleet is the mainstay.

French Nuclear Systems Under Development

On 18 June 1987 France committed to build a new class of ballistic missile submarines. Originally six were planned, to be commissioned by 2008.[6] The French also planned to have a new missile, the M5, ready in 1999. With an anticipated range of 11000 km, almost twice that of its predecessor M45 (> 6000 km), the M5 would greatly enlarge the region which any single boat could strike. The M45 carries 6 MIRVed warheads; the M5 could carry as many as 10 or 12.[7] If, as doctrine had it, three boats each carrying 16 missiles were at sea at any one time, the total force at sea would be 160 (or perhaps 192) warheads per boat, a total of 480 (or 576).

The nuclear force France now intends to deploy in 2005 will be somewhat less formidable and diverse than originally envisaged, though still significantly stronger than that of 1985. Fewer new ballistic missile submarines will be built; the M5 missile program has been delayed; Hadès has been effectively canceled; and France has taken an initiative to limit or halt nuclear weapons tests.

The principal modernization issues turn on four systems:

Ballistic missile submarines. Four new *Triomphant*-class SNLE-NG (Sous-marin Nucléaire Lanceurs d'Engins—Nouvelle Génération), not six, are now envisioned, to enter service in mid-1995,

5. Duval and Le Baut, above, pp. 238, 241.
6. *Jane's Fighting Ships*, 1990-91.
7. Robert S. Norris, Andrew S. Burrows and Richard W. Fieldhouse, *Nuclear Weapons Databook*. Volume V. *British, French, and Chinese Nuclear Weapons* (Boulder, Colorado: Westview, 1994), pp. 303-307.

1998, 2001 and 2005.[8] If existing SNLE of earlier classes remain fit for service, and proposed boats are not delayed, France could pace retirement of old boats to keep five SNLE—even six in some years—operational. (There is some discussion that only two boats might be at sea at a time. The formula given in the *Livre Blanc sur la Défense 1994* is that "alert levels, like the number of submarines at sea, vary with threat levels."[9])

M5 missile. This missile, intended to arm the new SNLEs, has been delayed until 2005. Since one boat would typically be in refit, only three sets of missiles are planned.[10]

ASMP/ASLP. The French government is weighing several aircraft-carried missile systems for future procurement. Two would be armed with conventional warheads. In December 1994 the Ministry of Defense authorized feasibility studies of the Matra anti-infrastructure Apache missile, a subsonic stealthy low-flying cruise missile of about 400 km range after launch. Aérospatiale will also develop a supersonic anti-ship missile (ANNG). These systems, however, are distinct from the follow-on to the ASMP medium-range air to ground missile now deployed with nuclear warheads. As of early 1995, the choice lay between a Tomahawk-style cruise missile proposed by Matra, the APTGD (arme précise tirée à grande distance), and the supersonic Aérospatiale entry Asura derived from the ASMP. The favored APTGD, subsonic, low-flying, stealthy, and equipped with bimodal radar and infrared guidance systems, would be very precise at a range greater than 400 km. Jacques Isnard reports the possibility that some 200 might be acquired.[11] Like the Tomahawk, APTGD could presumably be fitted with either a conventional or nuclear warhead.

Hadès missile. Hadès, a 500 km semi-ballistic missile, was intended to follow the then extant Pluton. France announced a halt to the program in June 1991, at which time twenty had been delivered

---

8. Assemblée Nationale N° 2935, 20 October 1992. Boucheron report. I:319.

9. *Livre Blanc sur la Défense 1994* (Paris: La documentation Française, 1994), p. 83.

10. Boucheron. I:321. The fourth *Triomphant*-class boat would still carry M45, or be in refit.

11. Jacques Isnard, *Le Monde* 17 December 1994.

and ten more were nearing the end of fabrication.[12]

The Cold War's end did not disturb the priority given to France's nuclear force. But it necessarily raised anew the question for which missions it was designed, against which "enemies" it might be directed. The main line of response was to leave the "enemy" undefined, reintroducing into the strategic characterization the phrase "*tous azimuths*" which had once served to avoid naming the Soviet Union and now served to avoid naming anyone. In late 1992 a further position was being advanced by some commentators on the political right: that France should be prepared to use nuclear weapons to deal with putative Third World tyrants. Although always a minority view, this position had enough persistence to provoke François Mitterrand to insist, speaking to senior French officials in 1994, that while he was president France would not make miniaturized nuclear weapons to use in limited conflicts. Instead, he said, France's nuclear forces would be reserved entirely to deter invasion of France or threats to its vital interests.[13]

France delayed deciding about the second and third legs of the triad, retaining for some time the 18 S3D missiles in fixed silos on the Plateau d'Albion. In August 1993 the French Air Force Chief of Staff, General Vincent Lanata, declared his preference for an air-launched nuclear missile capability, to be carried on the Mirage-2000N and then its successor Rafale. He envisaged "an adaptation of the present air-ground medium range missile (ASMP), or a version with a longer range (ASLP)."[14] General Lanata advanced a strategic, not budgetary, rationale, but he opened the door to foregoing the long-considered ASLP altogether.

An aircraft-delivered weapon, Lanata argued, made French nuclear capabilities more credible by offering a second way to penetrate defenses. Moreover, it would permit both political and operational flexibility of maneuver. This claim had internal political significance

---

12. Boucheron. I:328. In September 1991 President François Mitterrand announced that the system would be limited to 30 missiles and not deployed. In June 1992 Aérospatiale was notified that the program was at an end.

13. Reuters, 5 May 1994.

14. *Défense nationale*, August 1993, cited in *Le Monde*, 5 August 1993.

because some French politicians and strategists argued that the nuclear force should be readied for use against any Third World dictator who might use new offensive capabilities to threaten French interests.

> The evolution toward a capability against vital centers militates in favor of very precise systems, with a variable-yield warhead.[15]

French Nuclear Policy Today

In March 1994 France issued a White Paper on Defense, its first since 1972.[16] In many respects the document is a compromise, reflecting positions both of the center-right Government and of Socialist President François Mitterrand, and avoiding specific choices. Several key themes are, however, clearly stated.

French "*dissuasion*"—close to, but not exactly, "deterrence"—is sharply distinguished from plans for use:

> French nuclear strategy is a strategy of *dissuasion*, rejecting all confusion between dissuasion and use.[17]

With the end of the Cold War, the former justification for France's nuclear forces is "less pertinent." But "the nuclear era continues," and

---

15. *Ibid.* "L'évolution vers une capacité anti-centres vitaux milite en faveur de systèmes d'une grande précision, possédant une charge de puissance modulable."

16. *Livre Blanc sur la Défense*, Paris: La documentation Française, March 1994. The Commission on the White Paper chaired by Marceau Long, vice-president of the Council of State, included figures from the prime minister's office and relevant ministries. Among its twenty-nine members were chief of staff Admiral Jacques Lanxade, head of the defence ministry's armaments branch Henri Conze, and the director of military applications in the CEA, Roger Baléras. The analytic and strategic policy community contributed Thierry de Montbrial, director of IFRI, and Jérôme Paolini.

17. *Livre Blanc*, p. 79. If the translator abstains from the term "deterrence," it conceals that "dissuasion" and "deterrence" both work by persuading another party that it could in turn suffer awful devastation if it used nuclear weapons. But there is in the French something of an appeal to reason absent from the English "deterrence," which relies instead on "terror." The difference seems to lie in whether the other party is cast as a reasonable person or as an enemy beyond reason.

> we cannot ignore the permanence of a potential superpower on the east of the European continent.[18]

Division of former Soviet nuclear weapons among several successor states makes for more rather than less risk.

There may be new risks in the next century. There is a "strong probability" that a few more states will achieve a nuclear capability. Middle powers may prove capable of striking at Europe, or at France's strategic interests or forces abroad. Chemical or biological weapons may spread. But the authors conclude, significantly, that "this evolution in itself requires no doctrinal change on our part."

Nuclear disarmament measures should have no effect on the size of France's nuclear forces, which

> in conformance with the principle of sufficiency, is determined by the capacity to inflict unacceptable damage on any aggressor and not by attending to the balance of forces, which has nothing to do with nuclear arms.

"European nuclear doctrine" may be long coming, but should not be lost from view. Dialogue with Britain on this subject should be "pursued and deepened," but does not exclude conversations with other European partners. There will, however, be no "European nuclear doctrine" until there are "European vital interests," recognized both by Europe and by others.

> Until then, France has no intention of diluting its means of national defense in this domain under any pretext.[19]

Conventional forces cannot replace nuclear forces. This discussion is significant for two reasons. It registers the existence of an argument—perhaps among French strategists, but also with foreign advocates of denuclearization—about the conditions under which nuclear weapons could be eliminated. Then, it stakes France to a view rooted in "the lessons of History" which resists any challenge to French nuclear forces. Because the text contains the terms in which the claim for the sufficiency of non-nuclear arms is rejected, it is important to quote it in its entirety:

---

18. *Livre Blanc*, p. 80.

19. *Livre Blanc*, p. 81.

The success of theses on "conventional deterrence." These rest on the idea that certain sophisticated classical technologies confer on those who have them a radical superiority, permitting them to cut sharply, or even eliminate nuclear weapons from their defense. It is illusory and dangerous to pretend that they can have the effect, like nuclear arms, of preventing war. All the lessons of History testify to the contrary. These concepts valorise the conventional balance of forces, by nature unstable and based on strategies of use, preparation and the conduct of war. They suggest the possibility of resolving international problems by the use of force and drive the arms race. They are incompatible with our strategy. Far from replacing nuclear deterrence, "conventional" deterrence can only add to it.[20]

The authors then turn to dissuasion and nuclear force posture. Analysis confirms both the pertinence of the concept of "dissuasion" and the well-foundedness of France's choice for nuclear arms.

Nuclear weapons remain necessary as a "major element of the independence of France" and as a military precaution in the face of risk, the authors insist. Nuclear arms spare France from a conventional arms race, which would be contrary to her defense policy and "insupportable" financially.

They note the usual requirement of nuclear deterrence: the will and capacity to inflict unacceptable damage on an adversary. Moreover, nuclear weapons render general war "unthinkable." But the authors also recite the peculiarly French notion of a nuclear capability to issue a "final warning" if necessary.

Long-term credibility, the authors note, requires that France preserve its capacity for technological evolution. This is most likely a nod to those who insist that France retain lively capabilities in nuclear research and application, including the capacity to test. Then in the next sentence, deferring to those who hope tests will be halted, the authors insist that the program of test simulations is a "priority" which should be strengthened in coming years.

Nuclear forces should be sufficiently flexible and diverse to ensure that the French president would have options when required. "French political authority should always have the necessary means, and sufficient means, both secure and suited to whatever situations she might have to face." The means available should always be "above the threshold of sufficiency for the given threat, to avoid the political authority's finding itself at an impasse and paralyzed." Finally, "alert

20. *Ibid.*

levels, like the number of submarines at sea, vary with threat levels." So the policy opens the door to reducing the number of SSBNs (SNLEs) at sea to two, or even one, without committing that such a step will be taken.[21]

These are the authors' principal points on nuclear policy, but related subjects are taken up elsewhere in the *White Paper.* For example, they note the possibility of "protection" against attack and, in that context, call for study of means for wide-area aerial defense ("défense aérienne élargie").[22] Posing hypothetical scenarios, they include the possibility of a "major threat against western Europe," marking it as highly unlikely, but insisting the possibility "cannot be discarded, because it would present a mortal risk."[23] They discuss intelligence, especially the priority given to satellite systems.[24] Although France may cooperate with other European states in non-nuclear technologies and procurement, in everything related to nuclear systems—including missiles, warheads, penetration aids, intelligence, communications, and ballistic missile submarines—France must master design, construction and use.[25] France currently commits 3.38 percent of its Gross Domestic Product to defense, of which about 12.5 percent is attributable to nuclear dissuasion.[26]

British Nuclear Weapons: An Overview

Origins of the British Program

On 30 August 1941 Prime Minister Winston Churchill sent a minute to the Chiefs of Staff proposing a program of research on development of a 'uranium bomb'. Four days later Churchill's advisers recommended the program be given highest priority. With this action

---

21. *Livre Blanc*, pp. 82-83. See also the discussion of dissuasion at p. 111 and of ASW at p. 119.
22. *Livre Blanc,*, pp. 85-86.
23. *Livre Blanc, p. 96.*
24. *Livre Blanc*, pp. 105-107.
25. *Livre Blanc*, p. 152.
26. *Livre Blanc*, p. 172.

Britain became the first state to undertake to build an atomic bomb.[27]

This first official step was preceded by an analytic study by the Maud Committee, organized in April 1940, "an informal, academic group made up entirely of scientists and only loosely connected to the Whitehall apparatus."[28] The Maud Committee reported on 2 July 1941 that a bomb was possible and would take 30 months to build.[29]

This report already circulated the idea that Britain would require nuclear weapons after World War II.

> Even if the war should end before the bombs are ready the effort would not be wasted, except in the unlikely event of complete disarmament, since no nation would care to risk being caught without a weapon of such decisive possibilities.[30]

The decisions which led Britain to create the infrastructure for a *domestic* nuclear weapons capability, distinct from the plant and design laboratories in Canada and the United States in which British personnel worked during World War II, were made soon after the end of World War II. On 21 August 1945 Prime Minister Clement Attlee announced formation of an Advisory Committee on Atomic Energy whose mandate ran to nuclear development "whether for industrial or military purposes." On 29 October 1945 he told the House of Commons that a nuclear research laboratory would be established. Soon thereafter he estimated the cost of the facility at £1000 million and its annual budget at £500 million and anticipated other "substantial expenditure" in the future.[31]

British nuclear policy was decided in a Cabinet committee designated Gen 75, which met sixteen times during its life from August

---

27. The British nuclear program to 1970 has been ably canvassed by Andrew J. Pierre, on whose work I have drawn heavily in this section. Andrew J. Pierre, *Nuclear Politics: The British Experience with an Independent Strategic Force, 1939-1970* (London: Oxford University Press, 1972), pp. 9-10.

28. *Ibid.*, p. 15.

29. Norris et all, p. 18, citing Margaret Gowing, *Britain and Atomic Energy 1939-1945* (London: Macmillan, 1964).

30. Quoted in Pierre, above, p. 20. Pierre notes Michael Howard's comment, in his review of Margaret Gowing, *Britain and Atomic Energy, 1939-1941* (London: Macmillan, 1964) in the *Sunday Times* of 27 September 1964 that this has been "the basic principle of British policy ever since."

31. Pierre, above, p. 121.

1945 to January 1947. It initially consisted of the Prime Minister and six Cabinet members. The decision actually to build a bomb was taken by an even smaller group, designated Gen 163, on 8 January 1947.[32]

The decision was political: until 1955 Britain's nuclear program was "unrelated 'to strategic and tactical needs and probabilities.'"[33] In 1955 the British Government of Harold Macmillan committed to strategic defense of the United Kingdom, which led it to negotiate placing US Thor missiles in the UK under "dual-key" control.[34] Further key cooperative steps were negotiated and approved in the latter 1950s, as the UK continued to develop an indigenous capacity to design and build atomic and thermonuclear warheads.

Since the 1950s Britain has followed three delivery strategies. The first relied on "V-Bombers" (Valiant, Vulcan, Victor), committed in late 1952, with an initial Valiant operational capability in February 1955 and full nuclear capability in early 1957.[35] The final V-bomber was withdrawn from a nuclear bomber role on 31 December 1982.[36]

The second placed successive missiles aboard submarines: the Polaris A3T and then Polaris A3TK (Chevaline) on *Resolution*-class SSBNs, to be followed in 1995 by the Trident II (D-5) on *Vanguard*-class SSBNs. The Polaris decision followed soon after US cancellation of the Skybolt stand-off ballistic missile, which Britain had planned to deploy on the Vulcan bomber, in December 1962.

The *Resolution* first patrolled in June 1968.[37] Concerned that the Polaris A3T would not effectively penetrate Soviet antimissile defenses around Moscow, Britain began developing, in 1972, a warhead and 'penetration aid carrier' to defeat defenses. The combination of Polaris missile and purpose-designed payload, the Polaris A3TK

---

32. Norris et al., pp. 19-22, citing Margaret Gowing (with Arnold, L.), *Independence and Deterrence* (London: Macmillan, 1974), vol. 1, pp. 21, 182-183, and quoting at length her account of reasons for the British decision from p. 184.

33. John Simpson, *The Independent Nuclear State* (London: Macmillan, 2nd. ed. 1986), pp. 62-63, citing Gowing, above, vol. 1, p. 189.

34. Simpson, pp. 124-125.

35. Norris et al., pp. 142-143.

36. Norris et al., p. 145.

37. Norris et al., p. 101.

(Chevaline), was first deployed on patrol in mid-1982.[38] On 15 July 1980 Britain announced it would buy the Trident I (C-4) missile from the United States for deployment on a new class of SSBNs, and in March 1982 upgraded the proposal to Trident II (D-5).

Trident II will bring three capabilities significantly greater than those of the Polaris A3TK (Chevaline) it replaces, in range, warheads, and MIRVing. Its range is estimated between 7400 km and 11,000 km, dependent on payload; Polaris was limited to 4700 km.

The total number of warheads to be deployed has not been stated, but speculation centers on a maximum of 192,[39] which would mean three 16-missile four-warhead sets (assuming one boat in refit or repair at any time), or some mixed load—reflecting talk of the SSBNs assuming a "substrategic" role—totaling less than 192. In any case, the number is likely to be larger than the 96 warheads of the Polaris A3TK, three boats each carrying 16 two-warhead missiles, roughly twice as large.[40] In electing to mount fewer warheads, reducing payload weight, Britain could commit some missiles to more distant targets. Finally, the Trident warheads are MIRVed, unlike the Chevaline, which carried two warheads, which are not "independently targetable" but instead fall as a pair in the vicinity of a single target. As the House of Commons Defence Committee reported:

---

38. Norris et al., pp. 110-113.

39. In 1982 Britain announced that the aggregate number of warheads on the Trident D5 would not exceed the eight-warhead load originally intended for the Trident C4. Cf. Michael Quinlan, "British Nuclear Weapons Policy: Past, Present, and Future," in John C. Hopkins and Weixing Hu (eds), *Strategic Views from the Second Tier: The Nuclear Weapons Policies of France, Britain, and China* (La Jolla, California: Institute on Global Conflict and Cooperation, 1994). For three missiles sets of sixteen missiles that works to a maximum of 384, or 128 warheads per set. The 1992 Statement on the Defence Estimates described the stated maximum of 128 warheads (each) as "an upper limit, not a specification." This number was reduced further when the Secretary of State for Defence, Malcolm Rifkind, announced on 16 November 1993 that the number would be a maximum of 96 per boat (on average six warheads per missile). There is broad expectation, however, that the usual load will be four warheads per missile, giving 64 per boat and 192 total. Norris et al. accept this line of speculation. Norris et al., p. 66.

40. Britain said that the number of warheads on each A3TK (Chevaline) did not exceed the three on Polaris, but published estimates usually assume two. Three sets (among four boats) gives 16 x 2 x 3 = 96.

> Trident's accuracy and sophistication . . . represent a significant enhancement of the UK's nuclear capability. We have invested a great deal of money to make it possible to attack more targets with greater effectiveness . . .[41]

The general election of April 1992 occasioned debate on the size of the British force. Simply put, the governing Conservative Party committed to four boats, the Liberals to three, and Labour to two. Labour claimed that Royal Navy testimony had found the program workable with three Trident submarines, and that it could be workable with two.[42] With the Tories victorious, the fourth *Vanguard*-class SSBN was ordered.[43]

TABLE 2.2

The *Vanguard*-Class of British Ballistic Missile Submarines

#	NAME	STATUS AS OF 1 APRIL 1994
05	*Vanguard*	Accepted by Royal Navy in September 1993. Planning Trident test firings off Florida in mid-1994. Until it is operational, the British force consists of the remaining three Polaris boats, *Resolution, Repulse and Renown*.
06	*Victorious*	Launched September 1993. Contractor's sea trials to begin 1994.
07	*Vigilant*	Under construction.
08	(unnamed)	Under construction.

Source: Cm 2550. *Statement on the Defence Estimates 1994.* Presented to Parliament by the Secretary of State for Defence. April 1994. ¶ 406.

Although the operational requirement is that one boat—just one—be at sea, the four-boat *Vanguard*-class Trident program remains on course.[44] Completion and setting to sea of three or four *Vanguard*-

---

41. House of Commons. Session 1993-94. Defence Committee. Second Report. *Progress of the Trident Programme*. 4 May 1994. ¶26, p. xiv.
42. The Labour shadow foreign secretary, stating such testimony had been given by a Royal Navy admiral to a select committee. ITN report, CNN, 4 March 1992.
43. On 7 July 1992. *Defence Estimates 1992*.
44. Malcolm Rifkind, Secretary of State for Defence, said on 17 November 1993 that "a fleet of four submarines will not only provide assurance that one boat

class SSBNs by, perhaps, the year 2000 will equip Britain with a formidable force. It will carry many fewer warheads than it would have carried if each missile mounted the number first deployed by the United States (8) or—even more dramatically—the number theoretically possible (14-16). But many more targets will fall within its missiles' longer range and the boats can be hidden in broader seas farther from their principal targets.

The third British means of deployment has been aboard shorter-range aircraft, first as gravity bombs, and then as air-to-surface missiles. From 1962 to 1970 the nuclear-armed Blue Steel missile was deployed on Vulcan and Victor bombers.[45] By the mid-1990s older Canberra light bombers and Buccaneer and Jaguar strike aircraft no longer carried nuclear weapons, but 72 Tornado combat aircraft remained, each able to carry two nuclear bombs.[46] The UK has now given up a planned Tactical Air-to-Surface Missile (TASM), which would have significantly increased the nuclear capability of the Tornado. (The "substrategic" role is then shifted to Trident.)

British Nuclear Policy

In Spring 1952 Churchill directed the service chiefs to work out a "Global Strategy Paper." Their text "led Britain to become the first nation to base its national security planning almost entirely upon a declaratory policy of nuclear deterrence" and presaged Eisenhower's "New Look" policy.[47] Shortly after the paper's appearance, the Churchill government ordered quantity production of the V-bombers. A defense *White Paper* in 1955 set out Britain's commitment to

---

can always be at sea, but will also enable us to maintain cost-effective operating patterns." House of Commons. Session 1993-94. Defence Committee. Second report. *Progress of the Trident Programme*. 4 May 1994, p. 32. The *Statement on the Defence Estimates 1994*, p. 88, states that "Maintenance of an effective independent strategic deterrent involves . . . a minimum ballistic missile submarine (SSBN) force, providing assurance that at least one vessel can be at sea at all times . . ."

45. Norris et al., p. 96.

46. Norris et al., pp. 156-159. They estimate 100 WE177s deployed on this platform.

47. Andrew J. Pierre, *Nuclear Politics*, above, p. 87.

"nuclear deterrence and, in effect, massive retaliation."[48]

The Kennedy-Macmillan Nassau Agreement of 21 December 1962 reflects Kennedy's commitment to make Polaris available for Britain's planned new SSBN.[49] The agreement also envisages a "NATO nuclear force" to which elements of US, UK, and the "tactical nuclear forces now held in Europe" could be subscribed. The UK SSBNs and at least an equal number of US forces would be offered to the NATO multilateral force. But a caveat:

> The Prime Minister made it clear that except where Her Majesty's Government may decide that supreme national interests are at stake, these British forces will be used for the purposes of international defense of the Western Alliance in all circumstances.

Rationale in the 1980s and 1990s

The rationale offered for a Britain's nuclear force, set out in successive budget justifications, admits no doubt of the continued relevance of a nuclear deterrent. A private 1988 study, authored by officers of the Royal Institute of International Affairs, captures well the arguments made for maintaining a capable nuclear force:

> Defence is at the heart of British foreign policy: not only because the military instrument remains the ultimate support for foreign policy objectives, but also because of the important contribution which military power and pride make towards a nation's view of itself. The strength of popular support for the maintenance of a British independent nuclear deterrent force has not been diminished by perceptions of a weakening Soviet threat. The rationale for a British deterrent had, after all, as much to do with the preservation of Britain's international standing as a world power as with the intensity of the Soviet threat as then perceived. Together with the East of Suez commitment, it gave Britain the right to claim a special place in the counsels of Washington, and a seat "at the top table" in international diplomacy. The powerful symbolic association of military power with national pride was demonstrated again by the Falklands War, which fostered the image, both at home and abroad, of Britain as a country with a strong government and a clear sense of direction.[50]

---

48. Pierre, above, p. 156.

49. Statement on Nuclear Defense Systems. 21 December 1962. In Andrew J. Pierre, above, as Appendix B, pp. 346-347.

50. Christopher Tugendhat and William Wallace, *Options for British Foreign Policy in the 1990s* (London: Routledge and the Royal Institute of International Affairs, 1988), pp. 68-69. Tugendhat was Chairman, and Wallace the Deputy

After noting the pressure of budgetary constraints on future defense spending, they again insist on the centrality of Britain's nuclear forces:

> If arguments against reductions in Britain's conventional commitments are strong, arguments against cutting Britain's nuclear contribution are as strong, if not stronger. Britain's nuclear role remains a vital element in the country's claim to international standing. It commands firm support among the British public. In a period when the prospect of superpower arms reductions poses major uncertainties for European security, and when the credibility of the American nuclear guarantee to Western Europe is increasingly open to question, the justification for a European contribution to the Western Alliance's nuclear deterrent is extremely powerful. Neither the German nor the French governments would wish that European contribution to come solely from France; nor indeed would any other European government.[51]

Declaratory Nuclear Policy

The *Statement on the Defence Estimates 1993* sets out concisely Britain's basic force policy. This is "Military Task 1.1: Provision of an Effective Independent Strategic and Substrategic Nuclear Capability":

> ¶ 304. National nuclear capabilities, both strategic and substrategic, continue to underpin British defence strategy and provide the ultimate guarantee of our security.
>
> ¶ 305. Maintenance of an effective independent strategic deterrent involves: nuclear research, development, production and testing expertise and facilities; a minimum ballistic missile submarine (SSBN) force, providing assurance that at least one vessel can be at sea at all times, supported by secure, continuous real-time communications facilities covering the SSBN operating area; access to support and maintenance facilities for SSBNs, missiles and warheads; adequate conventional forces to safeguard deployment of the SSBN force; and conventional forces to safeguard at all times the physical security of nuclear assets as well as the command and control infrastructure. . .[52]

Director, of RIIA.

51. Tugendhat and Wallace, p. 77.

52. *Statement on the Defence Estimates 1993* (London: HMSO, July 1993), p. 24. ¶130 describes the "substrategic" capability, and ¶605 construction of the *Vanguard*-class Trident missile submarines. The statement also says that "the United Kingdom commits all its nuclear forces to NATO."

    In attributing "force elements" to several defence roles, the Ministry of Defence charges the "nuclear deterrent" role with 12 infantry battalions, a half "force element" of Royal Marines, and 3 ships (destroyers and frigates), in performance of duties to protect the deterrent force. *Ibid.*, p. 25.

The most salient claim made is that Britain commits to a *minimum* SSBN force, defined as a force which can have *one boat* at sea at all times. The four boats provide that assurance. One can be in refit, and therefore inaccessible; two could be in port, available to be put to sea with some delay, but certainly able to put to sea if required.

"Substrategic" Systems

In addition to its submarine-borne strategic nuclear missile force, Britain deploys only "the reduced number of WE177 free-fall bombs deployed on Tornado (aircraft)." Britain is preparing to shift the "substrategic" role to Trident at some point in the future. But why maintain a "substrategic" capability? The reason set out by the Secretary of State for Defence, Malcolm Rifkind, in a major policy statement, does not envision use in "limited" contexts, but instead as an element in strategic deterrence. As he puts it, Britain's use would be first use:

> . . . the ability to undertake a massive strike with strategic systems is not enough to ensure deterrence. An aggressor might, in certain circumstances, gamble on a lack of will ultimately to resort to such dire action. It is therefore important for the credibility of our deterrent that the United Kingdom also possesses the capability to undertake a more limited nuclear strike in order to induce a political decision to halt aggression by delivering an unmistakable message of our willingness to defend our vital interests to the utmost.[53]

Like the French doctrine of "*ultime avertissement*"—employing "substrategic" systems as a last warning—which it closely resembles, this strategic rationale raises a question about just what contingency plans may be in place. Without going into detail, it should be clear that initiating the use of nuclear weapons in a "crisis" is a dangerous step which invites response in kind and outcomes quite different from that anticipated by the Secretary of State for Defence.[54]

---

53. Malcolm Rifkind, "UK Defence Strategy: A Continuing Role for Nuclear Weapons?" Speech delivered 16 November 1993. House of Commons. Session 1993-94. Defence Committee. Second Report. *Progress of the Trident Programme*, 4 May 1994, p. 32.

54. The problem is not, despite Mr. Rifkind's characterization, one of "ensuring deterrence," since deterrence by its nature cannot be "ensured," but depends on a choice made by another party. In his scenario, no nuclear attack against Britain

European Nuclear Policy

François Mitterrand posed the issue of European nuclear policy in April 1992. By early 1994 the French response—for example, in the *Livre Blanc*—was cautious and cool.[55]

Britain has shied from the question from the beginning. Like France, however, it must address the question of how the European Union can have a common foreign and defense policy if nuclear weapons remain independently British and French. The question is somewhat different from that posed by NATO, a voluntary alliance, to which Britain "subscribed" its principal nuclear forces "except where Her Majesty's Government may decide that supreme national interests are at stake"—that is, when it would matter. It is different because defense is at the heart of Union.

In this vein the parliamentary assembly of the Western European Union—the European Union's defense arm—adopted a report calling on the WEU council of ministers to study the place of nuclear weapons in European security and how a common nuclear strategy could be found. It also asked ministers to set up a nuclear coordination group in WEU. The report's author, Armand de Decker, granting there was little interest in the issue at the moment, said "the debate on a European nuclear deterrent will be the moment of truth in the construction of European political union."[56]

---

or its allies has taken place. There has been "aggression" by a nuclear-armed state. Then the question is whether a nuclear-armed state which has up to that point withheld *nuclear* weapons but undertaken *conventional* aggression will be induced, by a nuclear demonstration, to both halt that aggression and continue to withhold nuclear weapons. Perhaps. And perhaps not.

Then the question is why Mr. Rifkind explains "substrategic" forces in this way. It avoids discussing other scenarios in which a single warhead might be used. It omits any acknowledgment of the "substrategic" force as a backup to *Trident*—a small but not altogether dismissible force—were the submarines to be destroyed or become vulnerable to detection. It keeps the way open to deploy modernized and more capable airborne forces in the future, without the additional capability seeming to be altogether new. Some combination of these rationales makes much more sense, within the deterrent paradigm, than the reason declared.

55. Cf. discussion of the *Livre Blanc* above.

56. De Decker, a Belgian, told the Assembly that European political union required that member states take part in developing the doctrine to assure their protec-

The national position was put by Gaullist MP Jacques Baumel, head of the WEU defense committee and concurrently vice-chairman of the defense committee of the French National Assembly. Baumel insisted that nuclear weapons were inherently national, under the control of statesmen legitimized by election. There was no chance countries—read Britain and France—would hand control over to an "unelected body."[57]

But a somewhat different tone was registered by Defense Minister François Léotard and French defense chief Jacques Lanxade. Léotard told an interviewer, not long after the June 1994 Franco-British security talks, that

> As the French nuclear deterrent was designed to ensure France's security and independence, any decision on its use can ultimately be made only on the national level . . . but that could change in the years ahead if the question of European political union is resolved and a true European defense identity emerges.[58]

Lanxade said in October that "France does not exclude the possibility of placing a nuclear deterrent force in defense of Europe, within the Western European Union":

> If . . . it is premature to speak of setting up a nuclear deterrent force at the service of Europe, it is not too early to approach the idea of risk-sharing and responsibilities which joint possession of nuclear weapons would imply.[59]

At the end of August 1994 Prime Minister Balladur said that setting in train the drafting of a White Paper on European defense policy would be a priority of France's chairmanship of the EU in the first semester 1995.[60] Jacques Chirac, elected French president on 7 May 1995, has not at this writing suggested any shift from the lines taken in 1994. During the presidential campaign he said that "a new type of

---

tion. A "common foreign and security policy"—envisaged by the Maastrict Treaty—could not develop if France and Britain insisted on defining their vital interests alone, under the protection of their nuclear umbrellas. "I am convinced that one day, sooner than you think, the EU will define its vital interests and the way of defending them." Reuters, 16 June 1994.

57. *Ibid.*

58. 14 June 1994, quoted in *Arms Control Reporter* 1994, p. 611.E-4.9.

59. *Ibid.*, citing *Sunday Telegraph* 11 June 1994, in FBIS-WEU 7.11.94.

60. *Le Monde*, 3 September 1994.

relationship between France and NATO (was) possible, and even necessary," but that he would not have France return to NATO's integrated military command.[61]

The Chinese Nuclear Weapons Program

In the months during which the Soviet Union was preparing and conducting its first nuclear test, the Chinese Communist Party, pressing civil war to a conclusion, seized state power and announced—on 1 October 1949—the People's Republic of China. With the bravado of the have-not, China discounted the political and military significance of nuclear weapons. Soon drawn into war with a nuclear power in Korea, China avoided public discussion of the military implications of nuclear weapons.[62]

Analysts argued that the principles set forth in Mao Zedong's military writings made it "difficult" for Chinese specialists to grasp and assert the strategic significance of the new weapons.[63] Protracted war, strategic withdrawal, withholding the strategic offensive until victory was certain, and subordinating the military to the political—among the most central elements of Maoist military practice—seemed unsuited to the nuclear era. Perhaps that was so. But we now know that on 14 September 1954 the Chinese Minister of Defense observed an extraordinary Soviet nuclear test, in which a 20 kiloton bomb was dropped from an aircraft and detonated at a height of 380 meters, and that within minutes units of some 44,000 Soviet troops dug into trenches were ordered into the blast zone.[64] The Chinese minister could well have concluded that soldiers could still fight after nuclear attack; he would not have learned the radiation effects, now believed to have been awful; but he certainly would have been impressed by the enormous power and destructive capacity of a nuclear bomb. China launched its nuclear bomb program a few weeks later.

---

61. *The New York Times*, 20 March 1995.

62. Alice L. Hsieh, *Communist China's Strategy in the Nuclear Era* (Englewood Cliffs, NJ: Prentice Hall, 1962), p. 7.

63. *Ibid.*, p. 9.

64. Fred Hiatt, Washington Post Service, in *International Herald Tribune*, 16 September 1994.

A Bomb Program: R & D with Soviet Assistance (1955- 1959)

Even in the turmoil of civil war and post-1949 construction, China found some resources for nuclear studies. The key figure was Qian Sanqiang, a nuclear physicist who in 1947 was appointed director of the Atomic Research Department of Academia Sinica. After the People's Republic was established, he became the director of an Institute of Physics in 1951 and an Institute of Atomic Energy in 1956.[65]

On 15 January 1955, at a meeting chaired by Mao Zedong, China decided to embark on a nuclear bomb program. Qian Sanqiang and other scientists explained to members of the Political Bureau the physics and geology on which a program would be based.[66] This decision coincided with the beginning of nuclear cooperation with the Soviet Union.

Shortly after the Chinese decision, the USSR Council of Ministers approved limited peaceful nuclear sharing with five countries, one of which was China. In return for raw materials for the Soviet nuclear program, China was to receive a research reactor—a heavy water reactor using uranium fuel at 2 percent U^{235}—and other assistance.[67]

The Korean War had shown the vulnerability of traditionally-

---

65. Chu-yuan Cheng, *Scientific and Engineering Manpower in Communist China, 1949-1963* (Washington: National Science Foundation, 1965), p. 238. Qian is also quoted as saying that a Nuclear Institute was created in 1949, with a dozen research scientists, whose number had grown "nearly tenfold" by 1955. *The Japan Times* (Kyodo-Reuter), 15 March 1978, citing a New China News Agency despatch.

66. John Wilson Lewis and Xue Litai, *China Builds the Bomb* (Stanford: Stanford University Press, 1988), pp. 38-39.

67. Anne M. Jonas, *The Soviet Union and the Atom: Peaceful Sharing, 1954-1958,* RAND Memorandum RM-2290, November 1958, pp. 12-15, cited in Alice L. Hsieh, *Communist China's Strategy in the Nuclear Era* (Englewood Cliffs, NJ: Prentice Hall, 1962), pp. 20-21. RAND Corporation analyst Hsieh speculates that designation of "peaceful uses" may have concealed Soviet intent to assist a Chinese weapons program, "a price that the Soviet Union may possibly have had to pay in order to secure Chinese acquiescence in a policy of caution dictated by the then existing military balance." However, Nie Rongzhen (see below) puts the beginning of Soviet cooperation with the weapons program at a later point.

armed Chinese forces. President Eisenhower claimed that deliberate intimations that the United States might use nuclear weapons had forced China to settle in the Korean armistice talks.[68] Marshal Peng Dehuai, named Minister of Defense in 1954, pressed a military modernization program, drawing lessons from the Korean War. In March 1955 the United States declared it would use tactical nuclear weapons should China attack Taiwan,[69] which must have sharpened China's attention to their destructiveness. By 1956 Chinese leaders were certainly alert to the change in strategic realities imposed by nuclear weapons, even if in defense they continued to rely on tested principles from an earlier period, consistent with the arms actually at their disposal.

Nie Rongzhen, soon to head China's program, has written memoirs telling of the early Sino-Soviet exchanges. China expected substantial Soviet support but was disappointed. Beijing raised "technical aid for China's missile research" with the Soviets in August 1956, but was largely rebuffed—Moscow agreed only to take 50 students—when the Soviets replied in September. Nie then proposed to the party Central Committee that China launch independent programs to acquire each of the essentials for a nuclear weapons capacity:

> I suggested to the Central Committee and the Central Military Commission that we start our own preparations for research to develop missiles, atomic bombs, new fighter planes and other sophisticated weapons, while striving to continue the negotiations with the Soviet Union, trying everything possible to get help. The Soviet government had agreed to train 50 missile specialists, and I said we should make the most of this chance.[70]

Nie's account makes it clear that he then had in mind a tactical weapon, a battlefield nuclear-tipped missile akin to fairly crude US weapons at the time:

---

68. Dwight D. Eisenhower, *Mandate for Change, 1953-56* (London: Heinemann, 1963), pp. 180-181, cited in Robert Neild, *How to Make Up Your Mind About the Bomb,* p. 118.

69. John Foster Dulles, "Report from Asia," comments of 8 March 1955 on return from the first meeting of the Manila Pact states, in *The Department of State Bulletin*, vol. 32, no. 821, 21 March 1955, pp. 459-460, cited in Hsieh, above, p. 27.

70. Nie Rongzhen, memoirs, excerpts titled "How China Develops Its Nuclear Weapons," in *Beijing Review* 29 April 1985, pp. 15-18.

> We were really in a quandary. According to the experts, it was no problem for Chinese engineers to design the (engine), shell bodies and aeromechanics of a rocket like the US Honest John. The problem lay in the complicated electronics, appliances, precision instruments and sensitive meters. China's development in these areas could not meet the needs of sophisticated weapons.[71]

Nor, it should be added, could China then produce the nuclear warhead which was the Honest John's *raison d'être*.[72]

Had Moscow's contribution been confined to receiving 50 students we would pay it little more attention. However, sometime between October 1956 and July 1957 the USSR "showed some signs of flexibility in offering technological aid," and in July 1957 Nie told I. V. Arkhipov that "we hoped his country would give technological aid to China's programme to develop sophisticated weapons." Moscow agreed. On 20 July a Chinese delegation was invited to negotiate the matter in Moscow. The Soviet ICBM was first tested in late August 1957. The nuclear delegation—including Nie—went in September, on 4 October the USSR launched Sputnik, and on 15 October, after 35 days of negotiations, the Chinese delegation signed an agreement "that the Soviet Union would aid China in such new technologies as rockets and aviation."[73] By some accounts the 15 October 1957 agreement also committed the Soviet Union to give China a prototype atomic bomb.[74] Nie does not say. The agreement was implemented "smoothly" through 1958 but—writes Nie in retrospect—did not come to much.[75] Indeed, it foundered on China's Great Leap Forward and

---

71. *Ibid.*, p. 15.
72. The Honest John, actively deployed from 1954 to 1974, was a tactical missile first deployed with a Mk-7 (W7) warhead, with a yield of 10-60 Kt. Thomas B. Cochran, William M. Arkin and Milton M. Hoenig (eds), *Nuclear Weapons Databook*, vol. 1. pp. 7-11. Thus Nie could in fact have been thinking of Honest John at the time.
73. Nie, above, p. 16.
74. "Statement by the Spokesman of the Chinese Government—A Comment on the Soviet Government's Statement of August 3." 15 August 1963. *Peking Review*, no. 33 (1963), 16 August 1963, pp. 7-15, p. 14. The relevant text:

    "As far back as June 20, 1959 . . . the Soviet Government unilaterally tore up the agreement on new technology for national defence concluded between China and the Soviet Union on October 15, 1957, and refused to provide China with a sample of an atomic bomb and technical data concerning its manufacture."
75. The delegation was led by Nie Rongzhen, Chen Geng and Song Renqiong.

ideological clashes between Moscow and Beijing which wracked their relations from 1958 onward.

Nie was not the only Chinese figure in Moscow during the key months of late 1957. Even Mao Zedong was there, attending a November conference of twelve governing communist parties. More germane, Guo Mojo led a scientific mission, Defense Minister Marshal Peng Dehuai met his Soviet counterpart Marshal Malinovsky on 4 November, and two days later a military mission left Beijing for Moscow.[76] It is a reasonable inference from Nie Rongzhen's account, however, that the Chinese side was throughout uncertain whether Moscow would be truly forthcoming. The Chinese must have debated to what extent the Soviets would deliver, and may have tested the Soviet side by making specific proposals. Writing in 1962, RAND analyst Alice Hsieh, after studying the composition of China's military mission and statements made at the time, speculated that the mission's aim was to discuss "the possibility of China's acquiring some kind of a nuclear capability" and that such a proposal "may have been raised and turned down by the Soviet side." She concludes:

> by the spring of 1958 it was clear that Peking was prepared to continue on the premise that the only road to an independent nuclear weapons capability was by way of a broadly based indigenous materials and development program—even though such a program relied on Soviet assistance.[77]

In retrospect, at least, Nie Rongzhen insists that China was right to undertake her own research program. (His words could, of course, be read as commentary on mid-1980s proposals to buy military

---

"After its signing, the agreement was implemented smoothly through 1957 and 1958. Although the Soviets only supplied us with a few outdated missiles, airplanes and material samples of other military equipment, along with the relevant technological material and some experts, all these won us time and enabled us to narrow the gap between our weapons technology and that of the advanced countries." Nie, above, p. 16.

76. Guo Moro, President of the Chinese Academy of Sciences, led a scientific mission which held talks with the Soviets from 18 October 1957 to 19 January 1958. A protocol on joint research, specifying 122 scientific and technological items, was signed. Hsieh states that "later reports simply suggested that key fields in this joint research were to be physics and the peaceful uses of atomic energy." Peng spoke with Marshal Malinovsky on 4 November, and the military mission left on 6 November. Hsieh, above, pp. 101-102.

77. Hsieh, above, p. 170.

systems abroad; certainly issues quite analogous to those which divided Peng Dehuai and Su Yu in 1955 and 1956 are present today.) His words confirm Hsieh's reading of the matter twenty years earlier. The CCP policy in 1957, he says, was essential to independence:

> Today, if we review the course we took during our development of sophisticated weapons, we are convinced that the policy of relying mainly on our own efforts, while seeking external assistance as an auxiliary as determined by the Central Committee, was not only correct, but vital. If we had relied solely on foreign aid or on purchasing foreign products for our weaponry, we wouldn't have made such quick achievements, our development would have become entirely dependent on others and would have made us vulnerable to outside manipulation.[78]

In any case, in mid-1959 the Soviet Union withdrew what aid it had given to China's nuclear program, according to a 1963 Chinese claim.[79] Remaining Soviet experts were withdrawn in 1960. Both moves were penalties for China's intransigent commitment to the Great Leap Forward and its implicit challenge to Soviet leadership of world communism.

The Bomb Program: R & D Without Soviet Help (1959 - 1964)

The Chinese research reactor began operation in mid-1958.[80] But with withdrawal of the Soviet specialists in 1959 and 1960, China was forced to consider how it would proceed. Moreover, China was in economic straits: the "three bad harvests" or "three lean years" of 1959-60-61 had become so acute that in January 1961 the CCP mandated severe austerity. These circumstances, Nie Rongzhen writes, raised questions about continuing the missile and nuclear weapons programs. Nie consulted with Mao Zedong, and in turn convened a meeting of specialists to assess China's position. They agreed to go forward, but "focusing on key problems," including medium-range and long-range missiles and nuclear weapons. Nie's conviction of the need for a nuclear deterrent, and Chen Yi's linkage of nuclear weapons to diplomacy, display motives altogether consonant with those of other states:

78. Nie, above, pp. 15-16.

79. See note 74.

80. New China News Agency, 30 June 1958, cited in Hsieh, above, p. 151.

> As for me, my opinion was always clear. To get rid of imperialist bullying, which China had suffered for more than a century, we had to develop these sophisticated weapons. At least then, we could effectively counterattack if China were subject to imperialist nuclear attack . . .
>
> Comrade Chen Yi said that even if we had to pawn our pants, China was still determined to make its own sophisticated weapons. He told me humorously many times that as foreign minister he still felt he couldn't straighten his back. If China could make the missiles and atom bombs, then he would have strong backing.[81]

The first Chinese nuclear test, on 16 October 1964, was a success:

> When Comrade Zhou proclaimed the good news, our eyes were moist with tears. Those present burst into long, thunderous applause. We warmly celebrated the great success.
>
> We also hailed the significant achievements we had made by relying on our own efforts. The superpowers' nuclear monopoly and their attempts at atomic blackmail had failed. The Chinese people would never submit to nuclear pressure. It was also a great victory for the Party's line of self-reliance. The facts clearly showed that the Chinese people had high goals, and were able to achieve what others had. Those who were present will never forget the excitement of that day.[82]

Foreign Assistance to the Nuclear Program

To what extent was China's nuclear weapons programme developed indigenously, and to what extent did it rely on foreign contributions? As explained above, China actively sought Soviet assistance in the period 1955-59. No doubt the assistance received—especially in the form of training in the Soviet Union—contributed to China's program. But China drew on other sources, not least of which was the fact that the United States had publicly demonstrated a bomb. Qian Sanqiang held a doctorate from the University of Paris and other Chinese recruited into the program had been trained in the United States. The degree to which Soviet assistance advanced the program, leading to a first test in 1964 instead of—say—1966 or 1970—cannot be judged without knowing much more than is now known, but Soviet refusal of assistance could at most have retarded the Chinese program, not denied China the bomb.

Something similar can be said of delivery systems. China's first

---

81. Nie, above, pp. 17-18.

82. Nie, above, p. 19.

nuclear-capable aircraft were adaptations of Soviet designs. China's building nuclear-powered submarines as platforms for solid-fuel nuclear-armed missiles was preceded by thirty years' experience with a fleet of some hundred diesel-electric submarines, largely transferred from the Soviet Union or built to a Soviet model. By the time China launched a nuclear-powered ballistic missile submarine the United States had sent such boats to sea for more than thirty years, their construction no doubt a subject of interest and conjecture among concerned Chinese. It is appropriate to emphasize Russia's passing missiles to China in the 1950s and training Chinese in missile technology. Nonetheless, China's capacity to solve the delivery problem by her own means should not be obscured.

On the other hand, would India have refused to sign the NPT (1968 or 1970) and detonated a nuclear device if China's first test had come not in 1964 but in 1974?

Targeting

China, like other nuclear weapons states, could target only what it could reach. Of course, a nuclear weapons state could, in principle, transport a nuclear weapon to another country by mundane means, such as merchant ships and trucks, but there is no public evidence that any has done so. With that caveat, China is confined to those targets within range of its missiles and aircraft capable of carrying a nuclear weapon.

China's first nuclear-capable missile was the DF-2, deployed in 1966, with a range of 1100 km and a payload of one 20 Kt weapon.[83] Lewis and Xue say "the Central Military Commission ordered it sited in Northeast China and targeted on cities and US military bases in Japan."[84] If this is correct, Japan became the surrogate target to deter US nuclear attack on China. Soviet cities could be reached by a nuclear-armed Tu-16 bomber, also first deployed in 1966, with a range of 5900 km.[85]

---

83. *SIPRI Yearbook 1987*, Table 1.8, p. 35.
84. John Lewis and Xue Litai, *China Builds the Bomb* (Stanford: Stanford University Press, 1988), p. 212.
85. *SIPRI Yearbook 1987*, Table 1.8, p. 35.

China's second nuclear-armed missile, the DF-3, was first deployed in 1971. The SIPRI[86] estimates for the DF-3 and DF-3A are shown in table 2.3.

TABLE 2.3
SIPRI Estimates of Chinese Land-Based Nuclear Systems

YEAR	MISSILE	NUMBER DEPLOYED	YEAR DEPLOYED	RANGE (km)	WARHEAD X YIELD
1987	DF-3	85-125	1972	2600	1 x 2-3 Mt
1993	DF-3A	50	1971	2800	1 x 3.3 Mt
1993	DF-4	20	1980	4750	1 x 3.3 Mt
1993	DF-5A	4	1981	13,000	1 x 4-5 Mt

Source: *SIPRI Yearbook 1987* and *SIPRI Yearbook 1993* (Stockholm: Stockholm International Peace Research Institute, 1987, 1993).

Lewis and Xue believe the DF-3 was deployed to target Soviet cities:

> Soviet cities now became the designated targets, and starting in 1971 the first DF-4 [*sic*] units moved to Qinghai (Xiao Qaidam and Da Qaidam) and other sites in Northwest China, closer to key Soviet targets.[87]

When China's next missile, the DF-4, was deployed in 1978, its longer range permitted siting in interior locations. The range was sufficient to hold at risk targets in the Soviet Union, Eastern Europe and India, depending on the launch location within China, but would not reach Britain or France.

Finally, China deployed the DF-5 with truly intercontinental range, extending coverage to all of Europe, but for which the only plausible target is the United States

For one fact we have a specific Chinese admission: Jiang Zemin and Boris Yeltsin signed a nuclear non-targeting agreement in September 1994 and declared they would no longer target each other's

---

86. Successive issues of the *SIPRI Yearbook* contain carefully compiled estimates of the nuclear forces of all nuclear weapons states. The *SIPRI Yearbook* data and the data in the five volumes of the *Nuclear Weapons Databook*, however, are compiled, as a first approximation, by the same people and are drawn from the same sources. In the case of China, which is least forthcoming about its forces, they must rely more than in other cases on inference and foreign sources.

87. Lewis and Xue, p. 213. Presumably DF-3 was intended.

territory.

By coupling a nuclear-armed missile to a submarine, China extends the missile's range, bringing under threat any region which the submarine can approach. The initial Chinese system, the JL-1 solid-fuel missile fired from SSBNs 09-02 and 09-03, has a relatively short range, but a longer range is planned for the JL-2, which will arm SSBN 09-04 (table 2.4).

TABLE 2.4

Lewis and Xue Estimates of Chinese Sea-Based Nuclear Systems

SOURCE	MISSILE	NUMBER DEPLOYED	YEAR DEPLOYED	RANGE (km)	WARHEAD X YIELD
Lewis & Xue[a]	JL-1	09-02: 12	1983; 1987	1 700	1 x 400 Kt
	JL-1	09-03: 12			
Lewis & Xue[b]	JL-2[c]	09-04: 20		8 000	1? x 400 Kt

a Lewis and Xue, *China's Strategic Seapower*, p. 120.

b Lewis and Xue, *China's Strategic Seapower*, p. 121, speculating on Chinese intentions from cited sources and inferring range from its being called a "long-range" missile. Number of missiles on 09-04 "not confirmed."

c The JL-2 will be a sea-based version of the DF-31 missile.

China issues no defence policy document like the French *Livre Blanc* and *Loi du Programmation Militaire* or the British annual *Defence Estimates*. US Secretary of Defense William Perry pressed China for greater openness when he visited there in October 1994.[88]

What Are Nuclear "Tests" Testing?

The nuclear test moratorium of 1992-95 and discussion of a CTB

88. *The New York Times* reported on 17 October 1994: "One goal is to persuade the Chinese to be more open about their military activities . . . The Chinese say their annual budget is about $7 billion, but Pentagon officials said that sum did not include major weapons programs and other military activities. 'We want to know what is behind Beijing's defense strategy, modernization and relations with Russia,' a senior Defense official said."

take nuclear tests to be sufficiently similar that it makes sense to consider "tests" as acts to be controlled. That may be. Nonetheless, nuclear tests have very different purposes, and the position of the Three—as French critics of the moratorium and Chinese officials repeatedly point out—is not at all that of Russia and the United States.

Nuclear weapons states have offered scant information about the precise purposes of their tests. Atmospheric tests, however, inject telltale isotopic evidence into the air, and underground tests create detectable seismic waves. By combining sensor evidence, official accounts, and an impressive marshaling of other public sources Robert S. Norris and his colleagues have assembled exhaustive test lists, in which they carefully identify both their sources and those points on which they remain unsure.[89]

The obvious first purpose is to prove a new design, or a variation on an already proven design. Although the first nuclear weapon design used in war had not been previously test-fired,[90] all Five have systematically tested weapon designs. It is generally understood, however, that a "straightforward" fission device can be designed with high confidence that it will perform as intended, without resort to an actual nuclear test detonation. Engineers fabricating a bomb on that basis would keep to proven and documented paths, employing computations to estimate effects, and then certifying the result by "cold" testing.[91] However, design requirements become much more demand-

---

89. Robert S. Norris, Andrew S. Burrows, and Richard W. Fieldhouse, *Nuclear Weapons Databook.* vol. 5. *British, French, and Chinese Nuclear Weapons* (Boulder, Colorado: Westview, 1994), Appendices 1-3. A Natural Resources Defense Council study.

90. The design tested at Alamogordo on 16 July 1945 was a plutonium device, the model for the bomb dropped on Nagasaki. No prototype of the uranium bomb dropped on Hiroshima had been tested.

91. In a "cold" test, an inert material, such as U^{238}, is substituted for the U^{235} or Pu. South African officials describe the test preparations observed in 1977 as plans for a "cold test," fully-instrumented, to test logistics for an actual detonation. David Albright, "South Africa and the Affordable Bomb," *Bulletin of the Atomic Scientists* July-August 1994, p. 41. An official deeply engaged in the French test program describes the passage of a design from conception to actual test detonation as including "tens" of "cold tests." Lucien Michaud, "Pourquoi des essais nucléaires?," in GREFHAN (Groupe d'Études Français d'Histoire de l'Armement Nucléaire), *Les Expérimentations Nucléaires Françaises* (Paris: GREFHAN, Institut de France, 1993), pp. 35-44, p. 38. In 1993 former

ing, and tolerances more precise, if one chooses to build a thermonuclear bomb or a very small bomb.

A second often-cited reason to pursue tests is to show that weapons fabricated some years earlier remain ready. It is true that a warhead is not "still," in that fissile material engages continuously in radioactive display, and that for any given design there is no experience of effects over time. An alternative exists: to dismantle the warhead carefully, subjecting it to close scrutiny.[92] There is a logical problem, too, to the argument that the inventory needs to be "confirmed" since the only weapon confirmed by destructive testing is the one tested, which is then no longer available.[93] On the other hand, the argument that it is politically useful to show *others* that one's deterrent forces work has, within the paradigm of deterrence or "dissuasion," a certain logical force.

A third reason to test is "safety." "Safety" experiments can be of two types. One—not requiring detonation—asks what would occur if the weapon were subject to fire or accident, or if the chemical high explosive accidentally exploded; radioactive material may be used to simulate a warhead.[94] The second—requiring detonation—asks if the warhead will actually fire despite measures, such as change to a "safer" chemical high explosive in the warhead assembly, to prevent unwanted detonations.

Pakistan Army Chief of Staff General Mirza Aslam Beg said that in 1987 Pakistan "carried out the test (of a nuclear device) in cold laboratory conditions and it was very successful." *International Herald Tribune*, 24 August 1994.

92. Geoffrey Beaven, Deputy Controller (Nuclear) in the British Ministry of Defense, has explained that scrutiny has led to the official judgment that the WE177 remains serviceable despite age: "(the) surveillance programme is an ongoing testing programme which looks at the aging effect on warheads as it occurs. We use that to predict how much life we think is left in the warhead. We extend the life as we inspect it and as we get knowledge of how it is aging. That has enabled us, as it has remained in service, to predict further life for the warhead." *Ibid*., Minutes of Evidence, ¶ 1254. The Defence Committee is quite clear that this is *examination*, not explosive testing. *Ibid*., p. xviii, ¶ 37.

93. Yet the argument is still heard. On 5 July 1993 UK Defence Secretary Malcolm Rifkind, speaking in the House of Commons, cited ensuring the "safety and reliability" of nuclear weapons as a reason for continued testing. Norris et al, *Nuclear Weapons Databook*, vol. 5, p. 53.

94. Britain conducted thirty-one experiments of this type in Australia from 1959 to 1961 under the names Vixen A and Vixen B.

A fourth reason to test is to observe how a warhead responds, and perhaps how detonation takes place, in an environment already suffused by the effects of the detonation of another nuclear weapon.

In the subsections which follow we will compare tests to systems, in effect asking what is "undone" as discussion of a Comprehensive Test Ban goes forward. In addition to matching tests to systems, we could also ask if tests can be matched to the warhead and delivery package characteristics which have been sought-after by system designers in some programs. Leaving aside early steps (fission and boosted fission in U and Pu versions, thermonuclear, and warheads then designed for lower weight/yield ratios and other "routine" optimizations), developed programs have sought these features:

(a) MIRVed payload (placing two or more "independently targetable reentry vehicles" in the same package)
(b) "variable-yield warhead"
(c) ABM penetration package (to foil defense measures))
(d) ERW ("enhanced radiation weapon," the "neutron bomb")
(e) substitution of IHE ("insensitive high explosive") for the chemical high explosive earlier used in many warhead designs, as a safety measure
(f) miniaturization, to achieve smaller and lighter warheads, sometimes as an element in MIRVing a payload
(g) "hardened" warhead (designed to survive a hostile environment)

Finally, the United States has used some tests to calibrate simulation techniques, and French designers wish to do so too. These technical achievements are eight widely sought designer desiderata.

In the period 1981-1994 a total of 11 British, 90 French, and 14 Chinese tests have been reported.[95] Since July 1963 Britain, the Soviet

95. These totals are subject to some uncertainty. For example, Norris et al. state that "at least" eight French tests were conducted in 1986. In addition, they list an additional eleven events, some of which they speculate may have been safety tests. "Safety tests are counted," they say, "even if there was no yield." (p. 416) The cutback, and then cutoff, of French tests and the measured pace of the Chinese program are shown by a year-by-year list of tests in the period 1981-1994:

Union (Russia), and United States have tested only underground. France last tested in the atmosphere on 15 September 1974 at Mururoa, and China on 16 October 1980 at the Lop Nor test site.

Britain

Of the 11 British tests 9 were of weapons in the 20-150 Kt range. The 1983 and 1991 tests were of less than 20 Kt. No purposes are firmly identified by Norris et al., but they report that the 1986 test was "said to be" Trident-related.[96] A reasonable inference from British procurement plans is that one or more tests confirmed the validity of the British-engineered Trident warhead, even if—as evidence suggests—Britain received extensive design support from the United States in bringing forth the warhead.[97] Weapons systems and missions known to have been under consideration may, at some future time, be

NUCLEAR TEST DETONATIONS 1981-1994

YEAR	BRITAIN	FRANCE	CHINA
1981	1	12	0
1982	1	9	1
1983	1	9	2
1984	2	8	2
1985	1	8	0
1986	1	8	0
1987	1	8	1
1988	0	8	1
1989	1	8	0
1990	1	6	2
1991	1	6	0
1992	0	0	2
1993	0	0	1
1994	0	0	2

Sources: 1981-93: Norris et al., p. 13 and Appendices 1, 2 and 3. 1994: wire service reports and Chinese statements.

96. Norris et al., pp. 402-403, n70.

97. Rear Admiral Richard Irwin, Chief Strategic Systems Executive, insisted on 16 March 1994 "We have done all the tests we need for Trident. We are quite confident that the Trident warhead is fully designed, completely tested, finished." House of Commons. Session 1993-94. Second Report. *Progress of the Trident Programme*. 4 May 1994. Minutes of Evidence, p. 14, ¶ 1232. The Trident warhead is "fixed yield and determined on manufacture," explicitly not variable yield. Irwin, *ibid.*, p. 12, ¶1211.

matched onto the test list:

(i) Trident: Trident II,
(ii) TASM (Tactical Air-to-Surface Missile): not identified,[98] and, speculatively,
(iii) Trident: "substrategic" variant or variable-yield warhead.[99]

But British officials declare that the "substrategic" warhead will be identical to the strategic warhead.[100]

---

98. Norris et al. believe "design work on the TASM warhead probably started in earnest in 1988" and that "preliminary designs were probably tested" noting three British tests in Nevada after 1988, p. 131. The TASM missile was canceled 18 October 1993. Statement by Malcolm Rifkind to the House of Commons.

99. A 1993 Defence Select Committee report envisions Trident missiles armed with a single warhead performing the "substrategic" mission, stating there is "no technical reason" why Trident cannot be configured to do this. Norris et al., p. 132, citing House of Commons (Defence Select Committee), *Report on the Progress of Trident* (London: HMSO, 6 July 1993). As noted above, however, the proven Trident warhead is fixed-yield.

100. House of Commons. Session 1993-94. Second Report. *Progress of the Trident Programme*. Minutes of Evidence, p. 13, ¶s 1219-1223. Efforts by members of the House of Commons Defence Committee to elicit the nature of the "substrategic" warhead led to this exchange:

(Mr. Home Robertson, MP) . . . I understand that the cost of modifying the warhead to give it a tactical role is going to be zero. Does that mean that the tactical warhead will have the same yield as its strategic counterpart . . . ?

(Mr. Geoffrey Beaven, Deputy Controller [Nuclear]) The existing warhead can fulfill a sub-strategic mission.

(Mr. Home Robertson) I bet it can, but would that not be a bit of an overkill?

(Mr. Beaven) Not necessarily.

(Mr. Home Robertson) Are there any modifications needed, despite the fact that there is no extra cost, or is that all classified?

(Mr. Beaven) The existing warhead will meet a sub-strategic role.

(Mr. Home Robertson) It is the same missile and the same warhead really?

(Mr. Beaven) Yes.

(Mr. Viggers, MP) So whether it is strategic or tactical is what you tell the recipient.

(Mr. Home Robertson) That will make them feel much better, will it not?

(Rear Admiral Richard Irwin) I think it will be easier to give you an answer on a classified basis.

(Mr. Home Robertson) They will feel better if they are hit by a tactical warhead, will they?

Britain has focused its limited resources on a handful of warhead designs. In part it could do so because US weapons complemented its own, and access to US design information spared inventing every step. The interplay between US and British programs has affected Britain's choice of "designer desiderata."

France

France, by contrast, conducted 90 tests in 1981-94. These are likely matched to known systems, in many cases, and sources such as the annual CEA reports offer claims, in general terms, confirming such purposes. Five warhead designs are now deployed, as shown in table 2.7.[101]

Not deployed, notably, is the TN90 warhead developed for the Hadès missile, of which 30 are "in store." Other proposed weapons systems to which tests were probably dedicated are:

(Sir Nicholas Bonsor, Chairman) We will go into private session at the end to cover that point.

Further efforts to draw out officials (*Ibid.*, p. 20,. ¶s 1313-1315.) on the "substrategic" variant suggest that some missiles might carry one warhead and others more. However many they carried, they could be used in a "strategic" or "substrategic" mode:

(Mr. Menzies Campbell, MP) Just to be clear, what one would do leaving the quayside . . . is that one would put a mix, as it were, into the arsenal.

(Rear Admiral Irwin) Yes.

(Mr. Campbell) There would be some strategic and some tactical, and you would make that decision, I think you told us last year, in advance before you leave the quayside? This is not a decision you make once you are in the water?

(Rear Admiral Irwin) you would have to configure it before you left. Having left, you can choose the way a missile is configured and say, "I will use that one sub-strategically." You can also use it strategically. If you configured it to only have one bang then its strategic side would be relatively small, but depending on how you configured it, it can make a bigger or lesser contribu tion.

(Mr. Campbell) But you have, as it were, to allocate. You have to create the match between missile and warhead before you go to sea.

(Rear Admiral Irwin) That is correct.

(i) M45 to go aboard new SNLE class: TN75;[101]
(ii) Matra aircraft-borne missile;
(iii) M5 to go aboard new SNLE class in 2005.[102]

TABLE 2.5
British Nuclear Weapons Tests
Selected Objectives

GOAL	ACTION
MIRV	The Chevaline was reportedly *not* MIRVed, but the Trident II will be. Since the system is or imitates a US system—the missile and reentry bodies are of US provenance, and the warhead is "probably a variation of American W76 warhead"—most warhead test requirements were met by the United States. Source: Norris p. 169.
penetration	Assurance that the British Polaris missile could penetrate missile defenses around Moscow underlay design and deployment of the "Chevaline," understood to combine "three or fewer" and probably two warheads and an array of decoys and devices to defeat defense. Source: Norris p. 163.
miniaturization	The Polaris A3TK Chevaline system was designed to defeat an anti-missile defense. To make space for the Penetration Aid Carrier a miniaturized warhead was developed. Source: Norris p. 163.
hardening	The Polaris A3TK Chevaline is reported to be hardened against ABM effects. Source: Norris p. 163.

Sources: Robert S. Norris, Andrew S. Burrows, and Richard W. Fieldhouse, *Nuclear Weapons Databook*. Volume 5. *British, French, and Chinese Nuclear Weapons* (Boulder, Colorado: Westview, 1994), p. 163: "The Penetration Aid Carrier (PAC) is a sophisticated maneuverable space-vehicle used for deploying the payload on differing trajectories (citing House of Commons, *Chevaline Improvements*, p. 1); the PAC is equipped with liquid and solid fuel propulsion, an on-board computer and a navigation system (citations); weight of PAC about 306-400 lbs (citing Freeman, *Lifting the Veil*, p. 32)."

101. The TN75 was first successfully tested in 1990, and "proved" in 1991. Norris et al., p. 416, citing the CEA *Rapport Annuel 1991*, p. 24, and *CEA Rapport Annuel 1992*, p. 61.

102. French parliamentary discussion of effects of the test moratorium cite the need to perfect a warhead for the M5 missile as one reason to resume tests.

In addition, France has designed and tested an enhanced radiation weapon ("neutron bomb")—for which there are no known present deployment plans—and is working to enhance and refine weapons.[103]

TABLE 2.6

French Nuclear Weapons Tests

Selected Objectives

GOAL	ACTION
MIRV	The TN 70 and TN 71 are designed for six-warhead MIRVed M4A and M4B SLBMs. Source: Norris p. 218.
"variable yield"	The TN 90 developed for Hadès is reportedly available in four yields up to 80 Kt. Source: Norris p. 5.
penetration	Penetration capabilities claimed for TN 71. Source: Norris p. 219, citing CEA *Rapport Annuel 1985*, pp. 77-79.
neutron bomb	An ERW warhead was developed for the Hadès missile. Source: Norris p. 273.
hardening	The TN 70, deployed in 1985, and TN 71 are "extremely hardened." Source: Norris p. 218. The TN-71 is sometimes called TN-71 D, for "durcie" (hardened). Source: GRIP.
calibration	Need for calibration of simulation is given as reason for further tests, for which approval was granted in June 1995.

Sources: Robert S. Norris, Andrew S. Burrows, and Richard W. Fieldhouse, *Nuclear Weapons Databook*, volume 5. *British, French, and Chinese Nuclear Weapons* (Boulder, Colorado: Westview, 1994). GRIP (Institut Européen de Recherche et d'Information sur la Paix et la Sécurité). *Memento défense-désarmement 1992* (Bruxelles: GRIP, January 1992), p. 123.

103. Norris et al., pp. 273, 213: "French weapons designers continue to work on a variety of features concerning warhead safety (including the incorporation of insensitive high explosives and the study of new liquid high explosives), security (against unauthorized use), variable yields, further improvements in yield-to-weight ratios, and hardening." On the new explosive, they cite CEA, *Rapport Annuel 1992*, p. 32.

TABLE 2.7

Deployed French Warhead Designs

WARHEAD	BASING	NUMBER: SYSTEMS
TN61	Silo-based IRBMs	18: "Plateau d'Albion"
TN70	Sub-borne SLBM	96: one set of 16 SLBMs (M4A) with 6 warheads each
TN71		288: three sets of 16 SLBMs (M4B) with 6 warheads each
TN80	Aircraft-borne ASMP	18: on 18 Mirage IVP aircraft
TN81		42: on 45 Mirage 2000N
		20: on 24 Super Étendard

China

China conducted fourteen tests in the period 1981-1994. Little about purpose can be inferred from publicly available data on the tests, but the relatively small number of tests must map onto the principal deployments China has made and might wish to make. A good measure of speculations current in Beijing in late 1994 is given by the resident *New York Times* correspondent's anticipation that China will test "the prototype for China's new submarine-launched ballistic missile [or] it may be a miniaturized warhead that could be bolted to China's first multiple-warhead missile able to reach Russian and American cities."[104]

TABLE 2.8

Chinese Nuclear Weapons Tests

Selected Objectives

GOAL	ACTION
MIRV	Anticipated. Source: Tyler 26 October 1994.
penetration	Lewis and Xue include penetration capabilities among warhead characteristics. Source: Lewis and Xue, p. 177.

104. Patrick E. Tyler, *The New York Times*, 26 October 1994.

Table 2.8 continued

neutron bomb	Norris et al. report that China's test of 29 September 1988 was "reputed to be" a test of an enhanced radiation bomb. Source: Norris et al., p. 421. Lewis and Xue state that in 1984 China made "critical breakthroughs" in neutron bomb design, and "over the next years . . . achieved success in testing these and other low-yield weapons." Source: Lewis and Xue, p. 235, citing *Shijie Ribao*, 9 November 1988.
insensitive high explosive (IHE)	An engineer in the Chinese weapons program told a US specialist in 1994 that the purpose of China's testing was to proof IHE. He also reported Chinese saying they had achieved a satisfactory set of warhead designs and intended to test no new designs.
miniaturization	Tests in the 1990s sought to develop "a new warhead with a much higher yield-to-weight ratio and with a capability of further miniaturization." Source: Lewis and Xue, p. 177. An unidentified Chinese "who worked inside China's ballistic missile program" said the 7 October 1994 test was to prove a new smaller but more powerful warhead required for its second-generation ballistic missiles. "China is testing its miniaturization program." Source: Tyler 8 October 1994.

Sources: Robert S. Norris, Andrew S. Burrows, and Richard W. Fieldhouse, *Nuclear Weapons Databook*. Volume 5. *British, French, and Chinese Nuclear Weapons* (Boulder, Colorado: Westview, 1994). Patrick E. Tyler, *The New York Times*, 8 October 1994 and 26 October 1994. John Wilson Lewis and Xue Litai, *China's Strategic Seapower* (Stanford: Stanford University Press, 1994).

Test Simulation

The nuclear program of each nuclear weapon state includes an extensive design and proofing capability. Designers and engineers have sought from the outset to exploit laboratory and modeling capabilities in order to short-cut design and reduce the number of required nuclear tests. Recurrent proposals of "test ban" have given further impetus to the quest for investigative methods short of actual nuclear detonation. The Five having agreed to negotiate a CTB is colored—for some if not all—by their enhanced simulation capabilities. Britain, the United States and France have all made plain their intention to press those capabilities still further.

The British position is set out authoritatively in a July 1994 Foreign Office memorandum, addressing implications of a CTB:

> We made plans for three tests at the Nevada Test Site in the period 1993 to 1996. . . . The loss of these tests, which were to provide information for the longer term, will have no immediate impact on our defence nuclear programme. It is however necessary to develop alternative technologies to provide, as far as possible through other means the information and assurance that nuclear testing would have given. Development of the necessary capabilities and programmes—sometimes referred to as Above Ground Experimentation (AGEX)—is underway, with the aim of providing the basis for continuing confidence in our design and predictive tools and our ability to ensure the continuing safety and reliability of our nuclear weapons. We are also further developing cooperation with both the United States and France.[105]

In fact, Britain began to hedge against a CTB by buying simulation equipment many years earlier.[106]

France's simulation program PALEN became a major focus of public debate at the end of 1993. In the course of this discussion a parliamentary committee prepared a report on PALEN, summarized in the next section, with a description of the equipment to be purchased and—in general terms—how it would be used.

In October 1994 the United States offered to provide China assistance in simulation, as an inducement to end tests. Secretary of Defense William Perry, in Beijing, said that his talks with his Chinese counterpart, Defense Minister Chi Haotian, focused on ways of using computer simulation to take the place of nuclear tests.

> The Chinese are pursuing that idea . . . and we discussed the possibility of exchanging information in that field, to the extent that we can do it without compromising security.[107]

---

105. House of Commons. Session 1993-94. Foreign Affairs Committee. *UK Policy on Weapons Proliferation and Control in the Post-Cold War Era.* Minutes of Evidence. 6 July 1994. Supplementary memorandum by the Foreign and Commonwealth Office, p. 28.

106. D. Fishlock, "Vulcan and Helen: Lasers of Unusual Power," *Financial Times*, 5 March 1981, cited in John Simpson, *The Independent Nuclear State: The United States, Britain and the Military Atom* (London: Macmillan, 2nd ed. 1986), p. 197.

107. Agence France Presse, 18 October 1994.

A senior Foreign Ministry official experienced in arms control acknowledged that China was interested in pursuing Perry's proposal to substitute simulation for tests, but observed that simulation, while attractive to the Five, could be viewed by non-nuclear weapons states as another form of proliferation. "Whereas it might be technically feasible," he said, "it may not be politically feasible."[108]

The French Plan to Simulate Nuclear Tests (PALEN)

President Mitterrand's decision in April 1992 to commit France to a nuclear test moratorium was accompanied by an instruction to the Commissariat à l'Énergie Atomique (CEA) to press forward with a program to simulate nuclear tests. This exercise, not far advanced when Prime Minister Pierre Bérégovoy announced Mitterrand's decision on 8 April 1992, was named PALEN: Préparation à la Limitation des Essais Nucléaires. It figured importantly in the debates of 1992-95 about whether France should sustain the moratorium, and how France should position herself vis-á-vis a proposed Comprehensive Test Ban.

A CTB would achieve four purposes: it would hinder established nuclear weapons states from confirming the validity of new weapon designs; prevent aspiring nuclear states from testing their first prototype; halt environmental harms of the tests themselves; and bar "flexing" tests intended to display the continued virility of the deployed force. The open literature does not make clear how far simulation can carry designers when the sought configuration or effect departs from designs proven by prior testing. Nonetheless, simulation is being sold to its public buyers, at least in France, as a set of techniques to offset the need for tests in design of new warheads. (The point of the French National Assembly report we introduce below is to insist that some tests are necessary, both to calibrate a simulation system and finally prove new warhead designs.) This path to evade the first purpose of a CTB is unavailable to nuclear aspirants, however, because they would not know how to simulate and would be barred from the weapons tests by which simulation techniques could be calibrated and assessed.

Twenty-three days after China's test of 5 October 1993, the

---

108. *Los Angeles Times*, 21 October 1994.

French National Assembly's Defence Commission established a panel to study the PALEN program.[109] Whether the panel's subsequent report is technically sound in all respects and captures other states' programs correctly will be subject to argument. Nonetheless, it reflects testimony from French (and other) specialists and its authors' political judgments. It is a revelatory document in the politics of French nuclear policy. We will, therefore, canvass it at some length.

The panel's report to the National Assembly begins by observing that there was reason to think Mitterrand's decision was opposed by the greater part of the French defense establishment, both military and political. As a result of the Chinese test, they say, the French public has come to question the moratorium's effect on French national security. Shall we be "good pupils," they ask, while the "bad pupils" scoff at the rules of good conduct?

The report follows several approaches in turn, which will be reviewed below. It describes analogous efforts to simulate nuclear tests in the United States. It considers the significance of Chinese testing. It spells out the purposes of the French testing program. It describes PALEN itself. The panel concludes as follows:

> we must say, with the greatest emphasis, that without new tests France is not sure to be in a position to procure a simulation system guaranteeing absolutely that it will remain master of its arms and thus assured of its security and independence.[110]

Jean-Michel Boucheron records a certain dissent from the panel's conclusions, but it otherwise supports the view that tests are required.

France and the United States Nuclear Program

The panel places emphasis on the United States' having already mastered the essential elements of simulation technology.[111] After

---

109. Assemblée Nationale. Commission de la défense. Rapport d'information n° 847. *La simulation des essais nucléaires*. René Galy-Dejean, Jacques Baumel, Jean-Michel Boucheron, Daniel Colin, Pierre Favre, and Pierre Lellouche. 15 December 1993.

110. *Ibid.*, p. 60.

111. US specialists have commented that the report "drew the wrong conclusions because it appeared to be premised on the mistaken belief that the United States has already developed, and intends to rely upon, a comprehensive 'simulation system' to replace the nuclear tests that will be banned under a CTB." R. L.

noting that previous moratoria had led to failures and delays in thermonuclear weapon design by the United States (November 1958 to September 1961) and United Kingdom (1966-73), the panel reviews the successive US simulation programs ATP (Augmented Nuclear Test Program), TBR (Test Ban Readiness) and SAFEGUARD. TBR coupled simulation methods with specific nuclear tests. It was akin to PALEN, but in 1992 was in its final phase.

> We know that the program enabled them to establish tables for the range 0 to 10 Kt covering the entire functional domain of ignitions and detonations from the feeblest energies, truly undetectable. With these data in hand, they can also derive the algorithms (programs) required for future simulations as well as the planned radiographic facility (DARTH) of the AGT (Above Ground Test) scheme.[112]

Between 1980 and 1989, they say, the United States conducted ten tests in which some hundred micro-charges were fired. "These tests of thermonuclear micro-charges had as their purpose to achieve a 'correlation' with experiments simulated with the laser NOVA at Livermore and to design a future laser of very high power for fusion experiments and, in the same vein, the definition of new thermonuclear stages." The United States, they say, may not have acquired all of the techniques needed for simulation, but has in hand the essentials.

SAFEGUARD includes provisions for conserving skills, maintaining the Nevada Test Site, and monitoring other states' programs (for example, within a CTB). It also includes, however, two technical elements—experiments which the panel presumably cites because of their similarity to features of the PALEN program:

> First there are «hydronuclear tests» undertaken at the Nevada Test Site which are nothing more than nuclear tests which release only very small amounts of fission energy and are therefore undetectable. Then they are developing, under the name AGEX (Above Ground Experiment) an extensive physics lab dedicated to simulation. It includes, for ignition, a radiographic accelerator called DARTH, now being built, which will permit measuring the movement of matter and its compression in «cold» hydrodynamic tests, that is those which do not release nuclear energy. For

---

Garwin, R. E. Kidder and C. E. Paine, "A Report on Discussions Regarding the Need for Nuclear Test Explosions to Maintain French Nuclear Weapons Under a Comprehensive Test Ban." Federation of American Scientists and Natural Resources Defense Council. January 1995.

112, Assemblée Nationale. Commission de la défense. Rapport d'information n° 847, above, p. 24.

physical simulation of levels of power, it will be necessary to use a megajoule laser (project NIF) as well as high-energy pulsed apparatus. From the beginning AGEX has been inseparable from nuclear tests. It is difficult to say today what effects the moratorium may have on this program.[113]

The United States may have said it will undertake no nuclear arms modernization program, but it is nonetheless—under the rubric of "prototyping"—engaged in research on new concepts, including mini-charges with special effects.

Comment on China

The panel offers several fragments and undigested observations about China: that its test preparations can be observed by satellite, that China could conduct numerous tests before NPT renegotiation, that members had wondered whether China might consider it normal to test for third countries. They discern a change in the US posture toward China's testing in the weeks after the 5 October 1993 test, indicating that the US would now accept the notion of several Chinese tests in 1994 and 1995. They then note an unverified report that the United States had sold China a supercomputer, ostensibly for civil purposes. The reader might conclude, and the panel may have so intended, that there was collusion between the United States and China, collusion which would enable China to modernize weapons despite the moratorium.[114]

Purposes of French Tests

The panel presents several reasons for French tests. They "permit validation of physics conceptions fundamental for nuclear arms," a particular area of physics largely unexplored. Without tests, the panel suggests, the warhead for the envisioned M5 missile would necessarily be larger and the system as a whole less than optimal. Tests also enable weapon designers to proof designs. They provide evidence of performance after a period of aging. They permit maintaining know-

113. *Ibid.*, p. 26.

114. *Ibid.*, pp. 33-34. But note the speculation in this volume that China has frozen weapon design, and that the purpose of its 1993-96 test program is to confirm those final designs and their initiation with Insensitive High Explosive (IHE).

how: by 2000 "almost all of the teams which conceived the TN 75 will have retired."[115] They reinforce dissuasion, "signifying to the whole world that our arms work."

PALEN

According to the report, PALEN is an ensemble of projects using calculation, X-rays, and lasers. CEA is determining what computers to buy, and will acquire them by 1997. It is also planning to buy a "radiographic accelerator" for entry into service in 1998, to obtain more detailed information than previously available. This X-ray machine is used to study instabilities in chain reactions under laboratory conditions. Lasers are used to simulate a nuclear explosion by focusing energy on a very small target of fissile material (deuterium-tritium), yielding a "thermonuclear micro-explosion." The CEA's largest current laser, PHEBUS, was the result of industrial cooperation with the United States. It envisages following the same route for the new machine, which will have an output 100 times greater than PHEBUS. The panel understands this device to be the heart of the PALEN program.

The Panel's Assessment of PALEN

The panel's account of PALEN must be understood as "friendly." It confines itself to setting out technical characteristics and requirements. The panel does not develop the counterargument that continuing investigation of warhead design might be of no *military* value, however much it explored physical unknowns or sustained a cadre of skilled weapons designers.

The report does, however, envision tests not only for PALEN, but to prove new designs. It notes that if tests were continued and authorization given for twenty-some tests, half would be committed to PALEN and half to enhancing warhead "stability and function," in particular warheads for the envisioned M5 missile or ASLP long-range stand-off missile. We can infer that reduced testing might,

115. The TN 75 is a miniaturized, hardened thermonuclear warhead which will present a smaller radar cross-section and therefore be hard for defenses to detect. It will only come into service in 1996. Norris et al., pp. 257, 259.

therefore, reinforce French hesitance to commit unreservedly to either M5 or a follow-on to the ASMP, though both programs could be adapted to warheads already in the inventory. On the other hand, PALEN awaits equipment to be delivered over the period 1998-2002, so that—as the panel observes—PALEN did not require prompt test resumption.

Current Status of PALEN

For 1995 PALEN has been allotted $183 million. On 21 April 1995 Prime Minister Edouard Balladur said France would build the "megajoule" laser at the Center for Scientific and Technical Studies in Aquitaine, beginning in 1996. It would "allow France to move forward with the design of nuclear weapons."[116]

President Jacques Chirac announced on 13 June 1995 that France would resume testing, from September 1995 to May 1996, after which tests would cease.

> I consulted all the experts, civilian and military, the responsible officials, to give me their feelings. They were unanimous in telling me that if we want to assure the security of our deterrent force, if we want to move on to the laboratory stage, that is the possibility to do in the laboratory experiments with computers, then we are obligated to finish this series of tests.[117]

France would test, he later explained, its "new warhead"—which *Le Monde* identifies as the TN75 for the M45 missile, for *Triomphant*-class SNLEs. Two tests would be dedicated to the "security, safety, and reliability" of explosive triggers and effects of aging. There would be four more—"in all, seven or eight tests"—which would "permit us to attain simulation technology."[118] So there seems to be room for two TN75 tests, if the first is not convincing.

---

116. Associated Press, 21 April 1995.

117. Associated Press, 13 June 1995.

118. *Le Monde*, 14 July 1995. [Compare, however, the CEA's claim to have "proven" the TN75 several years earlier (footnote 102).] Chirac said nothing about a warhead for the proposed M5 follow-on to the M45. Foreign Minister Hervé de Charette expressly denied France was testing to develop a new generation of weapons, or miniaturized weapons for use in situations which were unrelated to nuclear "dissuasion." *The Independent* [London], 13 July 1995.

Comparing the Three Nuclear Weapons Programs

Each of the Three began its nuclear weapons program for the same reason: conviction that true independence could be assured only with the bomb in hand. We have quoted the British Maud Committee's observation in 1941—before the US had launched its nuclear program—that in the aftermath of World War II "no nation would care to risk being caught without a weapon of such decisive possibilities."[119] The key decisions of 1947 (Britain), 1954 (France), and 1955 (China) were inseparable from the first ten years of the Cold War, in which true independence was believed to be at stake. Hiroshima was understood; and when France and China made their moves, the Soviet Union, too, was a nuclear state.

Their situations, nonetheless, differed dramatically. Britain, wartime ally of the United States, had been the first to see clearly the salience of nuclear weapons and then took part in a successful nuclear weapons program. Britain finally cast the die for an independent nuclear weapons program only after wartime nuclear collaboration with the United States had broken down, and the chances for international control appeared slim. Still, the Soviet Union had not yet exploded a nuclear device, and though Soviet troops were in eastern Germany, contention between the Soviet Union and the Western Allies had not yet been driven aground on the shoals of Berlin. Britain and the United States remained allies. Once Britain had tested, nuclear cooperation resumed.

France moved into nuclear energy—expressly including "military" applications—before 1945 was out. But by the time she embarked on the road toward nuclear weapons, in the early 1950s, one could say her motive was concern about the Soviet Union and Germany. Or that her motive was to avoid the humiliation of French submission to Germany.

China's leaders saw in 1955 that the United States could dictate terms on territorial issues—and perhaps others as well—unless China had an equivalent nuclear capability. But was China not protected by Soviet promises? In August-September 1958 precisely that issue arose between them, when China sought backing for an assertive policy in

---

119. Quoted in Andrew J. Pierre, *Nuclear Politics*, p. 17.

the Taiwan Straits: Moscow refused a guarantee. Only as the Sino-Soviet relationship broke down, from late 1958, did China find itself with two unfriendly nuclear superpowers at its border.

Britain, France, and China, however, faced the world from distinctly different positions:

• Britain achieved security and enlarged its influence through the United States. The dual problem in 1945 was, characteristically, how to keep America in the traces but reined in: ready to assert its weapons, but with prudence and purpose which also served British interests.

• France placed less weight on influence and more on autonomy. Unlike Britain, which resisted Hitler, France had given way. American and British troops liberated a subject people, a fact which the orchestrated relief of Paris by French contingents could blur but not erase. France had no natural ally, of any weight and capacity, on the European continent.

• China placed preeminent emphasis on security. From 1840 China had been repeatedly assaulted and occupied by foreign states. The problem for China in the 1950s was how to protect itself from foreign invasion or attack. The United States from the onset of the Korean War, and the Soviet Union from the breakdown of cooperation in 1958-60, both nuclear states, were the most likely to use force against China.

Differences in original purpose left their mark on the course of their nuclear programs. For example, Britain's reestablished relationship with the United States enabled her to abandon Blue Streak and obtain Polaris and Trident. Without access to US missiles, Britain would have had to design and build an indigenous missile system or give up on a "credible deterrent force."

France, like China, has built the "triad" of silo-based, airborne, and submarine-launched weapons. But Britain never deployed a silo-based nuclear weapon. Like China, but unlike Britain, France also created the industrial prerequisites not only for nuclear weapon fabrication but also for the array of means of delivery.

Britain and France went to SSBNs (SNLEs) when they could, because technology-driven strategic requirements compelled them to do so if they were to retain a credible force, and because they could acquire or develop the needed components and skills. They have moved more and more, especially since 1989, to rely on their submarine force for strategic missions. Moreover, they chose high-technology routes to manage penetration (Chevaline) and MIRVing.

China moved from aircraft to land-based missiles as the prime means of delivery. Missile technology, though hardly simple, was less complex than that of nuclear-powered submarines. China's limited access to technology forced the simpler delivery systems on her. Yet she also began early to face the technical challenge of designing and building a strategic submarine force.

China has kept early-model aircraft in service as nuclear delivery vehicles, and deploys liquid-fueled land-based missiles. These measures are compromises with necessity. Chinese missiles are—as best is known—single-warhead missiles carrying megaton warheads, suitable for devastation of "soft" targets such as cities even if the missile could not achieve precision accuracy.

Have the Three Truly Achieved Credible Deterrent Forces?

Since 1945 nuclear weapons have implied *not* fighting nuclear wars but, instead, sustaining *deterrent* relations. Each of the Three declares officially that its forces exist to deter (or dissuade). Deterrence, however, is inherently *relational.* A state leadership cannot deter by itself: it must stand in relationship to another state leadership, which observes the forces which could make good on a threat and decides that it will not move. Deterrence assumes a "rational" opponent.

A "credible deterrent" is a force so constituted, deployed and commanded that its holders *could* effect a counterstrike in revenge. The deterree asks: can they reach me? will enough of their force survive my strike that their harm to me would be "unacceptable"? and will they actually unleash the horrors which a revenge attack must call forth in turn? Among nuclear capable states the answers are typically "yes, probably, and possibly." And that is enough to deter. A leadership could judge the likelihood of counterstrike very small indeed and still be deterred.

A "credible deterrent" rests on these uncertainties. Deterrence is absent only when the means to strike back is not in place.

The effect of recent British and French nuclear force decisions is to approximate "minimum deterrent" forces, but in two distinct versions.

The British version, which relies on the United States for key elements, is *dependent in the longer-term.* And though it is in principle able to be deployed and fired independently, it is probably also *dependent on US intelligence for operations*. The French version is *independent and autonomous*, in both short-term and longer-term, but *constrained by intelligence shortcomings for operations*.

Britain and France, responding to the relative invulnerability of deep-diving nuclear-powered submarines, have copied the United States in placing the principal element of their deterrent aboard large SSBNs (SNLEs). This reflects the common judgment that land-based systems, whether dependent on aircraft or fixed-silo missiles, are vulnerable to location and attack.

Britain and France have wagered most of their nuclear weapons on the SSBN (SNLE). They must meet two criteria to win the gamble. Will the force be ready and available when "required"? Will it survive determined efforts by an enemy to destroy it? These criteria, in turn, reveal the two assumptions on which the wager depends. Both France and Britain assume that (i) at least one of the four SSBN (SNLE) will be operational on station, unhindered by mishap or sabotage, at any time. They also assume that (ii) over the anticipated lifetime of the class (the British *Vanguard*-class and French *Triomphant*-class) ASW capabilities will not defeat the ability of an SSBN (SNLE) to hide successfully.

"One boat at sea at all times" is the mantra of the British strategic submarine force. Why, then, have they built four boats? The principal stated reasons stem from the wear and tear on boats and crews. A second reason is to be able to put more missiles to sea. A third is to hedge against the enemy finding and destroying a boat on operational patrol. For a short time three, two, even one boat might be sufficient for "deterrence." But the fewest boats which will persuade admirals they can confidently keep "one boat at sea" over many years is four.[120]

120. Boats must alternate at sea, because crews must be brought home, and the second boat must be securely hidden before the first reveals itself. The incoming boat will require replenishment and maintenance. These are Boats #1 and #2.

But "one boat at sea" means little if its location can be found out. Is the second assumption—that SSBNs (SNLEs) can escape detection—sound? *The investments of Britain, France, and China in submarine-borne nuclear missile forces hinge on that assumption.* Although efforts to render SSBNs invisible go forward with urgence, I am frankly skeptical that anything as large as an SSBN, which must move and glow and reflect, will be able to resist determined efforts to find and follow its signs. The problem is that boats get the stealthiness available when they are built (or—where possible—refit), while the arts of sensing and signal processing advance continually.

The present US position is that SSBNs—if not tracked from port, if "clean" of alien devices, if sufficiently deep, and if operated as intended—cannot be found out except by chance. There is no persuasive evidence in the public domain to contest this claim as an accurate statement of the present relationship between concealment and detection. An assertion that the Soviet Union could track submarines—using synthetic aperture radar from space to follow the "heave" of a submarine as it passed through the ocean—prompted Senate and Parliamentary committee queries in both the United States and Britain. The responses convey something both of the attention paid such a claim and the official stance that SSBNs remain undetectable.[121] Eleanor Chelimsky, an official of the US General Accounting Office, testified to the Senate Committee on Governmental Affairs about a study of the US nuclear triad that

---

Once every ten or twelve years each boat will go into refit, an extended process which renders it inaccessible for two years or more. That is Boat #3. Boat #4 is a spare: if anything untoward happens to the first or second boat so that it cannot take its place in the rotation then Boat #4 will ensure "one boat at sea." In practice, all three boats not in refit are scheduled into the rotation.

121. On these claims, see Tim Beardsley, "Making Waves," *Scientific American*, vol. 268 no. 2, February 1993; and Hung P. Nguyen, *Submarine Detection from Space: Study of Russian Capabilities.* (Annapolis: Naval Institute Press, 1993). Gerard E. Marsh, reviewing the Nguyen book, argues that SSBNs are undetectable: "The navy runs what is known as the 'SSBN Security Program' . . . It has examined not only synthetic aperture radar detection of surface waves and ripples caused by the internal waves produced by passing submarines (the particular detection scheme Nguyen discusses), but infrared methods and other more esoteric schemes as well. All of the security program's evaluations support the view that, when operated appropriately, SSBNs are undetectable." *Bulletin of the Atomic Scientists*, vol. 50 no. 5, September-October 1994, p. 58.

> the submerged SSBN's are essentially invulnerable. They are even less detectable than generally understood, and there appear to be no current or long-term technologies that would change this.

Senator William S. Cohen questioned her in apparent allusion to the putative Soviet methods:

> *Ms. Chelimsky.* Yes, we have been briefed on it and we are very aware. In that case, we had no problem. We were given all the data that we needed . . .
>
> *Senator Cohen.* But you had everything, as far as non-aperture radar and other types of systems?
>
> *Ms. Chelimsky.* Right. There were many things that we could not write about, because they were too highly classified.
>
> *Senator Cohen.* But you had access?
>
> *Ms. Chelimsky.* Yes, we had access.[122]

In March 1994 a similar exchange took place between Menzies Campbell MP (defence spokesman of the Liberal Democrats) and Rear Admiral Richard Irwin (chief strategic systems executive), who was giving testimony to the House of Commons Defence Committee:

> *Mr. Campbell.* Since 1992 there have been rumors that the Russians had the capacity to detect submarines under water and, as I think you probably know, that has caused some controversy in the United States and some experiments followed upon these claims. Has the Ministry of Defence given any attention to these claims and, if so, what conclusions have been reached?

---

122. US Congress. Senate. Committee on Governmental Affairs. *Evaluation of the U.S. Strategic Nuclear Triad.* Hearing, 10 June 1993, p. 10. Eleanor Chelimsky presented the report as Assistant Comptroller General for Program Evaluation and Methodology, US General Accounting Office. In her prepared testimony she revealed something more of the GAO's assessment of possible threats to SSBNs (p. 41):

" . . the Soviet threat to the weapon systems of the land and sea legs had also been overstated. For the sea leg, this was reflected in unsubstantiated allegations about likely future breakthroughs in Soviet submarine detection technologies, along with underestimation of the performance and capabilities of our own nuclear-powered ballistic missile submarines. . . . Our specific finding, based on operational test results, was that submerged SSBNs are even *less* detectable than is generally understood, and that there appear to be no current or long-term technologies that would change this. Moreover, even if such technologies *did* exist, test and operational data show that the survivability of the SSBN fleet would not be in question."

Rear Admiral Irwin. Most certainly. We give a tremendous amount of attention to those claims, because if they were true they would have a very significant affect on our operational capability. The case is not proven and we believe that our submarines are extremely difficult to detect.

Mr. Campbell. Do I take it from that answer that the claims are, as it were, constantly under review? This has not been a question of hearing the allegation, dealing with it and dismissing, but in fact there is a continuing scrutiny as to whether or not there could be any substance in this claim?

Rear Admiral Irwin. Indeed there is, yes, at a very heavy level.

Mr. Campbell. If it were to be valid then, as you say, it would have a very considerable effect on the operating of the British nuclear deterrent?

Rear Admiral Irwin. Yes, if it is valid, it is not that they would have the capability instantly to see through a clear ocean, but what might be is that if they could localise the submarine by one means then they could localise it even more accurately with these other means. First of all, they have to find where the submarine is or has been. We are concerned about it, but we are not seriously worried about it.[123]

France too pays close attention to its SNLEs avoiding detection. The head of Project Coelacanthe, bringing forward the new *Triomphant*-class of French SNLEs (SSBNs), declared he had insisted most of all on achieving "acoustic discretion." This required suitable design of the boat and its propeller, machinery which produced the least possible vibration, and the development and proof of several measures to "filter" residual vibrations from reaching the sea.[124] The secondary leg of the French deterrent dyad is a stand-off missile. The combination of aircraft and stand-off missiles represents the most flexible and capable secondary system.[125] France's land-based missile is limited by its 3500 km range.

Britain, in addition to its strategic submarine capability, can

---

123. House of Commons. Session 1993-94. Defence Committee. Second Report. *Progress of the Trident Programme*. 4 May 1994. ¶s 1098-1100, p. 4.

124. Press release, "Exposé de l'Ingenieur Général de l'Armement Duval, Maitre d'Oeuvre Principal du Project Coelacanthe Devant les Journalistes Accrédités Défense, le 17 Décembre 1991. Le Programme des SNLE de Nouvelle Génération Type 'Le Triomphant.'"

125. This option would not be as attractive to Britain and France if they had not spent heavily on avionics. Consider the demonstrated vulnerability to modern interceptors of less capable aircraft (Gulf, Bosnia).

deliver nuclear weapons as gravity bombs.

China's capacity to strike the United States, Britain, or France could depend on as few as four DF-5 missiles, assuming its two SSBNs failed to sortie. All other pairs among the declared nuclear weapons states display a "credible deterrent." All Five could, in principle, deter Pakistan, Israel or India, in this sense.[126]

China, too, professes to practice minimum deterrence, with the aim "complete prohibition and thorough destruction" of nuclear weapons. Perhaps economic and technical constraints militated against any more ambitious path. Still, the effect is to keep British, French, and Chinese forces on the same scale.

---

126. Seymour Hersh argues that a prime aim and achievement of Israel's nuclear program was to hold the Soviet Union at risk of nuclear attack. Seymour Hersh, *The Samson Option* (London: Faber and Faber, 1993). Hersh asserts that Israel had missile and aircraft capability to reach the Soviet Union by the early 1970s, and additionally that "by 1973, Dimona's success in miniaturization enabled its technicians to build warheads small enough to fit into a suitcase; word of the bomb in a suitcase was relayed to the Soviet Union. . . . The Soviets understood that no amount of surveillance could prevent Israeli agents from smuggling nuclear bombs across the border in automobiles, aircraft, or commercial ships" p. 220.

Appendix 2.1

British Nuclear Policy

1. During the Cold War, NATO's nuclear weapons played an essential part in ensuring that major conflict never occurred. The knowledge that NATO might use the immense power of its nuclear forces in response to aggression removed any rational basis for a potential adversary believing that a war could be fought in Europe and won. Having established such a stable and secure framework for maintaining peace, we should not think lightly of dismantling it.

2. The artificial division of Europe has now gone but uncertainties and dangers remain. Russia will remain the pre-eminent military power in Europe, with large conventional and nuclear forces. We are working to build a new relationship with Russia and the states of central and eastern Europe, based on trust and mutual understanding. The joint declaration by the Prime Minister and President Yeltsin that their strategic nuclear missiles would be detargeted by 30 May 1994 is a reflection of growing confidence. The process as a whole will be helped by maintaining the stability in Europe provided by NATO's strategy, including the element of nuclear deterrence.

3. Complete and general nuclear disarmament remains a desirable ultimate goal, but nuclear weapons cannot be dis-invented. If at some point in the future a new global confrontation arose, the prospect of a race to re-create nuclear weapons would be profoundly destabilising. Moreover, the potential for nuclear proliferation would still exist. For a nuclear-free world to become a practicable objective, the international community would need to develop dependable solutions to these problems.

4. The Government has always been committed to maintaining only the minimum nuclear deterrent capability required for our security. We have long made clear that we will not use the full capacity of the Trident missile system, and that each submarine will carry no more than 128 warheads. In fact, on the basis of our current assessment of our minimum deterrent needs, each submarine will deploy with no more than 96 warheads, and may carry significantly fewer. It remains

our policy not to reveal precisely how many warheads will be carried within the new limit, but on current plans the total explosive power of the warheads to be carried on each Trident submarine will not be much changed from Polaris. Overall, the explosive power of the United Kingdom's operational nuclear inventory when Trident is fully in service will be more than 25% lower than the 1990 figure.

5. Trident was conceived as a replacement for our strategic nuclear capability. But the ability to undertake a massive nuclear strike is not enough to ensure deterrence. An aggressor might, in certain circumstances, gamble on a lack of will ultimately to resort to such a strike. We also need the capability to undertake nuclear action on a more limited scale in order to demonstrate our willingness to defend our vital interests to the utmost, and so induce a political decision to halt aggression without inevitably triggering strategic nuclear exchanges.

6. During the 1980s, continuing improvements in Warsaw Pact air defences led us to consider the early replacement of the WE 177 free-fall bomb with a sophisticated stand-off system. But the security situation has now changed, and we have concluded that replacing the WE 177 is not a sufficiently high priority in current circumstances to justify proceeding with a new nuclear system. We also intend to exploit the flexibility and capability of Trident to provide the vehicle for both the sub-strategic and strategic elements of our deterrent.

7. Judgments of this kind about future circumstances must inevitably be provisional. As insurance against potential adverse trends in the international situation, we will maintain a challenging programme of research at the Atomic Weapons Establishment. This will both sustain our ability to underwrite the safety and reliability of the warheads we have in service, and maintain our ability to develop and produce new warheads in the future.

(From the *Statement on the Defence Estimates 1994*, April 1994)

FIGURE 2.1
British Nuclear Missile Submarine Timeline

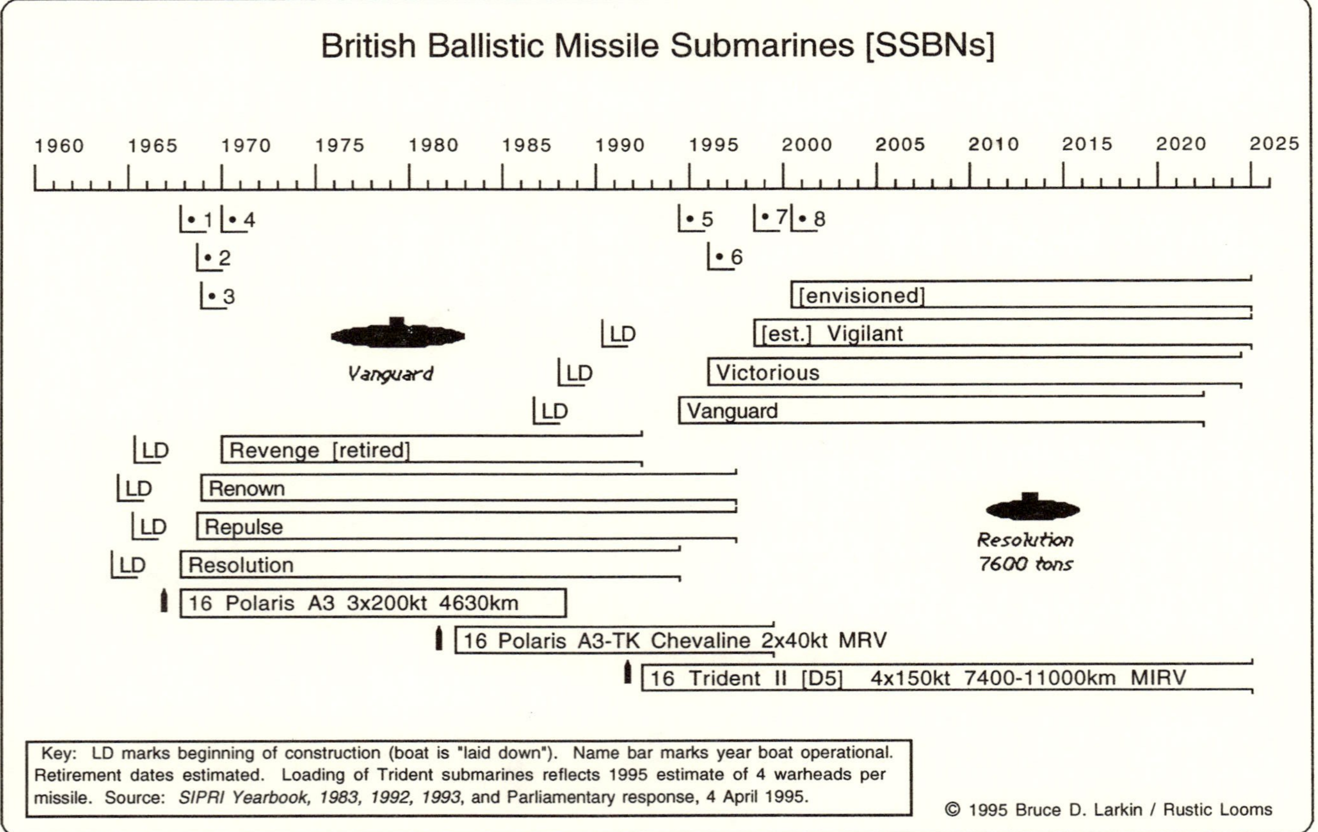
British Ballistic Missile Submarines [SSBNs]
1960
1965
1970
1975
1980
1985
1990
1995
2000
2005
2010
2015
2020
2025
• 1
• 4
• 2
• 3
• 5
• 7
• 8
• 6
[envisioned]
[est.] Vigilant
Victorious
Vanguard
Revenge [retired]
Renown
Repulse
Resolution
LD
LD
LD
LD
LD
LD
LD
Vanguard
Resolution
7600 tons
16 Polaris A3 3x200kt 4630km
16 Polaris A3-TK Chevaline 2x40kt MRV
16 Trident II [D5] 4x150kt 7400-11000km MIRV
Key: LD marks beginning of construction (boat is "laid down"). Name bar marks year boat operational. Retirement dates estimated. Loading of Trident submarines reflects 1995 estimate of 4 warheads per missile. Source: SIPRI Yearbook, 1983, 1992, 1993, and Parliamentary response, 4 April 1995.
© 1995 Bruce D. Larkin / Rustic Looms

FIGURE 2.2
French Nuclear Missile Submarine Timeline

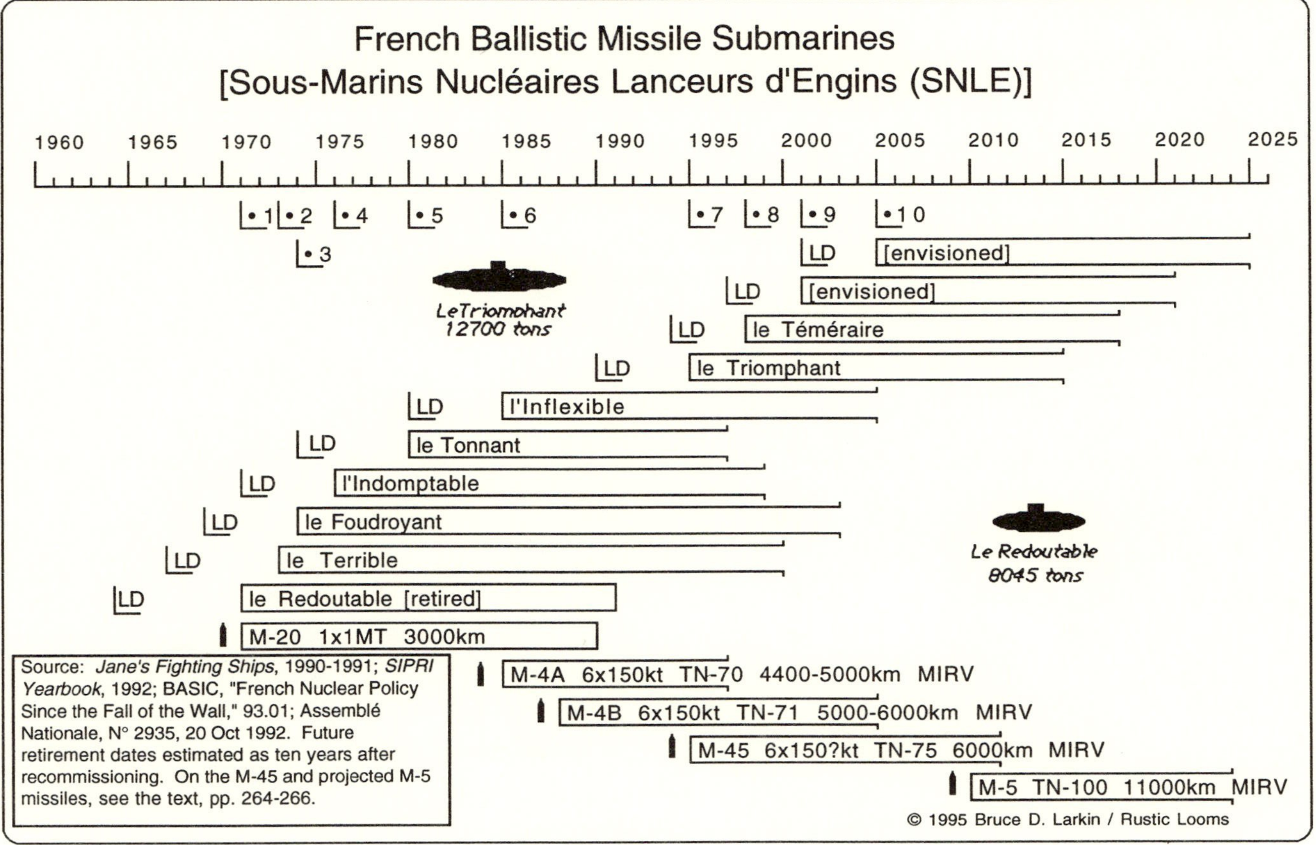

3

Test Ban and Non-Proliferation Regimes

Preliminaries

The United States opened the nuclear weapons era on 16 July 1945, when it tested the first plutonium device at Alamogordo, New Mexico. On 6 August 1945 it demonstrated the first uranium weapon, with which it destroyed Hiroshima.

Less than a year later, on 1 July 1946, the United States began nuclear testing at Bikini Atoll. Successive US tests merged nuclear engineering experimentation with weapons "proving." In all, the United States would test nearly a thousand times. Nuclear tests—almost 2000 nuclear explosions in all—continued into the 1990s, as the nuclear weapon states sought first to confirm and display their capabilities and then to refine designs.[1] The United States pioneered the design, engineering, testing, and militarization of a nuclear explosive device, in effect writing a script which others followed.

The atomic bomb at once raised the issue of control and abolition. Three months after Hiroshima, the leaders of the United States, Britain and Canada—Truman, Attlee, and Mackenzie King—met and agreed there should be a UN commission to eliminate nuclear weapons under effective safeguards, reinforced by inspection.[2] Their initiative led to the first resolution of the United Nations General Assembly, which created a UN Atomic Energy Commission mandated

---

1 The Stockholm International Peace Research Institute's *SIPRI Yearbook 1993* (Oxford: Oxford University Press, 1993) lists 1931 tests conducted by six countries (United States, Soviet Union, France, Britain, China, and India) through 1992. There have since been a handful of Chinese tests, and official revelation of hitherto unreported US tests. Of the reported tests, 492 are known to have been conducted in the atmosphere, and a further 31 Soviet tests announced in 1990 are considered by SIPRI to have been "probably atmospheric." Pp. 255-257.

2. Andrew J. Pierre, above, p. 113.

to "make specific proposals . . . for the elimination from national armaments of atomic weapons and of all other major weapons adaptable to mass destruction."[3] The Acheson-Lilienthal report of March 1946, commissioned by the US Secretary of State, and the proposal derived from it presented by the United States to the UN Atomic Energy Commission on 14 June 1946, the "Baruch Plan," proposed to accomplish this by global agreement distinguishing permitted from forbidden activities and securing "dangerous" steps—such as uranium mining and stockpiling—under direct control. They would tap nuclear power for electricity, but prohibit nuclear weapons.

The Soviet Union would not agree to the system of veto-proof sanctions on which the United States insisted. The two also disagreed whether controls should precede, or follow, the banning of nuclear weapons (which would deprive the United States of its small but unequaled nuclear arsenal). Some argue that Baruch's terms were too severe, barriers to agreement, but there is no evidence Moscow would have accepted controls before achieving nuclear weapons itself. The UN AEC held its final meeting on 29 July 1949. The Soviet Union tested a month later. With rejection of the "Baruch Plan" and hardening of the Cold War, arms control efforts were preempted by primacy accorded nuclear weapons development and deployment by the United States and Soviet Union, and then Britain, France, and China.

Despite failure of international control in the late 1940s, there have been recurrent moves to achieve some control. This chapter concerns test ban proposals, which would have presented a barrier to new and untested designs, and "anti-proliferation" measures to prevent the "spread" of nuclear weapons to aspirants. Those measures include the 1968 Nuclear Non-Proliferation Treaty and its links to the safeguards system of the International Atomic Energy Agency. In Chapter 4 we will turn to arms control measures to fix and cut existing nuclear weapons inventories.

Discussion of halting tests led to the 1963 Limited Test Ban Treaty, banning tests not confined underground. The proposed

---

3. Rotblat, Joseph, Jack Steinberger, and Bhalchandra Udgaonkar, *A Nuclear-Weapon-Free World: Desirable? Feasible?* (Boulder: Westview, 1993), citing United Nations (1970), "The United Nations and Disarmament 1945-1970," pp. 11-12.

"comprehensive test ban" was taken up again in the late 1970s, set aside during the Reagan years, and then has emerged in the 1990s as an agreed objective in the Conference on Disarmament.

Of course, the Limited Test Ban not only committed the signers not to test in the atmosphere, but also stigmatized non-signers who chose to test. In that sense it was a non-proliferation measure. Concern that a growing number of countries would engineer and deploy nuclear weapons was then addressed directly in the Nuclear Non-Proliferation Treaty (NPT), proposed by Ireland in 1961 and signed after lengthy negotiations in 1968. It entered into force in 1970. The NPT's requirement of review every five years and a conference after 25 years on its extension led to the 1995 NPT Review and Extension Conference. There weapons states' promises to negotiate an effective test ban were among the key steps by which they had laid a groundwork for indefinite NPT extension. Thus the two concepts of "test ban" and "non-proliferation" remain central to the global discussion of political steps to manage and end the danger posed by nuclear weapons.

At the end of the day, a treaty is agreed and sustained only by the continuing conviction *within* states parties that it is in their interest to do so. For the NPT this means that some states stay out, and that nuclear weapon states (with the declaratory exception of China) resist being drawn into discussion of abolition despite Article VI requirements. For the CTB it cautions us that all states, including Britain, France, and China, can withhold their consent. At this writing (June 1995) odds are for a CTB in 1996, but it may slip away, or be fatally defective.

Test Ban

The Soviet Union, United States, and United Kingdom, committing to negotiate a test ban, agreed to a test moratorium which began 31 October 1958.[4] Their negotiations—the three-party Conference on the Discontinuance of Nuclear Weapons Tests—took place at Geneva from 1958 to 1962. But France tested three times in 1960. The

4. John Simpson, *The Independent Nuclear State*.

moratorium was then ended by a Soviet test series beginning 1 September 1961, followed by US tests, which began 15 September.

However, in 1963 they agreed to end all but underground nuclear tests. This measure responded to public pressure against atmospheric testing, permitted their own weapons development to continue, but placed an onus on testing by aspirants (who were not technically able to test underground). The Partial Test Ban Treaty (PTBT)[5] banned nuclear weapons tests "in the atmosphere, in outer space and under water." China, known to be preparing its first nuclear test, reacted vigorously, stating that "manipulation of the destiny of more than one hundred non-nuclear countries by a few nuclear powers will not be tolerated."[6] Instead, Beijing counterproposed that all nuclear weapons should be destroyed.

The first Chinese test (16 October 1964) required that China address the inevitable criticism. Three days later Zhou Enlai sent a cable to all heads of government repeating the Chinese proposal for a world summit on prohibition and destruction of nuclear weapons.[7] He insisted China's motives and aims were peaceful, and that the nuclear program was altogether justified. China wished to distance herself from the Soviet Union and United States, but at the same time continue her test program.

On 14 June 1967 Beijing tested its first thermonuclear weapon. It has since maintained a regular, but measured, testing program. Its last atmospheric nuclear test took place in 1980.

The three signers of the PTBT resumed formal negotiation of a Comprehensive Test Ban in 1977, but upon Ronald Reagan's election in November 1980 their talks were suspended.[8] In any case, the

---

5. Signed 5 August 1963; entered into force 10 October 1963.

6. "Statement of the Chinese Government Advocating the Complete, Thorough, Total and Resolute Prohibition and Destruction of Nuclear Weapons (and) Proposing a Conference of the Government Heads of All Countries of the World, July 31, 1963," in *Peking Review* no. 31, 2 August 1963, pp. 7-8.

7. Zhou Enlai, "Cable to All Heads of Government Proposing a World Summit Conference on the Prohibition and Destruction of All Nuclear Weapons," in *Peking Review* no. 43, 23 October 1964, p. 6.

8. In 1982 the Reagan Administration announced its decision not to resume the negotiations. *Disarmament Facts 74* (New York: United Nations), April 1991, p. 11. In fact they came to a halt immediately after Reagan's election.

United States saw a test ban as a subordinate element in strategic weapons negotiations with the Soviet Union. Some ten years—and a realignment of US-Soviet relations—were required before a test ban could again be pursued.

The Soviet Union declared a moratorium on nuclear tests in October 1991. France followed with a moratorium in April 1992. From mid-1992, when the last US test took place, to mid-1995 only China tested (September 1992, October 1993, June and October 1994, and May 1995). Beijing has made it quite clear it intends further tests in 1995, and may test in 1996 until a CTB is concluded. France will test from September 1995 to May 1996.

The post-Reagan momentum for an outright ban on testing was set in motion by Mikhail Gorbachev's 15 January 1986 call for an end to nuclear weapons by the year 2000. Gorbachev proposed global elimination, bringing France, Britain, and China into the process at a second stage. If abolition could be seriously discussed, then certainly tests were also on the table.

On the other hand, if nuclear weapons advocates were to defend their programs against calls for abolition, and against dilution by a surge of new nuclear programs, a ban on testing—or at least discussion of a ban on testing—might be a way to keep the wolves of abolition and proliferation at bay. As a result, nuclearist and abolitionist interests joined in seeking terms for a test ban.

The key plays were made in Moscow, Paris and Washington. In Paris, François Mitterrand in April 1992 responded to the Soviet initiative by declaring a moratorium on French tests. Boris Yeltsin replied in July 1992 by extending the Soviet (Russian) test halt. After the summer 1992 US test series, pressure grew in the US Congress to force a halt. A bill enacted in early November 1992—attached to legislation which President Bush could not veto with comfort—compelled the President to present a plan for up to 15 tests between 1993 and 1996, with a ban then coming into place *if no other state tested*. By July 1993 President Clinton, in office almost six months, replied to Congress by ending US tests altogether—again *provided no other state tested.* His action meant, too, that there would be no UK tests, which since 1962 have been conducted at the Nevada Test Site.

CTB Negotiations in the Conference on Disarmament

The Clinton Administration's initiatives of June and July 1993 were followed by the UN Conference on Disarmament taking up the question of a Comprehensive Test Ban.[9] The CD resolved in August 1993 that it would begin to address the issue in January 1994. The talks began on 25 January, on the eve of Clinton's State of the Union message, and he took note of them. Consultations among the nuclear weapon states would continue at Geneva, outside the CD's own sessions.

Thus by the end of 1993 the declared nuclear states except China were subject to moratorium. All were alert to the relationship between their testing posture and the forthcoming NPT Review Conference, to convene in 1995. Failure to be serious about halting tests could imperil the non-proliferation regime. But a test halt could also become an internal issue in any of the nuclear weapon states.

In fact, the situations of the Three are not the same. Not only are their domestic politics of security quite different, but they stand in different positions technologically. France and Britain are deploying new generations of SSBNs (SNLEs) in many respects very similar, but Britain buys its missiles abroad; China is only beginning to solve issues of vulnerability and range in its seaborne deterrent force. These

---

9. The Conference on Disarmament (CD) has "a unique relationship with the United Nations." Its members are a subset of UN membership—39 in 1991—including the five declared nuclear weapons states. The CD is the fourth in a succession of disarmament forums: (1) Ten-Nation Committee on Disarmament (1959-1960); (2) Eighteen-Nation Committee on Disarmament (1962-1969); (3) Conference of the Committee on Disarmament (of 30 member states) (1969-1978); and (4) Committee on Disarmament (1979-1983), by which the present CD was known before adopting the name Conference on Disarmament. "It defines its own rules of procedure and develops its own agenda, taking into account the recommendations made by the General Assembly." *Disarmament Facts 74* (New York: United Nations, 1991), April 1991, p. 26.

In addition, there have been three UN General Assembly Special Sessions on Disarmament, in May-June 1978, June-July 1982, and June 1988. The unanimously-adopted Final Document of SSD I declared that nuclear weapons posed the "greatest danger to mankind" and set the ultimate goal to be "complete elimination of nuclear weapons." UN Document A/RES/S-10/2.

differences mean that each has distinct interests in the CTB negotiations.

The French Moratorium

The French debate over the moratorium of 1992-1995 opens a window on an underlying world of internal political maneuver, institutional voices, and the interplay of external and internal goals. The argument comes to turn—ostensibly—on whether weapons designs can be proven without exploding them and whether nuclear tests are a *necessary prerequisite* to design-proving computer simulations. Most of the discussion is enclosed in an envelope dedicated to protecting the nuclear weapons program. With some exceptions, initiatives which appear to limit nuclear weapons, or move toward their abolition, are proposed, endorsed, accepted, and negotiated by players whose intention is to conserve the national nuclear program against its critics. They may be prepared to accept some limitations now to maintain programs in the longer term.

Paris' story begins with the circumstances of President François Mitterrand's moratorium declaration in April 1992. Despite protests of political innocence by foreign policy specialists loyal to Mitterrand's socialist party, others saw a transparent appeal to Green voters, whose candidates had performed surprisingly well in recently held regional elections. The parties were positioning themselves for parliamentary elections, which took place in March 1993. But in mid-1993 Mitterrand insisted his aim was to limit nuclear arms: "End nuclear tests, and you can talk of ending nuclear over-armament."[10]

Many observers were puzzled by Mitterrand's holding the decision so close. Even his minister of defense, Pierre Joxe, not to mention the military, declared that they had not been consulted. Plans already underway for tests at Mururoa in the South Pacific had to be put abruptly on the shelf.

---

10. *Le Monde*, 16 July 1993, reporting a broadcast interview given by Mitterrand on Bastille Day. It is in this interview that Mitterrand says he sent letters to the heads of government of the United States, Russia and Britain telling them that "if you maintain this suspension of tests, or moratorium, France will do the same." But he does not mention China, though he describes his April 1992 action as conditional on the "nuclear powers" also foregoing testing.

The Commissariat à l'Énergie Atomique (CEA) was working on methods by which designs could be proved with few or no nuclear tests. The test moratorium led to "increased reliance" on this scheme, PALEN (Préparation à la Limitation des Essais Nucléaires).[11] PALEN's capabilities and the need for future tests was a focus of public controversy at the end of 1993.

Mitterrand's PS lost the parliamentary elections of March 1993, and the socialist government was succeeded by a center-right government led by the new Prime Minister, Edouard Balladur. In the French system, however, the President exercises ultimate authority in matters of foreign affairs and national security. The test moratorium remained in Mitterrand's hands.

France responded to US urging of moratorium extension, agreeing in June 1993 to extend the test ban. In the face of criticism from the military and Gaullist parliamentarians, Mitterrand and Balladur created a commission to assess the moratorium's consequences. Its seven members were described by the press as "known supporters of nuclear testing."[12] Center-right dispositions to keep testing drew strength from technical claims that some components of the PALEN simulation scheme itself would need to be calibrated by nuclear tests. On 12 September 1993 Minister of Defense François Léotard declared that France would resume tests if the experts said the moratorium cast doubt on the credibility of "dissuasion," "whatever the international situation." But if the experts said it did not, French testing would remain under moratorium.[13]

The Chinese test of 5 October 1993 forced the French internal debate into the spotlight. After the Chinese test Mitterrand said France would consult with the other nuclear powers, but that "I am not in favour in the present situation, with the information at my disposal, of resuming nuclear tests."[14] François Léotard was already on record

---

11. *CEA Annual Report, 1992*, p. 32. PALEN is discussed more fully in chapter 2.

12. Reuters, 5 October 1993.

13. *Le Monde*, 14 September 1993.

14. Reuters, 6 October 1993. A few days earlier the government announced that Balladur himself, in a clearly symbolic gesture, would bestow the insignia of Commander of the Legion of Honor on the Director of Military Applications of the CEA, Roger Baléras. *Le Monde*, 9 September 1993. Baléras, testifying before the Defense Commission of the Assemblée Nationale on 4 May 1993, had

that delaying further tests by a few years would not be a risk to France's security. When the French response was made public, it appeared to be a compromise between Mitterrand and Balladur. The Ministry of Defense had been instructed to take steps to maintain the existing nuclear stockpile, to be prepared to resume testing if necessary, and to continue to work on the PALEN simulation techniques. The Foreign Minister would consult with the United States, Russia, and Britain.[15] France's aims remained "to take part in the international arms control efforts . . . and keep at its disposal a credible and sufficient deterrent force, which it has today and must retain tomorrow to protect its vital interests."

The opening of CD talks on a CTB in January 1994 offered France an opportunity to set out her position. She discerned a common objective: to prevent nuclear proliferation and contribute to the disarmament process. But she flatly rejected a test ban designed to set in motion a process of denuclearization.

> We know that certain delegations nourish the hope that a test ban will set in motion a process leading in due course to the elimination of nuclear weapons held by the Five, by making for their obsolescence. Everyone knows that this notion is totally alien to us.[16]

A CTB should be—here the representative cites the 10 August 1993 CD decision—"universal and internationally and effectively verifiable." From this France drew several implications for the negotiation. Chief among them was that entry into force of a CTB should require participation of "all those States having a nuclear capacity and in particular the 'threshold' States." To that end the CD should be enlarged, so that ratification by all CD members would in effect be the condition for entry into force. We might call this the "universality criterion," that all must participate and all must agree. But it also

---

insisted tests were indispensable, and he was also one of the seven experts named by Balladur to assess the issue.

15. Reuters, 6 October 1993. Bernard Edinger wrote that the statement "appeared to be a compromise between Mitterrand, a Socialist keen to achieve a world ban on nuclear tests, and Balladur's Gaullist RPR party, which includes many who advocate an immediate resumption of French testing."

16. Statement of the French representative to the Conference on Disarmament, Geneva, 7 February 1994.

implies that France—or any other nuclear power—could bar a treaty. The consensus rule of the CD encourages the search for compromise and favors universality. The aim should be a treaty which can "receive the agreement of all, including of course the nuclear powers."

Then the French representative asked how nuclear powers can be expected to accept new constraints if the existing non-proliferation regime is violated with impunity. And if the NPT Review and Extension Conference were to fail to extend the NPT, France would think again about committing to a CTB.

That position cut across the judgment of many NPT extension advocates for whom a CTB was an achievable step to show good faith, addressing non-nuclear weapon states' objections to extension. France turned the table, asking instead that non-weapon states first prove their intent by NPT extension. This is the "NPT criterion."

Further, France required that the "fundamental conditions" of its agreement to the 10 August 1993 decision not be changed. Others should keep their commitments, as France had pointed out. This means—the representative recalls having clarified precisely on 29 July 1993—in particular "the principal acts which determine our assessment of the strategic situation," specifically the ABM and CFE treaties, START process and NPT treaty. We can call this the "performance criterion."

On the relationship between French tests and the negotiation, the representative declared that they were separate matters. One of the Five was negotiating without entering a moratorium and three had taken measures, after the Chinese test of 5 October 1993, to be able to go forward with tests. There was no incompatibility between France's taking part in CTB negotiations and an eventual resumption of French nuclear tests.

Finally, the French representative insisted on taking the time needed for a serious negotiation. It would not do to have a treaty on the cheap, especially if verification were slighted. Delegates must work for a treaty which, in contributing to non-proliferation, strengthens international security and at the same time preserves "the legitimate right of States to assure the credibility of their means of defense."

No one can object to the insistence that a CTB be serious—especially in matters of verification. Other French conditions are more contentious. The "universality criterion" and "performance criterion" would make a CTB hostage to any state which strove to achieve nuclear weapons, or to undo some provisions, for example, of the treaty on conventional forces in Europe. France wanted NPT extension to precede, not follow, CTB approval. Moreover, France argued for an "entry into force" requirement which meant a veto to France and each of the other nuclear weapon states. The net effect of these conditions can be read two ways. On the one hand, there is no doubt that a regime which met France's terms would be a stronger non-proliferation regime, and that a CTB which met France's conditions for entry into force would be more likely to endure. On the other hand, these conditions are so severe that they may readily fail. There is a third way to understand them: that they are initial negotiating positions, *desiderata* but not necessarily iron requirements. Would France, for example, accept a CTB which lacked the approval of a single nuclear aspirant?

In constructing these conditions, France makes out an argument which appears logical and consistent, but it is a false logic. NPT extension and the proposed CTB are not symmetric. Proliferation, or refusal of the proposal for indefinite extension of the NPT, does not undermine the rationale for a CTB. In fact, it may make it stronger, to the extent non-nuclear weapon states take the readiness of nuclear weapon states to sign a CTB as an index of their acceptance of common governance. On the other hand, a nuclear weapon state's refusal to sign a CTB would certainly undermine the case for effective NPT extension, since it would call into question that state's commitment to Article VI of the NPT. The force of argument runs in one direction, not both. This is so because what the nuclear weapon states give up in a CTB—tests of advanced designs—has no effect at all on their position vis-à-vis new nuclear weapon states. The status quo endows them—*with or without a CTB*—with the capacity to incinerate other states. (The French position on CFE compliance is subject to similar objections, in that not all compliance failures indict the worth of otherwise broad agreement.)

As to whether a CTB must be "universal," there is a serious questions about French insistence on universality. Does *nonadherence* matter if—as is widely asserted—a fission bomb can be confidently engineered without a weapons test? (The Hiroshima bomb design had not been explosively tested.) *Nonadherence* indicts not the CTB, but broader non-proliferation efforts. There might be other reasons for France to insist that the states with advanced nuclear programs sign: they are, after all, those whose forces France "dissuades." Paris has long displayed an intense allergy to others' defensive measures, which could nullify her force, and may judge their inability to test defenses against nuclear blasts a practical disincentive against their deployment.

Differences which could block a CTB were disclosed in April 1994 to a US correspondent by unidentified "US officials" privy to the closed-door negotiations. They confirmed that France said a CTB should follow, not precede, extension of the NPT. More surprisingly, France also reportedly argued that she should be allowed occasional nuclear tests—one every five to ten years—to confirm stockpile safety.[17]

On 5 May 1994 Mitterrand declared that France would not resume testing while he was President, and predicted that his successor would not resume testing "for fear of offending the whole world by relaunching nuclear overarming."[18] The PALEN program, he said, would have to achieve simulation without nuclear tests.[19]

Soon Mitterrand and Balladur made it clear the test issue was a major contention between them. Balladur said his government would not sign a CTB as long as it judged additional tests were "essential to the technical credibility of our deterrent force." He affirmed two key points of the French government position: that France would sign a CTB only if all other states able to produce nuclear weapons also signed; and he repeated the position that France's resuming tests

17. Thomas W. Lippman, Washington Post wire, 16 April 1994, citing a "background briefing" by US officials. The United States took a contrary view on both points. It urged a CTB as a step to encourage NPT extension, and opposed a "safety" loophole in a CTB.

18. Reuters, 5 May 1994.

19. *Ibid.* He pointed out it would have 10.5 billion francs ($1.6 billion) to do so.

would not be incompatible with negotiating a CTB.[20] Mitterrand defined the issue as a "major point of disagreement." "I informed the prime minister, the defense minister, and the foreign minister of my decision," Mitterrand declared in a television interview. "I said there would be no more nuclear tests so long as I am here. . . . We disagree. But in this case, it is the President of the Republic who decides. So I used my right."[21]

Balladur made one further key point: that France opposed any ban on nuclear weapons or moves that would challenge the status of current nuclear powers.[22]

The question of nuclear test resumption was carried into Parliament. Jacques Baumel, vice-chairman of the Defense Committee of the Assemblée Nationale, forced the issue by proposing an amendment to the defense budget. The government, in response, sought to placate Gaullist deputies, assuring Parliament that France remained able to test. Defense Minister François Léotard told the lower house that the budget contained funds for testing if it were ordered. Prime Minister Edouard Balladur assured the Assembly that France's "freedom to choose will be preserved." When Léotard subsequently said that Baumel's amendment would be withdrawn, he added that "this is a matter that should be left to the executive branch to decide."[23]

The French Government could simply have been trying to keep options open until after the April-May 1995 presidential elections. Until then the center-right government and Mitterrand socialist presidency had to accommodate one another. The French position at Geneva, for example, insisted the goal is a CTB (the voice of Mitterrand) while proposing that there be provision for a test every five or ten years (voice of the CEA and an important faction supporting the Balladur government). If this line of reasoning is correct, France instructed her CTB negotiators to preclude none of the likely

---

20. Paul Taylor, Reuters, 10 May 1994. Balladur did not specify exactly which countries would have to sign, but it would seem to mean more states than those believed to have nuclear weapons.

21. *Ibid.*

22. Emmanuel Jarry, Reuters, 10 May 1994.

23. Reuters, 25 May 1994.

positions France could take from mid-1995, while still presenting France as a foe of proliferation and advocate of serious, responsible and verifiable arms control measures. After Chirac's election France declared she would indeed resume testing, as explained in chapter 2.

United Kingdom and US Moratorium Policy

Before the Soviet and French initiatives, Britain had spoken judiciously about a comprehensive test ban as a longer-term objective. The initiatives forced Britain to specify its positions more carefully, with considerable latitude to continue testing, but some appearance of opening toward a CTB. Prime Minister John Major told Parliament on 22 March 1993:

> A comprehensive test ban would not in itself prevent a proliferator from producing and deploying a crude nuclear weapon without recourse to testing, and from obtaining materials with which to do this. But associated measures for verification and inspection, if sufficiently rigorous, and applicable to the states concerned, might constrain potential proliferators.

And he added:

> We support the ultimate goal of a comprehensive test ban.[24]

The Minister of State at the Foreign and Commonwealth Office, Douglas Hogg, said on 2 April:

> The Government's view is that we need to retain nuclear weapons, albeit in reduced numbers, and we need to ensure that they are safe. We must therefore review the case for testing against that requirement. It is also true that a comprehensive test ban has remained the British Government's long-term objective. In concert with other nuclear countries, we are reflecting whether it might be possible to bring forward that long-term objective or to abbreviate the timetable in some other way.
>
> Our long-term objective has been to subscribe to a comprehensive test ban treaty and we must now consider whether we can move more rapidly to the attainment of that policy.[25]

---

24. VERTIC. *Trust and Verify*, no. 36, March/April 1993.
25. *Ibid.*

Britain has given moratorium advocates no encouragement. Nonetheless, her hands are tied. Britain has no effective independence in test policy. She cannot test on her own, since she has no national facility, testing instead at the US Nevada Test Site. A US decision not to test implies Britain's being unable to test, unless London were to reconstitute an autonomous testing capability, a costly and politically difficult step which would contribute nothing to Britain's currently-planned nuclear force.

In October 1992 Congress required the US president to declare, the following year, a testing program of up to 15 tests in the period to 30 June 1996, of which 3 could be British tests.[26] (George Bush was then still in office and many thought he would be reelected.) Despite speculation as late as June 1993 that President Clinton would propose nine, his official response to Congress called for no tests at all. (Press reports indicated that there had been pressure to permit tests up to 1 Kt yield. A characteristic argument for such a floor is that if others' tests at low yields could not be detected, one should not unilaterally abandon the option.)

Britain may be tied to the Nevada test site, but she could lobby for a US test policy to her liking.[27] In a parliamentary reply in October 1992 the British Government termed the Congressionally-mandated moratorium "unfortunate and misguided."[28] In November 1992 a Government spokesman told the House of Commons that the Government believed a "minimal testing program" was "the best means of ensuring the safety and credibility of our deterrent."[29] But

---

26. H. R. 5373 stipulates that "The President may authorize the United Kingdom to conduct in the United States, within a period covered by an annual report, one test of a nuclear weapon if the President determines that it is in the national interests [sic] of the United States to do so. Such a test shall be considered as one of the tests within the maximum number of tests that the United States is permitted to conduct during that period."

27. Simon Tisdall reports that Britain unsuccessfully lobbied to test for safety purposes. *The Guardian*, 18 September 1993.

28. *The Guardian*, 18 December 1992.

29. Archie Hamilton, quoted in *The Guardian*, 25 November 1992.

Britain's motive may have been to test a new weapons design, as a major London paper reported.[30]

An Authoritative UK Statement of Policy

In July 1994 officials of the Foreign and Commonwealth Office, led by Minister of State Douglas Hogg, testified before the House of Commons' Foreign Affairs Committee on weapons proliferation and control. As part of the exercise the Foreign Office submitted a memorandum setting out UK policy.[31] It is a convenient reference guide to British positions, a careful and authoritative text. As a serious policy statement it also invites close scrutiny. In this section we canvass the FCO memorandum, to isolate and address those statements which shed light on British policy and intentions. The paper is divided into eight sections:

¶s 4-13	Nuclear proliferation, specifically:	
	5-6	NPT
	7	Nuclear Suppliers' Regime
	8-10	CTB
	11-12	Cut-off Convention
	13	IAEA
¶s 14-17	Chemical and biological weapons	
¶s 18-20	Missiles	
¶s 21-22	UN Special Commission on Iraq	
¶s 23-31	Conventional arms sales	
¶s 32-37	Dual-use goods	
¶s 38-39	Counter-proliferation	
¶s 40-47	Implementation of arms control agreements	

30. Rupert Cornwell, *The Independent*, 1 July 1993. Britain "has been wanting to test a new warhead version under design at the Aldermaston laboratory for use, defence sources say, both in the Trident submarine and for a new tactical "gravity bomb" which could be employed in a variety of roles. But, sensing the way the wind is blowing, British officials have been downplaying the importance of resumption." If this is correct, the warhead would replace the WE-177 and also provide Trident submarines with a warhead specifically tailored to a "substrategic" role.

31. House of Commons. Session 1993-94. Foreign Affairs Committee. *UK Policy on Weapons Proliferation and Control in the Post-Cold War Era.* Minutes of Evidence. 6 July 1994.

Non-Proliferation

The paper begins with a blunt statement of British aims ("HMG" stands for "Her Majesty's Government"):

> HMG's policy objective is, whilst retaining our own nuclear deterrent, to prevent the proliferation of nuclear weapons. . .
>
> HMG are committed through our membership of the NPT to limiting the possession of nuclear weapons to the five states defined in the NPT as nuclear weapon states (NWS) (ie the five who concluded a test explosion prior to 1967).[32]

The NPT and the Nuclear Suppliers' Regime are the main instruments of this policy. The UK seeks "unconditional and indefinite extension" at the 1995 NPT Review and Extension Conference. It is "resisting attempts" to condition NPT extension on completion of a CTB, new security assurances to non-nuclear states, or "target dates for the achievement of general and complete disarmament."[33]

The UK seeks a CTB "with the widest possible adherence, and with effective verification measures." A CTB requires the adherence of India, Iran, Iraq, Israel, Libya, North Korea, Pakistan, and Ukraine—and any other state "of proliferation concern":

> We therefore believe that ratification of the Treaty by all members of the Conference on Disarmament (which will include all the above-listed countries if plans for the Conference's expansion are put into effect) should be the condition for the Treaty's entry into force.[34]

---

32. *Ibid.*, ¶s 4-5.

33. *Ibid.*, ¶ 5.

34. *Ibid.*, ¶ 10. This issue was pursued by the Foreign Affairs Committee, taking evidence from Douglas Hogg and David Logan. The following exchange ensued:

    (Mr. Hogg) I think that our acceptance of the need for a Comprehensive Test Ban Treaty is premised on the assumption that there would be a general subscription to the Treaty as negotiated and if we found that a significant number of the participating countries would not sign up to it, then I think we would have to re-examine our policy on that. So you must assume that it is a pre-condition that everyone signs up to the Treaty. . .

    (Mr. Logan) . . . Our key concern, as the Minister has made clear, is that non-NPT parties such as the threshold States, who happen to be Members of the Conference on Disarmament, should sign and that is why we say all Members of the Conference on Disarmament. Above all, our concern is to get the nuclear weapon States and the threshold States.

(In the terms we developed discussing the French position, these constitute a "verification criterion" and a "universality criterion.")

Britain is "prepared to enter into negotiations" for a fissile material cut-off convention "with the aim of agreeing a convention . . . [not] prejudicing any of our substantial defense interests."[35] (Something akin to a "universality criterion" would also be applied.[36])

(Sir John Stanley) Minister, you slightly shaded in your answer what is said in the paper.

(Mr. Hogg) Very prudent of me!

(Sir John Stanley) . . . This may be an initial position by the British Government and we all understand that at an early stage in the negotiation, but the word "all" is quite clearly used there in your paper. In your verbal evidence you use a phrase—

(Mr. Hogg) Mr. Weasel was at the Despatch Box!

(Sir John Stanley) In your verbal evidence you used "a significant number" might dissent, might cause a change of policy.

(Mr. Hogg) Policy is all!

(Sir John Stanley) I think, Minister, what I am really putting to you is that if, say, Libya was the one country, to choose one example, or possibly North Korea—further away from the United Kingdom—that did not sign, would that really be a sufficient justification for the entire world not having the benefit of the Comprehensive Test Ban Treaty?

(Mr. Hogg) The truth is that is it not; policy is all, but at the end of the day you look at it in the round. The policy is all, but this matter will be ultimately a matter for collective discussion amongst colleagues and allies, but you must assume for the purposes of the policy as it is now established that the word "all" prevails, but naturally we will look at it in the round when the thing is finished.

(Chairman, Mr. David Howell) That is where you start from?

(Mr. Hogg) Yes. I do not think I can put it clearer than that.

35. In giving evidence, Brian Donnelly, Head of the Non-Proliferation Department of the FCO, explained what this meant (*Ibid*., p. 39):

"... we would continue to have certain requirements for fissile materials which will continue and which we will need to meet. One obvious example is highly enriched uranium for submarine propulsion. Another would be the ability to produce tritium, which is not strictly fissile material, but which would be necessary for the continued maintenance of our nuclear warheads into the future but which might need unsafeguarded material to produce it. So we would want to ensure that the terms of the convention did not inhibit our ability to continue to carry out these activities. We would also want to be sure that the cut-off was limited to the production of material and did not affect our ability to recycle existing material if that proved necessary."

36. *Ibid.*, ¶ 12.

Britain had "vigorously supported" action to strengthen IAEA's capability "particularly to detect undeclared nuclear facilities."[37]

Chemical and Biological Weapons

Britain "intends to ratify the CWC as soon as the necessary implementing legislation is in place." The United Kingdom is taking a "full role" in the work of the Preparatory Commission for the Organisation for the Prohibition of Chemical Weapons. It is also a party to the 1972 Bacteriological (Biological) and Toxin Weapons Convention.

Missile Proliferation

Measures against missile proliferation complement núclear non-proliferation. Impediments to acquisition of missiles and missile technology could postpone a new nuclear weapon state's achieving prompt and distant delivery capability. The British objective is

> to promote effective national controls on the transfer of ballistic missiles, their components and technology by the main producing countries. The main policy instrument is the Missile Technology Control Regime (MTCR).

The UK, the report states, is working with the US and others to "discourage" Indian deployment of the Prithvi missile and "to prevent the transfer to Pakistan of Chinese M-11 missiles."[38]

There is no intimation whatsoever of considering universal missile limitations or a "zero ballistic missile" regime. The MTCR does not constrain British missile acquisition.

Implementation of Arms Control Agreements

In this section the report considers START, CFE, and the Treaty on Open Skies. The UK has "welcomed" START I and II. With respect to Ukraine, the UK is "prepared to offer a security assurance on ac-

37. *Ibid.*, ¶ 13.

38. *Ibid.*, ¶s 19-20.

cession to NPT and to give technical help on weapon dismantlement."[39] CFE and Open Skies exercise verification techniques:

> Although not specifically linked to any existing arms control regime, the Treaty [on Open Skies] is an important adjunct to arms control verification since it permits signatories to overfly one another's territories at short notice to monitor military capabilities and activities. The Treaty is particularly significant in that it applies to the entire land area of each of its States Parties. Hence, unlike the CFE Treaty, Open Skies' provisions apply from Vancouver to Vladivostok.[40]

How Might the Three Hold Back in the CTB Talks?

The Three all have reasons to continue to test. Stated positions may conceal reservations. Delegations to the CD could stake out positions which made failure of the talks more likely, while diverting blame for failure to other parties or "intractable difficulties." They could insist on specific provisions which, though not unreasonable on their face, prepared for their withholding concurrence in the final text, or left them an "out" in a minimally consensual final text. In asking whether the positions the Three are taking include weakeners or spoilers, we would look for conditions which

1. would significantly dilute the CTB (such as an "escape clause" permitting low-yield tests, or periodic "safety and reliability" tests), or
2. require costly, elaborate, detailed, or difficult procedures, to which others will be unwilling to subscribe (such as costly verification terms), or
3. are politically offensive to one or more states (such as accepting "universality" of participation in the CD), or
4. require a technical performance not now achievable (such as real-time verification of low-yield tests), or
5. are likely to prove barriers to ratification in one or more participating states (for example, by requiring more intrusive inspection than their governments can defend at home).

---

39. *Ibid.*. ¶ 38. The UK subsequently gave just such an assurance in signing the "Memorandum on Security Assurances in Connection with Ukraine's Accession to the Treaty on the Non-Proliferation of Nuclear Weapons" in Budapest, 5 December 1994.

40. *Ibid.*, ¶ 45.

Plausible cases can be made for safety tests, and for foolproof verification by both remote "national technical means" and on-site inspections.

The Five declared weapons states have all stipulated preferred terms and conditions. Perhaps grounds are being prepared should they choose, as negotiations proceed, to withhold assent from the terms of a final text. Only the Five know just what is said behind closed doors. Observers are forced to construct from admissions and leaks just how the negotiations stand at any moment prior to final agreement. A *New York Times* 18 October 1994 editorial, in Appendix 3.1, offers a pessimistic version of the CD CTB negotiations.

The Five have lodged caveats, requirements and exceptions. Those recorded so far express criteria of (1) universality or (2) verifiability, or call for (3) an exception to permit some tests. For example, the United Kingdom insists that all members of the CD ratify a CTB before it comes into force. France takes the equivalent position that all nuclear capable countries being parties is "essential to the treaty's entry into force."[41] (Taken literally, these conditions would mean that refusal by even one such state would then block entry into force.) France requires—reasonably—that verification be "dependable and impartial." But how strict a requirement of "dependability" will be applied?

The reported French call for a "safety test" every five or ten years illustrates one type of exception. The United States had sought to test after ten years, but Clinton announced shortly before the NPT Review and Extension Conference opened that Washington would no longer press for that exception. A second exception would permit "peaceful nuclear explosions." A third would allow nuclear explosions with yields below some threshold, for example below the threshold of reliable seismic detection. Certainly any CTB which permitted such exceptions would be less than truly *comprehensive*.

---

41. Ambassador Gérard Errera (France). Ambassador Sir Michael Weston (United Kingdom). CD/PV.666, 25 January 1994.

The Chinese Position on a CTB

Foreign Minister Qian Qichen presented an authoritative but thumbnail statement of Chinese arms control policy to the UN General Assembly in September 1994. This statement (reproduced as Appendix 3.2) commits China only to *negotiations:*

> Negotiations should be undertaken with a view to concluding a comprehensive nuclear test ban treaty not later than 1996.[42]

Does this mean China will support *any CTB whatever its provisions* in 1996? That makes no sense. So we must understand that China's position is that it will sign a CTB in 1996 *if that CTB meets its approval*. Since the practices of the Conference on Disarmament require unanimous agreement to a final text, China need not fear being outmaneuvered; any proposed text that fails to meet Chinese approval will simply die. The strongest confirmation that China has *not* made a commitment to sign a CTB in 1996 is a statement attributed to an unidentified senior Foreign Ministry official with experience in arms control negotiation. He told journalists visiting Beijing that, indeed,

> China has made a political decision not to conduct nuclear tests after the signing of the Comprehensive Test Ban Treaty.

but then explained that

> It's an artificial date just to show there is political will.

How could this gesture be translated into a CTB signature? He said that the biggest barrier to a CTB was US opposition to "no first use":

> A U.S. commitment on non-first-use, as well as the commitment of other powers, would certainly help in China's participation.[43]

---

42. Speech of Qian Qichen, Vice-Premier and Foreign Minister, to the 49th Session of the United Nations General Assembly, 28 September 1994, in *Beijing Review* vol. 37 no. 41, 10-16 October 1994, pp. 29-32, p. 30.

43. *Los Angeles Times*, 21 October 1994.

The question then becomes whether China's stated positions on the terms of a CTB are, or are not, consonant with the requirements of other states.

On 24 March 1994 Chinese Ambassador Hou Zhitong told the CD that a CTB should "prohibit, at any place and in any environment, any nuclear weapon test explosion of any form which releases nuclear energy."[44] There are two ways to read this text. One stresses *any test explosion*, including those of small yield, whether at a test site or in the laboratory. In context—Hou is inveighing against loopholes—that is a persuasive reading. The second stresses *weapon* test, excluding "peaceful nuclear explosions," which are non-weapon tests. Even if the first reading were correct, implying an impulse toward a "strong" treaty, language that stringent could pose obstacles to verification, increasing the likelihood of *no* treaty.

Another theme open to two readings is China's insistence on no-first-use. Ambassador Hou said a CTB should contain "no first use" provisions. *Arms Control Today* comments that

> Including such a provision in the CTB Treaty would require the other four declared nuclear powers to reverse their current positions. A senior U.S. official, however, played down this issue. He emphasized that China is seeking a separate no-first-use pledge by the five declared nuclear powers in the CD's Ad Hoc Committee on Negative Security Assurances and has not pressed for any formal linkage with the CTB.[45]

Whether a "no-first-use" requirement is written into a CTB, or must be agreed elsewhere, if it is a condition of Chinese concurrence in a CTB then it constitutes a heavy demand on the other nuclear weapon states. Would they easily accede? To accede would mean *confining the mission for which nuclear weapons were purchased and deployed to exacting revenge if deterrence failed.* Although the Five all acknowledge deterrence (or "dissuasion") as the prime purpose for nuclear weapons, the military and nuclear establishments of Britain, France and the United States make their *internal case* for nuclear weapons on broader grounds. They do not limit nuclear weapons to deterring declared nuclear states. Instead, they talk of needing to have "insurance"

---

44. Conference on Disarmament. CD/PV.676. 24 March 1994. P. 20.

45. *Arms Control Today*, May 1994, p. 23.

against threats, of "action" against states which cannot be persuaded to give up programs to acquire nuclear weapons, of defending the "national sanctuary." Cold War Washington—and NATO—explicitly planned to use nuclear weapons against conventional breakthrough in Europe. Britain and France continue to write of "substrategic" options for their nuclear systems in the formal public justifications advanced for those programs. Russia may also conduct its internal arguments in something of this vein.

In this light, China's "no first use" requirement *could* prove crippling. It may be that China has no such intention, or wishes to leave a door open until later in the negotiations, or is really committed to compelling its nuclear partners to accept that the sole legitimate mission for nuclear forces is deterrence ("dissuasion").

Non-Proliferation Treaty (1968)

The Non-Proliferation Treaty was signed in 1968 and entered into force in 1970. It recognized two categories of states, "nuclear weapon states" and "non-nuclear-weapons states," and accorded each different rights and obligations. Non-nuclear-weapons states promised not to develop or receive nuclear weapons; the five nuclear powers agreed not to assist others in developing them. The non-nuclear states accepted ongoing non-nuclear status, but they got something in return: a commitment (Article VI) by the nuclear weapon states to engage in good faith negotiations toward complete and general disarmament, including nuclear disarmament.

The treaty also stipulated that after twenty-five years the Parties would consider for what term the NPT was to be extended, and whether there would be a single extension or a sequence of successive terms.

After the 1990 Review Conference—where no common decision could be reached—the nuclear weapon states positioned themselves to defend their nuclear forces, while keeping the non-proliferation regime in place as an obstacle to nuclear newcomers.

Before the 1995 NPT Review and Extension Conference Britain and France were on record favoring "unlimited extension" of the Non-Proliferation Treaty; China also declared itself for extension, though its position was not so clearly unqualified. In addition, all were taking part in the Comprehensive Test Ban talks.

The ostensible positions of all Three, then, favor arms control. However, "arms control" is not a clear-cut set of propositions. Instead, it has proven to be the set of measures which results from political negotiations and unilateral steps to manage arms holdings and practices. There have been strong displays of interest in specific measures. China and France stress their roles in bringing the Chemical Weapons Convention to a conclusion, and France hosted the signing ceremony. Mitterrand's April 1992 test moratorium initiative reshaped the issue *internally* as well as externally. China's long-standing call for a "no-first-use" pledge forces others to explain why they do not follow suit. Still, serious negotiations among the Five take place behind closed doors. There are few occasions when the Five must respond to expressions of disenchantment with their nuclear forces. The NPT Review Conferences present one such forum, even more important in 1995 because the issue of NPT extension was on the table.

International Atomic Energy Agency (IAEA)

The issue of "safeguards" was prompted by US President Dwight Eisenhower's proposed "Atoms for Peace" plan.[46] The US would share civil nuclear technology; in turn, recipients would accept conditions designed to prevent weapons proliferation. "The seminal accomplishment of the Atoms for Peace Program," Joseph Nye has written, "was the institution of a system of international safeguards administered by the International Atomic Energy Agency (IAEA)."[47] IAEA statutes were approved in October 1954 and entered into force in July 1957. By 1961 it had developed initial safeguards, and in 1965 set out a model safeguards agreement in document INFCIRC/66.

The 1968 NPT obligated signing non-nuclear weapon states to accept IAEA safeguards broader than those promulgated in

46. *Address by President Eisenhower Before the United Nations General Assembly*, 8 December 1953.

47. Joseph S. Nye. *The International Nonproliferation Regime*. Occasional paper no. 23. The Stanley Foundation, Muscatine, Iowa, June 1980.

INFCIRC/66. The applicable safeguards are spelled out in IAEA document INFCIRC/153, which records the terms approved by its Safeguards Committee in March 1971.[48] The NPT does not obligate nuclear weapon states to accept safeguards, an omission which prompted criticism and led the United States to accept, after some delay, voluntary IAEA safeguards of nuclear facilities except those with "direct national security significance." The Five are now all IAEA members.[49] Four have accepted IAEA safeguards in their civil nuclear

---

48. IAEA. The Structure and Content of Agreements Between the Agency and States Required in Connection with the Treaty on the Non-Proliferation of Nuclear Weapons. INFCIRC/153. *International Legal Materials* vol. 10 no. 4, July 1971, pp. 855-872. The texts of INFCIRC/66 (as revised through 1968) and INFCIRC/153 are also in Harald Müller, David Fischer and Wolfgang Kötter, *Nuclear Non-Proliferation and Global Order* (Oxford: Oxford University Press, 1994), pp. 190-201 and 213-229. On the differences between INFCIRC/66 and INFCIRC/153, see Müller et al., pp. 17-21, and Gary T. Gardner, *Nuclear Nonproliferation: A Primer* (Boulder, Colorado and London: Lynne Rienner, 1994, with the Program for Nonproliferation Studies, Monterey Institute of International Studies), p. 67 ff.

    NPT Article III § 1: "Each non-nuclear-weapon State Party to the Treaty undertakes to accept safeguards, as set forth in an agreement to be negotiated and concluded with the International Atomic Energy Agency in accordance with the Statute of the International Atomic Energy Agency and the Agency's safeguards system, for the exclusive purpose of verification of the fulfillment of its obligations assumed under this Treaty with a view to preventing diversion of nuclear energy from peaceful uses to nuclear weapons or other nuclear explosive devices. Procedures for the safeguards required by this article shall be followed with respect to source or special fissionable material whether it is being produced, processed or used in any principal nuclear facility or is outside any such facility. The safeguards required by this article shall be applied to all source or special fissionable material in all peaceful nuclear activities within the territory of such State, under its jurisdiction, or carried out under its control anywhere." Article III also fixes deadlines for beginning and completing negotiation of required agreements.

49. The IAEA approved China's application for membership on 11 October 1993, at an IAEA conference attended by a Chinese delegation. China formally entered the IAEA on 1 January 1984. Beijing promptly took hold. Ambassador Wang Shu presented his credentials to IAEA on 24 January. In early February Chinese experts gave papers at an IAEA symposium in Sofia on underground disposal of radioactive waste. On 6 June 1984 China was named a permanent member of the IAEA Board of Directors, in light of its advanced nuclear technology and production of raw materials. *China Quarterly* no. 97, March 1984, p. 184; no. 98, June 1984 p. 409; and no. 99, September 1984, p. 684.

programs, and China has agreed to place specific projects under safeguards.[50]

NPT Review and Extension Conference (1995)

The crux of global non-proliferation policy is the Treaty on the Non-Proliferation of Nuclear Weapons (NPT) (and IAEA safeguards which, under NPT Article III, adherents must accept). NPT Article X requires that there be a conference "to decide whether the Treaty shall continue in force indefinitely, or shall be extended for an additional fixed period or periods" twenty-five years after entry into force. Combined with a regular five-year review, the NPT Review and Extension Conference took place in New York April-May 1995.

The NPT is threatened by three hard problems. First, it is not universal; four non-signers (Israel, India, Pakistan and South Africa) are understood to have developed nuclear weapons, and a signer (Iraq) strove mightily to do so.[51] Second, it permits states to stockpile plutonium on the simple claim that they intend it as reactor fuel. Third, Article VI commits all states to "good faith" negotiation of disarmament:

> Each of the Parties to the Treaty undertakes to pursue negotiations in good faith on effective measures relating to cessation of the nuclear arms race at an early date and to nuclear disarmament, and on a treaty on general and complete disarmament under strict and effective international control.

---

50. Britain concluded a safeguards agreement with the IAEA in 1976. The text of the US-IAEA Safeguards Agreement is in US Arms Control and Disarmament Agency, *Arms Control and Disarmament Agreements* (Washington, DC: US ACDA, 1982), pp. 206-238. In 1981 France entered into an agreement with Euratom and IAEA on application of safeguards to declared French sites and materials. Similarly, the British agreement is with Euratom and IAEA. *SIPRI Yearbook 1993*, pp. 786, 787.

    Of the nuclear weapon states, Britain was subject to the no-transfer restrictions of the NPT. France did not sign the NPT until 1992, but declared in 1968 that it would act as if it had acceded. China too did not sign until 1992. However, France and China sent observer delegations to the 1990 NPT Review Conference. Müller et al., p. 60.

51. As noted above, South Africa has since declared that it has destroyed its nuclear weapons, and it has signed and ratified the NPT.

but after twenty-five years the nuclear weapon states have confined themselves to selected reductions, attributable wholly to military prudence, weapons obsolescence and a felt need to economize.

The US objective—behind which Russia, Britain, France, and in many respects China all lined up—was to obtain indefinite extension without compromising its nuclear force. The United States resisted amendment and claimed "good faith" performance of Article VI obligations. As the conference opening neared, the United States tried to respond to stated concerns: for example, dropping its CTB negotiating position that (some) tests should be permitted after ten years, and orchestrating a UN Security Council resolution of assurances to non-weapons states. The United States also insisted it would accept a majority vote if consensus could not be obtained, squeezing those opposed to indefinite extension (who had little doubt Washington could command a majority).

A pre-conference proposal of the Non-Aligned Movement identified six areas in which it sought "substantive progress" as a condition of agreeing to NPT extension:

- *Timetable*. Agreement on a time-bound framework for the total elimination of nuclear weapons.
- *Zones*. Adherence by the nuclear-weapon states to nuclear-weapon-free zone agreements, especially in the Middle East and Africa.
- *CTB*. Completion of a comprehensive test ban treaty.
- *Assurances*. Conclusion of a treaty providing legally binding positive and negative security assurances to non-nuclear-weapon states parties to the NPT.
- *Fissile Material*. Conclusion of a treaty banning the production and stockpiling of fissile material for nuclear weapons that is non-discriminatory, effectively verifiable and universally applicable.
- *Access to Nuclear Technology*. Guaranteeing free and unimpeded access to nuclear technology for developing non-nuclear-weapons states.[52]

These proposals present difficulties to the Three, as well as to Russia and the United States. On the issue of the *timetable*, the Non-Aligned Movement statement explicitly calls on China, France, and

52. Thomas Graham, Jr., "The United States and the Prospects for NPT Extension," *Arms Control Today* , vol. 25 no. 1, January-February 1995, pp. 3-6.

Britain to identify steps they will take to reduce their nuclear forces.[53] France and Britain show no readiness to commit to elimination of their nuclear forces. In that they are like the United States and Russia and—given their unreadiness—China too.[54] This proposal identifies the hard knot in Article VI and the inherently discriminatory character of the NPT.

The issue of *zones* encapsulates the issue of Israel: but Israel's reasons for a nuclear force look much like those offered by Britain and France. However much Britain and France inveigh against "proliferation" they are bound to be reluctant to press Israel.

On a *CTB*, all Three voice support for conclusion of a CTB, but it remains to be seen whether they will commit to a ban free from exceptions.

Because of the logical and practical difficulties with *assurances* which we have already discussed, they appear bound to continue to vex relations between nuclear and non-nuclear states. Until the Five sat down to work out a common position it seemed that they might invoke the UN Security Council to dodge any very specific *a priori* promises. The Three would commit to negative security assurances, subject (in the British and French cases) to some qualifications. They would not make a "positive security assurance" which committed them to use force—which could be nuclear force—to aid a state attacked or threatened with nuclear weapons.

A reasonable inference from British and French statements was that they would give no blank checks but would instead agree that in crises in which "positive assurances" would be invoked—"in case of the use or threat of use of nuclear weapons against a non-nuclear weapon state"—the issue should go to the UN Security Council, which would "act" in accordance with its obligations under the Charter. Of course, as each of them has a veto on Security Council action this would not tie their hands at all.

---

53. Acronym No. 4. *Strengthening the Non-Proliferation Treaty: Decisions Made, Decisions Deferred.* September 1994. P. 14.

54. The chief US negotiator at the NPT Review and Extension Conference said that "Countries are not telling the truth if they really think that we can have a serious negotiation about getting to a nuclear-free world. It is not possible under any foreseeable circumstance." Charles J. Hanley, Associated Press, 20 April 1995.

As enacted by the Security Council on 11 April 1995 the formula was much in that vein:

> in case of aggression with nuclear weapons or the threat of such aggression against a non-nuclear-weapon State Party to the Treaty on the Non-Proliferation of Nuclear Weapons . . . the nuclear-weapon State permanent members of the Security Council will bring the matter immediately to the attention of the Council and seek action to provide, in accordance with the Charter, the necessary assistance to the State victim;[55]

The resolution then introduces, however, pacific settlement, medical and humanitarian aid, compensation, states' expressed intention to "provide or support immediate assistance," and the Charter's affirming the right of individual and collective self-defense. None of this—especially in light of Bosnia—amounts to Security Council guarantees. The Five also gave negative assurances in the form of separate statements, a measure of their prickliness at any limitation but that of their own drafting, and the differences among them.[56]

The Three could accept a ban on production of *fissile material.* But they would reject a ban on "stockpiling" if that interfered with their capacity to remanufacture nuclear weapons. They would not accept requirements in the name of "non-discrimination" or "universal applicability" which did not respect their right to maintain capable forces.

At stake in the question of *access to nuclear technology*, of course, is whether states with weapons ambitions are shielding behind insistence their intentions are civil. The Three could agree that states should enjoy access to civil nuclear technology, provided the restriction to civil purposes had teeth. Britain and France would insist that the goals of the Nuclear Suppliers' Group and Missile Technology Control Regime not be compromised. It could prove very difficult to find terms which met both objectives.

---

55. UN Security Council Resolution 984, 11 April 1995.

56. The statements are in S/1995/261, S/1995/262, S/1995/263, S/1995/264 and S/1995/265.

The Outcome: Indefinite Extension, But . . .

The fault lines separating the Five from the most vocal NPT critics displayed themselves vividly when the NPT Review and Extension Conference met 17 April to 12 May 1995. But even the Five were not agreed on every point. The Conference opened with the United States, Russia, Britain, and France pressing for indefinite extension. Chinese Foreign Minister Qian Qichen, however, told the delegates that China could back NPT extension "for either an indefinite period or a series of fixed periods of no less than 25 years' duration." And he distinguished China's position from that of the others even more clearly in insisting that

> If the option for indefinite extension is chosen it must be made clear that such an extension should in no way be interpreted as perpetuating the nuclear-weapons states' prerogative to possess nuclear weapons.
>
> And, if the extension for multiple periods is chosen, we hold that each fixed period should not be less than 25 years.[57]

In any case, there should continue to be regular reviews.

As the Conference began a number of countries—among them Venezuela, Nigeria, Mexico, and Indonesia—pressed for something short of indefinite extension. They argued that the Five were failing to meet their NPT obligations and that only a shorter rein could keep pressure on them to disarm. They were also anxious to maintain the bargaining position which a consensus outcome would ensure them. Indonesia's UN Ambassador, Nugroho Wisnumurti, complained about the United States that "if indeed they want to push for a majority vote—and they already claim they have an overwhelming majority—then that will be the end of the NPT itself."[58]

By 9 May the United States had reportedly lined up at least 107 states for indefinite extension. *The New York Times* reported, however, that there were "persistent complaints of strong-arm tactics being used by the nuclear powers to win more votes." But the strategy of conference president Jayantha Dhanapala was to avoid a vote: "A voted decision on anything as important as this treaty would be a fatal

57. *The New York Times*, 19 April 1995.

58. *The New York Times*, 17 April 1995.

blow to it," he said on 9 May. "It would expose us as a divided house."[59] His effort to secure a result without vote proved successful, but not before Arab states insisted on language addressing Israel's nuclear program. The final package acknowledged the majority's preference for indefinite extension, alluded to Israeli nuclear weapons without specifically mentioning them, expressed the Five's readiness to conclude a CTB in 1996, and in language a shade more activist than Article VI called for

> the determined pursuit by nuclear-weapon states of systematic and progressive efforts to reduce nuclear weapons globally, with the ultimate goal of eliminating those weapons.[60]

The conferees sought expanded IAEA oversight of states' performance of their non-proliferation obligations, and ongoing annual review. There nuclear-weapon states could be held more closely accountable to perform "systematic and progressive efforts."

The package of proposals was agreed with 174 states taking part—only North Korea declining to join the result. But a number of states voiced reservations and criticisms, underscoring the fact that the outcome—while marking agreement not to hold NPT extension hostage—was certainly short of consensus.

MTCR and the Issue of Chinese Compliance

The Missile Technology Control Regime (MTCR) complements the NPT: the NPT commits non-nuclear signers not to acquire nuclear weapons, and the MTCR impedes access by all aspirants—NPT states

---

59. Barbara Crossette, *The New York Times*, 10 May 1995. Through 5 May only ten other states had agreed to Indonesia's call for rolling renewals every 25 years: Iran, Jordan, Malaysia, Mali, Myanmar, Nigeria, North Korea, Papua New Guinea, Thailand, and Zimbabwe.

    On US pressure, Crossette reported on 12 May 1995 that Venezuela's chief negotiator, Adolfo Taylhardat, resigned "after his Government suddenly changed its position from backing a limited and conditional extension to joining the United States in sponsoring a permanent renewal. In an interview, Mr. Taylhardat said this would not have happened if American pressure on Caracas had not been so intense."

60. *The New York Times*, 12 May 1995.

and non-signers alike—to the missile technology to deliver nuclear weapons swiftly from afar.

The main issue concerning the Three is China's status and alleged Chinese transfers contravening the MTCR. Unlike the NPT, a treaty open to all states, the MTCR is the voluntary undertaking of a few industrial states. China's MTCR position is that it had "adhered," where "adherence" is not "membership" and does not—for example—include taking part formally in negotiation of changes in the regime.

To illustrate how charges of MTCR violation vex the US-Chinese relationship, it is useful to trace the steps of that dispute. The first phase ended in February 1992, when China announced its adherence to the guidelines, and Washington removed some sanctions it had leveled against China in 1991.[61]

The second phase began in late 1992. On 5 December 1992 the press reported that China had sold "about two dozen" M-11 missiles to Pakistan and that the missiles arrived in Karachi on 20 November 1992. The report stated that

> In talks with the administration over the last few years, Chinese officials have acknowledged concluding a deal to sell the M-11 missiles to Pakistan, but argued that the contract had been signed before China was subject to the MTCR. But during Mr. Baker's trip to Beijing last year, China agreed that the regime's guidelines and parameters covered the M-11s.[62]

On 20 May 1993 US intelligence officials were reported claiming new evidence which "strongly suggests" China was continuing to export missile technology and hardware for the M-11 to Pakistan.[63] In August 1993 the United States imposed economic sanctions on China and Pakistan, including a two-year ban on the sale of sensitive US technology to China.[64] Two days later China said it might give up its

---

61. Lena H. Sun, Washington Post service, *International Herald Tribune*, 28 August 1993.

62. *Los Angeles Times* service, in *International Herald Tribune*, 5 December 1992.

63. *San Francisco Chronicle*, 20 May 1993.

64. *International Herald Tribune*, 26 August 1993. The despatch notes that the MTCR bars transfer of missiles with range exceeding 300 km or payload > 500 kg, but that China says the M-11 is not covered by MTCR guidelines. A further despatch in the *International Herald Tribune* on 28 August 1993 (from Lena H. Sun, *Washington Post* service) reports a 25 August 1993 US announcement that

commitment to keep to the MTCR guidelines in response to US sanctions,[65] and Deputy Foreign Minister Liu Huaqiu summoned US Ambassador J. Stapleton Roy to inform him that China viewed the sanctions as a "naked hegemonic act."[66] Moreover, said Liu,

> The Chinese government and people express their utmost indignation at such a move on the part of the U.S. government that compromises China's sovereignty, dignity and interests, and puts Sino-U.S. relations in serious jeopardy. . . .
>
> Now that the U.S. side has resumed these sanctions, the Chinese government has been left with no alternatives but to reconsider its commitment to the MTCR. . .
>
> [T]he US government shall be held fully responsible for all the consequences rising therefrom.[67]

It would be wrong to understand this dispute simply as a Chinese move to skirt controls, provoking US insistence that they keep their word. It was plain to those well-informed that the surface appearance reported by the press overlay a real dispute about just what China had agreed to do and about *whether China could be held, without explicit consent, to terms it had not taken part in drafting.* This was a dispute, then, about sovereignty and procedure, about consent and preemption. No doubt it was driven by a Chinese decision to transfer technology, whether from motive of policy or cash, or both. Its lesson, however, is that regimes rest on perceived interest, as was put very deftly by an experienced British diplomat in recounting this episode to members of Parliament.[68]

---

the United States had evidence China had shipped M-11 technology to Pakistan; the United States said this was prohibited by the MTCR. Sun explains:

"The Americans maintain that the missile exceeds the 1100 pound (500 kg) payload and 300-mile (500 km) distance limits set by the treaty. . . . The Chinese have not denied that certain items were shipped to Pakistan. But Beijing has maintained that it has not breached the specific arms control guidelines. . . . The shipment of missile-related technology that is the source of the dispute took place in December 1992, a few months after the Bush administration announced it was selling F-16 fighter jets to Taiwan."

65. *The Guardian,* 28 August 1993.

66. Xinhua She, quoted in Lena H. Sun, *Washington Post* service, *International Herald Tribune*, 28 August 1993.

67. *Ibid.*

68. Brian Donnelly, responding at length to a question from a member of the Foreign Affairs Committee of the House of Commons, captured this case with great clarity. (I have italicized the decisive comments):

In late 1994 China and the United States attempted to put this controversy behind them, but by mid-1995 it was once again aflame.

The Steps Ahead

The 1995 NPT Review and Extension Conference confirmed the importance attached to several ongoing negotiations and sought-for achievements. The key negotiations are set out in table 3.1, each associated with a set of rules which reinforce one another. These negotiations must also be considered in the context of bilateral talks between the United States and Russia, on the levels of their strategic nuclear forces, which we will consider in more detail in the next chapter.

One effect of anti-proliferation regimes, it should be noted, is to bring states other than Russia and the United States. into the negotiation of nuclear futures.

(Mr. Donnelly) If I may, Chairman, just to say that on the question of MTCR and China, as the Minister has quite rightly said, the essence of the supplier regimes is a certain degree of like mindedness amongst the members and a commitment to common proliferation goals and those who are outside it may or may not be willing to subscribe to those goals. What the Americans have tried hard to do with the Chinese is to persuade them to accept the MTCR guidelines as a matter of policy without actually committing themselves to be members of the regime and they did manage to bring the Chinese to accept, or to say that they would follow, the MTCR guidelines in their own export policy. *This was not the current version of the guidelines which have been modified in the last couple of years, but a slightly earlier version.* Then, however, there arose a dispute between the United States and China over whether these guidelines were in fact being adhered to in the context of Chinese exports to Pakistan, as a result of which—and it is a direct consequence of American domestic legislation—the Americans imposed sanctions on certain Chinese entities which are involved in missile production. On the question of whether that is proving helpful or not, I would have to say the jury is still out. *Certainly the Chinese still claim that the American sanctions are unjustified and that they are complying with the old MTCR guidelines*. . . . the Chairman of the MTCR has in the past been given mandates to talk to the Chinese to try and persuade them of the merits and *to persuade them to adopt the updated version of the guidelines.*

House of Commons. Session 1993-94. Foreign Affairs Committee. *UK Policy on Weapons Proliferation and Control in the Post-Cold War Era.* Minutes of Evidence. 6 July 1994.

Each of these initiatives has a focused purpose. That goal is sought in and for itself. Each is also part of the larger fabric of measures to halt proliferation and induce nuclear disarmament. As the NPT negotiations in New York in 1995 showed once more, however, the conditions for broad disarmament are not yet met.

There are two *sine qua non* of a thoroughgoing nuclear disarmament regime. First, all states which have nuclear weapons (or can build them) must agree they would be better off to give them up. Second, all must agree to the intrusive inspections and collective-security obligations required to sustain any non-nuclear future.

The non-nuclear future toward which NPT Article VI points would be marked by transparence, reassurance measures, substantial disarmament, and a recasting of the definition of a "state" which radically altered the sovereign attributes of the Westphalian state to arm and conceal.

In the meantime, there remains the question of existing nuclear weapons systems, which could be invoked in war.

TABLE 3.1

Ongoing Nuclear Arms Control Forums

PRINCIPAL NEGOTIATIONS	
NPT	In 2000, a further comprehensive NPT Review Conference. In 1997, 1998 and 1999, ten-day Preparatory Committee meetings which would "consider principles, objectives and ways in order to promote the full implementation of the Treaty, as well as its universality."[a]
START	The US-Russian Strategic Arms Reduction Talks. There is inevitable speculation on the terms of a prospective START III.
COMPLEMENTARY NEGOTIATIONS	
CTB	The Comprehensive Test Ban negotiation is being pursued in the Conference on Disarmament (CD) at Geneva.

Table 3.1 continued

	A statement adopted at the 1995 NPT Review and Extension Conference commits states to a Comprehensive Test Ban, to be concluded in 1996. However, they are not committed to any specific language.
Fissile Material Cutoff	This negotiation too takes place at the CD in Geneva. The 11 May 1995 conference statement called for a ban on production of plutonium and highly-enriched uranium . . . but only for military purposes.[b] Uranium at U^{235} concentrations for use as civil reactor fuel cannot be quickly converted to bomb use with existing technologies, but stockpiled Pu could be converted quickly by a state which had taken the preparatory steps to do so.
MTCR	Ongoing maintenance of the Missile Technology Control Regime is an important adjunct to the NPT, but takes place wholly outside the NPT framework.

a NPT/CONF. 1995/L.4. 10 May 1995.
b Text in NPT/CONF.1995/L.5, 9 May 1995.

To which agreed terms—whether in the form of shared understandings or treaty obligations—are nuclear forces to be subject? By what measures could the risks inherent in existing nuclear forces be reduced? Britain, France, and China are confronted by this question just as sharply as the United States and Russia, though the limelight of nuclear negotiations has centered on Moscow and Washington since the 1940s. We turn to this in the next chapter.

Appendix 3.1

Who's Delaying the Test Ban? Everyone.

More than 30 years after the U.S., the Soviet Union and Britain signed a Limited Test Ban Treaty halting nuclear tests in the atmosphere, they are finally getting around to negotiating a comprehensive test ban, barring tests altogether. But they and other nuclear-armed states seem to be looking for ways to limit the new treaty's comprehensiveness. That, in turn, is delaying a final draft.

Delay is precisely what Britain and France want. Both want to keep testing, and both hope that if negotiations drag on long enough, other states will lose interest. One of their delaying tactics has been to press for an exemption for so-called hydronuclear explosions that stop just short of a big bang. Although both countries argue otherwise, hydronuclear blasts are not needed to assure that warheads are safe and reliable; simulations using high explosives will suffice.

China, which has said it will accept a ban in 1996, is stalling while it completes a few more tests. It also seeks a loophole in the treaty permitting "peaceful" nuclear explosions. Washington and Moscow toyed for many years with the idea of using nuclear blasts to cut canals and tunnels through mountains, but all that ever came of it was India's attempt to pass off its 1974 warhead test as a peaceful nuclear explosion. In short, it became a pathway to proliferation.

The U.S. itself has proposed one of the most pernicious limits on the treaty. Washington would allow states to withdraw from the treaty after 10 years without even citing supreme national interests, as is customary. No reason would be needed, just 180 days' notice. Giving states so easy an out could effectively kill the treaty after 10 years.

The responsibility for energizing the negotiations and pointing them toward a truly total ban rests with the U.S. and Russia. They should stipulate that when the treaty says no tests, that means no hydronuclear tests and no "peaceful" explosions.

One way to accommodate the laggards, China and France, would be to delay full enforcement of the treaty until 1996, giving them time to complete a few more tests. But a treaty should be ready for signing by next spring. That will require more energetic efforts by Washington.

The New York Times, Editorial, 18 October 1994. Copyright © 1994 by The New York Times Company. Reprinted by permission.

Appendix 3.2

China Proposes Nuclear Package

The following is (excerpted from) a statement by Qian Qichen, vice-premier and foreign minister, and chairman of the delegation of the People's Republic of China, at the 49th Session of the United Nations General Assembly on September 28, 1994.

The world people have long lived in the shadow of a nuclear holocaust due to the all-out nuclear arms race between the two superpowers during the Cold War, resulting in a massive stockpiling of nuclear weapons. Now the international situation has drastically changed. Not only can we avert another world war, but the chances have increased for the complete prohibition and thorough destruction of nuclear weapons and for mankind to ultimately eliminate the threat of a nuclear war.

China has always stood for the complete prohibition and thorough destruction of all weapons of mass destruction. The Chinese government holds that a convention on the complete prohibition of nuclear weapons should be concluded in the same way as the conventions banning all biological and chemical weapons, respectively. As a signatory to the Treaty on the Non-Proliferation of Nuclear Weapons, China is in favor of its extension. Yet a mere extension of the treaty is obviously not sufficient. With a view to ultimately ridding mankind of the threat of a nuclear war and ushering in a nuclear-weapon-free world, the Chinese government proposes the following:

— All countries that possess nuclear weapons should pledge unconditionally not to be the first to use nuclear weapons, and should immediately start negotiations to conclude a treaty on non-first-use of nuclear weapons against each other;

— Efforts for the establishment of nuclear-free zones should be supported and all nuclear powers should undertake not to use or threaten to use nuclear weapons against any non-nuclear-weapon state or nuclear-free zone;

— Negotiations should be undertaken with a view to concluding a comprehensive nuclear test ban treaty not later than 1996;

— The principal nuclear powers should implement their existing nuclear disarmament treaties as scheduled and go on to drastically cut back their nuclear stockpiles;

— Negotiations should be undertaken to conclude a convention banning the production of weapon-grade fissile materials;

— A convention on the complete prohibition of nuclear weapons should be signed under which all nuclear powers should undertake the obligation to destroy all their nuclear weapons under effective international supervision; and

— International cooperation in the peaceful use of nuclear energy should be vigorously promoted simultaneously with the efforts to prevent the proliferation of nuclear weapons and step up the nuclear disarmament process.

The above points make up an integrated and interrelated nuclear disarmament process. We hold that all states, no matter whether they possess nuclear weapons or not, are entitled to participate fully in this process.

Since mankind has been able to make nuclear weapons and tap nuclear energy for peaceful purpose [sic] in the 20th century, we are confident that in the 21st century they will certainly be able to completely ban and destroy nuclear weapons and fully harness nuclear energy to enhance their own welfare. Before the advent of the new century, we stand ready to join the other nuclear as well as non-nuclear states to blaze the way toward this lofty goal and make our due contribution to its ultimate realization.

Beijing Review, vol. 37 no. 41, 10-16 October 1994.

Appendix 3.3

Decisions of the 1995 Review and Extension Conference of the Parties to the Treaty on the Non-Proliferation of Nuclear Weapons

17 April - 12 May 1995.

1. EXTENSION

NPT/CONF.1995/L.6

9 May 1995

EXTENSION OF THE TREATY ON THE NON-PROLIFERATION OF NUCLEAR WEAPONS

Resolution proposed by the President

The Conference of the States Party to the Treaty on the Non-Proliferation of Nuclear Weapons convened in New York from 17 April to 12 May 1995, in accordance with articles VIII, 3 and X, 2 of the Treaty,

Having reviewed the operation of the Treaty and affirming that there is a need for full compliance with the Treaty, its extension and its universal adherence, which are essential to international peace and security and the attainment of the ultimate goals of the complete elimination of nuclear weapons and a treaty on general and complete disarmament under strict and international control,

Having reaffirmed article VIII, 3 of the Treaty and the need for its continued implementation in a strengthened manner and, to this end, emphasizing the decision on strengthening the review process for the Treaty and the resolution on principles and objectives for nuclear non-proliferation and disarmament also adopted by the Conference,

Having established that the Conference is quorate in accordance with article X, 2 of the Treaty,

Decides that, as a majority exists among States party to the Treaty for its indefinite extension in accordance with its article X, 2, the Treaty shall continue in force indefinitely.

2. REVIEW PROCESS

NPT/CONF.1995/L.4

10 May 1995

STRENGTHENING THE REVIEW PROCESS FOR THE TREATY

Decision proposed by the President

1. The Conference examined the implementation of article VIII, 3, of the Treaty and agreed to strengthen the review process for the operation of the Treaty with a view to assuring that the purposes of the Preamble and the provisions of the Treaty are being realized.

2. The States party to the Treaty participating in the Conference decided, in accordance with article VIII, 3, of the Treaty, that Review Conferences should continue to be held every five years and that, accordingly, the next Review Conference should be held in the year 2000.

3. The Conference decided that, beginning in 1997, the Preparatory Committee should hold, normally for a duration of 10 working days, a meeting in each of the three years prior to the Review Conference. If necessary, a fourth preparatory meeting may be held in the year of the Conference.

4. The purpose of the Preparatory Committee meetings would be to consider principles, objectives and ways in order to promote the full implementation of the Treaty, as well as its universality, and to make recommendations thereon to the Review Conference. These include those identified in the Decision on Principles and Objectives for Nuclear Non-Proliferation and Disarmament adopted on 10 May 1995. These meetings should also make the procedural preparations for the next Review Conference.

5. The Conference also concluded that the present structure of the three main Committees should continue and the question of an overlap of issues being discussed in more than one Committee should be resolved in the General Committee, which would coordinate the work of the Committees so that the substantive responsibility for the preparation of the report with respect to each specific issue is undertaken in only one Committee.

6. It was also agreed that subsidiary bodies could be established within the respective Main Committees for specific issues relevant to the Treaty, so as to provide for a focused consideration of such issues. The establishment of such subsidiary bodies would be recommended by the Preparatory Committee for each Review Conference in relation to the specific objectives of the Review Conference.

7. The Conference agreed further that Review Conferences should look forward as well as back. They should evaluate the results of the period they are reviewing, including the implementation of undertakings of the States parties under the Treaty, and identify the areas in which, and the means through which, further progress should be sought in the future. Review Conferences should also address specifically what might be done to strengthen the implementation of the Treaty and to achieve its universality.

3. PRINCIPLES AND OBJECTIVES

NPT/CONF.1995/L.5

9 May 1995

PRINCIPLES AND OBJECTIVES FOR NUCLEAR NON-PROLIFERATION AND DISARMAMENT

Resolution proposed by the President

The 1995 Review and Extension Conference of the Parties to the Treaty on the Non-Proliferation of Nuclear Weapons,

Reaffirming the preamble and the articles of the Treaty on the Non-Proliferation of Nuclear Weapons,

Welcoming the end of the cold war, the ensuing easing of international tension and the strengthening of trust between States,

Desiring a set of principles and objectives in accordance with which nuclear non-proliferation, nuclear disarmament and international co-operation in the peaceful uses of nuclear energy should be rigorously pursued and progress, achievements and shortcomings evaluated periodically within the review process provided for in article VIII (3) of the Treaty, the enhancement and strengthening of which is welcomed,

Reiterating the ultimate goals of the complete elimination of nuclear weapons and a treaty on general and complete disarmament under strict and effective international control,

1. *Affirms* the need to continue to move with determination towards the full realization and effective implementation of the provisions of the Treaty, and accordingly adopts the following principles and objectives:

Universality

(1) Universal adherence to the Treaty on the Non-Proliferation of Nuclear Weapons is an urgent priority. All States not yet party to the Treaty are called upon to accede to the Treaty at the earliest date, particularly those States that operate unsafeguarded nuclear facilities. Every effort should be made by all States parties to achieve this objective .

Non-Proliferation

(2) The proliferation of nuclear weapons would seriously increase the danger of nuclear war. The Treaty on the Non-Proliferation of Nuclear Weapons has a vital role to play in the prevention of the proliferation of nuclear weapons. Every effort should he made to implement the Treaty in all its aspects to prevent the proliferation of nuclear weapons and other nuclear explosive devices, without hampering the peaceful uses of nuclear energy by the States party to the Treaty

Nuclear Disarmament

(3) Nuclear disarmament is substantially facilitated by the easing of international tension and the strengthening of trust between States that have prevailed following the end of the cold war. The undertakings with regard to nuclear disarmament as set out in the Treaty on the Non-Proliferation of Nuclear Weapons should thus be fulfilled with determination. In this regard, the nuclear weapon states reaffirm their commitment, stated in article VI, to pursue in good faith negotiations on effective measures relating to nuclear disarmament.

(4) The achievement of the following measures is important in the full realization and effective implementation of article VI, including the programme of action as reflected below:

(a) The completion by the Conference on Disarmament of the negotiations on a universal and internationally and effectively verifiable Comprehensive Nuclear Test Ban Treaty no later than 1996. Pending the entry into force of the Comprehensive Test Ban Treaty, the nuclear weapon States should exercise utmost restraint;

(b) The immediate commencement and early conclusion of negotiations on a non-discriminatory and universally applicable convention banning the production of fissile material for nuclear weapons or other nuclear explosive devices, in accordance with the statement of the Special Coordinator of the Conference on Disarmament and the mandate contained therein;

(c) The determined pursuit by the nuclear-weapons States of systematic and progressive efforts to reduce nuclear weapons globally, with the ultimate goal of eliminating those weapons, and by all States of general and complete disarmament under strict and effective international control.

Nuclear-weapon-free zones

(5) The conviction that the establishment of internationally recognized nuclear-weapon-free zones, on the basis of arrangements freely arrived at among the States of a region concerned, enhances global and regional peace and security is reaffirmed.

(6) The development of nuclear-weapon-free zones, especially in regions of tension, such as in the Middle East, as well as the establishment of zones free of all weapons of mass destruction should be encouraged as a matter of priority, taking into account the specific characteristics of each region. The establishment of additional nuclear-weapon-free zones by the time of the Review Conference in the year 2000 would be welcome.

(7) The cooperation of all the nuclear-weapon States and their respect and support for the relevant protocols is necessary for the maximum effectiveness of such nuclear-weapon-free zones and the relevant protocols.

Security Assurances

(8) Noting United Nations Security Council resolution 984 (1995), which was adopted unanimously on 11 April 1995, as well as the

declarations by the nuclear-weapon States concerning both negative and positive security assurances, further steps should be considered to assure non-nuclear-weapon States party to the Treaty against the use or threat of use of nuclear weapons. These steps could take the form of an internationally legally binding instrument.

Safeguards

(9) The International Atomic Energy Agency is the competent authority responsible to verify and ensure, in accordance with the statute of the Agency and the Agency's safeguard system, compliance with its safeguards agreements with States parties undertaken in fulfillment of their obligations under article III 1 of the Treaty, with a view to preventing diversion of nuclear energy from peaceful uses to nuclear weapons or other nuclear explosive devices. Nothing should he done to undermine the authority of the Agency in this regard. States parties that have concerns regarding non-compliance with the safeguards agreements of the Treaty by the States parties should direct such concerns, along with supporting evidence and information, to the Agency to consider, investigate, draw conclusions and decide on necessary actions in accordance with its mandate.

(10) All States parties required by article III of the Treaty to sign and bring into force comprehensive safeguards agreements and which have not yet done so should do so without delay.

(11) Agency safeguards should be regularly assessed and evaluated. Decisions adopted by its Board of Governors aimed at further strengthening the effectiveness of Agency safeguards should be supported and implemented and the Agency's capability to detect undeclared nuclear activities should be increased. Also States not party to the Treaty on the Non-Proliferation of Nuclear Weapons should be urged to enter into comprehensive safeguards agreements with the Agency.

(12) New supply arrangements for the transfer of source or special fissionable material or equipment or material especially designed or

prepared for the processing, use or production of special fissionable material to non-nuclear-weapon States should require, as a necessary precondition, acceptance of full-scope Agency safeguards and internationally legally binding commitments not to acquire nuclear weapons or other nuclear explosive devices.

(13) Nuclear fissile material transferred from military use to peaceful nuclear activities should, as soon as practicable, be placed under Agency safeguards in the framework of the voluntary safeguards agreements in place with the nuclear-weapon States. Safeguards should be universally applied once the complete elimination of nuclear weapons has been achieved.

Peaceful uses of nuclear energy

(14) Particular importance should be attached to ensuring the exercise of the inalienable right of all the parties to the Treaty to develop research, production and use of nuclear energy for peaceful purposes without discrimination and in conformity with articles I, II, as well as III of the Treaty.

(15) Undertakings to facilitate participation in the fullest possible exchange of equipment, materials and scientific and technological information for the peaceful uses of nuclear energy should be fully implemented.

(16) In all activities designed to promote the peaceful uses of nuclear energy, preferential treatment should be given to the non-nuclear-weapon States party to the Treaty, taking the needs of developing countries particularly into account.

(17) Transparency in nuclear-related export controls should be promoted within the framework of dialogue and cooperation among all interested States party to the Treaty.

(18) All States should, through rigorous national measures and international cooperation, maintain the highest practicable levels of nuclear

safety, including in waste management, and observe standards and guidelines in nuclear materials accounting, physical protection and transport of nuclear materials.

(19) Every effort should be made to ensure that the International Atomic Energy Agency has the financial and human resources necessary in order to meet effectively its responsibilities in the areas of technical cooperation, safeguards and nuclear safety. The Agency should also be encouraged to intensify its efforts aimed at finding ways and means for funding technical assistance through predictable and assured resources.

(20) Attacks or threats on nuclear facilities devoted to peaceful purposes jeopardize nuclear safety and raise serious concerns regarding the application of international law on the use of force in such cases, which would warrant appropriate action in accordance with the provisions of the Charter of the United Nations.

2. *Requests* that the President of the Conference bring this resolution, the decision on strengthening the review process of the Treaty, the decision on the extension of the Treaty and the Final Declaration of the Conference to the attention of the heads of State or Government of all States and seek their full cooperation on these documents and in the furtherance of the goals of the Treaty.

4. MIDDLE EAST

NPT/ CONF.1995/L.8

10 May 1995

Russian Federation, United Kingdom of Great Britain and Northern Ireland, and the United States of America: resolution

The Conference,

Reaffirming the purpose and provisions of the Treaty on the Non-Proliferation of Nuclear Weapons,

Recognizing that, pursuant to article VII of the Treaty on the Non-Proliferation of Nuclear Weapons, the establishment of nuclear-weapon-free zones contributes to strengthening the international non-proliferation regime,

Recalling that, the Security Council in its statement of 31 January 1992, affirmed that the proliferation of nuclear and all other weapons of mass destruction constitutes a threat to international peace and security,

Recalling also General Assembly resolutions adopted by consensus supporting the establishment of a nuclear-weapon-free zone in the Middle East, the latest of which is resolution 49/71 adopted on 15 December 1994,

Further recalling the relevant resolutions adopted by the General Conference of the International Atomic Energy Agency concerning the application of Agency safeguards in the Middle East, the latest of which is GC (XXXVIII)/ RES/21 of September 1994, and noting the danger of nuclear proliferation especially in areas of tension,

Bearing in mind Security Council Resolution 687 (1991) and particularly paragraph 14,

Noting Security Council resolution 984 (1995) and paragraph 8 of the Decision on Principles and Objectives for Nuclear Non-Proliferation and Disarmament adopted by the 1995 Review and Extension Conference of the Parties to the Treaty on the Non-Proliferation of Nuclear Weapons on 9 May 1995,

Also bearing in mind the Decisions adopted by the 1995 Revision and Extension Conference of the Parties to the Treaty on the Non-Proliferation of Nuclear Weapons,

1. *Endorses* the aims and objectives of the Middle East peace process and recognizes that efforts in this regard, as well as other efforts, contribute to, inter alia, a Middle East zone free of nuclear weapons as well as other weapons of mass destruction;

2. *Notes* with satisfaction that the report of Main Committee III (document NPT/CONF.1995/MC. III/ 1) in the 1995 Review and Extension Conference of the Parties to the Treaty on the Non-Proliferation of Nuclear Weapons has recommended that the Conference "calls on those remaining States not Parties to the Treaty to accede to it, thereby accepting an international legally binding commitment not to acquire nuclear weapons or nuclear explosive devices and to accept IAEA safeguards on all their nuclear activities";

3. *Notes* with concern the continued existence in the Middle East of unsafeguarded nuclear facilities, and reaffirms in this connection the recommendation in paragraph VI/3 of the report of Main Committee III urging those non-parties to the Treaty which operate unsafeguarded nuclear facilities to accept fullscope IAEA safeguards;

4. *Reaffirms* the importance of the early realization of universal adherence to the Treaty on the Non-Proliferation of Nuclear Weapons and *calls upon* all States of the Middle East that have not yet done so, without exception, to accede to the Treaty on the Non-Proliferation of Nuclear Weapons as soon as possible and to place their nuclear facilities under fullscope IAEA safeguards;

5. *Calls upon* all States in the Middle East to take practical steps in appropriate fora aimed at making progress towards, inter alia, the establishment of an effectively verifiable Middle East zone free of weapons of mass destruction, nuclear, chemical and biological and their delivery systems and to refrain from taking any measures that preclude the achievement of this objective;

6. *Calls upon* all States party to the Treaty on the Non-Proliferation of Nuclear Weapons and in particular the nuclear weapon States to extend their cooperation and to exert their utmost efforts with a view to

ensuring the early establishment by regional parties of a Middle East zone free of nuclear and all other weapons of mass destruction and their delivery systems.

4

Reducing Inventories

In the preceding chapter we introduced arms control measures to block the spread of nuclear weapons and end nuclear testing. We focused on the Non-Proliferation Treaty and non-proliferation regime, and negotiations for a comprehensive nuclear test ban. Britain, France, and China are concerned about these measures. They want to hinder proliferation, but they also want—with the qualifications introduced in chapter 3—to remain free to test new weapon designs or to calibrate test simulators.

We now turn to measures to cut—even eliminate—nuclear weapons. As we noted above, proposals to abolish nuclear weapons were advanced by Canada, Britain, and the United States in the 1940s. The heart and core of Mikhail Gorbachev's 15 January 1986 call was to eliminate all nuclear weapons by the year 2000, a plan which envisaged drawing Britain, France and China into cuts after the Soviet Union and the United States had taken significant steps. Former US Secretary of Defense and World Bank head Robert McNamara advocates sharp cuts in US and Russian warheads to "at most" 100-200 each, a number now exceeded by each of the Three.[1]

Much of the argument about "security" in cuts turns on what others hold. As a consequence, British, French and Chinese inventories will matter more and more as Russian and US numbers fall. If the Three are ever to negotiate their nuclear holdings, it will be only after they have seen Russia and the United States accept ever sharper cuts than hitherto announced. Moreover, the Three have nuclear weapons in large part—though they might have acquired them in any case—in the conviction that nuclear weapons are an "equalizer" against any misplaced ambition of the United States or the Soviet Union (Russia). And, as we all know, the Five could do terrible damage to each other. So it is appropriate to consider in this text the

---

1. *The New York Times*, 23 February 1993.

main steps taken by the United States and Russia (Soviet Union) to manage their nuclear relationship, because it will shape how the Three understand their political and security environments.

The mainstream US-Soviet (Russian) negotiations have centered on control, and then reductions, in the number of strategic nuclear systems they deploy, and collateral stability measures. The key steps in counter-proliferation and quality constraint were the PTBT and NPT. The foremost measures to reduce nuclear inventories and maintain "deterrent stability" are the ABM Treaty and the succession of SALT and START accords.

The START II Baseline

Soviet-US negotiations on bilateral nuclear weapons limitation and reduction have resulted in six important treaty texts: ABM Treaty and SALT I Interim Agreement (1972), SALT II Treaty (1979), INF Treaty (1987), START I (1991) and START II (1993).[2]

The ABM Treaty codified a sharp limit on deployment of anti-ballistic missile systems which—if they had worked—would have upset the mutual vulnerability which "deterrence" required.

SALT and START set limits on deployable strategic systems, by type and number. The aim was to prevent costly procurement, maintain an effective balance of threats, and—in START—cut numbers, especially of destabilizing silo-based systems with several warheads on one missile. These measures did not address many forms of modernization, though they did register types of systems which both were quite willing to forego, and they left Russia and the United States each with massive destructive capabilities.

---

2. 1. ABM Treaty: Treaty Between the United States of America and the Union of Soviet Socialist Republics on the Limitation of Anti-Ballistic Missile Systems. Signed 26 May 1972. Entered into force 3 October 1972. 2. SALT I Interim Agreement: Interim Agreement Between the United States of America and the Union of Soviet Socialist Republics on Certain Measures with Respect to the Limitation of Strategic Offensive Arms. Signed 26 May 1972. Entered into force: 3 October 1972. 3. SALT II Treaty: Treaty Between the United States of America and the Union of Soviet Socialist Republics on the Limitation of Strategic Offensive Arms. Signed: 18 June 1979. (The SALT II Treaty was never ratified.) 4. INF Treaty: Signed: December 1987. 5. START I Treaty: Signed 31 July 1991. 6. START II Treaty: Signed 3 January 1993.

The INF Treaty banned ground-based systems with ranges from 500 km to the conventional threshold of "strategic" systems, 5500 km. It was prompted by deployment in Europe of increasingly capable nuclear systems in the 500-5500 km range, the Soviet SS-20 and US Pershing II missile and the US GLCM (Ground-Launched Cruise Missile). These posed special problems. They could strike "strategic" objectives, saving long-range systems for other targets. Further, the Pershing II could strike Moscow only minutes after firing.

The breakthrough INF agreement did away with all nuclear-armed missiles in the ranges covered. The parties agreed to destroy existing missiles and put inspection in place to ensure new sets were not produced. These moves signaled that medium-range and intermediate-range ground-based nuclear missiles were now judged disadvantageous. Moscow and Washington concluded that it was better they were not deployed at all than deployed. The INF Treaty did not remove all nuclear weapons from Europe. It did not prevent Europe being targeted by US or Russian weapons. Still, it made clear that nuclear systems were not necessarily useful enough to justify their cost and risk and that states could negotiate their elimination.

The United States and Soviet Union deployed some 10,000-12,000 "strategic" warheads apiece in the mid-1980s. Under START I they will cut several thousand warheads each, to levels of roughly 6500. START II imposes even further cuts in the range 3000-3500 warheads. Cuts are likely to reach 3200 (Russia) and 3500 (United States) by the year 2003 (or 2000 if the United States were to assist Russia in the process).

So the START process changes the global strategic environment, the world in which Britain, France, and China deploy their nuclear systems. France and China, especially, will welcome the cuts; Britain will at least welcome Russian cuts. They remain alert, however, to the fact that Russia and the United States will retain capable systems, in large numbers. Moscow and Washington pursue many avenues of modernization—including work on theater anti-ballistic missile (ABM) systems and anti-submarine warfare (ASW) techniques—which could nullify smaller nuclear forces.

They must ask, too, whether the START II agreements will be implemented. If they are, there will be calls for the Three to join further cuts and explore disengagement measures. If they are not, the argument for the Three independent nuclear forces will be stronger internally, more resistant to proposals for disengagement. Failure of START could come about, for example, if Ukraine refused to adhere to the NPT and surrender the nuclear weapons on her territory, or if there were a radical nationalist takeover of the US or Russian government. We must assume, therefore, that in Beijing, Paris, and London very close attention is being paid to the START process.

START II Implementation

START I was signed by the United States and Soviet Union on 31 July 1991. Vexing complications were introduced by the breakup of the Soviet Union, which left nuclear weapons on the territories of Belarus, Ukraine and Kazakhstan. Moscow moved promptly to organize command of those forces under the rubric of a Commonwealth of Independent States, but that did not resolve what is to happen to the weapons or how successor republics would acquit Soviet treaty obligations.

The key document binding the Soviet successor states to START I is the Lisbon Protocol, signed by the United States, Russia, Belarus, Ukraine and Kazakhstan on 23 May 1992. Belarus, Ukraine, Kazakhstan and Russia assume the Soviet obligations under the treaty. Belarus, Ukraine and Kazakhstan commit to adhere to the NPT as non-nuclear weapon states "in the shortest possible time."[3] When the Russian parliament approved START I on 4 November 1992 it made certain stipulations, among them that Belarus, Ukraine and Kazakhstan complete their adherence to the NPT.[4]

START I must be effected before the negotiated and agreed START II terms are implemented. This means that the major cuts in strategic systems envisioned by START II could have been derailed by failure of Belarus, Ukraine or Kazakhstan to meet the conditions of the Lisbon Protocol. Even had that happened, of course, the United

---

3. Text in *SIPRI Yearbook 1993* (Oxford: Oxford University Press, 1993), pp. 574-575.

4. Carnegie Endowment for International Peace and the Monterey Institute of International Studies. *Nuclear Successor States of the Soviet Union*, no. 1, May 1994, p. 2.

States and Russia could still have engaged in cuts as deep as those set out in START II. At this writing, however, Belarus, Ukraine, and Kazakhstan are on track toward denuclearization.[5]

---

5. *Belarus*. The first successor state to act was Belarus. On 3 February 1993 Belarus' parliament ratified the 1991 START I treaty, and on 22 July 1993 it became a party to the NPT as a non-nuclear weapons state. By one count, 54 single-warhead SS-25s remained in Belarus in April 1994; transfer to Russia had begun, and was to be completed by mid-1996. (Carnegie Endowment for International Peace and the Monterey Institute of International Studies. *Nuclear Successor States of the Soviet Union*, no. 1, May 1994, p. 4, citing [on transfers] testimony to the Senate Armed Services Committee of Assistant Secretary of Defense Ashton Carter). By late August 1994 Belarus reported less than 40 warheads remaining on its territory. (Foreign Minister Vladimir Senko, quoted by Reuters, 26 August 1994).

   The nuclear weapons remaining in Belarus are under Russian jurisdiction and control.

   Belarus is taking the next step in its NPT obligations, negotiating a full-scope safeguards agreement with the IAEA. The nuclear weapons to be transferred to Russia lie outside that agreement (*Ibid*., p. 4).

   Commentators observe, however, that Belarus has moved more swiftly than Ukraine and Kazakhstan to meet its obligations. (*The New York Times*, editorial, 9 February 1993.)

   Kazakhstan. Kazakhstan early ratified START I (2 July 1992) and joined the NPT on 14 February 1994. Like Belarus and Ukraine—though Ukraine has not yet adhered to the NPT—Kazakhstan is negotiating a full-scope safeguards agreement with the IAEA. Nuclear weapons which were in Kazakhstan as Soviet weapons would not be subject to IAEA inspection under such an agreement. (Carnegie Endowment for International Peace and the Monterey Institute of International Studies. *Nuclear Successor States of the Soviet Union*, no. 1, May 1994, p. 2.)

   As of May 1994, 1290 of the 1410 nuclear warheads listed in Kazakhstan in the START I Memorandum of Understanding remained there. Russian press reports state that all will be transferred to Russia by mid-1995. (*Ibid*., p. 5, citing [on impending transfers] Radio Free Europe/Radio Liberty Daily Report, 4 May 1994). An undetonated Soviet nuclear device in a test shaft at Semipalatinsk was destroyed on 31 May 1995. Associated Press, 31 May 1995.

   Semipalatinsk is thought to have been a base for Soviet strategic bombers carrying nuclear-armed air-launched cruise missiles. As Semipalatinsk lies only a few hundred kilometers from the Chinese border, these aircraft were no doubt of interest to Chinese air-defense planners. Removal of the bombers to Russia is a marginal improvement for China, though at least some of the ALCMs which armed them are reportedly in storage at Semipalatinsk. (*Ibid*., p. 5 and map. The START I Memorandum of Understanding listed 370 ALCMs in Kazakhstan.)

   Ukraine. Despite Ukraine's signature of the Lisbon Protocol, pledging to sign

---

and ratify START I (as a successor state to the Soviet Union) and the Non-Proliferation Treaty, Ukraine's government and parliament was laggard in moving to those steps. Instead, nuclear weapons became a subject of nationalist claims, as well as bargaining chips over compensation. One expression of Ukraine's reticence to sign and ratify was given by the chair of Ukraine's foreign relations committee, Dmitro V. Pvlychko, who said, as reported by *The New York Times* on 19 November 1993, that

"We're moving toward nonnuclear status, step by step, and only under guarantees of security and aid. We'll fulfill our obligations under Start I. But we don't have the financial ability to destroy the weapons themselves. The main point is to get money and that is why we're moving cautiously. We're not avoiding our obligations. Ukraine doesn't want to be a nuclear power, but we can't give these weapons up like we gave up the tactical ones without compensation. If the West wants us to give them up quickly, they need to give us assistance."

Negotiations on the weapons in Ukraine continued into 1994. In December 1993 *The New York Times* reported that Ukraine Deputy Prime Minister Valery Shmarov said 17 of the 46 SS-24s had been "deactivated," their warheads taken off and moved away from the launchers. "We are prepared to remove all SS-24's from military alert," he said, "but only if conditions discussed at these talks (with Russia) are fulfilled." Twenty of the SS-19s were reportedly also being dismantled Issues on which Ukraine is said to have declared "conditions" included the amount of money aid to finance dismantling, what would be done with dismounted warheads, and what security provisions might be offered Ukraine. (*The New York Times*, 21 December 1993.)

However, on 3 February 1994 the Ukrainian parliament approved START I without conditions and also approved the Lisbon Protocol. The logjam appeared broken following an agreement signed by the presidents of Ukraine, Russia and the United States on 14 January 1994 setting a deadline for removal of all nuclear weapons from Ukraine to Russia. Dismantlement of nuclear systems, warhead removal and storage are reportedly underway. The three-party statement of January 1994 stipulated that all SS-24s in Ukraine—46 with 460 warheads, more than a quarter of all warheads in Ukraine—would be deactivated by mid-November 1994. (Carnegie Endowment for International Peace and the Monterey Institute of International Studies. *Nuclear Successor States of the Soviet Union*, no. 1, May 1994, p. 3, 10-11.) On 16 November 1994 the Ukrainian parliament voted 301-8 to accede to the NPT. On 5 December 1994 Russia, Britain and the United States signed a "memorandum" on security assurances to Ukraine, which incorporates a qualified negative assurance and a commitment to seek UN Security Council action were Ukraine to become object of a nuclear attack or threat. (Sherman W. Garnett, "Ukraine's Decision to Join the NPT," *Arms Control Today*, vol. 25 no. 1, January/February 1995, pp. 7-12.) The negative assurance reaffirms, with specific reference to Ukraine, their commitment "not to use nuclear weapons against any non-nuclear-weapon state" party to the NPT; the qualification is "except in the case of an attack on themselves, their territories or dependent territories, their armed forces, or their allies, by such a state in association or

• • •

If the measures envisioned at Lisbon are carried out, START II may well be realized. There are at least two other uncertainties, however, which must be borne in mind. START could be derailed if Russian internal politics adopted the views of START's critics, believed to be numerous in the military and nuclear systems. Implementation also faces severe practical problems: can these systems be disassembled safely, in the large numbers planned, within the planned time? and what is to be done with the resultant plutonium and uranium?

Although START is not sure, calls for participation by the Three in nuclear weapons disengagement and reductions are certain to be forthcoming in some form. We now turn to the policies of the Three with respect to negotiated reductions.

France

France watched US-Soviet bilateral arms negotiations, judging the results by their effects for France. David Yost observes that the ABM Treaty met French interests, since an effective anti-missile system would have cast doubt on some elements of France's capacity to deter the Soviet Union.[6] Of course, France agreed with US rejection of Soviet calls to count French nuclear forces with US forces in negotiating numbers for SALT I and II. Yost points out, however, that although France gave qualified endorsement to SALT II, some French analysts found fault with it, charging that it codified a shift in the strategic nuclear balance favoring the USSR, did not limit the SS-20 or Backfire bomber, and in some details could hinder NATO force modernization.

François Mitterrand voiced the French position authoritatively before the UN General Assembly in 1983.[7] He opened the possibility

---

alliance with a nuclear-weapon state.")

6. David Yost, "France," in Fen Osler Hampson, Harald von Riekhoff, and John Roper (eds.), *The Allies and Arms Control* (Baltimore: Johns Hopkins University Press, 1992), pp. 162-188, pp. 174-175.

7. 28 September 1983. UNGA A/38/PV.9 (PROVISIONAL) 29 September 1983, the provisional verbatim record of the UNGA session of 28 September 1983.

of French participation in strategic arms limitation talks, but with great discretion, laying the weight of his remarks on the "conditions for progress":

> We cannot reject the idea—and I do not—that the five nuclear Powers should together debate when the time comes a permanent limitation of their strategic systems. We must therefore set out clearly the conditions for progress in this field.

He first required superpower reductions to a level more like that of France:

> The first of these conditions is the correction of the fundamental difference, in terms of type and quantity, between the armaments of the two major Powers and those of the others, and the difference between a country that might use them to assert its power and a country which might be forced to make use of them for its own survival.

A second condition centered unmistakably on Soviet conventional preponderance in Europe:

> The second condition flows from the wide gap between conventional forces, particularly in Europe, a gap which has become even wider, I fear, because of the existence of chemical and biological weapons, the manufacture and stockpiling of which must be prohibited by a convention.

The third stemmed from the vulnerability of France's nuclear deterrent to technologies which might blunt or nullify it:

> The third condition is the cessation of the escalation in anti-missile, anti-submarine and anti-satellite weapons.

Mitterrand went on—in implicit response to Reagan's proposal in March of 1983 to create the "Star Wars" system—to note there was now "no curb on the development of anti-missile weapons in space" and to call for a ban on satellization of "any type of weapon," not only nuclear weapons.

The second condition was met by the Treaty on Conventional Forces in Europe (CFE) and the Chemical Weapons Convention, but the first and third remain at issue. Mitterrand restated the French position in February 1992 at the close of talks with Boris Yeltsin, when he told a joint news conference that France was prepared to join talks on nuclear arms reduction only after the United States and Russia carried out a further phase of deep cuts in their arsenals. But he did not commit to joint negotiations:

> Once these cuts have reached a certain level, in a fixed time frame, France could join these negotiations.[8]

He offered no specifics, but did praise Russia's disarmament initiatives, saying these already had enabled France to modify some defense programs.

When France declared its test moratorium (8 April 1992) it said it would retain its independent nuclear deterrent as "the keystone of our defense policy," but would continue to press for global arms reductions. Eight months later, welcoming the START II accords between Russia and the United States, the French Ministry of Foreign Affairs confirmed France's readiness to act in accordance with the "conditions" laid down by President Mitterrand in his 1983 speech to the UN General Assembly:

> France confirms that, at the appropriate moment, and in accordance with the conditions she has long laid down—which the President of the Republic spelt out before the United Nations General Assembly in 1983—she will be prepared to shoulder her share of responsibility in the process of monitoring and reducing nuclear weapons.[9]

Understanding what France might be willing to negotiate at some time in the future requires, however, a sense of voices on behalf of a continuing French nuclear capability. A month after China's October 1993 test, as preparation of France's *Livre Blanc* on defence went forward, debate on nuclear policy sharpened. Among figures in this debate is Jacques Baumel, vice-chairman of the Defense Commission of the National Assembly and an RPR deputy for Hauts-de-Seine. His is the strongest voice on behalf of new missions for nuclear weapons:

> The very notion of an absolute nuclear weapon has changed over the past 30 years. It has now both lost its legitimacy and been trivialized. It is just another weapon of mass destruction.. . . . The French doctrine, hitherto restricted to the strategy of massive countercity strikes, should move toward more selective capabilities, directed against specific military forces or sensitive installations. It will require

8. Wire service despatches, 7 February 1992.

9. Statement of the Spokesman of the Ministry of Foreign Affairs, Paris, 30 December 1992.

more accurate weapons which are difficult to intercept, and very mobile with a reduction in collateral effects.[10]

Le Monde takes this to mean aerodynamic vectors like Matra's Apache cruise missile and supersonic vectors like Aérospatiale's stand-off missile ASMP (and, had the decision been to build it, an ASLP). Baumel continues that

> logic dictates that our country should maintain dual deterrence, that of our missile-launching submarines for countercity attacks and also that of a second flexible component, which would be mobile and very accurate and would comprise air-to-surface or surface-to-surface missiles of the medium-range air-to-surface missile type on board Rafale planes, on ships, or cruise missiles with dual conventional and nuclear capabilities.

and regretted that Britain had abandoned an ASLP (TASM).

Jacques Isnard, *Le Monde* military correspondent, identifies such views in the general staffs and at the CEA as well as in parliament. They take for granted the need to modernize strategic missiles, but also advance new doctrine:

> Abandoning a countercity deterrence known as a no-war deterrence or deterrence "by the weak of the strong," which it has had since the sixties when it needed to deter the Soviet Union, France would move to a doctrine of the use of sophisticated nuclear weapons, with variable or directed power, which their critics compare to battlefield munitions and which would aim to wipe out the potential of unreasonable states, invoking a counterforce strategy known as deterrence "by the strong of the crazy."

France would have such a kiloton or sub-kiloton weapon, Isnard states, simply by making operational the fission primary of existing thermonuclear warheads. Isnard anticipated that doctrinal argument would have to be faced in the *Livre Blanc*, to appear in early 1994.[11]

When it was published, however, such new missions were

---

10. *Le Monde*, 6 November 1993. Translation in JPRS-TND-93-037.

11. Jacques Isnard, *Le Monde*, 6 November 1993. In a biting critique of "the sorcerer's apprentices of a new nuclear doctrine," Jacques Amalric writes in *Liberation* 11 November 1993 that "it is impossible, by definition, to deter the insane with certainty" and accuses advocates among politicians of being "more concerned with the coming presidential election than with the perfecting and financing of . . . conventional smart weapons that would make it possible to cope successfully with the 'crazies'." JPRS-TND-93-037.

rejected. The *Livre Blanc* does posit a hypothetical scenario in which its forces might face, in a regional conflict, "weapons of mass destruction" and observes that the intervention force would be supported by France's qualitative superiority in means of destruction, a superiority resting largely on "technological advance." Nuclear weapons go unmentioned.[12] Elsewhere, the collective authors insist "French nuclear strategy is a strategy of dissuasion, rejecting any confusion between dissuasion and use."[13]

China

The PTBT prompted China's first comprehensive comment on nuclear weapons. On 31 July 1963, in a biting critique of the US-Soviet-British signing of the Partial Test Ban Treaty, China advanced a proposal calling on the nuclear weapon states to withdraw nuclear weapons abroad, end all tests, halt export and import of nuclear weapons and technical data, and establish an (ill-defined) "nuclear weapon-free zones of the Asian and Pacific region" embracing China, Japan, the United States and the Soviet Union, and other zones. These measures were to be preliminary to "complete prohibition and thorough destruction of nuclear weapons." (The complete text of the statement of 31 July 1963 is reproduced as Appendix 4.1.)

More than a year later, announcing its first nuclear test, China set down principles for nuclear arms control which have remained henceforth in the Chinese lexicon. They reflect the change that China now spoke as a nuclear state, if not yet in the strict sense a nuclear *weapon* state. One principle took up the theme already set out in 1963: achieving "complete prohibition and thorough destruction of nuclear weapons." In English usage we would simply say "abolition." The second: China solemnly declared it would "never at any time and under any circumstances be the first to use nuclear weapons." This is the position abbreviated in English usage as "no first use." China also called for a summit conference to agree "as a first step" toward complete prohibition and thorough destruction "not to use nuclear weapons, neither to use them against non-nuclear countries and

12. *Livre Blanc*, pp. 115-116.

13. *Ibid.*, p. 79.

nuclear-free zones, nor against each other."[14] Thus China's position in 1964 centered on no-first-use as a first step toward abolition.

China's 1964 analysis did not stop there. China insisted that "nuclear war can be prevented."

> We are convinced that nuclear weapons, which are after all created by man, certainly will be eliminated by man.[15]

Already the nuclear states' adopting "no first use" was stipulated as a precondition to end proliferation:

> If those countries in possession of huge quantities of nuclear weapons are not even willing to undertake not to use them, how can those countries not yet in possession of them be expected to believe in their sincerity for peace and not to adopt possible and necessary defensive measures?

Beijing gained the Chinese seat in the United Nations in Fall 1971, opening the possibility China could take part in UN-sponsored disarmament discussions. Beijing immediately put itself on record. Chinese UN Ambassador Qiao Guanhua, in his maiden speech, charged that "the superpowers, while talking about disarmament every day, are actually engaged in arms expansion." And he declared China's position:

> China will never participate in the so-called nuclear disarmament talks between the nuclear powers behind the backs of the non-nuclear countries. China's nuclear weapons are still in the experimental stage. China develops nuclear weapons solely for the purpose of defence and for breaking the nuclear monopoly and ultimately eliminating nuclear weapons and nuclear war. The Chinese Government has consistently stood for the complete prohibition and thorough destruction of nuclear weapons and proposed to convene a summit conference of all countries of the

---

14. The Chinese proposal:

    "That a summit conference of all the countries of the world be convened to discuss the question of the complete prohibition and thorough destruction of nuclear weapons, and that as the first step, the summit conference should reach an agreement to the effect that the nuclear powers and those countries which may soon become nuclear powers undertake not to use nuclear weapons, neither to use them against non-nuclear countries and nuclear-free zones, nor against each other."

    Chinese Government Statement. October 16, 1964. "China Successfully Explodes its First Atom Bomb." *Peking Review* no. 42 (1964), 16 October 1964, Special Supplement.

15. *Ibid.*

> world to discuss this question and, as the first step, to reach an agreement on the non-use of nuclear weapons. The Chinese Government has on many occasions declared, and now on behalf of the Chinese Government, I once again solemnly declare that at no time and under no circumstances will China be the first to use nuclear weapons.[16]

Three days later China conducted a nuclear test.[17] Qiao Guanhua followed on 24 November with a major speech on disarmament, urging that a Soviet proposal for a world disarmament conference not be put to the vote. Citing regions in which the question of "paramount importance" was not disarmament but "the defence of national independence and sovereignty and the winning of the right to national existence," China insisted that adopting disarmament measures

> without distinguishing the aggressors from the victims of aggression and those who threaten others from those who are threatened can only lead the question of disarmament on to a wrong path and benefit imperialism.

The partial test ban and the nonproliferation treaty were "camouflage" for the superpowers' nuclear expansion. China developed nuclear weapons only because she was "under the nuclear threat of the two superpowers." What should be done? Qiao repeated the call for a world conference on "complete prohibition and thorough destruction" of nuclear weapons; a non-use agreement would be the "first step" in the conference; and to realize the ultimate aim of "complete prohibition and thorough destruction" the United States and Soviet Union should "first of all" agree to two steps: no-first-use and withdrawal of nuclear weapons to their own territories. The precise language of the withdrawal requirement was

> Dismantle all nuclear bases set upon the territories of other countries and withdraw all their nuclear armed forces and all nuclear weapons and means of delivery from abroad.[18]

---

16. Qiao Guanhua, Speech to the UN General Assembly, in *Peking Review*, no. 47, 19 November 1971, pp. 5-9, p. 9. Qiao also insisted "we will never become munitions merchants," a position which has been superseded.
17. "New Nuclear Test," announcing test of 18 November 1971. *Peking Review*, no. 48, 26 November 1971, p. 4.
18. Qiao Guanhua, 24 November 1971, in *Peking Review*, no. 49, 3 December 1971, pp. 14-16.

If this last provision meant that the seaborne deterrent force of the United States and Soviet Union would have to withdraw to home waters, negating its *raison d'etre*, there must be a question about the seriousness of China's intent. However, there was no mistaking China's plans to continue testing, in the absence of an agreement to destroy nuclear stockpiles.[19]

Then in 1972 Beijing was confronted by the need to vote on a proposal co-sponsored by 52 small and medium-sized states creating a Special Committee to examine government views on a world disarmament conference. Of the 35-nation Special Committee Beijing declared that

> although China will not participate in the special committee . . . the Chinese delegation can agree to maintain contact with the special committee and exchange views on the question of disarmament.[20]

The next major step taken by China was to sign (21 August 1973) and ratify (12 June 1974) Protocol II of the Treaty of Tlatelolco. Adherence hardly restricted China from any action she would soon take. And Beijing was at pains to point out that its joining the Treaty did not imply a departure from its rejection of the Non-Proliferation Treaty. On the other hand, it used signing as an occasion to insist that the superpowers "must be asked to undertake to observe and implement" two Chinese-drafted provisions, one of which would

---

19. Chen Chu, remarks to the First Committee of the UN General Assembly, on China's being "compelled" to develop nuclear weapons. Summary and excerpts in *Peking Review* no. 51, 17 December 1971, pp. 19-20.

20. *Peking Review*, no. 48 1 December 1972, p. 9. Nonetheless, China voted in favor of the resolution.

    There were, however, maneuvers to force China's hand. The original draft stipulated that members would include the veto powers, but after objections by China that was changed to those named by the President of the General Assembly. The President, a Pole, reserved a seat for each of the nuclear powers, including China, and China cried foul. "China Not to Take Part in World Disarmament Conference Special Committee," in *Beijing Review* no. 3, 19 January 1973, pp. 8-10. On 9 January 1973 Huang Hua, China's Permanent Representative to the United Nations, issued a statement that China "will not take part in the work of the special committee on the world disarmament conference and firmly opposes the forcible reservation of seats for China or any other countries which have no intention to take part in the work of the special committee."

prohibit the transportation of nuclear weapons through Latin American territorial waters or airspace.[21]

Chinese statements on the occasion of Chinese nuclear tests in the 1970s echoed themes which had long been at the core of Chinese declaratory policy concerning its nuclear program and elimination of nuclear arms:

> The conducting of necessary and limited nuclear tests by China is entirely for the purpose of defense and for breaking the nuclear monopoly by the superpowers, with the ultimate aim of abolishing nuclear weapons. The Chinese Government declares once again that at no time and in no circumstances will China be the first to use nuclear weapons. The Chinese Government and people will, as always, work together with the other peoples and peace-loving countries in the world in the common struggle to achieve the lofty goal of complete prohibition and thorough destruction of nuclear weapons.[22]

---

21. *World Armaments and Disarmament, SIPRI Yearbook 1976* (Stockholm: Stockholm International Peace Research Institute, 1976), p. 433. The relevant portions of the Chinese statement upon signing are these:

    "China will never use or threaten to use nuclear weapons against non-nuclear Latin American countries and the Latin American nuclear-weapons-free-zone; nor will China test, manufacture, produce, stockpile, install or deploy nuclear weapons in these countries or in this zone, or send her means of transportation and delivery carrying nuclear weapons to cross the territory, territorial sea or airspace of Latin American countries. It is necessary to point out that the signing of Additional Protocol II to the Treaty for the Prohibition of Nuclear Weapons in Latin America by the Chinese Government does not imply any change whatsoever in China's principled stand on the disarmament and nuclear weapons issue and, in particular, does not affect the Chinese Government's consistent stand against the treaty on non-proliferation of nuclear weapons and the partial nuclear test ban treaty. . .

    "The Chinese Government holds that, in order that Latin America may truly become a nuclear-weapon-free zone, all nuclear countries, and particularly the super-powers, which possess huge numbers of nuclear weapons, must first of all undertake earnestly not to use or threaten to use nuclear weapons against the Latin American countries and the Latin American nuclear-weapons-free zone, and they must be asked to undertake to observe and implement the following: (1) dismantling of all foreign military bases in Latin America and refraining from establishing any new foreign military bases there; (2) prohibition of the passage of any means of transportation and delivery carrying nuclear weapons through Latin American territory, territorial sea or air space."

    Ibid., p. 463.

22. Press Communiqué announcing Chinese test of 23 January 1976. *Beijing Review*, no. 5, 30 January 1976, pp. 3-4.

Since 1978 disarmament has been more actively pursued in the UN system. In that year the UN General Assembly held a First Special Session on Disarmament (SSD I).[23] SSD I established a Committee on Disarmament (replacing the Conference of the Committee on Disarmament): China first took its seat in this body in February 1980. (China remained outside the *Ad Hoc* Committee on the World Disarmament Conference, about which it had protested in 1973. It "maintained contact," however.) China participated in the Group of Governmental Experts to Study the Institutional Arrangements Relating to the Process of Disarmament, authorized by a 1979 General Assembly resolution, through the person (in 1980) of Yang Hushan.[24] SSD I also reactivated its Disarmament Commission, composed of all UN members, as a subsidiary deliberative organ of the General Assembly. In 1983 China joined the International Atomic Energy Agency.[25]

China took part in SSD I—it was, after all, as universal as the UN itself—and submitted a full working paper on disarmament. Its calls upon the superpowers are familiar: no-first-use, withdrawal of armed forces from abroad, arms race cessation and staged "drastic" cuts in nuclear weapons.[26] On 15 May 1979 China put forward, at the UN Disarmament Commission, a "Proposal on the Elements of a Comprehensive Programme of Disarmament." Similar in content to previous proposals, it does declare more imaginatively the point at which China might *begin to negotiate* destroying its nuclear stocks: when the US and USSR had realized "substantial progress" in destroying their nuclear weapons

> thus closing the huge gap between their nuclear arsenals and those of the other

---

23. On SSD I, see *World Armaments and Disarmament, SIPRI Yearbook 1979* (Stockholm: SIPRI, 1979), ch. 11.

24. US Arms Control and Disarmament Agency, *Documents on Disarmament 1981* (Washington: United States Arms Control and Disarmament Agency), p xxvii. China's entry was effective on 1 January 1984.

25. *China Quarterly* (London), no. 97, March 1984, p. 180. China applied on 5 September 1983 and was admitted 11 October 1983.

26. "Chinese Delegation's Working Paper on Disarmament," in *Beijing Review*, no. 24, 16 June 1978, pp. 22-24.

nuclear states to the satisfaction of the majority of states .[27]

Thus China had already taken part in two special, but "universal," forums on disarmament before taking its place at the (Geneva) Committee on Disarmament on 5 February 1980. At Geneva the Chinese delegate, Zhang Wenjin, offered a somewhat different measure of the point at which China would be prepared to negotiate away her stocks: the superpowers were to reduce their nuclear arms "until the huge gap between them and the other nuclear-weapon states is reduced to the minimum," after which others would be "asked" to join in destroying weapons. This is a more careful, and perhaps a deliberately adjusted, phrasing.

China's readiness to enter multilateral discussions of disarmament corresponded with Deng Xiaoping's achieving control of the CCP Political Bureau. From mid-1978 through 1979 and 1980 Deng displaced Hua Guofeng and those judged hostile to economic reform and further opening to the West. By the time of the Second Special Session on Disarmament (7 June to 10 July 1982) China had become an experienced participant. China's position here was that if the US and USSR "took the lead" in halting testing, improvement and production of nuclear weapons and in reducing their inventories by half, China would be ready to join all other nuclear states in proportionate reductions by agreed procedures.[28] The main lines of China's mid-1990s positions were being put in place.

In 1985 China repeated that she was ready to take part in an international conference to discuss "steps leading to the complete prohibition and destruction of all nuclear weapons," provided that the US and USSR "took the initiative" in nuclear disarmament.[29] A lengthy statement of China's position in mid-1985 distinguished short-term and long-term goals, now arguing that in "taking the lead" the superpowers should

> [stop] testing, improving and manufacturing nuclear weapons, and substantially

27. "China's Stand on the Question of Disarmament," in *Beijing Review* no. 22, 1 June 1979, pp. 16-17.

28. *World Armaments and Disarmament, SIPRI Yearbook 1983* (Stockholm: SIPRI, 1983), pp., 540-541, citing UN document A/S-12/AC.1/11.

29. *Beijing Review* no. 16, 22 April 1985, pp. 7-8.

[reduce] their nuclear arsenals. Afterwards, other nuclear countries should also take corresponding measures and reduce their arms proportionately. Before this, all nations with nuclear weapons should undertake not to use nuclear weapons first, and not to use or threaten to use such weapons against non-nuclear nations. They should also reach agreement on non-use of such weapons against one another.[30]

Chinese calls for other steps, including prevention of an arms race in outer space, were clearly directed at the Reagan Administration's Star Wars program. In discussing China's objections to the non-proliferation treaty, her commentator argues that "vertical proliferation is more important." ("Vertical" proliferation is technological enhancement and greater numbers of nuclear weapons. The NPT works only against "horizontal" proliferation.) The commentator quotes Zhao Ziyang who had declared that

China is critical of the discriminatory Nuclear Non-Proliferation Treaty, and has declined to accede to the treaty. But China by no means favours nuclear proliferation, nor will it engage in such proliferation by helping other countries develop nuclear weapons.

It is important to stress how much has changed since China detonated its first nuclear test in 1964. Then the argument justifying China's own tests was put forward under the banner of opposing the "nuclear monopoly" of the United States, Soviet Union, and Britain. It was a measure to "oppose the US imperialist policy of nuclear blackmail and nuclear threats." In 1995 China is a full participant in the Non-Proliferation Treaty, publicly committed against proliferation, and often acting in concert with the United States. But the appeal to "no first use" now addresses the contradiction in the Non-Proliferation Treaty between nuclear weapon states and non-nuclear weapon states.

On the very day of China's first test—16 October 1964—China's leadership sent a message to all those who had taken part in the test, including scientific and technical personnel and PLA officers and men. It called on them to "reach new summits of science and technology" and to "strengthen national defence," but it also instructed them to "strive for the complete prohibition and thorough destruction of nuclear weapons!"[31] At a time when China's adversaries had deep

30. Xia Yishan, "China Pushes for Total Disarmament," in *Beijing Review*, no. 21, 27 May 1985, pp. 15-19, p. 17.

31. Message of the Central Committee of the Chinese Communist Party and the

inventories of nuclear weapons and China still no deliverable capability, abolition would certainly have served China's security. A similar argument that abolition remained in China's national interest could be made in 1995.

If arms control occupied the time of PLA officers and scientific personnel in 1965 or 1966, their activity was well-hidden. However, at the beginning of the 1980s China's leadership reassessed the world situation. Dangers were not as they had been seen. Moreover, China's nuclear program had matured. China could enter UN-sponsored arms control talks with no fear that China's security would thereby be threatened. To stay outside those talks, on the other hand, would have been increasingly difficult to justify.

Whether in the 1980s Chinese who dealt in nuclear policy were observing the leadership's 1964 mandate to "strive for complete prohibition and thorough destruction" or—with reservations about abolition—were simply on the watch for China's interest, they certainly became participants in arms control conversations. The PLA conducted its contacts on these matters in part through the Chinese Institute of International Strategic Studies.[32] The Chinese intelligence community providing information to the State Council sought informed views through its Institute of Contemporary International Relations. And China's nuclear weapons designers, the scientists and engineers who brought China's nuclear weapons into being, opened channels to their counterparts in other nuclear weapon states. Not only did personnel from Lawrence Livermore Laboratory and Los Alamos Scientific Laboratory visit Chinese nuclear weapons laboratories and the Chinese test site, but the Chinese Academy of Engineering Physics and its Institute of Applied Physics and Computational Mathematics systematically sought contacts and sponsored international seminars on nuclear arms control.

Does China really want "complete prohibition and thorough destruction" of nuclear weapons? Chinese differ in their judgments. There may, of course, be advocates of China's keeping nuclear weapons "no matter what." And any specific proposal will be

---

State Council of the People's Republic of China. 16 October 1964. *Peking Review*, no. 43 (1964) 23 October 1964, p. 5.

32. Earlier the Beijing Institute of International Strategic Studies.

imperfect, and will require that China accept risks. There will be grounds for holding back.

Still, China has set out a framework of terms and conditions with unusual care, and has urged abolition for more than thirty years. If other states actually took abolition or nondeployment seriously, concerned Chinese will weigh whether their security would be served by such a regime. The CTB negotiations provide a test. If CTB negotiations are not blocked by other states, China will have to decide whether to commit to the consensus terms of a final text: at that point the relative strength of nuclearist and non-nuclearist advocates will be much clearer.

Britain and Reduction

Margaret Gowing attributes to Britain the first post-war impetus for international control. Small groups of Britons and Americans had thought about control before the war ended but "they had not got very far." Control was "uppermost," however, in the mind of Prime Minister Clement Attlee, who wrote in August 1945 that

> The only course which seems to me to be feasible and to offer a reasonable hope of staving off imminent disaster for the world is joint action by the USA, UK and Russia based upon stark reality. We should declare that this invention has made it essential to end wars.[33]

There was, she comments, "no sign of any American initiative on international control."[34] Attlee proposed to meet Truman in Washington. He sought guidance before departing. A committee chaired by the Secretary of the Cabinet considered three forms of controlling atom bombs: flat prohibition, production only by an international organization, or production only by the "Big Three" (United States, Soviet Union, and Britain) or the "Big Five" (additionally France and China). Judging that major powers could not be barred from making the bomb, they suggested a prohibition on *use*, backed up by collective retaliation.

---

33. Margaret Gowing, assisted by Lorna Arnold, *Independence and Deterrence: Britain and Atomic Energy, 1945-1952,* vol. 1. *Policy Making* (New York: St. Martin's Press, 1974), pp. 64-65.

34. *Ibid.*, p. 65.

Attlee did not accept this proposal, but it illustrates that autumn's debate. In September 1945 Attlee wrote to Truman that possibility of retaliatory attack was "the only deterrent," that the underlying scientific discoveries "are now common knowledge," and even observed of plutonium that "the harnessing of atomic energy as a source of power cannot be achieved without the simultaneous production of material capable of being used in a bomb." Fundamentals of nuclear weapons were already well-understood.[35]

The Washington Declaration, issued by Attlee, Truman, and Canadian Prime Minister Mackenzie King on 15 November 1945, translated Attlee's concerns into a call for UN discussion of proposals for control. In order to "attain the most effective means of entirely eliminating the use of atomic energy for destructive purposes and promoting its widest use for industrial and humanitarian purposes" they called for a Commission to recommend specific proposals to the United Nations on four points:

(a) For extending between all nations the exchange of basic scientific information for peaceful ends,

(b) For control of atomic energy to the extent necessary to ensure its use only for peaceful purposes,

(c) For the elimination from national armaments of atomic weapons and of all other major weapons adaptable to mass destruction,

(d) For effective safeguards by way of inspection and other means to protect complying states against the hazards of violations and evasions.[36]

British Foreign Secretary Ernest Bevin and his US and Soviet counterparts met in Moscow 16-26 December 1945, agreeing to propose the Commission's establishment with exactly those terms of reference.[37] The General Assembly created the UN Atomic Energy Commission, but it proved unable to reach conclusions which both the United States and Soviet Union would accept.

---

35. *Ibid.*, pp. 78-81.

36. Washington Declaration. 15 November 1945. *Department of State Bulletin*, vol. 13, no. 334, 18 November 1945, pp. 781-782, p. 782.

37. *Department of State Bulletin*, vol. 13, 30 December 1945, pp. 1030-1032. France, China and Canada joined in proposing the Commission's creation to the General Assembly.

These earliest British efforts for nuclear arms control coincided with the beginnings of her autonomous weapons program. Gowing explains that

> Mr. Attlee's own position illustrated the paradox. As he prepared to go to Washington he talked of the abandonment of power politics and of faith in the United Nations. "The new World Order," he had written, "must start now." But he was also intent on making Britain's own atomic position as strong as possible, in particular by forging the strongest possible nuclear link with the United States. Official advice had been insistent on this. The Chiefs of Staff had emphasized that in the event of failure to secure international agreement, the possession of atomic weapons "of our own" as deterrents would be vital to British security. They wanted the British production of weapons to start without delay.[38]

When the issue of joint control with the Soviet Union was again foremost, approaching the test moratorium of 1958, British policy sprang from sources much like those of 1945. She would be a player alongside the Americans. She doubted Soviet intentions, but was prepared to explore them. And she wanted her own deterrent—in 1957 and 1958 a confirmed thermonuclear deterrent. Washington proposed a ten-month test suspension in July 1957, to give time to achieve a test ban agreement and an end to nuclear weapons manufacture. John Simpson captures the British dilemma:

> The British government, under intense domestic pressure to cease testing, had no choice but publicly to support the United States proposal, yet ministers were probably relieved that Soviet opposition prevented the plan being agreed, as if the weapon cut-off proposal had been immediately implemented it would have left the United Kingdom in possession of some 20 completed Blue Danube weapons and two thermonuclear test devices. [British Prime Minister] Macmillan described this situation as "the terrible dilemma in which we find ourselves, between the Scylla of test suspension and the Charybdis of 'cutoff' of fissile material."[39]

By late 1958 Britain had met its main objectives. It had a promise from Eisenhower of information on further points of thermonuclear weapon design.[40] Simpson explains neatly how pursuit of a test ban would then further British security aims, enabling London to

---

38. Gowing, *Independence and Deterrence*, vol. 1, p. 72.

39. John Simpson, *The Independent Nuclear State: The United States, Britain and the Military Atom* (London: Macmillan, 2nd ed. 1986), p. 107.

40. *Ibid.*, p. 143, citing Macmillan, *Riding the Storm*, pp. 561-562.

> accept the superpower testing moratorium with equanimity, leaving France and China on the other side. Macmillan and his cabinet then concentrated on a three-pronged strategy to consolidate Britain's international security position. This comprised the achievement of the national atomic and thermonuclear weapon stockpile goals as rapidly as possible; the signing of a comprehensive test ban agreement and possibly a fissile material cut-off, to achieve the internationalist aims of both a halt in the arms race and the exclusion of further states from the nuclear club; and the pursuit of all measures which would limit the ability of the two superpowers to develop methods of neutralising atomic and thermonuclear weapons, and thus once more relegate Britain to an inferior military position. . . . [D]isarmament and arms control measures, after 1958 . . . were seen as the most effective way of sustaining the military credibility of the British inventory of strategic nuclear weapons.[41]

We have noted in chapter 3 Britain's participation in the talks which led to the Partial Test Ban Treaty (1963) and the inconclusive CTB talks of 1977-80.

Nonetheless, both the SALT negotiations and those for a CTB had possible implications for the British weapons program. John Simpson identifies fear of possible SALT II limitations on MIRV technology transfer as a major reason for Britain's undertaking the Chevaline scheme (which fitted warheads in a British-made reentry vehicle with advanced penetration aids).[42] Later, Carter's advocacy of CTB, and Soviet proposals in the SALT II negotiations to bar either party from making strategic technology transfers, were viewed askance by some Ministry of Defence officials, and prompted the MoD to buy AWE Aldermaston laser equipment for simulation of weapons physics.[43] Like the other weapons states, Britain would explore laboratory means to continue work even if a CTB were agreed.

In the SALT and START negotiations the United States resisted Soviet efforts to bring British (and French) weapons into the calculus. For its part, Britain has carefully steered clear of any firm undertaking to place its nuclear weapons into negotiation. At the same time, British and French procurement restraint—buying fewer SNLEs in the French case, and fewer missiles in both cases, than they had earlier intended—clearly was in step with the rhythms of reduction being

---

41. *Ibid.*, p. 145.

42. *Ibid.*, p. 173.

43. *Ibid.*, p. 197, citing D. Fishlock, "Vulcan and Helen: Lasers of Unusual Power," *Financial Times*, 5 March 1981.

codified in START.

Nonetheless, Britain's agnostic posture was restated forcefully in Government statements to the House of Commons' Foreign Affairs Committee in July 1994. The Foreign Office stipulated that

> HMG have set up no specific trigger point or criterion for entering UK strategic weapons into future strategic arms reduction negotiation. We shall keep the case for doing so under regular review, having regard to progress on the implementation of the START Treaties and other developments in the strategic environment.[44]

---

44. House of Commons. Session 1993-94. Foreign Affairs Committee. *UK Policy on Weapons Proliferation and Control in the Post-Cold War Era.* Minutes of Evidence. 6 July 1994. Memorandum submitted by Foreign and Commonwealth Office, ¶ 42. A member of the Foreign Affairs Committee, Mike Gapes, characterized ¶ 42 as "ambiguous" and asked "is it not the fact that the British Government, it could be argued, is dragging its feet." Douglas Hogg denied this was so, claiming that President Yeltsin had said while visiting London that he did not think British nuclear weapons should be put on the table since they were of comparatively small order.

    (Mr. Hogg) . . . So we are not under any pressure at the moment from anybody, the Americans and the Russians or the Chinese, for that matter. . . . (I)f there was continuing reduction of strategic weaponry following treaties beyond the START agreements, the point might come where we put ours into the equation. That point has not come and I do not think I can usefully speculate in what circumstances it would come, but I am not shutting the door to it absolutely.

    Minutes of Evidence, pp. 39-40.

Appendix 4.1

Statement of the Chinese Government Advocating the Complete, Thorough, Total and Resolute Prohibition and Destruction of Nuclear Weapons Proposing a Conference of the Government Heads of All Countries of the World July 31, 1963

A TREATY on the partial halting of nuclear tests was initialled by the representatives of the United States, Britain and the Soviet Union in Moscow on July 25.

This is a treaty signed by three nuclear powers. By this treaty they attempt to consolidate their nuclear monopoly and bind the hands of all the peace-loving countries subjected to the nuclear threat.

This treaty signed in Moscow is a big fraud to fool the people of the world. It runs diametrically counter to the wishes of the peace-loving people of the world.

The people of the world demand a genuine peace; this treaty provides them with a fake peace.

The people of the world demand general disarmament and a complete ban on nuclear weapons; this treaty completely divorces the cessation of nuclear tests from the total prohibition of nuclear weapons, legalizes the continued manufacture, stockpiling and use of nuclear weapons by the three nuclear powers, and runs counter to disarmament.

The people of the world demand the complete cessation of nuclear tests; this treaty leaves out the prohibition of underground nuclear tests, an omission which is particularly advantageous for the further development of nuclear weapons by U.S. imperialism.

The people of the world demand the defense of world peace and the elimination of the threat of nuclear war; this treaty actually strengthens the position of nuclear powers for nuclear blackmail and increases the danger of imperialism launching a nuclear war and a world war.

If this big fraud is not exposed, it can do even greater harm. It is unthinkable for the Chinese Government to be a party to this dirty fraud. The Chinese Government regards it as its unshirkable and sacred duty to thoroughly expose this fraud.

The Chinese Government is firmly opposed to this treaty which harms the interests of the people of the whole world and the cause of world peace.

Clearly, this treaty has no restraining effect on the U.S. policies of nuclear war preparation and nuclear blackmail. It in no way hinders the United States from proliferating nuclear weapons, expanding nuclear armament or making nuclear threats. The central purpose of this treaty is, through a partial ban on nuclear tests, to prevent all the threatened peace-loving countries, including China, from increasing their defence capability, so that the United States may be more unbridled in threatening and blackmailing these countries.

U.S. President Kennedy, speaking on July 26, laid bare the substance of this treaty. Kennedy pointed out that this treaty did not mean an end to the threat of nuclear war, it did not prevent but permitted continued underground nuclear tests, it would not halt the production of nuclear weapons, it would not reduce nuclear stockpiles and it would not restrict their use in time of war. He further pointed out that this treaty would not hinder the United States from proliferating nuclear weapons among its allies and countries under its control under the name of "assistance," whereas the United States could use it to prevent non-nuclear peace-loving countries from testing and manufacturing nuclear weapons. At the same time, Kennedy formally declared that the United States remains ready to withdraw from the treaty and resume all forms of nuclear testing. This fully shows that U.S. imperialism gains everything and loses nothing by this treaty.

The treaty just signed is a reproduction of the draft treaty on a partial nuclear test ban put forward by the United States and Britain at the meeting of the Disarmament Commission in Geneva on August 27, 1962. On August 29, 1962, the Head of the Soviet Delegation Kuznetsov pointed out that the obvious aim of the United States and Britain in putting forward that draft was to provide the Western powers with one-sided military advantage to the detriment of the interests of the Soviet Union and other socialist countries. He pointed out that the United States had been using underground tests to improve its nuclear weapons for many years already, and that should underground nuclear tests be legalized with a simultaneous prohibition of such tests in the atmosphere, this would mean that the United States could continue improving its nuclear weapons and increase their yield and effectivity. The Head of the Soviet Government Khrushchov also pointed out on September 9, 1961, that "the programme of developing new types of nuclear weapons which has been drawn up in the United States now requires precisely underground tests," and that "an agreement to cease only one type of testing, in the atmosphere, would be a poor service to peace; it would deceive the peoples."

But now the Soviet Government has made a 180 degree about-face, discarded the correct stand they once persisted in and accepted this reproduction of the U.S.-British draft treaty, willingly allowing U.S. imperialism to gain military superiority. Thus the interests of the Soviet people have been sold out, the interests of the people of the countries in the socialist camp, including the people of China, have been sold out, and the interests of all the peace-loving people of the world have been sold out.

The indisputable facts prove that the policy pursued by the Soviet Government is one of allying with the forces of war to oppose the forces of peace, allying with imperialism to oppose socialism, allying with the United States to oppose China, and allying with the reactionaries of all countries to oppose the people of the world.

Why should the Soviet leaders so anxiously need such a treaty? Is this a proof of what they call victory for the policy of peaceful coexistence? No! This is by no means a victory for the policy of peaceful coexistence. It is capitulation to U.S. imperialism.

The U.S. imperialists and their partners are with one voice advertising everywhere that the signing of a treaty on the partial halting of nuclear tests by them is the first step towards the complete prohibition of nuclear weapons. This is deceitful talk. The United States has already stockpiled large quantities of nuclear weapons, which are scattered in various parts of the world and seriously threaten the security of all peoples. If the United States really will take the first step towards the prohibition of nuclear weapons, why does it not remove its nuclear threat to other countries? Why does it not undertake to refrain from using nuclear weapons against non-nuclear countries and to respect the desire of the people of the world to establish nuclear weapon-free zones? And why does it not undertake in all circumstances to refrain from handing over to its allies its nuclear weapons and the data for their manufacture? On what grounds can the United States and its partners maintain that the United States may use nuclear threat and blackmail against others and pursue policies of aggression and war, while others may not take measures to resist such threat and blackmail and defend their own independence and freedom? To give the aggressors the right to kill while denying the victims of aggression the right to self-defence—is this not like the Chinese saying: "The magistrate may burn down houses but the ordinary people cannot even light their lamps"?

The Chinese Government is firmly opposed to nuclear war and to a world war. It always stands for general disarmament and resolutely stands for the complete prohibition and thorough destruction of nuclear weapons. The Chinese Government and people have never spared their efforts in order to realize this aim step by step. As is known to the whole world, the Chinese Government long ago proposed, and has consistently stood for, the establishment of a zone free from nuclear weapons in the Asian and Pacific region, including the United States.

The Chinese Government holds that the prohibition of nuclear weapons and the prevention of nuclear war are major questions affecting the destiny of the world, which should be discussed and decided on jointly by all the countries of the world, big and small. Manipulation of the destiny of more than one hundred non-nuclear countries by a few nuclear powers will not be tolerated.

The Chinese Government holds that on such important issues as the prohibition of nuclear weapons and the prevention of nuclear war, it is impermissible to adopt the method of deluding the people of the world. It should be affirmed unequivocally that nuclear weapons must be completely banned and thoroughly destroyed and that practical and effective measures must be taken so as to realize step by step the complete prohibition and thorough destruction of nuclear weapons, prevent nuclear war and safeguard world peace.

For these reasons, the Government of the People's Republic of China hereby proposes the following:

(1) All countries in the world, both nuclear and nonnuclear,

solemnly declare that they will prohibit and destroy nuclear weapons completely, thoroughly, totally and resolutely. Concretely speaking, they will not use nuclear weapons, nor export, nor import, nor manufacture, nor test, nor stockpile them; and they will destroy all the existing nuclear weapons and their means of delivery in the world, and disband all the existing establishments for the research, testing and manufacture of nuclear weapons in the world.

(2) In order to fulfil the above undertakings step by step, the following measures shall be adopted first:

a. Dismantle all military bases, including nuclear bases on foreign soil, and withdraw from abroad all nuclear weapons and their means of delivery.

b. Establish a nuclear weapon-free zone of the Asian and Pacific region, including the United States, the Soviet Union, China and Japan; a nuclear weapon-free zone of Central Europe; a nuclear weapon-free zone of Africa; and a nuclear weapon-free zone of Latin America. The countries possessing nuclear weapons shall undertake due obligations with regard to each of the nuclear weapon free zones.

c. Refrain from exporting and importing in any form nuclear weapons and technical data for their manufacture.

d. Cease all nuclear tests, including underground nuclear tests.

(3) A conference of the government heads of all the countries of the world shall be convened to discuss the question of the complete prohibition and thorough destruction of nuclear weapons and the question of taking the above-mentioned four measures in order to realize step by step the complete prohibition and thorough destruction of nuclear weapons.

The Chinese Government and people are deeply convinced that nuclear weapons can be prohibited, nuclear war can be prevented and world peace can be preserved. We call upon the countries in the socialist camp and all the peace-loving countries and people of the world to unite and fight unswervingly to the end for the complete, thorough total and resolute prohibition and destruction of nuclear weapons and for the defence of world peace.

Peking Review, no. 31, 2 August 1963, pp. 7-8.

5

Coordinations

This chapter concerns coordination among the five nuclear weapon states. Our purpose is to illustrate something of the breadth and intensity of coordination, as it bears on future nuclear arms control and abolition.

Experience in Difference and Coordination

The Five have not yet met together to negotiate joint nuclear cuts, but they meet and negotiate in a number of forums. Some concern nuclear issues expressly. In others nuclear weapons and the parties' nuclear-weapon status are implicitly present.

China's was a silent presence when the United States, Soviet Union and United Kingdom negotiated the Partial Test Ban Treaty (1963). One aim of the PTBT was to delegitimate any Chinese test and corresponding nuclear program. China responded with vehemence. Fifteen months later China tested, establishing itself as a nuclear weapon state.

In tracing the British program we saw that the first official finding that a nuclear weapon could be built was British. Britain and Canada contributed to the joint effort proven at Alamogordo. Soviet participation in the UN Atomic Energy Commission talks from 1946, before Moscow had detonated a test device, did not result in international control and abolition. But Moscow joined with Washington and London in talks on a test ban in the late 1950s, the talks which ultimately led to the PTBT.

The Five are the Permanent Members of the UN Security Council. The Charter entrusts to the UNSC responsibility to respond to threats to international security. Each of the five has the authority to block action by the Security Council by declining to concur—the "veto power." They meet in formal sessions, but also privately, in meetings held typically at one or another of their UN missions. The subject is not often nuclear weapons, but it may be. The temperate tone and content of UNSC resolutions on North Korea's refusal to permit IAEA inspection of sites in 1993 and 1994 can only be explained as the outcome of behind-the-scenes negotiations with China, which publicly opposed stronger measures.

The Five meet in the General Assembly. They take part in the Conference on Disarmament (Geneva). They are members of the International Atomic Energy Agency. Three are members of NATO (US, UK, and France) and a fourth (Russia) participant in NATO fringe activities.

Of course, the "veto Five" and the "nuclear Five" have not always been neatly the same. Beijing was denied China's seat in the United Nations until 1971. France—stressing her autonomy—for many years declined to join the disarmament negotiation in Geneva, and from 1966 to the present has not taken part in the integrated military command of NATO. When the Non-Proliferation Treaty was debated in 1968, France did not give assurances like those given by Britain, the United States and the Soviet Union and the corresponding UN Security Council resolution 255,[1] and did not join the treaty, although she did say she would act in keeping with its terms. France and China both signed and ratified the NPT in 1992.

Perhaps there were occasions prior to 1991 when representatives of the Five met privately to discuss nuclear issues among themselves, but they held acknowledged meetings twice in 1991.[2] They planned further meetings at Geneva in the context of the Conference on Disarmament's CTB negotiations, which began in January 1994.

The 1994 CD CTB negotiations envision parallel talks in Geneva among the Five, even as the non-nuclear-weapons states will assuredly also caucus. France proposed such talks.[3] At the start of the CD negotiations on 7 February 1994 France declared that there was "no incompatibility" between the CD's multilateral negotiation and private talks

---

1. See the discussion of assurances and Resolution 255 in chapter 1.
2. Paris 8-9 July 1991, London 17-18 October 1991. The statement issued at the end of the London meeting described their subject as "issues related to conventional arms transfers and to the non-proliferation of weapons of mass destruction." *Newsbrief*, no. 16, Winter 1991/92, p. 16 (Programme for Promoting Nuclear Non-Proliferation, University of Southampton).
3. Statement of the Spokesman of the Ministry of Foreign Affairs, Paris, 30 December 1992.

among the Five, which were simply "natural."[4]

An authoritative Chinese analyst insists that "political coordination between the permanent members of the UN Security Council is necessary to guarantee the non-proliferation mechanism." The Five "may take proper steps through consultation" on supporting nuclear-free zones, arms control, and nuclear no-first-use.[5]

Disarmament and non-proliferation are not the only nuclear weapons subjects, however, which Britain, France and China have discussed with the United States and Soviet Union (Russia), or in bilateral contacts themselves. Several quite different types of issues have been broached:

Transfer of Technical Information

- Between the US and UK
- From the USSR to China
- From the US to France (the "Ullman claims")[6]

Transfer of U^{235}, Pu and Tritium

- Between the US and UK[7]
- Between USSR and China[8]

---

4. Intervention of the French representative, 7 February 1994.

5. Bu Ran, *Beijing Review*, vol. 37 no. 51, 19-25 December 1994, pp. 19-21.

6. Ullman, Richard H., "The Covert French Connection," *Foreign Policy,* Summer 1989, pp. 3-33. Ullman describes secret exchanges between the United States and France, under which the United States transferred information to France on several key subjects, including miniaturization, missile guidance, and targeting. The irony lies in the seeming contradiction between France's autonomous program and engaging in "exchange of technical information" with the United States. For the French denial that obtaining information compromises nuclear independence, see the Ministry of Defense statement quoted in Pascal Boniface, "France," in Boniface ed., *L'Année Stratégique 1990* (Paris: Stock/IRIS, 1990), p. 30.

7. John Simpson, *The Independent Nuclear State* (London: Macmillan, 2nd. ed. 1986), pp. 200-201.

8. Before the Sino-Soviet split, the Soviet Union created a reprocessing facility at Urba, 1300 km northeast of Almaty, in Kazakhstan, for the express purpose of reprocessing nuclear material for the Chinese nuclear program. *The Independent*, 26 November 1994, citing Ivan Chasnikov, head of a Kazakhstan parliamentary committee on radiation ecology. (Note also that Chinese supply of uranium ore to the Soviet Union was a key element of their initial coopera-

Dual-Key Nuclear Weapons Sharing

- US nuclear weapons from the US -> France
- US nuclear weapons from the US -> UK

Sale of Equipment for Simulation and Delivery Systems

- US Cray computers for simulation -> France
- French missile test equipment -> China[9]

Safety and Stability Exchanges

- Possibly among all Five
- UK and US assistance to Russian tactical nuclear weapons storage and dismantlement

Operational Planning

- US, UK and France in NATO
- US-UK targeting coordination

Intelligence Sharing

- US, UK, and France in NATO context[10]
- US and UK
- Possibly between the US and China

Management of Environmental Consequences and Public Criticism of Nuclear Weapons Programs as Environmentally Unsound

- Initially, through PTBT ban on atmospheric testing

---

tion in the 1950s.)

9. Lewis and Xue, *China's Strategic Seapower*, p. 191, records purchase from France of equipment to measure the performance of the first generation SLBM JL-1 during boost phase.

10. For example, the US, UK and France take part in "a special consultative group at which all 16 Allies are represented (which) meets regularly at NATO to exchange views and information on nuclear weapons in the former Soviet Union." House of Commons. Session 1993-94. Foreign Affairs Committee. *UK Policy on Weapons Proliferation and Control in the Post-Cold War Era.* Minutes of Evidence. 6 July 1994. "Memorandum submitted by Foreign and Commonwealth Office," ¶ 6 (iii).

- At sea, in discussion of dumping prohibitions

Shared Test Facilities

- UK nuclear weapons testing at US Nevada test site

Non-Proliferation Initiatives

- US, USSR, and UK in NPT, joined (1992) by France and China
- US, UK, and France in the Missile Technology Control Regime[11]
- US, USSR, UK and France in the Nuclear Suppliers' Group
- US and USSR to denuclearize Belarus, Ukraine and Kazakhstan
- US, Russia, China, UK, and France in the UN Security Council (for example, on measures regarding North Korea)[12]

Cooperation on Non-Explosive Surrogates for Testing

- US and UK[13]
- UK and France[14]

---

11. Russia and China, though not members of the MTCR, have agreed to respect the MTCR guidelines.
12. On 30 May 1994 the UNSC adopted a statement on North Korea's imbroglio with IAEA and inspection of its nuclear facilities "worked out earlier" among the Five, according to *The New York Times*, 31 May 1994. The private debate "centered on how tough the statement should be. American officials said France sought to make explicit the threat of economic sanctions if North Korea failed to comply, but China balked." The resultant statement "carries less weight than a resolution but was politically palatable to the Chinese."
13. "We will be sharing information with the United States." See following note.
14. On 28 April 1994, in written replies to the House of Commons Committee on Defence, the Ministry of Defence reported:

    "We have recently held discussions with the French authorities over co-operation in the development and use of facilities to enable proper stewardship of our nuclear weapons to be maintained should a Comprehensive Test Ban be agreed. A number of areas of common interest have been identified, and proposals for further exchanges are being considered. AWE facilities are not currently used by the French but this is not ruled out for the future.

    "There has of course been extensive co-operation with the US across a wide range of nuclear issues for many years. This has included the use of UK facilities by US organizations and vice versa."

- US and France[15]
- US and China[16]

This list suggests that coordination, far from being rare, has been repeated and extensive.

Do the Five also have ties to the three "undeclared" nuclear weapon states (Israel, India and Pakistan)? Did they support South Africa's abandoned program? Have they assisted other aspirants (Iraq, Iran, North Korea perhaps)? Four preliminaries:

1. All aspirants have relied heavily on the published reports of declared programs.[17]
2. Many personnel in aspirant nuclear weapons programs have

House of Commons. Session 1993-94. Defence Committee. Second Report. *Progress of the Trident Programme*. 4 May 1994. Written Evidence. "Memorandum submitted by the Ministry of Defence . . . (29 April 1994)," p. 47.

On "alternative technologies" to replace explosive testing, Britain has declared that "We are also further developing cooperation with both the United States and France." House of Commons. Session 1993-94. Foreign Affairs Committee. *UK Policy on Weapons Proliferation and Control in the Post-Cold War Era*. Minutes of Evidence. 6 July 1994. "Supplementary Memorandum by the Foreign and Commonwealth Office," p. 28. Mr. Douglas Hogg precised, in responding to the Chairman of the House of Commons Foreign Affairs Committee on "alternatives to nuclear testing," that "We will be sharing information with the United States and I hope we can co-operate with the French in this area. It is particularly important for the French." Minutes of Evidence, above, p. 38. It would appear that, if the Minister of State in the Foreign Office is fully informed, Britain had proposed cooperation to the French but as of 6 July 1994 no substantive cooperation—apparently to take the form of "information sharing"—had yet been achieved with France.

15. The United States is the source of key pieces of equipment for the French program, equipment not otherwise available.

16. The United States proposed in October 1994 to assist China by providing information about test simulation. (See chapter 2.)

17. This logic extends to delivery systems as well as nuclear weapons. The chief designer of China's first two nuclear-powered submarines urged that the Chinese SSBN be designed to travel at a lower speed than its attack-submarine predecessor, because "the Chinese knew that the French had built a small, low-speed, nuclear missile submarine, and that the low speed reduced its noise emissions and made it less susceptible to detection." Lewis and Xue, *China's Strategic Seapower*, p. 68.

trained or been employed in declared states.

3. Aspirants have bought in international markets, sometimes in deliberate violation of export controls, sometimes exploiting inattention or unconcern on the part of sellers.
4. The non-proliferation culture known today has been forged over time. Actions forbidden by treaty or agreement today (such as transfers in violation of the 1970 NPT) were not violations at an earlier time.

Seymour Hersh has made out a strong case that France aided the Israeli program, and that the United States turned a deliberately blind eye toward it. Israel invites the strongest charges of links from the Five to an aspirant. Pakistan's quest for components and Iraq's widespread buying abroad are well established. There are strong suspicions that South Africa received assistance from Israel.

Beyond these understandings, however, the record is rather meager and uncertain. Charges rely on undisclosed government intelligence sources. In some respects alleged delicts are themselves ambiguous. For example, what can be made of Chinese transfers of research equipment to Iran or Algeria, not in violation of any IAEA requirements? But the important point to bear in mind is that aid to the Israeli program took place thirty and more years ago, and that discovery in 1991 of Iraq's advanced program set in motion the UN Special Commission and an entirely fresh judgment about the vigilance required to prevent clandestine weapons programs from going undisclosed.

Dual-Key Deployment and Coordination in NATO

One of the oddest arrangements of the Cold War placed designated nuclear systems under "dual-key" control. On the soil of an American ally in western Europe, these systems were *in some respects* in the custody of the allied military and *in some respects* in the custody of US military officers. In principle, neither party could fire them alone. The result was to include the European ally in prospective nuclear operations, while maintaining the position that no transfer from US control had (yet) been made.

Dual-key basing in the United Kingdom was initiated in 1959,

result of an initiative in late 1956 and an agreement in February 1958. The United States would supply the missiles; Britain would maintain the missiles and man the sites.

> The warheads would be supplied by the United States, and remain totally in United States custody on the bases until orders were received that the missiles were to be readied for firing . . .
>
> British and American officers had separate firing keys for each missile, and both had to be inserted before its engines would start.[18]

France also participated in "dual-key" access to US nuclear warheads. Until de Gaulle withdrew France from the NATO integrated military command on 7 March 1966, French units in Germany—aircraft and ground forces—were readied to use US nuclear warheads if required.[19]

Twenty years later there were reported to be 2013 US warheads deployed in Europe for non-US use. These were scattered among seven countries (Belgium, Germany, Greece, Italy, Netherlands, Turkey and the United Kingdom). The United States deployed another 3911 in Europe under its own control. Of those 5924, about 3400 were in West Germany, and of those 1500 warheads were designed to be fired from artillery pieces.[20]

Over the same period mechanisms to coordinate west European nuclear capabilities for deterrence and war were worked out in NATO. Fourteen nations take part in the NATO Nuclear Planning Group. Arkin and Fieldhouse explain how NATO and US nuclear planning for Europe is carried out:

> European nuclear planning is shared between the U.S. European Command, headquartered at Stuttgart-Vaihingen, and the NATO International Military Staff, and in turn by three NATO nuclear commands: Allied Command Europe (ACE), in Casteau-Mons, Belgium, Allied Command Atlantic (ACLANT), in Norfolk, Virginia, and Allied Command Channel (ACCHAN), in Northwood, England. (Citing US Congress. House Appropriations Committee. FY 1985 DOD, part 1, p.

---

18. John Simpson, *The Independent Nuclear State* (London: MacMillan, 2nd. ed. 1986), pp. 124-125, citing M. H. Armacost, *The Politics of Weapons Innovation: The Thor-Jupiter Controversy* (New York: Columbia University Press, 1969). Britain also deployed tactical systems to be used with US warheads, including battlefield missiles in Germany. Simpson, p. 156.
19. Norris et al., pp. 188-189.
20. William M. Arkin and Richard W. Fieldhouse, *Nuclear Battlefields* (Cambridge, Massachusetts: Ballinger, 1985), pp. 102 ff.

511). Together they produce NATO's equivalent of the SIOP: the Nuclear Operations Plan (NOP), officially known as SACEUR SUPPLAN 10001A (Supreme Allied Commander Europe Supplementary Plan).[21]

The NATO elements of this process are guided by the NATO Military Committee, and that in turn by the North Atlantic Council.[22]

Britain—but not France—is a member of the NATO Nuclear Planning Group. John Baylis suggests that "Britain probably has been able to play an influential role" in the NPG as the only European nuclear power there.[23] On the "protracted military and political debate" over "flexible response" between its proposal in 1962 and adoption by NATO in 1967, G. M. Dillon judges that British defense decision makers played a central part.[24] On the other hand, France remains very much a major European state, and a nuclear power. The conventional focus on de Gaulle's 1966 withdrawal from NATO's integrated military command also misleads, as John Fenske points out with great clarity:

---

21. Arkin and Fieldhouse, *Nuclear Battlefields*, p. 96.

22. G. M. Dillon, "Britain," in G. M. Dillon ed., *Defence Policy Making: A Comparative Analysis* (Leicester University Press, 1988), pp. 9-52, p. 48, offers a concise summary of NATO defense policy-making structure:

    "In permanent session at the level of Permanent Representatives the (North Atlantic Council) meets at least once a week . . . The Council's Defence Planning Committee (DPC), dealing with matters directly related to defence, meets both in permanent session at the Permanent Representative level and twice yearly at Defence Minister level. Nuclear issues are discussed in the Nuclear Planning Group (NPG) in which fourteen countries are now represented, and in the more exclusive High Level Group (HLG).

    "On the military side NATO's Military Committee is the highest military authority in the alliance. It functions on a continuous basis through the operation of Permanent Military Representatives (with the exception of France, which withdrew from NATO's integrated military command structure in 1966, and Iceland, which has no military forces), but convenes twice yearly at the Chiefs of Staff level. The Military Committee is supported by an International Military Staff."

    Further discussion of European structures, including NATO and its Nuclear Planning Group, appears in chapter 7.

23. Ken Booth and John Baylis, *Britain, NATO and Nuclear Weapons* (London: Macmillan, 1989), p. 276.

24. G. M. Dillon, "Britain," in G. M. Dillon ed., *Defence Policy Making: A Comparative Analysis* (Leicester University Press, 1988), pp. 9-52, p. 26.

in practice France has maintained abundant contacts with NATO ever since leaving the integrated military command in 1966. In 1967 the Ailleret-Lemnitzer Agreement, and in 1974 the Valentin-Ferber Agreement, established plans for the participation of French troops alongside NATO, if the political authorities so decide. French elites willingly maintain the convenient fiction that France is "outside NATO" as a way of saying that it is not in the NATO integrated military command. They have been telling their people more frequently in recent years that France is a faithful member of the Atlantic Alliance, bound by the North Atlantic Treaty to come to the aid of other signatories subject to aggression. On the other hand, they do not talk any more than necessary about France's continued membership in many NATO structures, including the North Atlantic Council (the top decision making body) and the air defence warning system NADGE (NATO Air Defence Ground Environment).[25]

Coordination of Nuclear Reductions in NATO

NATO—with full British participation—has effected significant cutbacks in nuclear deployments, in effect implementing US-Soviet agreements to reduce nuclear systems. The communiqué of NATO's Nuclear Planning Group meeting of 17 October 1991 delineates these measures clearly:

> 4. The principal objective of our meeting was to agree a new sub-strategic nuclear force posture and stockpile level which responds to the changing security environment in Europe. . . . there is no longer any requirement for nuclear ground-launched short-range ballistic missiles and artillery. In this context, we welcomed President Bush's recent decision, and the reciprocal response by President Gorbachev, to withdraw and destroy the associated nuclear warheads worldwide. We also welcomed the decision to withdraw all tactical nuclear weapons from surface vessels, attack submarines and land-based naval aircraft, and to destroy many of these weapons.
>
> 5. In addition to the elimination of ground-launched nuclear systems, the number of air-delivered weapons in NATO's European stockpile will be greatly reduced. The total reduction in the current NATO stockpile of sub-strategic weapons in Europe will be roughly 80%.
>
> 6. These unilateral measures, which are additional to the substantial reductions already made in recent years, accord with our long-standing policy of maintaining only the minimum level of nuclear forces required to preserve peace and stability. Nuclear weapons will continue for the foreseeable future to fulfil their essential role in the Alliance's overall strategy, since conventional forces alone cannot ensure war prevention. We will therefore continue to base effective and up-to-date

---

25. John Fenske, "France," in G. M. Dillon ed., *Defence Policy Making: A Comparative Analysis* (Leicester University Press, 1988), pp. 147-170, p. 163.

sub-strategic nuclear forces in Europe, but they will consist solely of dual-capable aircraft, with continued widespread participation in nuclear roles and peacetime basing by Allies. Sub-strategic nuclear forces committed to NATO continue to provide the necessary political and military link to NATO's strategic nuclear forces and an important demonstration of Alliance solidarity.

British-French Nuclear Cooperation

Could Britain and France achieve economies or enhanced security by cooperation in nuclear weapons? In procurement? Deployment? Operations? Is some form of "sub-minimum deterrence" possible for states which envision sharing security futures?

French President François Mitterrand raised the question of a common European nuclear doctrine in January 1992.[26] Western Europe was considering the Maastricht Treaty, moving toward European Union, and envisioning a common security policy. As this discussion has evolved, both British and French officials talk of their forces as prospectively "European," but neither envisages relinquishing any degree of national control.

But Britain and France could cooperate *bilaterally*. In October 1992 Britain announced that Paris and London had held "exploratory and informal" discussions on "coordination of their nuclear deterrent policies."[27] France suggested that they coordinate their nuclear policies as a step toward an EC nuclear force.[28] These approaches led to a Joint Commission on Nuclear Doctrine and Policy, set up in November 1992 and made permanent in July 1993. Sessions are confidential, but the defense correspondent of the *Independent* reports that

26. "Only two of the twelve have nuclear forces. For their national policies they have a clear doctrine. Is it possible to conceive a European one? This will quickly become one of the major questions of the construction of a common European defense." Mitterrand, New Year press conference, 1 January 1992, as reported in *British American Security Information Council, 1992 Annual Report*, p. 8.

27. British Secretary of State for Defence Malcolm Rifkind, on 20 October 1992. *Le Monde*, 22 October 1992.

28. French Prime Minister Pierre Bérégovoy. PPNN *Newsbrief*, Winter 1992, no. 20, p. 10, citing news reports of 2 October 1992.

> the Commission has reviewed British and French approaches to nuclear deterrence in the light of the expected proliferation of nuclear, biological and chemical weapons.
>
> The idea of a "European dimension" to deterrence has been studied but the idea of sharing nuclear deterrent patrols—French ballistic missile submarines deterring attack on Britain and vice versa—has been ruled out as it undermines the whole idea of an "independent deterrent." There has also been discussion of France and Britain collaborating on the next generation of nuclear powered torpedo submarines.[29]

Comprising senior Defense Ministry and Foreign Ministry officials, the Joint Commission meets several times a year.[30] Defense issues are also reportedly key topics in the "annual" Franco-British summits, most recently in July 1993 and November 1994.

These discussions address European defense and nuclear doctrine. They can also deal with more discrete programs. At the 1994 meetings John Major and François Mitterrand agreed to establish a small Euro Air Group to plan possible future joint air operations. France reportedly wants British participation in a European imaging satellite—for intelligence-gathering independent of the United States.[31] *Le Monde* commented on its front page that the summit "reinforced military cooperation between London and Paris" and that "this perspective is new for Great Britain, whose strategic links with the United States have long been exclusive."[32] The summit was to receive a "very academic" report on defense doctrine prepared by the joint commission:

> The report in question does not open for a moment any precise path, even if, on one side or another of the Channel, people speak of a notion of sharing—someday—of patrols by the SSBNs of the two navies or the eventuality of building nuclear attack submarines in common. It's just not there, and nuclear "coverage" of Europe by Great Britain and France remains in the realm of speculation.[33]

If this relationship builds, it could overcome past French disappointment at Britain's October 1993 cancellation of TASM, the one nuclear *procurement* measure the two explored sharing. It also

29. Christopher Bellamy, *Independent* (London), 18 November 1994.

30. *Ibid.*

31. Editorial, *Independent* (London), 18 November 1994.

32. *Le Monde*, 19 November 1994.

33. Jacques Isnard, *Le Monde*, 19 November 1994.

remains to be seen whether their joint cooperation will extend to other sensitive areas which have been the subject of speculation, especially ASW techniques. Observers also must ask whether "independent" French and British judgments that they can operate with one boat at sea (Britain) or two (France),[34] so preserving their autonomous deterrent capability, do not take into account that together they will have two or more at sea.

Commentators have observed that Britain is hampered by its close nuclear relations with the United States, which has been wary lest secrets travel through Britain to third parties; and that France so values the autonomy of her nuclear program that she would jealously protect it even when engaged in cooperation. But times have changed. The Cold War over, US nuclear primacy in Europe has ebbed. Europe is building the European Union. And in Yugoslavia France and Britain have practiced a politics of constraining their commitments abroad to conserve political assets and freedom of action at home. Future British and French governments may judge that independence within the European Union requires a similarly close concerting of nuclear policy.

Politico-Military Cooperation Among the Five

In each crisis demanding UN Security Council action since the end of the Cold War, the Five have consulted with one another. Enough is reported in the press and officially acknowledged to establish both the capacity for coordination and the force of a prospective veto. In considering how the Five might negotiate with respect to nuclear weapons cuts or disengagement, we can learn something about their practices and experience by looking at the record.

The Gulf War began with Iraq's invasion of Kuwait on 2 August 1990. The United States sought a series of UN Security Council resolutions, leading up to the 29 November 1990 authorization to use force to undo the occupation of Kuwait. Iraq had been a Soviet client and several hundred Soviet military advisers were in Iraq during the fall of

---

34. France's declaratory policy is that "alert levels, and the number of (strategic) submarines at sea, are adjusted to the threat." *Livre Blanc sur la Défense 1994*, chapter 4, § 1.2.

1990. The Soviet Union and China took different positions. Moscow approved coalition action and contributed a small naval presence in the Gulf. On the crucial issue of the enabling resolution, however, Moscow pressed to delay expiry of the warning from 31 December to 15 January, to which Washington acceded. China did not join the coalition and did not vote "aye" on the 29 November resolution, but also withheld a veto.

After Kuwait was recaptured and the 100-hour ground assault halted, the United Nations imposed a regimen on Iraq which included finding and destroying Iraq's programs in weapons of mass destruction. The work was done jointly by the UN Special Commission and the International Atomic Energy Agency, with the support of all UNSC veto powers and extensive Russian participation.

On Bosnia—and former Yugoslavia more generally—the Soviet Union (Russia) took engaged positions which supported a UN presence while urging on specific matters that the Council adopt positions more responsive to Serbia. For example, when the French initiative of February 1994 (for qualified enforcement of "safe havens" in Sarajevo and Tuzla) won US support and NATO endorsement, and was set in motion, Russia called for a meeting of the Security Council to consider further the issue of enforcing withdrawal of artillery pieces or guaranteeing security of the Tuzla airstrip by air attack. Moscow had earlier urged lifting economic sanctions against Serbia. China throughout exercised the strong "non-interference" plank of her foreign policy, but did not stand in the way of measures to which the other four could agree.

More cautionary is the history of the Missile Technology Control Regime. Underlying Chinese resistance to limitation of its missile sales, and correspondingly sharp and public US criticism, has created a record of exchanges, on which we can draw, which is unusually detailed. After years of avoiding the NPT and MTCR, Chinese officials in June 1991 first indicated a readiness to consider adherence. The occasion: talks with US Under Secretary of State Reginald Bartholomew in Beijing on proliferation issues, talks which were prompted by increasingly insistent reports that China intended to transfer M-9 missiles to Syria and M-11 missiles to Pakistan.[35] Soon thereafter Congress stipulated that the President report—before Congress considered renewing most favored nation status—on China's willingness to adhere to the MTCR before.[36]

On 17 August 1991 China announced that it would sign the NPT.

Bartholemew returned to Beijing in September, and again—this time accompanying Secretary of State Baker—in November. China committed, in Baker's words, to "observe the guidelines and parameters" of the MTCR; NCNA and *Beijing Review* wrote of expressed Chinese willingness to "observe the MTCR guidelines and parameters *in actual transfers*"[37] (Emphasis added). As a condition, China insisted that Washington lift three sanctions imposed on China on 16 June 1991. We will consider whether the phrase "in actual transfers" was intended to diminish or qualify the commitment.

China also used the occasion of Baker's visit to declare a timetable for NPT adherence. The Standing Committee of the National People's Congress would consider it in late 1991, and the formalities of formal accession would be undertaken within three months after that.[38]

Chinese Analyses of the MTCR

Within a few days of Baker's return to Washington, China published a critical analysis of the MTCR. It applauds as "positive" meetings of the five veto powers in Paris (July 1991) and London (October 1991). At Paris the Five

---

35. *Washington Post*, 19 June 1991, p. A22. (Cited in Timothy V. McCarthy ed., *A Chronology of PRC Missile Trade and Developments*, International Missile Proliferation Project, Monterey Institute of International Studies, 12 February 1992.)

36. 29 July 1991. *Arms Sales Monitor*, July-August 1991. (Cited in McCarthy ed., above.)

37. On the Baker-Bartholemew visit of December: *Washington Times* 16 November 1991, pp. A1, A17; 18 November 1991, pp. A1, A10; *Washington Post*, 16 November 1991, pp. A21, A23; 18 November 1991, pp. A1, A17; *New York Times*, 18 November 1991, pp. A1, A5; *Beijing Review*, 25 November - 1 December 1991, p. 7; *Milavnews*, December 1991, p. 2. (Cited in McCarthy ed., above.)

38. *Beijing Review*, vol. 34 no. 47, 25 November - 1 December 1991, p. 7.

> agreed that they would support a freezing and eventually a total ban on ground-to-ground missiles in the Middle East as one of the steps to justly, reasonably, comprehensively and equitably prevent proliferation of nuclear weapons.[39]

In so introducing a discussion of the MTCR, the author in effect distinguishes between forums in which China has taken a role and those to which it was not initially invited.

The measures stipulated in the MTCR exchange of April 1987 "are designed to safeguard unilaterally the security and interests of Western nations":

> Developing countries are denied the access to aeronautical and aerospace high technology. Furthermore the (MTCR) group has so far failed to provide a just and effective supervision and verification mechanism. The spread of missiles and missile technology by arms merchants in the member states is usually permitted by business authorities in those countries. Regions haunted by conflicts, actual or potential, are still regarded as markets promising huge profits for them.[40]

We can imagine that these arguments were among those made to Messrs. Baker and Bartholemew during the eighteen hours they talked with Chinese leaders. And we can also imagine that they were told "the only effective measure to prevent missile proliferation is to adopt a comprehensive, fair and reasonable policy" based on three linkages:

> 1. The measures should be linked to the establishment of a comprehensive, fair and reasonable regime of non-proliferation of weapons. . .
>
> To limit the transfer of missiles but not limit the transfer of other offensive weapons are [*sic*] biased. For third world countries which lack effective air defence capabilities, the threat from offensive weapons like fighter bombers is greater than that from missiles.
>
> 2. They should be linked to comprehensive, fair and reasonable disarmament measures. . .
>
> The United States and the Soviet Union, as the two largest arms-exporting countries, share special responsibility for large-scale reductions of transfers of offensive weapons to the Middle East and the lowering of the arms level in the region.
>
> 3. They should be linked to the comprehensive, fair and reasonable settlement of regional conflicts.[41]

---

39. Bu Ran, "Missiles: Proliferation and Control," in *Beijing Review*, vol. 34 no. 48, 2-8 December 1991, pp. 12-15, p. 12.
40. *Ibid.*, p. 13.
41. *Ibid.*, pp. 14-15. One story about the meaning of "in actual transfers" is told by

The initial promise of Chinese adherence to the MTCR was not fully realized, as we pointed out, discussing the MTCR as a counter-proliferation initiative, in chapter 3. The United States and China fell out over allegations that China was shipping M-11 missiles to Pakistan. Their argument turned on whether, as the US charged, the missiles' range reached the distance proscribed under the MTCR or, as China insisted, it did not. The "range" of a missile is not a simple function of its initial state, but may be altered by enhancements or by mounting a lighter payload than initially envisaged. The United States and China professed to have resolved their differences on this issue when Warren Christopher and Qian Qichen met in Washington in October 1994.

Soon thereafter, however, US officials described an "offer" made to China: if China fully disclosed past M-11 technology exports to Pakistan, Washington would forgive China's violations and waive sanctions. But if later evidence showed China had concealed past activities, then the United States would impose sweeping sanctions.[42] If China were to agree, US-Chinese understandings of the MTCR would begin with a clean slate.

North Korea, the IAEA, and the UN Security Council

North Korea's putative nuclear weapons program forced the Five to consult on IAEA policy and UN Security Council resolutions. For

---

William Safire the columnist with an eye cocked on China. (*The New York Times*, 5 March 1992) On 17 November, fresh from his Beijing talks, Baker claimed "clear gains in the fields of proliferation and trade." This meant, he said, that China would not export M-9 missiles to Syria. Safire:

"One week later, if my information is correct, the Chinese secretly agreed to help the Syrians construct their own missiles locally. This included the supply of Chinese equipment needed to assemble the advanced weaponry.

"The plot: China would live up to the letter of its agreement with the U.S.—holding back the Pershing-type M-9's—but violate its spirit by making it possible for Syria to deliver destruction in a locally produced missile of equivalent range. . .

"[On 23 February 1992] .Beijing announced that 'China will act in accordance with the Missile Control Technology Regime . . . in its export of missiles and missile technology.'"

42. *International Herald Tribune*, 15 November 1994, despatch from Elaine Sciolino of *The New York Times*.

example, US-China negotiations were conducted between China's deputy UN representative, Chen Jian, and the US Assistant Secretary of State for Political and Military Affairs, Robert Gallucci.[43] (Gallucci was also charged to negotiate with the North Koreans on some occasions when direct US-North Korean talks took place.) In this case, China's aim was to use the implicit threat of Security Council veto to force the other Five into a more temperate resolution than they would otherwise have preferred. Gallucci also met French, British, and Russian diplomats.[44]

Conclusion

In this chapter we show two paths along which cooperation between nuclear weapon states has traveled. There are several significant episodes in which one helped another achieve or enhance nuclear capabilities. There are also now several dramatic cases in which nuclear weapon states have cooperated to reduce arsenals and reduce the likelihood of unwanted nuclear war. These are numbered among the empirical steps in disengagement.

If we take these two approaches and consider future paths, two large possibilities appear. In one, the nuclear weapon states *cooperate to maintain their relative nuclear monopoly.* They work to keep the status quo. In the second, they cooperate to achieve disengagement and denuclearisation, but certainly under terms judged to maintain and enhance security.

The years 1995 and 1996 will tell a great deal. Writing before the CTB negotiations are concluded, we can imagine several distinct outcomes. In one, the CTB fails or is importantly diluted. One of the Five argues that verification is inadequate, or that it must be allowed tests of yield lower than 1 kt, or that it must be permitted "safety" tests.[45] The negotiations collapse, or the < 1 kt tests are granted, or an

---

43. Reuters, 31 March 1994.

44. Alan Elsner, Reuters, 31 March 1994.

45. At this writing (June 1995) the possibility remains that one or more of the nuclear-weapon states might insist on a "safety" loophole. This is so despite President Clinton's announcement that the United States would withdraw its declared wish for some tests ten years hence. In abandoning the prospect that a CTB would permit "exceptional explosions," Britain used language which

important number of non-nuclear weapon states judge a "safety and reliability" reservation unacceptable. None of the Five "breaks ranks." Among the non-nuclear weapon states will be a sense that the Five somehow concerted their positions in order to thwart any reduction of their nuclear autonomy. At the NPT Review and Extension Conference the nuclear weapon states had agreed to stress a disarmament objective, but refused to agree to any "date certain" for abolition. Conclusion of many non-weapon states: The Five, fixed in domestic judgments that their nuclear programs must be protected and sustained, constitute a nuclear cabal.

The second outcome would be quite different: a CTB with *no* explosive nuclear tests, rigorous verification, and no blatant loopholes. China would agree to sign in 1996—not before—and would then bring her tests to a halt. The Five would take Article VI obligations seriously, in keeping with the texts agreed at the NPT Review and Extension Conference. The non-nuclear weapon states would believe this outcome credible because of some joint recognition among the Five that they did not gain by threatening one another. They would use both the five-year NPT reviews and the greater scope of the Preparatory Committee to press again in 2000.

Whatever path is followed, the Three will have had ample opportunities to put before Russia and the United States the question whether the nuclear status quo does in fact best assure security.

---

would construct a new loophole around the phrase "responsibility of ensuring the safety and reliability of its nuclear weapons." Thus UK Ambassador Weston spoke as follows to the Conference on Disarmament on 6 April 1995:

"But the UK, in common with the other nuclear weapon states, will continue to bear the responsibility of ensuring the safety and reliability of its nuclear weapons. This point was stressed in the statement that I made on behalf of the UK and France on 8 March in Working Group 2. At that time, we retained the bracketed reference to exceptional explosions in the draft Article on Scope.

". . . we are now prepared to withdraw the phrase on exceptional tests. We would therefore agree to this being deleted from the revised version of the Rolling Text. This is no way diminishes our responsibility to ensure the safety and reliability of our nuclear weapons. I would like to state for the record that we consider that the Scope Article should not be interpreted as prohibiting the UK, in common with the other nuclear weapons states, from fulfilling its responsibility to maintain the safety and reliability of its nuclear weapons."

Trust and Verify, no. 56, April 1995. The editors state that France has also said it agrees with removal of the bracketed phrase.

6

Verification and Transparency

Joint disarmament and arms control measures require effective verification and ongoing assurance. States will mount their own efforts to test compliance. Some of those efforts will be deeply clandestine. But there remain many steps, collective or coordinated, for which cooperation is required. For example, the United States and Soviet Union (Russia) have demonstrated in implementing the INF Treaty how cruise missile production prohibitions can be assured by monitors at the factory gates. Verification provisions for the Chemical Weapons Convention include carefully designed on-site inspection rights.

The Five have been jointly engaged, with other countries, in mapping out a verification regime for the proposed CTB. How could non-compliance be detected? And would the probability of detection be sufficiently high? The work is organized through the Conference on Disarmament. An expert's committee has designed an array of seismic monitors and set out just what such an array could do.

There is something of Alice in Wonderland in this. Well-informed designers of a *fission* weapon need not test it. There are many other signals of a new nuclear weapons program to prompt an on-site inspection. And the most advanced simulation work is supported by tests of very low yields, some so low that no network could detect them. If the Five can agree on a CTB they will be able to agree on a monitoring system and verification practices, but—like the CTB itself—they will be of greater symbolic than practical value.

The exercise, however, serves as a kind of training room for the three difficult verification tasks which must be addressed by disengagement and abolition regimes:

1. What is the baseline inventory?
2. Are agreed restrictions and prohibitions being observed?
3. Are there unacknowledged programs?

Odds are that British, French, Chinese, Russian, and US intelligence services regularly talk with each other about known weapons programs, to gauge their status, and about evidence of aspirant intentions. Moreover, since March 1991 it is established that IAEA cannot enforce an effective non-proliferation regime without access to prime current intelligence on suspected sites and activities. The Five are not the only possible source of such information, but are among the most important.

The United States and Soviet Union exchanged counts of their nuclear delivery systems in the SALT I and SALT II negotiations of the 1970s. To get the greater security of agreed levels they had to give up the "military secret" of numbers. In December 1993 German Foreign Minister Klaus Kinkel proposed an international register of nuclear weapons. The idea was reportedly ill-received in Paris, London and Washington, but a strong case for it has been made by a leading German arms control analyst.[1]

Is verification a *technical* or a *political* matter? Certainly it is a technical issue just what events and conditions a given sensing system can detect and discriminate, and whether it gives reliable measures. Whether verification is *adequate*, however, is a political judgment, for in a complex case it can never be perfect, yet verification which falls quite short of "perfection" may still give adequate assurance in the practical world. One rule of thumb, therefore, is that *verification must be as intrusive as the most skeptical party requires*. This means that some combination of observers in place and prompt on-site inspections, letting the most skeptical party see as much as it has the patience to look at, is what is required for adequate assurance. Does this mean that every facility must be—in principle—open? Probably it does. Does it mean that every document must be available for inspection? It does not. Does openness of facilities mean that trade secrets could be compromised? Yes, and there should be recourse for compensation.

As we have written above, Britain, France and China have all practiced secrecy in their nuclear programs. China—which to this day treats as state secrets information given to high school students in the rest of the world—may resist the open doors which verification

---

1. Harald Mueller, "Transparency in Nuclear Arms: Toward a Nuclear Weapons Register," in *Arms Control Today*, October 1994, pp. 3-7.

requires.

At the height of the Cold War, the Soviet Union and the United States agreed to verify strategic arms cuts using "national technical means": they would use cameras and radios to scan each other. The capacity to look into another state has grown even keener since that time. Four of the Five—all except Britain—place satellites into orbit to observe the Earth, some of them carrying highly sophisticated observing equipment. Reconnaissance satellites cannot establish the baseline nuclear weapons inventory of France or China, but they can identify activity at known storage sites and evidence of any structure built or goods moved above ground.

Verification: Reconnaissance Satellites

One motive to arm is fear of what cannot be seen. If states could see—from above and by inspecting suspect sites—fear would have reduced force. States might still profess "need" for nuclear weapons, but their arguments would have to be based either on refutable claims, or on vague complaints about the future. Everyone's being able to see creates a new opportunity for disengagement and denuclearization.

Early military reconnaissance used film returned to earth, which had the virtue of high resolution. Sustained observing in periodic passes over many months, however, favored transmitting digitized data, which could be immediately accessible. Trends in sensors, compression, transmission, and post-processing on the ground, including the capacity to scan the same location at different frequencies and at different times and tease information from more than one image, promise increased transparence.

Precise satellite imagery, once a state monopoly, is becoming a commercial affair. This shifts the decision-maker's world in several ways. Preparations for large-scale conventional attack cannot be concealed. The movements of surface ships are known. Under good conditions aircraft can be confirmed to be on the ground. Large-scale construction enterprises can be concealed only with difficulty.

These changes affect the micropowers' nuclear positions. Consider, first, the argument that even small nuclear inventories deter nuclear attack. Refined surveillance means micropowers are less likely to conceal successfully land-based missiles and aircraft; and we can imagine refinements compromising submarine-based systems. If system numbers are small, then, a "secure second-strike capability" would be less attainable, and nuclear weapons less certain to deter a willing attacker. Now consider a different argument, that nuclear weapons are the ultimate insurance against the state being overrun by conventional forces. Under transparency, prospective conventional aggressors lose surprise and, as a result, there is time for conventional collective security to be mobilized.

In both cases, being able to see reduces the likelihood of *false fears*, on which so many frictive hostilities have been based, and creates new opportunities for *assurance by revelation*.

If these arguments are correct, the cumulative effect of sharper intelligence from space is to reduce the value of nuclear weapons systems. They are more exposed if few, and less necessary for non-nuclear-deterrent missions.

Commercialization

Satellite imagery is commercially available. A government or private party can buy archived imagery or order new images. "Some conditions apply," not least of which is the readiness of the camera owner to deal. Imaging capability will improve and the number of vendors in the market grow, so that states, consortia, or international organizations seeking to meet verification objectives will not be confined to US, Russian, French, or Chinese military imagery, which they may be denied.

At the present time buyers can go to three sources: US Landsat, French SPOT, and Russian KVR-1000. Landsat (30 m) and SPOT (10 m) images are relatively low-resolution. Only the KVR-1000, sold commercially with an equivalent ground sample distance (GSD) of 2 m, are high-resolution. (In addition, the United States has announced release of more than 800,000 "Corona" images taken between 1960 and 1972, to be completed by August 1996.[2]) France has reportedly

2. At the time they were taken, these were the best military reconnaissance images available to the United States. (Landsat images became available in 1972). The resolutions of the released images range from 560 feet to 6 feet, improving as the systems were refined. The images will be sold in photographic form and made available free on the Internet at [http://edcwww.cr.usgs.gov/dclass/]. *The*

opposed commercial distribution of high-resolution images, concerned about security implications.[3] Satellite imaging permits not only clear pictures, but data for mapping, including topographic mapping.[4]

New ventures are in the works. WorldView, a California company, plans to supply photographs from a single satellite in 1996 with a resolution of "under three meters."[5] Their scheme envisages users being able to call up high-resolution images for display on their own workstations. They appear to promise worldwide availability of their most recent images. Other companies include Eyeglass International, a consortium of firms which have supplied US intelligence capability, and a Lockheed subsidiary, Space Imaging Incorporated.[6]

Vipin Gupta, addressing arms control verification, observes that

> States could become more self-reliant in their ability to verify an adversary's

---

New York Times, 25 February 1995. *Boston Globe* service, 26 June 1995.

3. Vipin Gupta, *New Satellite Images for Sale: The Opportunities and Risks Ahead* (Livermore: Lawrence Livermore National Laboratory, Center for Security and Technology Studies, 28 September 1994), pp. 5-7, citing Peter B. de Selding, "French Doubt Market for Sharper Images," *Space News*, vol. 5 no. 12, March 21-27 1994, pp. 1, 20.

   SPOT-1 was launched 22 February 1986, SPOT-2 22 January 1990. SPOT-3 was scheduled to be launched in 1993. A SPOT-4 is envisioned. Fernand Verger, Isabelle Sourbès, Raymond Ghirardi, and Yvette Palazot, *Atlas de Géographie de l'Espace* (Antony and Montpelier: SIDES-RECLUS, 1992), pp. 204-205.

   Gerbert A. Yefremov, head of Mashinostroyeniya, which built the Soviet Union's spy satellites, said he was working with US investors to sell satellite images. The firm also seeks Western partners to further develop earth-imaging satellites. *The New York Times*, 2 May 1994.

4. By passing twice over the same region and using active radar imaging, NASA hopes to achieve topographic maps accurate in elevation to 6 m or less. *The New York Times*, 8 October 1994 (AP). "These 'stereo' views will allow researchers to detect changes in the Earth's surface as small as a half-inch" they report, attributing the claim to the NASA project manager.

5. John Markoff, *The New York Times* 12 February 1993, citing unnamed sources "familiar with the project." The company is WorldView Imaging Corporation, Oakland, California. Markoff reports WorldView's receiving a license from the US National Oceanic and Atmospheric Administration to undertake the required satellite launches. The company's founder, Walter Scott, headed the Lawrence Livermore Laboratory SDI projects "Brilliant Pebbles" and "Brilliant Eyes" before leaving the laboratory in 1991.

6. Vipin Gupta, above.

> compliance with an agreement. In the absence of a formal or informal accord, commercial remote sensing satellites could provide valuable, independent data on force structures for use in arms control negotiations as well as insight on the verifiability of specific provisions. Pre-verification exercises could also be undertaken to test the feasibility of establishing compliance to proposed restrictions.[7]

He also cautions that greater availability of high-resolution imaging could work the other way, sharpening conflicts and straining alliances. Militaries are sensitive to the ways in which sensing capability could be used against them.

The French Program

French Defense Minister Pierre Joxe, who served until early 1993, strongly supported major enhancements of France's satellite capability. Its principal components are shown in table 6.1.

French specialists are keenly aware of others' satellite capabilities. A 1987 IFRI study of anti-satellite weapons[8] prepared under the direction of Pierre Lellouche reviews systems in space: a US electronic listening satellite (launched from the spaceship Discovery) monitoring the Soviet Union from a geostationary orbit, Soviet active and passive ocean reconnaissance satellites, and the US KH12 optical reconnaissance satellite "which can distinguish at any time of day an object less than a meter on a side and transmit the result in real time, particularly useful for detection of mobile ICBMs."

French purposes are set out succinctly by Pierre Latron, a key figure in the military space program.[9] They plan to reinforce their intelligence capability:

---

7. *Ibid.*, p. 23.

8. *La Guerre des Satellites: Enjeux Pour la Communauté Internationale* (Paris: l'Institut Français des Relations Internationales, 1987), pp. 34-35. The study was prepared under the direction of Pierre Lellouche with the assistance of Yves Boyer, Eva Kulesza and Jérôme Paolini.

9. Pierre Latron from 1987-90 was director of the Hélios satellite program, and from 1990 responsible for preparation and development of all French military space programs (except telecommunications). N°2501 Assemblée Nationale. N°213 Sénat. 18 December 1991. Paul Loridant, *Rapport sure les Orientations de la Politique Spatiale Française et Européenne*. II. Contributions des Experts. Pierre Latron, "l'Espace Militaire." Expertise N° 6.

> Augmenting the number of satellites, development of an infra-red observation capability, creating radar satellites and electronic listening satellites permitting us to mount a system of observation which is able to furnish images at higher frequencies, whatever the weather conditions, and to measure indices of force activity.

TABLE 6.1
French Satellite Programs

PROGRAM	PURPOSE
Hélios	Imaging at visual and infra-red frequencies. Hélios-1A, limited to daytime clear-weather imaging, launched 7 July 1995. Hélios-1B could be launched in 1996. Hélios-2, due around 2000, will offer higher resolution and infra-red imaging. Hélios includes 14.1% Italian and 7% Spanish participation. Sources: *Armées*; *Le Monde*.
Syracuse II	Communications. Syracuse I was launched in the early 1980s, providing secure communications—principally for naval ships "from the Antilles to the Indies." It has been replaced by Syracuse II, with a first satellite into orbit in 1991 and a second in 1992. Source: *Armées*.
Horus [formerly Osiris]	Radar imaging [also at night and through cloud cover], due about 2005. Sources: *Armées*; *Le Monde*.
Zenon	Planned electronic listening satellite. Cerise, an experimental microsatellite, part of studies of electromagnetic signals in low orbit, was piggy-backed aboard the Hélios-1A launch. Sources: *Armées*, *Le Monde*.

Sources: *Armées d'Aujourd'hui*, N°172 Hors Série. *Le Monde*, 8 July 1995. Hélios-1 is estimated to cost 7.8-8 billion 1994 francs, Hélios-2 11-11.5 billion francs, and Horus 12-15 billion francs. *Le Monde*, citing reports by Deputy Jean-Michel Boucheron and Senator Jacques Golliet.

Latron sets out military uses of space which France could envisage. In addition to three complementary types of images (visible light, infra-red, and radar), military satellites provide radar detection ("surveillance of fleets at sea, surveillance of aerial movement") and electronic listening ("technical analysis of intercepted signals, from telecommunications systems and radars" and "interception of communications and analysis of the content of messages").

Military oceanography, Latron explains, takes as its particular subject those ocean zones which display variable conditions of sound propagation. In that context, he notes studies of ocean "height" from satellites bearing high-precision altimeters, citing as examples the Franco-US TOPEX-POSEIDON and the European ERS-1 satellites.[10]

Concerning arms control, he takes satellite observation as "only one component of a system of verification," since it can only see what is visible and is subject to deception and camouflage. It will always be necessary to conduct on-site inspections.

Middle- and long-term military space plans are fixed in a classified document titled "Plan Pluriannuel Spatial Militaire" (PPSM) by the Groupe d'Etudes Spatiales in the Ministère de la défense. First drawn up in 1984, it is updated every two years. The plan then being drawn up—not yet approved at that juncture by the Minister of Defense—envisaged successively more ambitious objectives: first (from 1996) getting Hélios data more quickly, more suitable for tactical needs; then (from 2000) setting forth toward a more complete system, including observation on many bands (visible light, infra-red, radar) and "embarking on specialized satellites." He envisages prompt transmission, either to a national center or directly to theaters of operations. Further yet (from 2010/2015) the systems will need to be renewed, to attain more precise information with even less delay.

Britain

Britain has no imaging satellite program, spending small sums on earth observation and other subjects principally through the European Space Agency.[11] It would be surprising if the United Kingdom did not have access to US photographic coverage. (On the other hand, their French counterparts acknowledge Britain's "vast military telecommunications network." Britain does eavesdrop from space.)

---

10. The French Ministry of Defense contributed 125 million francs to development in France of the POSEIDON altimeter. Latron, p.12.

11. Fernand Verger, Isabelle Sourbès, Raymond Ghirardi, and Yvette Palazot, *Atlas de Géographie de l'Espace* (Antony and Montpelier: SIDES-RECLUS, 1992), p. 115.

China

By contrast to Britain, China has vigorously pursued satellite reconnaissance. For example, in 1982 China launched its twelfth satellite; it followed a path with orbital characteristics like those of Soviet and US photographic reconnaissance satellites and a capsule was recovered five days after launch.[12]

Multinational Observing

An observer satellite—probably a system of satellites—could be operated by a consortium or a global body, producing images for arms control verification and perhaps other purposes, such as environmental assessment, as well. A 1990 study by a UN Group of Experts set aside, on grounds of cost and organization, suggesting that the United Nations itself mount a verification capability. Nonetheless, the Chair of the Group of Experts commented that

> it was widely recognized that United Nations access to sophisticated overhead imaging would be especially important if the United Nations were to have the ability to move into a variety of areas on short notice and perform essential verification tasks.[13]

In the meantime, however, France sees a role in disarmament for the Western European Union satellite center, created in June 1991 on French initiative. Pierre Latron expected the center to receive not only commercially available images but also Hélios images made available by the Hélios partners, France, Italy and Spain. A study group was put in place within WEU to consider different observations systems—optical and radar—which the WEU might support.[14] Germany appears ready to commit to the consortium. Freed to take part in international military activities by a decision of its Constitutional Court in July

12. *SIPRI Yearbook 1983* (Stockholm: Stockholm International Peace Research Institute, 1983), pp. 431-432.
13. Fred Bild and Peter Jones, "Multilateral Verification: Opportunities and Constraints," in *Disarmament*, vol. 13 no. 2, 1991, pp. 69-82, p. 76. The report: "Study on the Role of the United Nations in the Field of Verification." UNGA A/45/372, 28 August 1990.
14. N°2501 Assemblée Nationale, above, p. 15.

1994, Germany was courted as a prospective contributor to the costs of Hélios-2 or Horus. Showing off Hélios-1 to his German counterpart, French Defense Minister François Léotard declared that "France has made a choice decidedly European. Space is a fundamental element for a European defense policy."[15]

Pros and Cons of Overhead Transparency

The argument for a multilateral image source is that no national source can be trusted. The selection of images may be misleading. The image itself could be doctored. Access could be withheld. Even if national images were used, it would be important to confirm them against an independent source.

The argument against high resolution for hire is that it would pinpoint targets. Just as the US bought SPOT imagery during the Gulf War, so some other country in a future war could buy images showing US encampments, radars, other facilities, and even movement. Clearly this objection favors those who can achieve high resolution by their own means, who wish to preserve their "imaging monopoly."

In this clash between "transparence" and "concealment," transparence must win, because the technology to achieve sufficiently high resolution grows more accessible. With access non-nuclear states will be in a better position to judge whether verification of disengagement or abolition is convincing. The United States may still see better than others, but others will see well enough.

Would greater transparence jeopardize China's deterrent force, during a transition from present deployments to disengagement or abolition? Probably not. It was with just this vulnerability to satellite detection in mind that China's leadership decided in 1967 to put the deterrent to sea.[16]

Satellite reconnaissance technology also creates opportunities for *concerted verification* of disengagement or abolition by the Five, pooling technical capabilities.

---

15. Jacques Isnard, *Le Monde*, 15 January 1995.

16. John Wilson Lewis and Xue Litai, *China's Strategic Seapower: The Politics of Force Modernization in the Nuclear Age* (Stanford: Stanford University Press, 1994), p. 143.

On-Site Inspection

On-site inspection is the absolute *sine qua non* of any arms control regime in which cheating is possible and salient. Prompt inspection—or ongoing observation—would be necessary to ensure no breakout from a radical disengagement regime. Since the condition of effective mutual restraint is assurance that other parties are not exploiting your restraint to do you harm, you must be able to be satisfied that they are not. On-site inspection offers the means to resolve doubt about whether an activity is harmful, or whether any activity at all is taking place at a designated site. And it is demonstrative, useful to assure a public.

A complementarity exists between sources of initial warnings—traditional intelligence-gathering, technical means, "societal verification"—and focused attention on a site. On-site inspection is not possible if the site is not identified.

If the number of suspect sites is manageably small and the prohibited activity concerns large physical operations, monitors can determine with certainty whether prohibited activity is taking place at a site. But there are limits to what on-site inspection can achieve. For example, the UN Special Commission, though in principle free to make on-site inspections, cannot access or control conteact among those who have taken part in the Iraqi weapons program, nor be sure to what extent design activity and planning continue.

Britain, France, and China do not participate in the US-Soviet (Russian) verification practices set out in the INF Treaty, but Britain and France participate fully in the CFE Treaty, and they are all signers of the Chemical Weapons Convention.

CW Convention

The CW Convention provision for on-site inspections could not be more explicit:

> Article IX. §8. Each State Party has the right to request an on-site challenge inspection of any facility or location in the territory or in any other place under the jurisdiction or control of any other State Party for the sole purpose of clarifying and resolving any questions concerning possible non-compliance with the provisions of this Convention, and to have this inspection conducted anywhere without delay by

> an inspection team designated by the Director-General and in accordance with the Verification Annex.[17]

Other techniques will also be used. A Working and Expert Group of the Preparatory Commission for the Organisation for the Prohibition of Chemical Weapons is charged with responsibility to work up detailed verification procedures.[18]

BW Convention

The Bacteriological (Biological) and Toxin Weapons Convention (1975) includes no verification regime. Britain and others have urged that verification measures be added to the Convention. Work to that end is taking place. In the meantime,

> the UK is conducting a series of practice inspections in the biotechnology and pharmaceutical industries to examine verification procedures and to explore the implications for industry of intrusive inspections.[19]

Conclusion

It remains to be seen how verification of the CW Convention and BW Convention will be given effect, especially in states accustomed to protecting state secrets or private industrial secrets. At the minimum, each suspected violation will create case experience.

Our purpose here is to note the centrality of verification. Without it there can be no assurance. Remote sensing offers new opportunities. No method provides absolute freedom from risk, but carefully designed and artful means of verification and self-revelation could reduce risk of non-compliance to levels lower than the level of risk run under present nuclearist practice.

---

17. Convention on the Prohibition of the Development, Production, Stockpiling and Use of Chemical Weapons and on their Destruction. *SIPRI Yearbook 1993* (Oxford: Oxford University Press, 1993), pp. 735-756. However, §15 ensures the inspected state advance warning of at least 12 hours.

18. House of Commons. Session 1993-94. Foreign Affairs Committee. *UK Policy on Weapons Proliferation and Control in the Post-Cold War Era.* Minutes of Evidence. 6 July 1994. Memorandum submitted by Foreign and Commonwealth Office, ¶ 15.

19. *Ibid.*, ¶ 16.

7

National Structures and Civil Society

Here and in the two chapters which follow I set out internal concerns—including views of external threats—which can be discerned today and will persist, however modified, into the future. The institutions introduced here will persist; future civil society will be rooted in the civil society of today; and issues with which future polities will grapple will be seen as consequences, in part, of their situations today.

Each of the Three is taken up in turn. I will point out corresponding European institutions, since Britain and France are in the European Union.

Britain

Central Politics

The present Conservative government (July 1995) depends on a House elected on 9 April 1992, which provided John Major a slender majority of eighteen seats (a "swing" of only nine). By British practice a General Election must be called within five years of the last. To exploit whatever advantage there may be in its choice of election date, the Conservatives would—on present indications—let time run, hoping that Labour's lead in today's soundings would decline. If not forced earlier, the government could wait until late 1996, or even the beginning of 1997.

As in the United States, of course, the electoral system and voter disinterest lead to governments elected by minorities of those who could qualify to vote.[1]

---

1. Ronald Reagan won the presidency against Jimmy Carter in 1980 with the votes of fewer than 30 percent of those eligible to register and vote. Conservative candidates for the House of Commons in 1992 received a minority of votes cast, and won eleven seats (and thus their majority in the House) by majorities of 585 or less, an aggregate of fewer than 3000 votes. John Stevenson, *Third Party Politics Since 1945* (Oxford: Blackwell, 1993), p. 123.

Labour has not held the prize of governance since 1979. If a Labour majority were won in 1996 or 1997 it would, still, be no more formally accountable than the Conservative governments of Margaret Thatcher and John Major. Moreover, secrecy envelops nuclear weapons. And Labour has a special sensitivity on the subject, stemming from its internecine quarrels around "unilateralism" and the studied efforts of the Tories, over decades, to paint Labour as disqualified on defense.

Parties: Labour Party

In the fifteen years since 1980 Labour has recast itself on the nuclear issue. The "unilateralist" left led the party to electoral disaster. Its mandate delegitimated, center-left support drawn off to the Social Democrats, it was forced to give way. Proposing abandonment of Britain's nuclear weapons was not the path to government.

Britain's Labour Party remains committed to placing British nuclear arms into negotiation, should Labour govern. But this policy—devised for the April 1992 general election—is Labour's remnant nod to disarmament. Neil Kinnock called in 1987 for terminating Polaris and canceling Trident, but in May 1989 told his party Executive Committee that he would never again propose unilateral nuclear disarmament.[2] The subsequent leaderships of John Smith and (from mid-1994) Tony Blair have moved Labour even more clearly toward a centrist posture.

The Labour Party's declaratory posture does not foretell exactly what policies Labour would follow in Government, but a close reading suggests the internal debate: distinctions drawn, commitments made, issues skirted or avoided. The annual Labour Party Conference (1994) passed two germane resolutions, one a bland statement ("carried") which speaks to the electorate and a second more assertive text, carried on a card vote, which explicitly addresses the Labour front

---

2. Len Scott, "Spirit of the Age or Ghost from the Past? Labour and Nuclear Disarmament in the 1990s" in *The Political Quarterly*, vol. 62 no. 2, April-June 1991, pp. 193-203, p. 193, citing *The Guardian* 10 May 1989 and "Meet the Challenge—Make the Change": The Final Report of Labour's Policy Review for the 1990s, London, Labour Party, 1989, p. 87.

bench.[3] Their differences in tone suggest long-standing internal party disputes. The first welcomes "opportunities" for "peaceful and co-operative relations between east and west" but cautions that

> Britain must also retain the military and industrial capacity to meet a wide range of potential risks to security.

The second calls for "ensuring greater world peace and security."

Both speak of lower defense spending, but the first is hesitant, and cautious:

> Conference believes that the new international environment should provide the scope to reduce defence spending among all industrialised countries in the medium term, on the basis of international agreements on force reductions including both conventional and nuclear weapons.

It cautions that cuts beyond those already projected by the present Government "would fall directly on services personnel and defence capacity." Spending has "already fallen towards the average European level." (Reaching the European average has been a Labour aim.)

The second resolution invokes previous commitments to the European average, and focuses not on a downward trend but a "present high level of arms expenditure" by Britain which "runs counter to trends of other NATO countries." Britain spends for defense "at least one per cent more of our national income" than European neighbors and "Britain's economy cannot sustain such a high level of arms spending."

The first text stresses the relationship of defense to jobs: job effects of budget cuts, plant closures, conversion and diversification. Except for the suggestion cited above that agreements to reduce conventional and nuclear weapons are a *precondition* for further defense spending cuts, this text is silent on arms control. It adopts the device of saying the next Labour government should "base its defence plans on a comprehensive defence review" to avoid elaborating such plans before an election. (The Liberal Democrats adopt the same device.) Moreover, a Labour government should also base its plans on

---

3. Labour Party Conference, Blackpool, 3-7 October 1994. The first resolution is Composite 48, the second Composite 49. Labour posts current documents on the web at [http://www.poptel.org.uk/labour-party/].

"maintenance of international agreements": a Labour Britain, the text implies, would not leave NATO, but would also continue to be aware of obligations under the NPT.

Delegates left it to the second text to declare explicit measures and goals regarding nuclear weapons (although this text too addressed jobs and military conversion):

- *Nuclear disarmament.* Conference "welcomes all genuine attempts to reduce nuclear weapons."
- *Nuclear tests.* Similarly, all "genuine attempts" to end testing. Britain should "stop testing all nuclear weapons immediately."
- *Trident.* The Conference "condemns" the Trident programme, a "massive expansion of this country's nuclear weaponry" which "flouts the Non-Proliferation Treaty." It calls on the Labour front bench to "stand by the condemnation of Britain's Trident programme" voiced by the 1993 Labour Party Conference. It "reaffirms" the 1993 decision that

  > scrapping of the Trident weapons programme is an essential step towards the elimination of nuclear weapons worldwide and all other weapons of mass destruction and continues to call for the next Labour government to decommission the Trident missiles system . . .

- *Trident and the Non-Proliferation Treaty.* A further paragraph calls for action *now*: Britain should go to the NPT Review and Extension Conference of April-May 1995 "unencumbered by its present nuclear capacity." By "scrapping Trident" the UK could bring a "chance of success" to the NPT negotiations.

It is important to bear in mind that these are Conference texts, not decisions of the parliamentary Labour Party or Labour's National Executive Committee. They show a persistent interest among some Labour adherents in "scrapping Trident" without declaring terms or conditions, but also show that Conference was prepared to commit to Britain's maintaining a diverse and capable military, centrally linked to NATO. Britain's nuclear weapons program has gone forward under Conservative and Labour governments alike. The radically different tones of the two Conference resolutions coexist uneasily, but no doubt voice shared wishes of an electoral coalition, which could be expressed in a Labour Government's joining disarmament moves if the terms were right. The "right terms" would have to include other states' accepting measures which objectively reduced residual threats to Britain. For without that, Labour would be exposed to electoral defeat by a Conservative Party unrestrained by any wish to credit Labour with statesmanship.

Parties: Conservative Party

The governing Conservative Party distances itself from bargaining away Britain's nuclear arms. The British position set out in the *Statement on the Defence Estimates*, 1992, is that

> if, in time, the US and former Soviet arsenals were further reduced substantially, and there had been no significant improvements in defensive capability, we would consider what further contribution we might make to arms control.

which committed Britain and the governing Conservative Party to nothing at all. In fact, the Conservative government has abandoned nuclear systems judged obsolete, withdrawn some weapons and put them in store, and decided (18 October 1993) not to go ahead with a long-discussed new stand-off missile. All of these fit the category "further contribution," offset by enhancement of Britain's sea-borne nuclear forces which has gone forward. Nuclear weapons and the Trident force are at the heart of Conservative strategy:

> **Nuclear Deterrence**. Conservative defence strategy will continue to be underpinned by nuclear forces—the ultimate guarantee of our country's security. Our nuclear weapons remain essential for our own, and NATO's security . . .
>
> . . . Our policy has been determined by one consideration alone: to possess the minimum number of warheads required to inflict unacceptable damage, in retaliation, upon any would-be nuclear aggressor.
>
> . . . It is simply misleading to claim that, if Trident is a minimum nuclear deterrent, then Polaris must be inadequate. Polaris is indeed adequate in 1992, but Trident must be operational until well into the 21st century, and throughout its long service must be capable of deterring any level of nuclear aggression. There are enormous uncertainties ahead, including: the development of more effective ABM defences, political instability within the Commonwealth of Independent States, and

the dangers of nuclear proliferation both within the CIS and more widely.[4]

For the Conservative Party, nuclear weapons policy is also a benchmark to distinguish the Conservatives from Labour and Liberal Democrats. Only a continued Conservative majority, they argue, ensures the security of Britain.[5] Labour and Liberal Democrats—however much they conceal it—are anti-nuclear. Partisan party publications are unambiguous on this point, putting at the top of their list of "key attacking points" against Labour on defense and foreign affairs that

> *Labour cannot be trusted to maintain Britain's defences in this dangerous and uncertain world.* They refuse to endorse the concept of nuclear deterrence and plan massive defence cuts.[6]

There is an "entrenched anti-nuclear element in the Liberal Party" which would say that "the time to relinquish the deterrent is now." "Labour and Liberal Democrat defence policies are almost indistinguishable."[7]

The section of *The Campaign Guide 1994* on defense and foreign affairs runs some fifty pages, setting out positions in great detail, many illustrated by quotations from Conservative ministers. Apart from passing reference to the START process and CSCE, four lines are given to arms control: there will be an NPT Review Conference, and "Britain favours a substantial, preferably indefinite, extension."[8]

---

4. Conservative Research Department. "Defense in a Changing World," in *Politics Today*, no. 10, 31 August 1993, pp. 304-305.

5. "We are the only Party unambiguously committed to the preservation and modernization of the United Kingdom's independent nuclear deterrent. Britain's nuclear forces will remain the ultimate guarantee of our country's security. Our new Trident fleet will give us the modern, flexible minimum deterrent that we need—and provide excellent value for money." Conservative Party. *The Campaign Guide 1994*, pp. 576-577.

6. *Ibid.*, p. 306. In another document they put it that "Labour have not clearly accepted the *principle* of nuclear deterrence." (Italics in original.) Conservative Party. *The Campaign Guide 1994*, p. 622. This party campaign guidance stops just short of calling Labour "unilateralist," heading discussion of Labour nuclear policy "Unilateralism under another name?"

7. Conservative Party. *The Campaign Guide 1994*, pp. 626, 624.

8. *Ibid.*, pp. 591-592.

If this document is any measure, the Conservative Party does not see its future in voters drawn to arms control.

Parties: Liberal Democrat Party

The Liberal Democrat Party is a bare force in the House of Commons (23 seats in 1994), but its position—in effect somewhere between the Tory right and Labour left—tells something about how viable postures are understood by politicians working their constituencies. Its intermediate place—and the unlikelihood of its governing except as a coparticipant—enable the Liberal Democrat party to explore alternatives which the Conservative Party rejects and Labour is unwilling to discuss. Moreover, any change in the center of gravity of British nuclear policy would require changed perceptions by the very voters to whom the Liberal Democrats appeal. So its distance from today's political authority requires us to explore the Liberal Democrats' origins and policies.

The Liberal Party, a major force before World War I, receded in the 1920s as the Labour Party advanced. After World War II the Liberal's very existence as an electoral party was in doubt. It struggled on, reduced to a half-dozen seats in the House of Commons and as little as 2.5 percent of the vote in a general election (October 1951). Eight years later, under fresher leadership, it achieved 5.9 percent (October 1959). Working to improve organization and position over the next fifteen years the Liberal Party was gradually recreated, winning almost 19 percent of the vote (October 1974) and 13 seats.

The House was divided, and in 1977 Labour and Liberals struck a temporary alliance (the "Lib-Lab Pact") to preserve a Labour government.

The election of 1979 was a turning-point in British politics. It ended Labor's government and introduced the Thatcher era. The Liberal Party secured 11 seats with 13.8 percent of the vote, which seemed to promise more near-marginal existence. But on 10 November 1980 Michael Foot, long committed to unilateral nuclear disarmament, was elected leader of the Labour Party. Disputes within Labour about policy and intra-Party democracy culminated on 26 March 1981 in formation of a breakaway Social Democratic Party. Though small—14 MPs—the SDP implied possible realignment in

British politics. In April the SDP and Liberals set out terms for an alliance, which became an electoral force first tested in 1983. John Stevenson, a British political analyst, places Labour's non-nuclear policy at the center of its failure, and by implication the Alliance's strong showing:

> Labour's manifesto was described by one Shadow Cabinet member as "the longest suicide note in history." It pledged the Party to leave the Common Market, adopt a non-nuclear policy, increase public expenditure and impose further nationalization. The result was a Conservative triumph on the basis of 42 per cent of the vote. Labour plummeted to its worst figure since 1918, to 28 per cent, while the Alliance showed a strong surge in the last few days of the campaign to end at just over 25 per cent.[9]

Nonetheless, nuclear issues were to figure in a major dispute between the SDP and Liberals in 1986. According to Stevenson, "strong unilateralist and pacifist elements" among the Liberal rank-and-file took exception to SDP figures speaking out about a new phase in deterrence "based on a 'Euro-bomb.'" The Liberal Assembly—defying party leadership—passed a non-nuclear stipulation at its September 1986 Assembly, casting doubt on the Alliance position.[10]

After election failure in 1987 the two Alliance partners moved to fuse. The fused party[11] contested elections with still only limited results: 6 percent of the vote in the European Parliament elections of June 1989, and 20 seats on 18.3 percent in the next General Election (March 1992). The Labour Party by 1992 had adopted a multilateralist position on nuclear disarmament.[12]

The party's Working Group on Security Policy, chaired by the late Lord Bonham-Carter, drafted in June 1994 a working paper for debate at the Liberal's regular conference in September.[13] They

---

9. John Stevenson, *Third Party Politics Since 1945: Liberals, Alliance and Liberal Democrats* (Oxford: Blackwell, 1993), p. 82.

10. *Ibid.*, p. 83. And, at p. 96: ". . . many Liberals suspected the SDP's radical credentials. To them David Owen seemed more interested in preserving an independent nuclear deterrent and the 'social market' than in proportional representation or regional government," the latter traditional Liberal interests.

11. Under successive names: (March 1988) Social and Liberal Democrats, (September 1988 short form) Democrats, (short form) Liberal Democrats.

12. Stevenson, *Third Party Politics Since 1945*, above, *passim*.

13. *Shared Security: Security and Defence in an Uncertain World.* Policy Paper

proposed these positions on issues germane to nuclear weapons:

- Liberal Democrats propose a new round of strategic nuclear talks, to include the UK, France and China, as well as Russia and the United States, as soon as there is a CTB in hand:

> Liberal Democrats . . . call for further negotiations to reduce and if possible eventually eliminate holdings of nuclear weapons by the five recognised nuclear weapon states. We have called consistently for the UK to be ready to enter negotiations to reduce its own nuclear weapon stockpile, in line with its obligations under Article VI of the NPT.

- While other states possess nuclear weapons Britain should continue to deploy "a minimal nuclear force."
- Britain should threaten to use nuclear weapons only "in self defence as a deterrent against the use or threat of use of nuclear weapons." Use must always be "proportional" and not be "directed at" civilian targets.
- While Britain has nuclear weapons their "deterrent purpose" is in two forms. Strategically: "as a weapon of last resort against nuclear attack." Substrategically: "to protect British or WEU/NATO forces from nuclear attack."
- Trident can perform both roles. When Trident is "operational," other British nuclear weapons should be "withdrawn." The four Trident boats should not deploy more warheads "than at present are deployed on Polaris," a maximum of 192. And,

> It may well be possible that an appropriate level of minimum deterrence can be provided by a reduction below even the number of warheads currently deployed on Polaris. A greater degree of integration in nuclear weapons policy—covering such matters as patrolling—between the UK and France is also desirable; we welcome the current negotiations with France.

- The number of warheads deployed "should be stated explicitly and be open to independent verification."

As long as others have nuclear weapons, however, Britain would maintain a "minimum force." The terms are somewhat more dodgy

---

No. 6. June 1994.

about what "threat of use" and "use" of that force might be. Is a "weapon of last resort against nuclear attack" used only *after* an attack has been made? or is it used preemptively *before*? Similarly, are troops "protected from nuclear attack" simply by the *deterrent threat* to use nuclear weapons substrategically, or must they be used *preemptively*?

The Liberal Democrat position is articulated around an extended discussion of the NPT and CTB. We might term their view a *qualified abolition position.*

- Liberal Democrats "fully support the aims of Article VI of the NPT. . ."
- But a "nuclear weapons free world" is a "long term goal." (They are careful not to commit themselves to denuclearization now.)
- Nonetheless the choice between abolition and a world of "minimal forces" should be expressly canvassed:

> . . . some eminent strategists see this goal of a nuclear free world as having important security benefits and of being achievable within 20-30 years. The security benefits of a nuclear-free world, as opposed to a world where some states retain a minimal force of nuclear weapons, should be studied by military planners and strategic thinkers as a matter of urgency.

- A "comprehensive and universal" CTB, with a "strong verification system," should be readied for signing before the NPT Review and Extension Conference of 1995.
- Liberal Democrats support "indefinite extension" of the NPT, while calling for stronger verification including intrusive IAEA on-site inspection.
- There should be an end to production of plutonium for weapons purposes and highly enriched uranium for any purpose; plutonium should be stored under international supervision; and BNFL's plutonium separation should not be expanded.

This is a paper of a party seeking public office. It does not spell out the minimum acceptable verification provisions of a CTB, for example, nor does it make clear whether "strengthening" of IAEA verification rights and capabilities should be a precondition of NPT extension. What we do find is a set of specifics which the Liberal Democrats propose Britain offer as signs of good faith Article VI compliance: five-party strategic arms talks, disengagement from WE 177 deployment, CTB signature *before* the NPT conference, putting British plutonium stocks under international supervision.

Finally, the drafting group committed itself to a satellite reconnaissance scheme:

- It would be "useful" to institute a WEU satellite surveillance programme, both as an anti-proliferation measure and to help enforce arms control agreements. They suggest combining French launch vehicles and British instrumentation.

What would these positions mean if the Liberals were faced with votes in which their seats in the House of Commons mattered? Another hint—but only that—was given by Liberal Democrat leader Paddy Ashdown after a briefing from US officials and political figures prior to a visit to the United States. Ashdown felt and reported pressure from the United States that Britain give up some of its Trident force. And he voiced it in a manner critical of Thatcher-Major policies:

> This is America the protector about to become the whip-cracker. This will be harsh reality for those who have always vested our defence and security interests in America. It will also underline the increasing urgency with which we, in Britain, need to consider integrated European defence security measures.[14]

Central Governance

The Prime Minister heads government. Of six key Ministerial Committees of the Cabinet which he chairs, three concern nuclear policy: Defence and Overseas Policy, Intelligence Services, and—most directly—Nuclear Defence Policy. In principle the Prime Minister and Cabinet stand accountable to Parliament. But a British government secure in its majority is akin to a conspiracy between its members and the Parliamentary majority which elects it. The

---

14. *Independent on Sunday* (London), 19 February 1995.

Government proposes legislation. Ministers are questioned in the House but they need not, and often do not, give substantive replies. Ambition subordinates majority members to the Government of the day, on which they depend for ministerial preferment.

Offsetting the privacy of majority party government are institutional measures to protect public purpose. Monies must be accounted. Government is carried on by a professional civil service. The House operates committees, including the Defence Committee and the Foreign Affairs Committee, which hear evidence and publish the transcripts of their open sessions. These mitigate the government's substantial capacities for secrecy. Nonetheless, under press of time, and where "national security" is engaged, consequential decisions can be and have been taken in private by very small groups around the Prime Minister.[15]

The Secretary of State for Defence ("defence minister"), and other ministers who assist, are political persons, typically without experience in defense policy. In defense, as in other areas, policy is formed, defined and administered by the Government heavily reliant on the professional civil service, the staff of the Ministry of Defence. Expertise in policy, weapons systems, procurement, and nuclear strategy resides in the ministry and in the military forces which it controls. The British nuclear weapons establishment, designing and producing British nuclear weapons, is now also subject to administration by the Ministry of Defense.

The question germane to this study is "what role does the Ministry of Defence play in maintaining Britain's nuclear commit-

---

15. On secrecy in British government see Richard Rose, *Politics in England* (London: Macmillan, 1989), pp. 94, 208-210. Citing John Lloyd, "The Ferret," in *New Statesman*, 30 January 1987, p. 12, Rose quotes an off-the-record comment of Margaret Thatcher's press secretary, Bernard Ingham: "There is no freedom of information in this country; there's no public right to know. There's a commonsense idea of how to run a country and Britain is full of commonsense people. Bugger the public's right to know. The game is the security of the state, not the public's right to know. . ." Norris et al., p. 66, summarize: "Far more so than in the United States, British policy decisions about the acquisition, deployment, and employment of nuclear weapons are made by very few people and conducted in great secrecy. For example, only four or five Ministers in an Ad Hoc Cabinet Committee may be involved in an important decision, with no participation (or even knowledge) by other Ministers, Parliament, or the public."

ment?" Serious efforts to set out decision-making within the ministry underscore its insistence on secrecy.[16] The formal posture that the ministry simply carries out instructions of the Government of the day must give way to an appreciation of the force of policy experience, information, and ongoing management of programs which extend across the lives of successive governments. A better guide to the Ministry's role in argument is suggested by Lawrence Freedman's discussion of British targeting policy in the 1980s as Trident was being anticipated, in which he tells us that "the view that it was neither necessary nor wholly proper to concentrate on Soviet cities"—as the Chevaline program had been designed to do—"was associated with Michael Quinlan, the leading civil servant on nuclear issues at Whitehall."[17] If the interplay between targeting requirements and strategic capabilities were effectively addressed anywhere we would expect it to be within the Ministry of Defence (MoD). And Quinlan was not simply a specialist on nuclear issues, but in due course Permanent Under-Secretary, the senior civil servant in the ministry.[18]

In 1985 a Defence Arms Control Unit of twelve members, civilian and military, was established in the Ministry of Defence.[19] McLean describes its duties:

> A new Policy Review Section is being added to the Unit, which considers itself a "policy division," working out what aspects of a problem are major policy issues. The Unit liaises with the Foreign Office Arms Control and Disarmament Department, and the Defense Department; with NATO disarmament policy via the Special Consultative Group; and with the United States Department of Defense and

---

16. See especially Scilla McLean (with assistance from Tony Thomson and MacDonald Graham), "Britain," in Scilla McLean ed., *How Nuclear Weapons Decisions are Made* (Houndsmills, Basingstoke, Hampshire: Macmillan, 1986), pp. 85-153, on which this and further sections on British institutions and decision-making have drawn.
17. Lawrence Freedman, "British Nuclear Targeting," in Desmond Ball and Jeffrey Richelson (eds), *Strategic Nuclear Targeting* (Ithaca: Cornell University Press, 1986), pp. 109-126, p. 124.
18. McLean identifies the Permanent Under-Secretary as "the channel for all civilian advice to the Secretary of State ('defence minister'). It is one of the most prestigious and powerful posts in the British civil service."
19. McLean, above, p. 109. Before the reorganization of January 1985 these duties had been assigned to Defence Secretariat 17. This section is directly responsible to the Permanent Under-Secretary. *Ibid.*, p. 135.

> State Department via joint working groups . . .[20]

The second Ministerial location of arms control policy discussion is the Foreign and Commonwealth Office ("Foreign Office," "ministry of foreign affairs"), which addresses these subjects through the cited Arms Control and Disarmament Department. The question is: how are differences between positions of Defence and the Foreign Office resolved? McLean:

> While arms control policy must be "cleared" with the Ministry of Defence (MoD), defence policy need not be cleared for its arms control implications.[21]
>
> Through the process of clearance, the MoD exerts considerable influence, verging on a veto, over FCO [arms control] policy. The emphasis of its work is on protecting present and future weapons policy options.[22]

Since 1951 a junior Minister in the Foreign Office has been charged with responsibility for arms control.[23]

Nuclear Command and Control

Authority to fire a nuclear weapon reportedly rests with the Prime Minister and a single deputy, who must agree. According to Christopher Bellamy of *The Independent* the deputy is probably the Secretary of State for Defence. They stand at the head of a "firing chain." Bellamy says the "two-man rule" applies "all the way down the chain." And reporting the departure of HMS *Vanguard* from Faslane to Coulport, where thermonuclear warheads would be attached to its sixteen Trident missiles, Bellamy quoted Commander Peter Wilkinson, who was to captain *Vanguard* on its first operational patrol: "I have 100 per cent confidence in the safety and security of the firing chain system—that there will be no mistakes."[24]

---

20. *Ibid.*, p. 109.
21. *Ibid.*, p. 133.
22. *Ibid.*, p. 135.
23. *Ibid.*, p. 133.
24. *The Independent*, 26 November 1994.

The Military

The Defence Council, comprising ministers, chiefs of the defence staff and service chiefs, and senior MoD civil servants, is the MoD's summit policy group. It is chaired by the Secretary of State for Defence.[25]

The January 1984 reorganization created a Unified Defence Staff of four groups. The Strategy and Policy group, Scilla McLean writes,

> handles all longer-term defence policy and strategy and military nuclear policy work (with the exception of the day-to-day running of the strategic nuclear force, which is the responsibility of the Navy) including NATO, UK nuclear strategy, nuclear security, weapons, targeting and deployment. There are two departments, one handling military aspects of nuclear policies, the other handling the political, parliamentary and academic aspects of defence policy.[26]

A Defence Intelligence Staff, with a 1994-95 budget of £60 million, concerns itself with "purely military subjects" such as defence doctrine and orders of battle, but also

> looks at the proliferation of nuclear, chemical and biological weapons and ballistic missiles; scientific and technological developments of application to defence, and the transfer of technology; arms sales, arms control and verification issues; and defence industries and infrastructure.[27]

A Chief of Defence Intelligence "coordinates" the work of DIS, and he and his deputy sit on the central Joint Intelligence Committee. The deputy is also Director General of Intelligence (Assessments), who is charged with making intelligence assessments, including those of defense-related political and economic issues. A Director General of Scientific and Technical Intelligence is responsible for scientific and technical assessment of ballistic missiles, nuclear, biological and chemical issues, space vehicles and defense industries.[28]

---

25. *Ibid.*, p. 104.

26. *Ibid.*, p. 107.

27. Cm 2550. *Statement on the Defence Estimates 1994*. Presented to Parliament by the Secretary of State for Defence. April 1994. P. 41.

28. *Ibid.*, pp. 41-42.

The Nuclear Weapons Establishment

The British weapons production system is its Atomic Weapons Establishment (AWE), which since 1973 has functioned under the Procurement Executive of the Ministry of Defence. Its principal centers are AWE Aldermaston (warhead design), AWE Burghfield (production, components, and nuclear weapons assembly), AWE Cardiff (components), and AWE Foulness (non-nuclear testing).

In 1944 the United States and Britain created the Combined Development Trust to allocate jointly supplies of uranium. Britain obtained uranium from South Africa and had an option on half of the deposits in the Belgian Congo.[29] They initially relied on the gaseous diffusion method and by 1957 were drawing significant quantities from a plant at Capenhurst. Production ended in 1963. Britain has not produced highly-enriched uranium (HEU) since 1963, instead buying it from the United States; a gas centrifuge plant at Capenhurst was completed in 1984, but no weapons-grade material may have been produced.[30] Plutonium was drawn from two reactors at Windscale (later renamed Sellafield) from 1951 to 1957, and after 1957 from production reactors at Calder Hall and Chapelcross.[31]

Proposals for nuclear weapons procurement are made in the Procurement Executive of the Ministry of Defence. Staff of the Deputy Chief of the Defense Staff (Systems) prepare a "Staff Target." This is

> also discussed by a relatively new committee, the Senior Nuclear Group, chaired by the Chief of the Defence Staff and the Permanent Secretary. This group fulfills no formal executive role but takes a panoramic view of the interaction of nuclear policy and procurement with other aspects of the department's business.
>
> . . . The decision to move from one stage to the next (Feasibility Study, Project Definition, Full Scale Development, Production) rests with Ministers who will be advised by the Equipment Policy Committee (NUCLEAR) (EPC(N)).[32]

---

29. Andrew J. Pierre, p. 128-129.

30. David Albright, Frans Berkhout and William Walker, *World Inventory of Plutonium and Highly Enriched Uranium 1992* (Oxford: Oxford University Press, for SIPRI, 1993), p. 64.

31. Albright et al., p. 41. See also Norris et al., pp. 76-78.

32. Norris et al., *ibid.*

It is in the AWE that Britain undertakes whatever work it does in warhead design and—by extension—simulation of nuclear events. Britain's efforts to maintain a design and development capability without nuclear tests are presumably lodged in the Mathematical Physics Department of AWE Aldermaston.[33] It is a reasonable presumption that this group has contributed opinions to formation of British policy in the CTB negotiations.

TABLE 7.1

Britain: Sources of Nuclear Weapons Components

Nuclear warheads	
Uranium^{235}	Stockpiled
Plutonium^{239}	AWE/BNFL
Design	AWE
Fabrication	AWE
Delivery Systems: Submarine-Borne Missiles	
Missiles	US
Missile guidance system	US
Reentry vehicles	US
Missile servicing capabilities	US
Platform: Ballistic Missile Submarine (SSBN)	
Submarine	Market
Reactors	Market
Turbines	Market
Electronics	Market
Refit capabilities	UK
Platform: Aircraft: Tornado	
Airframe	Market
Engines	Market
Avionics	Market
Navigation System	Market
WE 177 Free-fall bomb	AWE

33. The Mathematical Physics Department is cited in McLean, above, p. 119. Until mid-1987 the AWE was known as the Atomic Weapons Research Establishment (AWRE). On AWRE and AWE, see Norris et al., p. 68.

TABLE 7.2
Britain: Industrial Providers by Weapons Platform

Platform: SSBN [a]			
Submarine	VSEL (Vickers Shipbuilding and Engineering Limited)		
Reactors	Rolls-Royce		
Turbines	GEC		
Electronics			
Rockwell			Navigation systems
Plessey Marine			Sonar &c.
Plessey			Computers
Ferranti			Computers &c.
Gresham CAP			Command & control
Platform: Aircraft: Tornado [b]			
Airframe	Panavia (Consortium)		
Aeritalia		Italy	Wings
British Aerospace		UK	Fuselage
MBB (Messerschmitt-Bolköw-Blum)		FRG	Fuselage
Engines	Turbo-Union (Consortium)		
Rolls-Royce		UK	
Motoren und Turbinen		FRG	
Fiat		Italy	
Avionics	GEC		
	Smith		
Navigation System	Ferranti		

a VSEL will build all four *Vanguard*-class SSBNs. Details from Norris et al., p. 166.
b Norris et al., p.157.
Source: Norris et al.

Industry

Industry's manifold relations to nuclear weapons policy imply, for this inquiry, four questions. Can Britain produce the weapons and delivery systems it uses? Are British producers dependent on the nuclear program? Are British producers subject to foreign influence or control? And how intimate are relations between British producers and those with whom they deal in the armed forces and the Ministry of

Defence? We cannot give complete answers to these questions, but we can say enough to suggest consequences of arms spending, including nuclear weapons spending, for British industry.

Our strategy will be to identify the *main requirements* of Britain's nuclear program and the *principal suppliers*. We simplify yet further by identifying those met from the United States, or through the ongoing activities of the Ministry's Atomic Weapons Establishment. In the table which follows, entries are for strategic systems now being procured (*Vanguard* class SSBN and Trident D-5 missile) and the one extant aircraft platform—Tornado. Tornado is no longer being procured. There are plans for upgrading some Tornado's in the inventory, but no follow-on aircraft has been publicly discussed.

Britain's sourcing system and the lead firms in meeting market requirements are listed in tables 7.1 and 7.2. Our schematic in tables show the procurement structure underlying several important facts:

1. The AWE itself incorporates several key production steps, including those to separate and machine Pu^{239}, complemented by BNFL's newly-enhanced Pu separation capabilities (THORP).

2. The Trident system—except for the warhead—is an off-the-shelf purchase from the United States. British industry has no experience in large-scale launch vehicles, whether for space launch or long-range nuclear weapon launch.

3. VSEL's submarine-building capacity is dependent upon a stream of orders to build one submarine—either an SSN or SSBN—every eighteen months. Fewer orders than that would increase the cost per boat and make it more difficult to maintain the capacity.[34] On

34. House of Commons. Session 1992-93. Defence Committee. Sixth Report. *The Progress of the Trident Programme*. 16 June 1993, p. xiii:
"The timing of the contracts for SSBNs 07 and 08, and of their construction by VSEL, have been strongly influenced by non-military considerations, in particular by the state of contract negotiations and VSEL's long-term industrial requirements. ... This year Rear Admiral Irwin told us 'We deliberately slipped SSBN 07 to give a better profile of work at Vickers and in doing so we arranged the programme for SSBN 08 to tie in with that, again to give the best programme of work at Vickers.'"

the other hand, British aircraft manufacturers make and sell aircraft for the international market. No British airframe capacity is dependent on orders for nuclear platforms.

4. The electronics and avionics portions of large-scale weapons systems are a growing part of cost and complexity. In the nature of the industry, more sourcing is done from abroad, and units assume access to foreign components and services.

5. In short, Britain can build aircraft and manufacture nuclear weapons. British Aerospace and GEC Marconi, to mention two principal firms, embody expertise across a broad range of military applications. In that sense, Britain is no more "dependent" on foreign supply than all others in an interdependent high-technology market. Producing an indigenous large-scale missile, however, would require years of work, though Britain produces small ones, and has working models of large ones in hand.

In present circumstances, delay served VSEL's interests. Nonetheless, VSEL is dependent on the SSBN orders into the 1990s. Britain made a choice of tempo two decades ago around the rate of one new boat each 18 months. Anticipating the new *Vanguard* class, new SSN construction was fit into the schedule, and then Britain laid down the four SSBNs in quick succession. The SSBN force creates part of the need for SSNs,[35] and together they provide enough work to keep VSEL in business.

British firms have acquired interests in arms producers abroad, and surrendered some interests to foreign firms. Firms producing nuclear systems are among them, but there is no clear pattern and the scale is relatively small. For 1990-91, for example, GRIP reports 34 instances of acquisition or taking control in the armament sector, including four in which a foreign firm acquired a British interest, and two of British firms acquiring foreign stakes. Thomson-CSF made

---

35. Four of twelve SSNs are explicitly allocated to the strategic nuclear program, in Britain's rather elaborate (if sometimes strained) allocation of force elements to defense roles. Cm 2550. *Statement on the Defence Estimates 1994*. Presented to Parliament by the Secretary of State for Defence. April 1994, p. 28.

three purchases, of which buying half of Ferranti's acoustic ASW activities most concerns strategic systems: but it results in a sharing, or pooling, of common interest in the subject.[36] Nothing in recent experience suggests British concern that it might be losing essential elements of its military productive capacity.

Civil Society

Civil society consists not only of organized non-state constructs but the population itself as well, engaged in ongoing conversation about the future of society, the state, and more often "public" concerns directly affecting individuals. It is difficult to measure the extent of conversation, though it must be reflected—not quite clear how—in "public opinion," which we take up in the next section. We can say about civil society something of the quality of some examples of public nuclear discourse and the scale of organized expression of civil societal concern about nuclear issues.

For the British case, an exemplar of an accessible public text which takes argument as its subject, setting forth judgments and reasons, is Robert Neild's *How to Make Up Your Mind About the Bomb*.[37] Neild, a British economist and arms control specialist, goes to some trouble to position his arguments outside the struggles diverting Labour:

> The notion that unilateral and multilateral policies for disarmament are mutually exclusive is surprisingly common. It is the result of internal feuds within the Labour Party in which the terms "unilateralist" and "multilateralist" have been used vulgarly as slogans by rival factions. It is clearly nonsense. While pursuing multilateral measures of disarmament, the achievement of which depends on the agreement of other countries, it is necessary to decide what level of arms to maintain; and that means you need to have a unilateral policy . . .[38]

Neild proposes (1981) that Britain renounce nuclear weapons, rid itself

---

36. GRIP (Institut Européen de Récherche et d'Information sur la Paix et la Sécurité • European Institute for Research and Information on Peace and Security). *Memento défense-désarmament 1992: L'Europe et la sécurité internationale.* Les dossiers du GRIP. N° 168-171, April-July 1992, pp. 238-240.

37. Robert Neild, *How to Make Up Your Mind About the Bomb* (London: Andre Deutsch, 1981).

38. *Ibid.*, p. 125.

of US bases, but remain in NATO. Britain would urge the United States and Soviet Union to undertake "radical nuclear disarmament" by steps which could be unilateral, perhaps registering for some time in a "minimum deterrent."[39]

The Campaign for Nuclear Disarmament (CND) is the best-known anti-nuclear movement. In 1983, growing sharply in response to the issue of new nuclear deployments (the NATO "two-track" decision of December 1979 and US plans to deploy nuclear-armed Pershing II and cruise missiles), CND reached 54,000 national members and 250,000 attached to local groups.[40] The Greenham Common peace camp women, independent of CND, campaigned before the gates of a missile base. CND activists assumed an international dimension with formation in 1980 of European Nuclear Disarmament, which encouraged protest activity across Europe.

Civil society includes too those who lose jobs and trade when military programs are cut back. Closures can pit one locality against another, one group of workers against another. The 1994 shutdown of a major ship refit yard did just that. Gradual drawdown of British military personnel affects soldiers and seamen, but social effects are diluted over time.

Public Opinion

Much of the British public accepts Britain's nuclear forces. The political parties reflect that in not challenging Britain's deterrent head-on. Liberal Democrats and Labour profess a wish to see it gone, but with qualifications. The main qualification is that zero nuclear weapons must be general. This has the effect of shifting the choice to any state which has nuclear weapons and insists on keeping them.

---

39. *Ibid.*, pp. 126-130.

40. Geoffrey Lee, "Nuclear Weapons and the Peace Movement," in Bill Jones (ed), *Political Issues in Britain Today* (Manchester: Manchester University Press, 3rd. ed. 1989), pp. 316-337, p. 321.

    Richard Rose marks CND as a "complete outsider"—with no influence in Whitehall—because "its goal is absolute—Britain's unilateral abandonment of nuclear weapons—and has been rejected by successive Labour and Conservative ministers of Defence." Richard Rose, *Politics in England* (London: Macmillan, 5th ed. 1989), p. 232.

The British public, to the extent it engages the issue at all, agrees that it is right and necessary to keep nuclear weapons as long as others have them.

Robert Neild understandably regrets the "vulgar slogans" of unilateralism and multilateralism, excluding dual strategies, but they pervade British discussion of nuclear weapons. The Gallup Poll of 12-17 November 1986 found 28 percent of men and 35 percent of women endorsing unilateral nuclear disarmament. By party preference, 11 percent of Conservative, 34 percent of Alliance (the form Liberal Democrats took at the time), and 50 percent of Labour respondents endorsed giving up nuclear weapons. They were forty percent of young respondents (18-34) but only 30 percent of the old (65 plus).[41]

In 1989 MORI asked "if all nuclear weapons are abolished by the year 2000, do you think this will make Britain safer, less safe or about the same as now?" The responses, by party preference, are shown in table 7.3:

TABLE 7.3

Britain: Would Abolition Make Britain Safer?

Percent	ALL	Con	Labour	Dem	SDP
Safer	37	29	45	44	28
Less safe	20	28	13	14	22
Same as now	39	40	37	39	43
Don't know/no answer	4	3	5	3	7

Source: MORI poll of 2025 adults aged 15+ at 144 constituency sampling points throughout Great Britain. *British Public Opinion*, May 1989, p. 5.

A MORI poll conducted 20-24 September 1991 reported that 27 percent of respondents either "agreed" or "tended to agree" that "Britain should get rid of its nuclear weapons even if other countries keep theirs." But 39 percent "agreed" or "tended to agree" that "Britain should keep its nuclear weapons even if other countries get rid of theirs."

So we can say that in the late 1980s and early 1990s two-thirds of the British public accepted nuclear weapons. How would they judge

41. Richard Rose, *Politics in England* (London: Macmillan, 5th ed. 1989), pp. 161, 262, 355.

abolition? Only 20 percent thought Britain would be "less safe" in a non-nuclear world.

France

Central Politics

For fifty years the British Parliament has chosen Prime Ministers from either the Labour or the Conservative party. Labour, for one period, required Liberal support to govern, and John Major's slim 1992 majority was abetted by Unionist MPs from Northern Ireland. Striving takes place within parties and individuals come forward through ministerial service.

The lines of French central politics are very different, in three respects. The parties, over time, are more fluid, subject to redefinition, and more numerous. Electoral alliance assumes greater importance. And there exists a strong tradition of intra-party groups around individuals, clientilist factions focused on the prominence and advancement of the figure at their center. Senior figures maintain their personal secretariats as they move in and out of government and party posts.

The term of a French president is seven years, barring incapacity or death, so the political timetable of the early 1990s focused on the presidential election of spring 1995. Who would the nominees be?

At stake was authority in foreign affairs and defense for the seven years 1995-2002.[42] Maneuver for the presidency bears directly

---

42. Under the 1958 Constitution, the President appoints the Premier, presides over the Council of Ministers, and is "the guarantor of national independence, of the integrity of the territory, and of respect for Community agreements and treaties." (Articles 8 and 5) He or she commands the armed forces and "presides over the higher councils and committees of national defense." (Article 15) The President negotiates and ratifies treaties. (Article 52) Should "the institutions of the Republic, the independence of the Nation, the integrity of its territory or the execution of its international engagements be menaced in a grave and immediate manner" and normal government function be interrupted, the President shall take what action the circumstances demand. (Article 16) Mitterrand has insisted that the Constitution accords the president primacy in defence and foreign affairs, and Prime Minister Balladur (1993 - 1995), though from the opposition, has not contested that. The French text is in Assemblée

on French nuclear policy.

- Whether the President acts out of partisan political calculation or belief it serves French interest, he has latitude for initiative in arms control. Mitterrand illustrated that in ordering, in April 1992, French suspension of nuclear tests.
- Although party differences on France's nuclear forces narrowed radically in the run-up to PS victory at the beginning of the 1980s, differences remain. Evidence of this lies in Pierre Joxe's having sought to protect the arms control steps taken by the PS government as its days waned in early 1993.
- Within *each of the parties* differences exist on the weight to be accorded defense and on the role of nuclear weapons. This is one area among many in which the ambitious maneuver. But because the President leads in defense, whether a candidate is "presidentiable" turns in part on party and electoral judgments of defense posture.

Two issues debated in 1992-1995—nuclear posture and weapons test policy—illustrate relationships among parties, President, and nuclear weapons. In late 1992 advocates staked out positions on defining France's nuclear policy in the new world post-1989. For what purposes should France hold nuclear weapons? What forces did those purposes imply? French analysts, talking to me about the internal debates, stressed that advocates of the three principal positions could be found in each of the major political parties.[43] It would be wrong, they

---

Nationale, DIAN 44/94, *Constitution du 4 octobre 1958*. September 1994.

43. The three positions were—roughly—*status quo*, *status quo* with selective draw-down of forces, and *status quo* plus new missions (capabilities suited to the "new threats" from emerging states). Other visitors to Paris heard much the same thing, as a BASIC report on French nuclear policy in early 1993 makes clear. "French Nuclear Policy Since the Fall of the Wall," BASIC Report 93.1. They characterize the positions in this way (pp. 21-22):

"One school of thought still holds to the . . . doctrine of *dissuasion du faible au fort* and wants to maintain the status quo. This approach tends to be quite isolationist, placing primary importance on protecting the sanctuary of French territory through nuclear deterrence. . .

"A second group of nuclear strategists is shifting focus toward the perceived threat from the South. . . . [N]uclear strategy would be that of the 'strong to the

insisted, to imagine the parties had consistent positions on these issues. Nonetheless, on the test moratorium there was a strong expectation that Mitterrand's departure and replacement by a center-right president would clear the way for France to test again.

Authority of the presidency is such a prize that candidates of the center-right have risked dividing their forces rather than give way before the election—and as a consequence have lost the presidency twice to François Mitterrand, the Socialist Party leader, in 1981 and 1988. Would the center-right, then, choose or negotiate a *single* candidate for the presidency, or would two or more figures divide the vote on the first ballot? And, then, with what effects?

Approaching the March 1993 parliamentary election there were three principal parties: on the left, the Socialist Party (SP), identified with President Mitterrand, which led the Government; on the center-right, the centrist Union for French Democracy (UDF), identified with former President Giscard d'Estaing, and the stronger "neo-Gaullist" Rassemblement pour la République (RPR), identified with former Prime Minister Jacques Chirac. A center-right landslide ensured an RPR-UDF government. Edouard Balladur was named Prime Minister. The Socialists appeared unable to recapture direction.

When the election of April-May 1995 took place, Chirac and Balladur did both press their candidacies. Socialist Lionel Jospin, surprising many, survived the first round of voting; Balladur did not; but Chirac won the presidency on the second round. As we have noted, within a month he approved nuclear test resumption.

Central Governance

Like Britain, however, France makes choices largely through a consensual process, in which professional specialists have weight and for which metaphors of "stream" and "momentum" are apt, but punctuated by selected ministerial initiatives.

This system turns strongly on the central role of the President in

---

weak' . . .

"A third group advocates the maintenance of a strictly sufficient minimum deterrent . . . This group calls for deep cuts and a reconfiguration of the French arsenal. . . President Mitterrand seems inclined toward this position with its use of the phrase 'strict sufficiency' in the new *Projet de Loi*."

the Fifth Republic, instituted under de Gaulle's guidance in 1958.

When test resumption was suddenly placed on the table by China's 5 October 1993 test Defense Minister Léotard insisted that the issue would be dealt with broadly, with the implication that there would be wide internal consultation. "This decision will be taken in coming months by the whole French executive," Léotard said. "It is not tomorrow, nor the day after. We have a deterrent capacity that is not threatened by the testing halt."[44]

The Ministry's internal organization reflects the usual requirements of discussion and policy formulation which mark all hierarchic bureaucratic bodies. The Minister of Defense presides, the prime point of contact with the broader government and politics.

Arms policy and conventional military procurement is organized in the Délégation Générale pour l'Armement (DGA) of the Ministry of Defense. Nuclear warhead procurement, however, lies with the Direction des Applications Militaire (DAM) of the Commissariat à l'Energie Atomique (CEA). CEA also oversees civil nuclear power. The Délégue who heads the DGA is a key figure, with great authority, and sits as well on the board of the CEA.

Longer-term reflection on policy within the Ministry of Defense is lodged in the Délégation aux Affaires Stratégiques, which includes military officers, engineers from DGA, and analysts borrowed from civilian research centers.

The President's constitutional authority in defense matters is exercised through the Conseil de Défense, which he chairs, and which consists of the Prime Minister and key ministers, the military heads of services, and three senior advisers.[45] Its deliberations are secret.

---

44. Reuters, 6 October 1993.

45. François Nectoux (drawing on work of David Schorr), "France," in Scilla McLean (ed), *How Nuclear Weapons Decisions are Made* (London: MacMillan, 1986), pp. 154-185, pp. 177-178. The ministers (1986) are those of Defense, Foreign Relations, Economy and Finances, Research and Industry and the Interior. The senior advisers are the Secrétaire Générale de la Défense Nationale (SGDN), Secrétaire Générale de l'Elysée, and the Chef de l'Etat-Major Particulier.

The Military

The military is intimately participant in formation of strategic policy. As noted above, the service chiefs take part in the Conseil de Défense, where they have access to the President.

The Etat-Major Particulier, ranking military officers, are the military with most frequent contact with the President. They oversee creation of the daily "engagement codes" by which the President would order nuclear weapons used.[46]

A distinctive feature of the French system is that procurement—the realm of the DGA—is in the hands not of military officers but of graduates of the Ecole Polytechnique further specialized in armament. François Nectoux, describing this system, explains that

> Most of the administrators and engineers at CEA's Direction des Applications Militaires, and practically all of them at the Ministry of Defence's DGA are not only graduates of Polytechnique but have gone on to become Ingénieurs Généraux de l'Armement (IGA's).
>
> This phenomenon helps to explain some of the weaknesses of the armed forces within the defence community. Outside the Etats-Majors, most of the key positions are held by IGAs, not by soldiers—and high ranking officers are often bitter about this.[47]

The Nuclear Weapons Establishment

The central organ in the French nuclear system is the Commissariat à l'Énergie Atomique (CEA), created by decree of 18 October 1945.

Although CEA's mandate extended from the outset to military applications, France only committed to accelerated production of the bomb at a cabinet meeting conducted by Prime Minister Pierre Mendès-France on 26 December 1954. Two days later General Albert Buchalet became head of a Bureau d'Etudes Générales within the CEA, subsequently the Département des Techniques Nouvelles (May 1956) and present-day Direction des Applications Militaires (DAM)

---

46. *Ibid.*, p. 180.
47. Nectoux, above, p. 157.

(12 September 1958).[48] DAM has "exclusive responsibility for the research, development, testing and production of French nuclear warheads."[49] In 1993 the Director was Roger Baléras.

DAM's work is distributed among six Centre d'Etudes: Centre d'Etudes de Limeil-Valenton (warhead design), Centre d'Etudes de Valduc (warhead production and dismantlement waste), Centre d'Etudes de Ripault (detonators and stockpile maintenance), Centre d'Etudes Scientifiques et Techniques d'Aquitaine (militarization of nuclear warheads), Centre d'Etudes de Bruyères-le-Châtel (metallurgy, chemistry, seismology, analysis of nuclear explosions), and Centre d'Etudes de Vaujours-Moronvilliers (high-pressure shock wave studies).[50] In 1994 DAM employed 5784 persons, a third of CEA staff, and defense constituted 42.1 percent of the CEA budget.[51]

CEA produces all required fissile material, and the materials tritium, deuterium and lithium used in fusion weapons. A CEA subsidiary, the Compagnie Générale des Matières Nucléaires (COGEMA), was created on 19 January 1976 to conduct all aspects of nuclear materials production.[52]

France found uranium ore in metropolitan France in November 1948, and also obtained uranium in Madagascar, Niger, and Canada. France's first plutonium-producing reactor (G1) went critical on 7 January 1956. According to the CEA Administrator-General, France ceased plutonium production in 1992.[53] However, on 3 August 1994 France approved restarting the Superphénix fast-breeder reactor, designed as a plutonium source, but idled four years previously for repairs.[54]

---

48. Norris et al., p. 183.

49. *Ibid.*, p. 197.

50. *Ibid.*, pp. 199-200.

51. Jean-Paul Hébert, *Production d'armement: Mutation du système français* (Paris: Documentation française, 1995).

52. Through the group CEA-Industrie CEA has 89.16% control (1994) of COGEMA. Jean-Paul Hébert, *Production d'armement*, above.

53. Norris et al., *ibid.*, pp. 202-203.

54. *International Herald Tribune*, 4 August 1994. Restarting was initially confined to strictly limited purposes.

TABLE 7.4

France: Sources of Nuclear Weapons Components

Nuclear warheads [a]	
Uranium^{235}	COGEMA
Plutonium^{239}	COGEMA
Design	CEA/DAM
Fabrication	CEA/DAM
Platform: Triomphant-*Class SNLE (SSBN)*	
Submarine Hull and Integration DCAN Cherbourg	DCN
Reactors	Market
Turbines	Market
Electronics	Market
Refit capabilities	DCN
Delivery Systems: Submarine-Borne Missiles	
Missiles	Market
Missile guidance system	Market
Reentry vehicles	Market
Delivery Systems: Stand-off Missile	
ASMP Stand-off missile	Market
Platform: Aircraft: Super Etendard	
Airframe	Market
Engines	Market
Avionics	Market
Navigation System	Market
Nuclear capability: ASMP	
Platform: Aircraft Carrier Charles de Gaulle	
Hull and Integration DCAN Brest	DCN
Reactors	Market/CEA
Propulsion	Market
Radars	Market

TABLE 7.5

France: Industrial Providers by Weapons Platform

Platform: SNLE (SSBN) Triomphant-*class*	
Reactors	Technicatome
Electronics	
Sonar	Thomson Sintra
Delivery Systems: Submarine-Borne Missiles	
Missiles	Aérospatiale
Guidance system	SAGEM
Delivery Systems: ASMP Stand-Off Missile	
Missile	Aérospatiale
Propulsion	ONERA, SNPE
Inertial guidance	SAGEM
Guidance computer	ESD, SAGEM
Platform: Aircraft: Super Etendard	
Airframe	Dassault
Engines	SNECMA
Avionics	SFENA
Radar	Dassault Electronique
	Thomson CSF
Navigation System	SAGEM
Platform: Aircraft: Mirage 2000N	
Airframe	Dassault
Engines	SNECMA
Radar	Dassault Electronique
	Thomson/CSF
Inertial guidance	SAGEM
	ESD-SAGEM
Platform: Aircraft Carrier Charles de Gaulle	
Reactors	Technicatome
	CEA
Propulsion	ECAN
Radars	Thomson-CSF

Source: Norris et al.

The procurement structure is shown in tables 7.4 and 7.5. French procurement invites several further observations:

1. The government-owned shipyards at Ile Longue (Brest) and Cherbourg depend on ongoing naval construction programs.[55]
2. The aircraft serving as nuclear platforms are models of warplanes which, in other configurations, have been sold abroad in significant numbers. (Table 7.6)
3. Arms—including non-nuclear systems and exports—are important contributors to the sales of these firms. Consider the largest French arms manufacturers (including state-run DCN), whose 1989 arms sales total about US $17 billion. (Table 7.7).
4. What portion of their sales is attributable to nuclear systems? Absent a comprehensive set of accounts, we can compare aggregate program estimates for key programs to get some sense of the scale. (Compare the 1989 French defense budget allocation to Title V (capital expenses) of FFr 53.8 billion.[56])

TABLE 7.6

France: Nuclear-Capable Aircraft

AIRCRAFT	TOTAL	TOTAL FRENCH	FRENCH NUCLEAR-CAPABLE[a]	TOTAL FOR EXPORT
Super Etendard	85	71	20 (+)	14
Mirage-2000	334	205	165[b]	129

a The number deployed in the early 1990s. as nuclear-armed aircraft. More units were deployed to carry nuclear weapons in the 1980s.

b Includes 75 2000N and 90 dual-capable 2000D. Norris et al. report 42 2000N aircraft deployed with an ASMP.

Source: GRIP. *Memento défense-désarmement 1992*, p. 288; Norris et al., pp. 283-284 and 320-321.

---

55. A new yard was built at the Cherbourg naval dockyard to build the *Triomphant*-class SSBNs. Norris et al., p. 258.

56. Jean-Paul Hébert, *Stratégie Française & Industrie d'Armement* (Paris: FEDN, 1991), p. 126, citing M. Blin, Sénat, doc. n° 88, tome III, annexe 45, 21 November 1988. Hébert also lists the eight nuclear forces projected for the future by the Loi de la Programmation Militaire for 1987-91 (Missiles M5, M4, S4, missile refit of M4, the SNLE, 68 Mirage 2000N, Hadès missile (now dropped) and 90 ASMP) at a total cost of FFr 272.9 billion (US$47.7 billion). *Ibid*, p. 27.

TABLE 7.7
France: Arms Sales as Proportion of All Sales
Selected Firms

FIRM	SECTORS	ARMS SALES 1989	1989 (MILLION US$)	%
Thomson SA	Elec Miss	4 320	12 027	36
Thomson-CSF	Elec Miss	4 120	5 282	78
DCN	Ships	3 630	3 626	100
Dassault-Breguet	Aircraft	2 200	3 059	72
Electronique Serge-Dassault	Electronics	0 500	0 645	78
Aérospatiale	Airc Miss	2 190	4 969	44
CEA Industrie		1 820	5 254	35
SNECMA Group	Engines	1 260	3 371	37
SNECMA	Engines	0 530	2 108	25
GIAT	Land	1 020	1 056	97
Matra Group	Miss Other	0 870	3 462	25
Matra Défense	Electronics	0 710	0 710	100
SAGEM Group	Electronics	0 410	1 628	25

Source: GRIP. *Memento défense-désarmement 1992*, pp. 232-233.

TABLE 7.8
France: Cost of Selected Nuclear Systems

PROGRAM	COVERAGE	COSTS (BILLION US$)
Triomphant SSBN	Four boats (excl. missiles)	13.1
MSBS M5 SLBM	Three sets: 3 * 16	7.7
ASMP	For completed program of 90	1.4
Rafale	281 aircraft, of which "possibly" only 60 will be nuclear-armed	32.47
	(Unit cost, including R & D:)	~ 0.1

Source: Norris et al., passim. A nominal conversion rate of FFr 5.1725 = US$1 was applied where no conversion was given.

> Bearing in mind that these programs are carried on over many years, we can nonetheless speak of the current SSBN(SNLE)/SLBM building program as the equivalent of about a year's arms sales of France's leading arms firms. The nuclear-attributable costs of the Rafale aircraft, the next generation air platform, will be the equivalent of perhaps five months' sales.

Relations between government and industry are intimate. Vincent Lanata, two months after retiring as French air force chief of staff, moved with the consent of the Ministry of Defense to join Aérospatiale, to coordinate its program for the next-generation transport aircraft.[57]

Civil Society

Anti-nuclear activism has been slight. There was no French equivalent of the "Freeze Movement" in the United States and, of course, no plan to deploy US Pershing IIs or Ground-Launched Cruise Missiles in France. However, when France announced a resumption of nuclear testing in June 1995, it occasioned a street march which drew several thousand demonstrators.[58]

Greenpeace maintains a serious presence which nettles the nuclear establishment and the Navy—the *Rainbow Warrior* is not forgotten—but it is not broad-based. However, shortly before Chirac announced France's test resumption, another *Rainbow Warrior* was clearing Auckland harbor bound for Mururoa, and in the process paying tribute to the photographer killed when French agents blew up the *Rainbow Warrior* in 1985.[59]

When, in the early 1980s, the US Conference of Catholic Bishops voted to acknowledge nuclear deterrence only as a most temporary waystation to abolition, their French counterparts stressed the necessity to arm in order to block evil.

No doubt sharp cuts in nuclear programs, if not compensated by

---

57. *Le Figaro*, 3-4 September 1994.

58. AP put the marchers at "as many as 10,000." 20 June 1995.

59. Reuters, 13 June 1995.

other military spending, would have serious economic consequences. These would fall heavily in Brittany, where naval construction is concentrated. However, substantial program cuts, introduced gradually, have not provoked serious challenge to government.

If both advocacy and opposition are "flat" in France by comparison to other countries, that is quite consistent with the reports of opinion polls.

Public Opinion

How does the French public judge France's nuclear forces? And how is that judgment distributed by party affiliation? The French polling organization SOFRES conducted a poll in May 1993 for the French military. Asked if the nuclear force should be reinforced, "modernized," kept as is, or reduced, 44 percent of respondents said it should be reinforced or "modernized," and only 20 percent that reductions should be begun:

TABLE 7.9
France: What Future For French Nuclear Forces?

Nuclear Forces	Reinforce	"Modernize"	Maintain *status quo*	Begin Reduction	No Opinion
All French	5	39	30	20	6

Support for reduction came more strongly from those under 34, while those with a memory of World War II were the strongest advocates of "modernization", as shown in table 7.10.

Finally, although as one might expect those favoring reduction identified more with the Left, while a majority of those identifying with the parties of the resurgent Center-Right coalition (UDF and RPR) favored "modernization," there was some support for reduction on the Right and substantially more support for reinforcement and "modernization" on the Left:[60]

60. SOFRES. *L'état de l'opinion 1994*. (Paris: Éditions du Seuil, 1994), p. 109.

TABLE 7.10
France: What Future? By Age Groups

By Age	Reinforce	"Modernize"	Maintain *status quo*	Begin Reduction	No Opinion
18-24	5	29	34	28	4
25-34	5	33	31	27	4
35-49	4	40	32	19	5
50-64	4	45	29	14	8
65 - +	4	49	25	12	10

TABLE 7.11
France: What Future? By Declared Party Preference

By Party Prefer-ence	Reinforce	"Modernize"	Maintain *status quo*	Begin Reduction	No Opinion
PC	10	19	24	32	15
PS	2	30	36	28	4
GE	3	26	33	36	2
Verts	3	12	47	25	13
UDF	5	51	25	16	3
RPR	4	57	26	10	3
FN	19	42	21	13	5

Notes: PC: Parti Communiste. PS: Parti Socialiste. GE: Génération Ecologie. Verts: Verts-Ecologie. UDF: Union pour la Démocratie Française. RPR: Rassemblement pour la République. FN: Front National.

SOFRES reports several other illustrative results. Were a French ally, such as Germany, invaded would that justify putting life at risk? Forty-six per cent agreed it would.[61] Asked if they would say of themselves that they were "anti-militarist" 61 percent replied "not at all"

61. *Ibid.*, p. 111.

and only 14 percent either "completely" or "very" anti-militarist.[62]

A separate poll among 16 to 24 year-olds asked them to describe themselves as "close to" or "distant from" the various political parties: only the two ecological parties could muster more than a quarter "close," and more than half reported themselves "far" from all other groupings.[63]

The left—and especially the governing Parti Socialiste—lost massively in the parliamentary elections of March 1993. Only a handful of PS deputies survived. In canvassing possible reasons for such a sweeping defeat, SOFRES considered the possibility that the PS's abandonment of traditional socialist positions had contributed to its losses. Was it reproached for its "realism"?

In nuclear weapons matters, very little. Only 5 percent of respondents, and 7 percent of those who identified themselves as close to the Left, identified with the criticism of the PS that it had maintained French nuclear forces.[64]

A reasonable reading of these figures is that there is no strong public support, from any major segment, for France's giving up nuclear weapons. On the other hand, there is a discernible generational difference, younger people being readier to reduce, and least ready to enhance, nuclear forces, and distanced from all parties, Left and Right, which have joined in the governing consensus.

Europe

Are French and British nuclear weapons also European weapons? And if they are, who will decide whether to maintain, withdraw, store, or abandon those systems? The obvious starting-point is that Britain and France both insist their nuclear capabilities are and will remain

62. *Ibid.*, p. 114.

63. *Ibid.*, p. 167. This poll was taken 25-27 January 1993, about two months before the March 1993 election. Many observers thought Génération Ecologie and Les Verts would poll well, perhaps (taken together) nearly 20 percent. Between late 1992 and the election the two self-destructed. Even with that in mind, however, the party preference figures of the 16-24 year-olds are striking. Only 24 percent termed themselves "close" to the socialists. They were "far" from the communists (73 percent), socialists (59 percent), UDF (64 percent), RPR (63 percent) and the right-wing National Front (67 percent).

64. *Ibid.*, pp. 78-79.

under national control. There would be no issue, except for the fact that Britain has pledged its strategic nuclear forces to a largely-European alliance—subject, it is always necessary to note, to their withdrawal if Britain chose to do so—and that both Britain and France are committed to the European Union and the Maastricht Treaty's anticipation of a common foreign and security policy. Can you have a common European security policy which leaves use or non-use of nuclear weapons in the hands of Britain and—separately—France?

Central Politics

The European Community was reborn on 1 January 1994 as the European Union. It is governed by a Council of Ministers representing states, a Commission of one or two Commissioners from each state which acts as a kind of cabinet to the President of the European Commission, and the European Parliament—granted greater powers by the Maastricht Treaty but hitherto sharply limited—of Members chosen in popular elections. The elected members typically ran as party candidates in their home states. On arrival at Parliament in Strasbourg, they adhere to groupings, which then act as parties. After the elections of 1994 the largest group in Strasbourg was the Socialist group, which chose as its leader a Labour Party MEP from Britain.

Central Governance

There is no European "defense ministry" and no "defense minister." The defense component of the European Union is provided by the Western European Union (WEU), distinct from NATO but recognized by NATO as its "European pillar." The EU Maastricht Treaty envisions a "common foreign and security policy" for the EU, but just what that may prove to be, or even how it would be arrived at, is only beginning to be seriously addressed.[65] The concept now being

65. In this vein the communiqué of the Ministerial Meeting of the North Atlantic Council, NATO's governing body, issued 1 December 1994 welcomed "endorsement by the WEU Council of Ministers in Noordwijk of preliminary conclusions on the formulation of the common European Defence Policy" and "the WEU's decision to initiate reflection on the new European security conditions, including the proposal put forward by France that this should lead to a white paper on European security." *NATO Review*, vol. 42 no. 6 December

considered to manage the dual existence of NATO and WEU for conventional operations would provide "separable but not separate military capabilities that could be employed by NATO or the WEU."[66]

In practice, NATO—through the nuclear force contributions of the United States and Britain, and despite France's non-participation in NATO's integrated military command—has been the central forum of West European nuclear planning. NATO is governed by the North Atlantic Council, typically through a gathering of foreign ministers in Ministerial Session. The defense ministers also meet. Nuclear decisions are the province of the NATO Nuclear Planning Group, which considers force proposals from its sub-committee designated the "High Level Group." Communiqués are issued after meetings of the Nuclear Planning Group, but "activities of the High-Level Group are unpublicised and no communiqués of its meetings have ever appeared."[67] In addition, in 1994 NATO created a Joint Committee on Proliferation and two expert groups, a Senior Politico-Military Group on Proliferation and a Senior Defence Group on Proliferation, charged to consider "means available to prevent and respond where necessary to proliferation" of weapons of mass destruction.[68] NATO supports arms control initiatives in language consonant with the declared

---

1994/ no. 1 January 1995, pp. 26-28, § 14. NATO Secretary General Willy Claes called for "the closest cooperation between NATO and the WEU, on the basis of complementarity, transparency and no duplication of military structures . . . A strong European pillar will enable our European Allies to take greater responsibility for their common security and defence." *Ibid*., p. 7.

66. Communiqué, above, § 15.

67. Scilla McLean, "Britain," in Scilla McLean (ed), *How Nuclear Weapons Decisions are Made* (London: Macmillan, 1986), pp. 142-143. McLean states that the "High-Level Group" consists of senior defence ministry personnel, chaired by the US Assistant Secretary of Defence for International Security Affairs. Britain is represented by the Deputy Under-Secretary of the Ministry of Defence in charge of Plans and Policy.

    The NATO Secretary General is Chairman of the Nuclear Planning Group. It functions under a Nuclear Planning Directorate which, according to a 13 April 1994 NATO explanation, "is responsible for coordination of work on the development of NATO defence policy in the nuclear field and the work of the Nuclear Planning Group." The Director of Nuclear Planning is Chairman of the NPG Staff Group.

68. Communiqué, above, § 17.

policies of Britain, France and the United States.[69]

The Military

The EU member states' militaries exist as autonomous forces, through which defense of EU states could be promptly undertaken in case of need.

European states are, however, represented in four security organizations: United Nations (UN), North Atlantic Treaty Organization (NATO), West European Union (WEU), and the Conference on Security and Cooperation in Europe (CSCE). Each of these bodies has some bearing on options available to European states.

NATO predates the EC/EU; it includes Canada and the United States, not EC/EU members, and military forces under its aegis are commanded by a US general officer. Not all EU members are in NATO: Ireland and the three who joined the EU on 1 January 1995—Sweden, Finland, and Austria—have remained apart from military blocs. Although NATO has coordinated conventional defense preparations, it is distinguished by explicitly concerning itself with nuclear weapons deployment and prospective use. British and US nuclear weapons have been, and some remain, allocated to NATO. France has not taken part in the integrated military command of NATO since 1966.

France prefers the West European Union as frame for military cooperation, a preference stiffly resisted by Britain. WEU does not include the United States. The touchy problem of just which forces would "march" in case of attack, and under which jurisdiction, has been side-stepped by national policies which suggest that at the moment of danger units would be "at the disposal" of both NATO and WEU. WEU also has an Assembly with parliament-like features.

---

69. Most recently, see Communiqué, above, §§ 17-18: "We remain fully committed to the indefinite and unconditional extension of the Treaty on the Non-Proliferation of Nuclear Weapons (NPT) . . . We attach great importance to the negotiation of a universal and verifiable Comprehensive Test Ban Treaty. It is also important to achieve a universal ban on the production of fissile material for weapons purposes. Ws continue to consider as essential tasks the early entry into force of the Chemical Weapons Convention and the elaboration of measures to strengthen the Biological Weapons Convention . . ."

The CSCE—through which the Treaty on Conventional Forces in Europe was negotiated—has set limits on permissible non-nuclear forces in designated categories, including personnel, tanks, and aircraft. Out of the CFE Treaty and related negotiations a fabric of observation and notice is being developed. CSCE has weak means to act politically in case of threats to the peace, but no authority to gather or command military forces.

Public Opinion

The narrow margin by which the Maastricht Treaty was voted in 1993—in France a fraction of a percent carried approval—had not been envisioned a year earlier when the locomotive toward Union appeared to be on track. In the run-up to key national referenda stress was on "subsidiarity": in effect, keeping local control of local matters. In some countries, then, very large minorities of those voting expressed skepticism about the European project.

Nuclear weapons were not a significant issue in French domestic discussion prior to the vote, which hinged much more on economic expectations. Britain did not put the issue to referendum.

In Summary

No doubt Britain views NATO as an instrument to keep the United States engaged in Europe and—because of the special US-UK ties—so enhance Britain's role. In a Europe-only Europe Germany and France would have much greater sway. France did not—it is important to recall—leave NATO when it gave up taking part in the integrated military command. Its leadership continues to express adherence to the principles of autonomy which dictated its "departure." Commenting on Minister of Defense François Léotard's attending the NATO Defence Minister's meeting in September 1994, the first time France had been represented since 1966, *Le Monde* insisted that French policy remained as before: Mitterrand and Balladur were agreed that French forces were not to be reintegrated into the "*automatismes*" which characterized the NATO command.[70] But *Le*

70. *Le Monde*, 6 September 1994.

Monde also noted that it is taken for granted French troops in the Eurocorps—the cooperative venture of France, Germany, Belgium and Spain—would be at the disposal of NATO if required.

France has throughout explained its nuclear forces as a national project, though it toyed with tactical weapons which one imagines could have been used, to defend Germany, on German soil. Britain, however, has ventured "European" explanations to justify the force. It confronted Moscow with a "second centre of decision-making," should the Russians have concluded the United States would not risk for Europe. It was a contribution to NATO. These explanations seem strained, nor is it clear that the non-nuclear members of NATO have urged Britain—or France—to protect them with nuclear weapons.[71]

China

China's central governance proceeds through two parallel hierarchic structures, one Party, the other Government. Key decisions emanate from the Chinese Communist Party. Government is subordinate. What "politics" there is takes place within party, state, and military structures. It is doubtless intense. It is also, for the most part, secret.

Central Politics

In the fifteen years since Deng Xiaoping emerged from post-Mao political maneuvers to become the preeminent Party figure, he has stamped China with "economic reform," rapid modernization of industry and communication, military modernization, "market socialism," and political and economic relations far and wide, but also with continued Party ascendance and the profound repression symbolized by 3-4 June 1989 ("Tiananmen").

The central term of Party politics is negotiation between the Center and its constituencies, in which the Center's designation of high officials, and the constituencies' representations to the Center, proceed within the limits imposed by their mutual dependence. Some constituencies are organizational, some provincial, and some

---

71. Similar arguments are made by Robert Neild, *How to Make Up Your Mind About the Bomb* (London: Andre Deutsch, 1981), pp. 98-99, relying with approval on Lawrence Freedman, *Britain and Nuclear Weapons*, p. 140 ff.

functional; and among the functional constituencies, the People's Liberation Army (PLA) has usually been well-represented at the Party Center.

Formally, the analog of the Cabinets elsewhere is the State Council, the principal organ of executive government presided over by a prime minister. Li Peng has been prime minister since 1988. But it is in the Party structure that the core of governance can be found: a Political Bureau elected by the Central Committee, and the Central Committee in turn elected—once in five years—by the National Party Congress. These elections proceed by ballot, which may be secret, but selection of the 2000-odd members of the National Party Congress is itself the result of political negotiations, carefully prepared.

Central Governance

Just as Britain, for example, places key defense decisions in the hands of a small committee of the Cabinet, to which a designated council of senior defense officials reports, so it is understood that China's nuclear program has been governed by a group of senior officials, including Political Bureau members, to which the Central Military Commission reports.

From 1962 the program was overseen for some years by the Special Central Commission (also cited as the Fifteen-Member Special Commission), whose chairman was Prime Minister Zhou Enlai.[72]

The Central Military Commission may now be the final authority to supervise the nuclear program and exercise launch decision. Lewis and Xue conclude that "Only the chairman of the [Central Military] commission has the authority to commit China to nuclear war."[73] Deng Xiaoping became its chairman in June 1981. Its chair now (June 1995) is Jiang Zemin, who heads the Chinese Communist Party as its General Secretary. The Central Military Commission had been a *party*

72. The Commission was created by the Political Bureau on 17 November 1962, and given the name Central Special Commission in March 1965. Lewis and Xue, *China's Strategic Seapower*, p. 79. Zhou Enlai died in January 1976.

73. John W. Lewis and Xue Litai, *China's Strategic Seapower* (Stanford: Stanford University Press, 1994), p. 125, citing Guo Qingsheng, "China Has a Nuclear Counterattack Capability—A Visit to China's Strategic Missile Units," *Liaowang*, April 22, 1985, p. 24.

organ. In June 1983, however, a *government* organ by the same name and with identical membership was established by the National People's Congress.[74]

Leading military figures have often been among those elected to the party's Political Bureau by the CCP Central Committee. But of the four active-duty full generals in 1993, only one (Liu Huaqing) sat on the CCP Political Bureau. According to *Cheng Ming*, in July 1993 Jiang Zemin promoted six generals to the topmost rank. Then—with approval of the CCP Central Committee—he provided that they would be entitled to sit in meetings of the Political Bureau, as non-voting members. Two other full generals would also do so. Of the ten, four were not members of the Central Military Commission: henceforth they would attend its meetings. One vice-chairman of the Central Military Commission (Liu Huaqing) was already a member of the Political Bureau and its seven-member Standing Committee. The other vice-chairman (Zhang Zhen) would henceforth attend the Standing Committee without vote.[75] These steps set in place a ten-

74. *China Directory 1985* (Tokyo: Radiopress, 1985), p. 162. Kenneth Lieberthal explains that the PLA "does not answer to the government," but to the Party, and that "the government Military Affairs Commission is a hollow shell." *Governing China* (New York: Norton, 1995), p. 205.

75. *Cheng Ming* (Hong Kong), 1 September 1993, pp. 12-13, translated in FBIS-CHI-93-171, pp. 46-48. On ranks, see also *China Directory 1994* (Tokyo: Radiopress, October 1993).

The ten full generals, duties, and memberships (• indicates a new entitlement):

FOUR ORIGINAL ACTIVE-DUTY GENERALS	POST	POLITICAL BUREAU	CENTRAL MILITARY COMMISSION
Liu Huaqing	Vice-Chairman, CMC	Member and Member, Standing Committee	Vice-Chairman
Zhang Zhen	Vice-Chairman, CMC	• attend, and attend Standing Committee	Vice-Chairman
Chi Haotian	Minister of National Defense	• attend	Member
Zhao Nanqi	Commandant, Academy of Military Science		• attend

member military leadership in proximity to the Party center. In another move to bridge civil and military, Jiang reportedly announced that Zou Jiahua, a deputy premier charged with national defense, would attend both the Political Bureau and the Central Military Commission.[76]

A further echelon of organs has been created by the Central Military Commission to guide and advise on design and production of nuclear weapons and delivery systems. These bodies, shown in table 7.12, have been successively reorganized, in part in response to program requirements, and certainly as a reflection of internal political contests. In its current form, as the Committee of Science, Technology and Industry for National Defence, it has since 1982 presided over military reforms marked by adoption of new weapons technology and an emphasis on enhanced technological skills.[77]

• SIX NEWLY-PROMOTED ACTIVE DUTY GENERALS	POST	POLITICAL BUREAU	CENTRAL MILITARY COMMISSION
Zhang Wannian	Chief of the General Staff	• attend	Member
Yu Yongbo	Director, PLA General Political Department	• attend	Member
Fu Quanyou	Director, PLA General Logistics Department	• attend	Member
Zhu Dunfa	Commandant, PLA National Defense University	• attend	• attend
Zhang Lianzhong	Commander, PLA Navy	• attend	• attend
Cao Shuangming	Commander, PLA Air Force	• attend	• attend

76. *Ibid.*

77. See Lewis and Xue, *China's Strategic Seapower* and *China Builds the Bomb*, for data in table 7.12 and many other details about these organizations, their charters, and contention for authority.

TABLE 7.12

China: Successive Entities Coordinating Defense Science and Technology

FOUNDED	NAME	KEY FIGURES TERMINATION
1958 October	DSTC Defense Science and Technology Commission	Nie Rongzhen On 29 July 1982 merged into COSTIND.
1959 December	NDIC National Defense Industrial Commission	He Long In September 1963, merged into NDIO.
1961 November	NDIO National Defense Industry Organization	Luo Ruiqing Restored in September 1973, replacing the Leading Group. On 29 July 1982 merged into COSTIND.
1969 December	National Defense Industry Leading Group	Qiu Huizuo "Replaced the long-defunct NDIO." In turn, replaced by restored NDIO in September 1973.
1982 July	COSTIND Committee of Science, Technology and Industry for National Defense	Chen Bin

The Military

The People's Liberation Army manufactures the aircraft and missiles with which China's nuclear weapons would be delivered and deploys and operates delivery systems. (The navy is a part of the

PLA.)

The military unit responsible for land-based nuclear systems is the Second Artillery Corps. In 1993 it was commanded by Lt. General Yang Guoliang, one of 189 members of the CCP Central Committee.[78]

Lewis and Xue identify a Nuclear Submarine Flotilla (1975) and later a Nuclear Submarine Corps created to command SSBN operations, and initially headed by the first captain of China's first SSBN (401), Yang Xi.[79] They describe a base near Qingdao comprising multiple shelters, offering partial protection against nuclear attack, from which China's SSBNs operate.[80]

The Nuclear Weapons Establishment

The Chinese structure is not as well-delineated as those of Britain and France. Oversight and direction proceed from the Party center to the Central Military Commission. In turn it is dependent on the People's Liberation Army for requirements definition and the Commission on Science, Technology and Industry for National Defense (COSTIND), which "supervises weapons research and development and coordinates the military with the civilian sectors of the economy."[81]

The CMC and COSTIND direct the actual work. Norris et al. have not identified which entity does serial production of warheads. Laboratory and testing tasks are located in the Chinese Academy of Engineering Physics ("Ninth Academy").

The Chinese bomb program was undertaken by decision of a meeting on 15 January 1955.[82] Organization took on more tasks, and grew more complex, with time. In 1956 the work was lodged under a Third Ministry of Machine Building, renamed the Second Ministry in 1958. Its main sections are identified in table 7.13. The centrally-

---

78. *China Directory 1994*, above, p. 213.
79. John W. Lewis and Xue Litai, *China's Strategic Seapower* (Stanford: Stanford University Press, 1994), p. 125.
80. *Ibid.*, pp. 123-124.
81. Norris et al., p. 342.
82. *Ibid.*, p. 331.

important Ninth Academy continues today under the name Chinese Academy of Engineering Physics.[83] Weapons testing took place at the Lop Nor test site, instituted on 16 October 1959.

TABLE 7.13

China: Components of the Second Ministry of Machine Building

Ninth Bureau (Nuclear Weapons Bureau)[a].

(i) Beijing Nuclear Weapons Research Institute

(ii) Northwest Nuclear Weapons Research and Design Academy (Ninth Academy)[b]

(iii) Nuclear Component Manufacturing Plant

Fuels Production Bureau. Produced fission and fusion materials.

(i) Gaseous Diffusion Plant (Lanzhou)

(ii) Nuclear Fuel Processing Plant (Jiuquan, Subei Xian, Gansu)

(iii) Nuclear Fuel Component Plant (Baotou)

Construction Bureau.

a Li Jue headed both the Ninth Bureau and the Ninth Academy.

b The Ninth Academy opened in 1963. Before it was ready, design work was done at the Beijing Nuclear Weapons Research Institute.

"San Xian" (Third Line) inland production capabilities were created in large measure as a hedge against industry's vulnerability to attack, concentrated as it was close to the Soviet Union and the coast. On economic criteria, constructing San Xian plant and infrastructure was a massive waste, diverting desperately-needed investment to military purposes in remote sites where building was difficult. Nonetheless, it provided an opportunity for the nuclear program to build more advanced production capabilities, such as those identified in Table 7.14.

83. The Director of the Chinese Academy of Engineering Physics until 20 January 1994 was Hu Renyu. He was followed on that date by the previous Deputy Director, Hu Side.

TABLE 7.14

China: "San Xian" Uranium and Plutonium Processing Systems

Plutonium production capability. Two main components:

(i) Pu production reactor and chemical separation plant (Guangyuan, Sichuan)

(ii) nuclear fuel component plant (Yibin, Sichuan)

Uranium concentration capability (about 1975):

(i) gaseous diffusion plant (Heping (Jinkouhe), Sichuan)

TABLE 7.15

China: Ministry Sources of Delivery Systems

SUBJECT	MINISTRIES OF MACHINE BUILDING	AFTER 1981-82 CHANGES
Aircraft	Third	Ministry of Aviation Industry
Electronics	Fourth	Ministry of Electronics Industry
Munitions and armaments	Fifth	Ministry of Ordnance Industry
Naval construction	Sixth	China State Shipbuilding Corporation
Ballistic missiles	Seventh	Ministry of Space Industry
Space systems	Eighth	(Merged into Ministry of Space Industry in 1981)

Source: Adapted from David L. Shambaugh, "China's Defense Industries," in Paul H. B. Godwin ed., *The Chinese Defense Establishment: continuity and Change in the 1980s* (Boulder: Westview, 1983), p. 54.

Industry

State organs do all Chinese design and procurement. Much of the governmental structure overseen by the State Council consists of ministries in industry, agriculture and transport. Economic reform of the 1980s is proceeding but very slowly among state firms which manufacture for the civil market. Although there appears to be pressure on all industrial units to find marketable products, the state's interest in defense industry probably ensures its retention under direct state control.

In late 1994 China announced, however, a dramatic shift of 300,000 persons from military nuclear to civil nuclear work, with the emphasis on electricity. A nuclear plant official said that

> Most of the nuclear factories are closed or have stopped operation. Military production has been reduced to the minimum on State orders, and development of nuclear electric power is our main task.[84]

He did not say whether these cuts would have any effect on weapons production, but he did say that "China will keep a task force of nuclear scientists and engineers as is commensurate with its status as a nuclear power."

In table 7.16, FPB designates the Fuels Production Bureau of the 2° Ministry of Machine Building. The table shows only the more modern delivery systems, though earlier systems remain deployed, and among the three SSBNs built or being built provides information for the first, SSBN 09-02:

TABLE 7.16

China: Industrial Providers of Warheads, Delivery Systems and Weapons Platforms

Nuclear warheads[a]	
Uranium 235	2° Ministry
FPB: Gaseous Diffusion Plant, Lanzhou, Xinjiang	
Plutonium 239	2° Ministry
FPB: Nuclear fuel Processing Plant, Jiuquan, Subei Xian, Gansu	
Design	2° Ministry
9° Bureau: 9° Academy (later Chinese Academy of Engineering Physics)	
Fabrication	2° Ministry
FPB: Nuclear Fuel Component Plant, Baotou	

84. UPI 25 September 1994, citing *China Daily*, which reported remarks of the China National Nuclear Corporation, Jiang Xinxiong.

Table 7.16 continued

Delivery Systems: Submarine-Borne Missile

Julang-1 (JL-1) Missile

1978: Seventh Ministry. First Academy.[b]

Final assembly: Plant 307 (Solid Rocket General Assembly Plant), Nanjing[c]

Missile design

Initial design: Ministry of National Defense. Fifth Academy (created October 1956). In January 1965 became the Seventh Ministry. From December 1978, the Seventh Ministry's Second Academy.[d]

Rocket engine

Seventh Ministry. Fourth Academy (Solid Rocket Motor Academy).[e]

Reentry vehicles

Various units of the Seventh Ministry and Academy of Sciences.[f]

Electronics

Fourth Ministry.[g]

Guidance and Flight Controls

Initial design: Seventh Ministry, Fourth Academy (Solid Rocket Motor Academy).[h]

Platform: Ballistic Missile Submarine (SSBN) 09-02

Submarine

Sixth Ministry.[i]

Reactors

Second Ministry.[j]

Delivery System: DF-5 ICBM

Missile

Wanyuan Industry Corporation[k]	Beijing

Boosters

Zhang Zhong Machinery Factory	Shanghai

Platform: Aircraft: Hong-7[l]

Airframe

Xian Aircraft Company	Xian

a Norris et al., passim.

b Lewis and Xue, *China's Strategic Seapower*, p. 163.

c *Ibid*., p. 184.

d	*Ibid*., pp. 130, 138, 183.
e	*Ibid*., pp. 138 ff.
f	*Ibid*., pp. 179-180.
g	*Ibid*., p. 162.
h	*Ibid*., p. 157.
i	*Ibid*., pp. 103 ff.
j	*Ibid*., p. 33.
k	Norris et al., p. 341. Also known as Capital Machinery Company.
l	Norris et al., p. 393.

Several similarities between the Chinese procurement system and those of other nuclear states are evident:

1. Like their British and French counterparts, Chinese aircraft and missile manufacturers build for export.

2. And like their Russian and American colleagues, Chinese nuclear weapons engineers and collateral production specialists are in quest of cognate projects in the civil sector.

Civil Society

The first Chinese nuclear protest known to us took place on 6 December 1985 in Urumqi, the principal city of Xinjiang. Agence France Presse reported that student demonstrators voiced several complaints—for example, of discrimination against Uighur students—and among them a call for an end to nuclear tests at Lop Nor. These protests reportedly stemmed from an inquiry into Lop Nor undertaken by students in the Department of Biology of the University of Xinjiang. Hundreds, perhaps thousands, are said to have been arrested after the 1985 demonstrations.[85] The Urumqi demonstrations echoed

85. Isabelle Maltor and Dongfang Ouyang, "Nouvelle donne régionale pour le Xinjiang," *Le Monde Diplomatique*, November 1993, p. 22. They cite an Amnesty International report of 13 November 1992, reported in *Le Monde* 17 November 1992. The 6 December demonstrations were briefly reported by Agence France Presse. Other nationalist, but not nuclear, protests have been reported. Robert Delfs, *Far Eastern Economic Review*, v 148 n 18, 30 May 1990, p. 10, cites a clash with protesters on 5-6 April in Kizilsu Kirghiz Autonomous Prefecture near Kashgar. Cited in Clement C. Yang, "China and the Central Asian Nightmare," *Journal of Contemporary China*, Spring 1994, pp. 88-95, p. 92.

among Xinjiang students in Beijing.[86] Further student protests against tests at Lop Nor are reported to have taken place in 1991, after an "incident."[87]

The crucial question for China is whether its nuclear program will proceed step by step, supported by sufficiently stable central authority and thus subject to that authority's control. Or will China be another Soviet Union, sundered into its component regions or provinces? Another Yugoslavia? Changes of such a degree would radically alter the context of China's nuclear weapons and raise critical control issues.

China differs from the Soviet Union in that there is a long history of central government and—for much of the population—a common (written) language. Roughly 93% of China's population is ethnic *Han*. Though not all Han speak "*guoyu*" (the "national language") as their native language, many reading characters in regional dialects, the written language is common and *guoyu* taught throughout.

Nuclear protest in China's far-west Xinjiang Province is part of larger anti-Han sentiment. There is limited evidence of a Uighur separatist movement and anecdotal evidence that Xinjiang's population chafes under rule from Beijing. Even if Beijing were not attentive to faraway test protests, it is ever alert to any sign of provincial or ethnic separatism. Xinjiang, China's "New Frontier," is home to several non-Han ethnic groups whose members share ethnicity and Islam with populations in the newly independent states of Uzbekistan, Turkmenistan, Kazakhstan and Kyrgyzstan.[88] Journalists report nationalist and anti-Chinese sentiment reaching the form of armed

86. Beijing students in 1985 weighed a show of numbers to call attention to economic complaints. The 1985 protests took place at the time of the 50th anniversary of the 1935 December 9th Movement. In 1935 students had challenged the Guomindang's apparent unreadiness to resist Japan and had given impetus to the nationalist role of the Chinese Communist Party.

Beijing students from Xinjiang were reported to have demonstrated in late December 1989. They met twice with Chinese leaders, but were said to have been "dissatisfied" with the result. *Cork Examiner*, 30 December 1985.

87. Maltor and Ouyang, above.

88. Visiting Central Asia in 1994, Li Peng did not visit Tajikistan. China claims a tract in Gorno-Badakhshan, part of Tajikistan. Reuter, 19 April 1994.

revolt.[89] What in Xinjiang might be a call for an end to discrimination against Uighurs becomes, when voiced in a nationalist context, a call to sunder Xinjiang from China.[90]

Chinese Premier Li Peng visited Uzbekistan, Turkmenistan, Kazakhstan and Kyrgyzstan in April 1994. A Uighur separatist movement has operated in Kazakhstan's capital. The position taken by his host in Kazakhstan, of course, stressed non-interference. A Kazakhstan environmental group, the Nevada-Semipalatinsk Movement, planned to protest, during Li Peng's visit to Kazakhstan, against Chinese nuclear testing in Xinjiang.[91] But Kazakhstan's Nazarbayev was not to be drawn into identification with Chinese separatism. Li Peng appreciated Nazarbayev's having said, at the time of Li Peng's visit to Kazakhstan, that Kazakhstan wouldn't allow the "East Turkestan" faction to act against China from Kazakhstan.[92]

When Li Peng reached Uzbekistan his policies in Xinjiang were acknowledged by the Uzbek leader, Islam Karimov, who said "we cannot overemphasize the role which China plays in this particular region in preventing separatist feelings and establishing peace and stability."[93] Non-Han separatism has a certain life of its own which, if

---

89. For example, Michel Jan, *Le Figaro*, 4 September 1994, citing an armed revolt at Baren, near Kashgar, in April 1990.

90. Reports identify at least two groups in Kazakhstan urging independence of Xinjiang ("Eastern Turkestan"). James Kunge quotes Kakharman Khojamberdi, president of a registered Inter-republic Uighur Association, as saying "Our main task is to protect the human rights of Uighurs and to bring about independence for Eastern Turkestan." Khojamberdi does not support violence in Xinjiang. But another does: Yusupbeg Mulisi, head of a United National Revolutionary Front for Eastern Turkestan, told Kunge that "In March we decided to use all possible means, including terrorism, to bring about a revolution in Xinjiang." Reuter, 17 April 1994.

    On reported demonstrations in twelve xian of Xinjiang Province on 8-12 November 1993, see *China Focus*, a publication of the Princeton China Initiative, vol. 2 no. 3, 1 March 1994, p. 3. They identify no nuclear demands, but cite demonstrators shouting "Xinjiang belongs to the Uighurs!"

91. Reuter, 17 April 1994. According to the reporter, a foreign environmental specialist in Kazakhstan said "radiation levels along the border were high because winds carry the fall-out from the blasts westward toward central Asia." But since 1981 China has tested underground.

92. *China Daily*, 27 April 1994.

93. Reuter, 19 April 1994.

China's center were fully preoccupied elsewhere, could lead one or a few provinces to break away.

There is ample evidence of political repression by Beijing in Tibet and every reason to believe that Tibetans would prize independence.

The other disintegration scenario has China's rich provinces declaring autonomy from their poorer cousins. Distinctive economic regions do exist around Guangzhou (Canton), and nearby Hong Kong, and around Shanghai. The entire eastern coast is distinguishable from much of the hinterland. Growth rates differ between provinces, because resource endowments differ and some can trade more easily than others.

A third disintegration scenario identifies the weak link at the Center and in the Chinese Communist Party itself. On this speculation, the present trend to decentralization and greater provincial initiative would continue, tipping the balance ever-more toward provinces and localities. Under attack for corruption and incapacity, the Party would find itself with fewer economic resources as well. Self-preservation would require that it devote what Party and State resources it controlled to internal organizational ends. And it could not neglect the People's Liberation Army, whose allegiance to the Center would be a critical determinant of continued Party authority.

Will any of this happen? The question is probably misstated. Much of this is happening, and it will become more accentuated, but it *need not* cripple the Center or lead to actual breakdown of the state *because there are powerful reasons for keeping a unified Chinese state*. Provided provinces and localities can carve significant effective autonomy—with freedom over major economic decisions and how they choose leadership and set main policy—it is useful for them to maintain a unified state. China has a voice in the world: Guangdong or Sichuan would not sit as a Permanent Member of the Security Council. There are nuclear weapons to consider, both their continued development and management, and the question of policy toward other nuclear states—today Russia and India.. All the reasons why Europe is moving toward union are reasons for China to maintain union, including the merits of a large internal market. And, finally, from China's own earlier experience in the century there is the warning of warlordism: domestic peace for any one province requires that there be domestic peace for all.

So the most likely outcome is that China will not fall apart, but that there will be an unusual degree of decentralization and increasing economic difference between regions.

These changes need not prevent Beijing from maintaining a single centrally controlled nuclear program with forces which were gradually refined and developed. Like Britain and France, China faces budget pressure, with shrinking relative tax revenues available to the Center. To the extent its *raison d'etre* is associated with security, the PLA, and nuclear weapons, the Center will be willing to pay what it must for their continued identification with it.

Conclusions

This chapter identifies the institutions most closely associated with the nuclear weapons programs of the Three and those political parties and movements most likely to voice themselves in any argument about nuclear futures. No simple conclusion emerges. What does seem clear, however, is that the sources of persisting in the status quo are strong and deeply-entrenched. The rationale of each nuclear program has been set out for many decades. They have been funded, against competing demands. Public justifications have been made and repeated. Britain's Conservative Party even sets up deterrence as a "principle" in which one can believe, a test of right reason. So the momentum is very strong.

On the other hand, this review shows several surprising facts. The number of industrial units in Britain and France which are heavily dependent on the nuclear program is small. A more complex discussion of nuclear weapons could emerge in Great Britain, if only because the Conservative Party is at low ebb politically. The need to explain national nuclear programs in a Europe of common security compels Britain and France to entertain a discussion which otherwise might not take place. In China, much hinges on whether political issues become *at all* a question of public debate. Will the agenda remain in the hands of the Political Bureau, or will there grow—even within the confines of an unreported discourse—provincial calls for resources now going to defense?

8

Costs and Risks

If nations could stock and deploy nuclear weapons at little or no cost or risk, few voices would call for disengagement and abolition. Beginning with Mikhail Gorbachev's speech of 15 January 1986, however, prominent public figures in both Russia and the United States have urged step-by-step accomplishment of very deep cuts and even complete abolition. There are serious men and women, incontestably familiar with the strategic calculus, who judge the costs and risks of nuclearism to be too high.

In taking up the 1995 NPT Review and Extension Conference and Article VI of the NPT, we have discussed the argument of non-nuclear states that nuclear weapons should be abolished. If there are advantages in having nuclear weapons, the non-nuclear weapon states do not profit from them, or profit only as dependent protectorates of nuclear weapon states. In either case they must tolerate being vulnerable to nuclear attack.

In this chapter we will assess costs and risks, to nuclear weapon states, of their nuclear inventories. Then in the next chapter we will examine the security arguments for nuclear weapons, looking at specific "threats" which leaders of the declared nuclear weapon states claim they face—or plausibly may believe they face. We set these two assessments side by side to recreate the ambivalence of most nuclear advocates: "of course nuclear weapons are a bad thing, but security imperatives compel us to keep them in the world as it is." It is important to consider both terms of this argument, because the harms are serious, and because security concerns are powerful and often reasonable.

Public Health Hazards and Environmental Harms

It is now well-understood that judging the social utility of a nuclear program—weapons, propulsion or electricity—requires a judgment of the effects of the radioactive material on people and on other species. Under some rubric such as "nuclear waste management" the physical material which emits harmful radiation must be somehow contained. Or, if it is not, those materials enter the environment. In any case, some unwanted emissions will inevitably occur.

Three facts make this an especially vexing issue. First, radioactive material can be widely dispersed, as it was by the hundreds of atmospheric nuclear tests undertaken by the five declared nuclear weapon states, in the atmosphere or through ground water. Many individuals may touch, breathe, or ingest it. This occurred in the civil nuclear program at Chernobyl. Second, effects of low-level radiation are not well-established. The results of high-level exposure are visible and dramatic, as they were at Chernobyl, where some died and many were desperately ill with radiation sickness. But there is not strong agreement about the effects of radiation diluted in the oceans or the atmosphere, which may be experienced by an individual as a small insult, a small increment to unavoidable "background" radiation.[1] Third, the material may emit radiation for a long time.

Of the harms we will consider in this chapter, this is the most uncertain, because of the inconclusive science about low-level experience. At the same time, it is a harm about which we must be especially cautious, because dispersion can reach large numbers. No person, and no member of any other species, could escape the risk of encountering nuclear material injected into the air by weapons tests.

Making nuclear weapons requires handling radioactive isotopes of uranium, plutonium and other elements. The physical processes—principally mining, uranium enrichment (increasing the concentration of U^{235}), plutonium production and separation, Pu^{239} concentration, milling and waste disposal itself—contaminate the equipment in which they take place and chemicals which are used. In addition, nuclear reactors of a nuclear weapons program, whether built to produce plutonium or tritium, or power submarines and aircraft carriers

---

1. On the most recent findings, however, see "Direct Estimates of Cancer Mortality Due to Low Doses of Ionising Radiation: An International Study," *The Lancet*, vol. 344, 15 October 1994, cited in *Le Monde* 2 November 1994, which reports a study of 96,000 persons who have worked in the nuclear industry. Jean-Paul Dufour comments that the report "seems to show that the partisans of prudence are correct."

dedicated to nuclear missions, are integral elements of a nuclear weapons program. "Spent" reactor fuel—like that produced by nuclear power plants—contains radioactive isotopes.

Human exposure during mining, processing and milling, and exposure to "waste," is typically less dramatic than exposure at Hiroshima, Nagasaki, and even Chernobyl. Since no human activity is risk-free, proponents of nuclear systems argue that the harm to humans from nuclear reactors, for example, is of an order similar to that of power generation by burning coal, or ongoing automobile transport. They further insist that technical means exist, or can be devised, to limit radiation exposure among workers and store radioactive waste safely.[2]

A more pessimistic view stresses that nuclear systems—civil and military—risk future Chernobyls and, even if they operate as designed, produce radioactive waste that must be stored, at further risk of harm. Citing the high toxicity and long half-life of plutonium—an inevitable product of both civil and military reactors—critics insist that the environmental costs of nuclear programs are potentially severe and, for practical purposes, eternal.

We cannot resolve here the issue between those who hold that "nuclear is sufficiently safe" and their critics who argue that "nuclear is too dangerous." There is no doubt nuclear weapons programs have placed many individuals at risk.[3] Management of U^{235} and plutonium is only now becoming a subject of open discussion among the declared nuclear weapon states.

---

2. Discussing the "culture of safety" promoted by the nuclear power sector, *Le Monde* correspondent Jean-Paul Dufour paraphrases the point of view prevalent in EDF and CEA: "Our plants are infinitely more safe and less deadly than the coal mines of yesteryear or the French highways." *Le Monde*, 16 November 1994, reporting on the Second International Colloquium on the Science of Danger, organized at the Sorbonne by the Institut européen de cindyniques.

3. We have mentioned Hiroshima and Nagasaki. Military exercises took place around nuclear tests in the United States and Soviet Union. Nuclear detonation aside, if one accepts that the risk of release of nuclear material from a nuclear weapon—that is, a rupturing or a chemical explosion—is not zero, and that radioactive material released would harm people who encountered it, then the *risk* is real for all those living in localities where nuclear weapons are stored or through which they are transported.

Britain

As Britain has conducted weapons tests abroad (Australia, Christmas Island, Nevada), the principal domestic issues have concerned reactor and reprocessing products. Most recently, controversy has centered on a new Thermal Oxide Reprocessing Plant (THORP) at the Sellafield nuclear complex, opposed by critics of plutonium extraction. The Conservative government of John Major has decided to start the plant.[4]

Reprocessing "spent" reactor fuel is not a perfect procedure. Albright et al. report that, although in "modern" reprocessing plants more than 99 percent of plutonium in spent fuel can be captured,

> At Sellafield it has been estimated that between 2 and 3.5 tonnes of plutonium are contained in a variety of plutonium contaminated solid wastes which have accumulated at the site over the past 40 years.[a] A 1986 (British) government report showed that about 1.8 tonnes of plutonium were held in stripped fuel cladding and other plutonium contaminated materials (PCM) produced in magnox reprocessing.[b] This is equivalent to losses of 4-5 per cent in magnox reprocessing.[c] [5]

The point of reprocessing is to extract plutonium. Plutonium's high toxicity makes its presence in waste an issue. But the product itself, of course, is the same highly toxic element. Plutonium's toxicity and the need to avoid a critical event impose stringent requirements on handling and storage. The British Department of Energy stated that as of 31 March 1990 31 tonnes of plutonium separated from Britain's magnox reactors were stored at Sellafield.[6]

---

4. THORP started its first phase of active commissioning on 17 January 1994. Programme for Promoting Nuclear Non-Proliferation. *Newsbrief.*, no. 25, 1st Quarter 1994, p. 10.

5. David Albright, Frans Berkhout and William Walker, *World Inventory of Plutonium and Highly Enriched Uranium 1992* (Oxford: Oxford University Press and the Stockholm International Peace Research Institute, 1993.), pp. 18, 85. Magnox fuel is uranium metal fuel clad with magnesium oxide (magnox). Their notes: "a. Hinkley Point "C" Inquiry, Transcript of evidence day 98, UK, 1989, p. 17. b. HMSO, *Radioactive Waste Management Advisory Committee Seventh Annual Report*, London, September 1986, figure 3. c. These large losses are chiefly the result of the mechanical decladding of magnox fuel. Selective chemical decladding used for oxide fuels tends to reduce plutonium losses to ≤1 per cent."

6. Albright et al., p. 93, citing Department of Energy, *News Release 195*, 18

THORP is designed to keep Britain in the business of capturing plutonium and other radionuclides from spent reactor fuel. One of THORP's intended customers is Japan, which would then stockpile the returned plutonium, ostensibly to fuel power-generating reactors. Opposition to THORP springs from a double concern about the plutonium—which could be converted to weapons use—and the heterogeneous radioactive waste left over.[7] Critics also charge coastal contamination.[8]

THORP has sent one deputy to the European Parliament. In the 16 June 1994 election of MEPs in Ireland, the most striking outcome was the electoral success of Green Party candidate Ms. Patricia McKenna, who attributes her success to voters' wanting "action on THORP" in the form of an Irish government legal challenge to the installation, across the Irish Sea.

One source of concern, then, is inadvertent loss of radioactive material into the environment. The second concerns management of designated waste, by long-term containment or disposal. Containers may fail. Disposal assumes that the method of disposal is "safe." The United Kingdom has favored dumping radioactive material at sea.

In November 1993 participants in the London Dumping Convention—an agreement originally adopted in 1972 which already banned dumping high-level radioactive waste at sea—agreed to ban low and intermediate radioactive waste as well.[9] Senior British

---

October 1990. The 1991 figure was 33 tonnes. "Separated plutonium requires extensive physical protection and safeguarding, and as a toxic material needs special precautions so that it does not endanger health." Albright et al., p. 21. Sellafield and four other UK reprocessing plants are operated by British Nuclear Fuels Limited (BNFL). Until coprocessing of civil and military material ended in 1986, the weapons program provided a portion of the work for these plants, but less than 10 percent. THORP will be the second of two large-scale plants on the Sellafield site. Norris et al., p. 78.

7. Concern extends not only to known product but also to the adequacy of reporting. Paul Leventhal and Daniel Horner insist that "France and Britain deny [the IAEA] the access it needs to certify the accuracy of plutonium measurements." *The New York Times*, 25 January 1995.

8. Albright et al., p. 91n, say "liquid radioactive discharges from Windscale/–Sellafield and from reactor sites were reaching their authorized limits because increasingly contaminated pond water was being washed out to sea (or into a lake in the case of Trawsfynnydd)."

9. The London Dumping Conventions formal title is Convention on the Prevention

officials said that they still had not decided how to dispose of ten nuclear-powered submarines due to be decommissioned by the year 2000, prompting *Guardian* correspondent Paul Brown to conclude they wished to retain the option of "cutting them up and dumping them at sea."[10] Joined by Belgium, four nuclear weapon states—Britain, China, France and Russia—abstained in November, but by February 1994, when the agreement came into force, all but Russia had agreed to keep to its terms. The International Maritime Organization said that Russia had pledged to "endeavour to avoid pollution of the sea by dumping of wastes." Britain, however, stipulated that it would reopen negotiations if opinion appeared to have shifted to favor marine radioactive dumping. Reuters attributed Britain's position to its need to dispose of the old submarines.[11]

While dumping low-level radioactive waste at sea was in fashion,

---

of Marine Pollution by Dumping of Wastes and Other Matter. From 1983 parties to the London Dumping Convention followed a moratorium on dumping low-level nuclear waste. Gareth Porter and Janet Welsh Brown, *Global Environmental Politics* (Boulder: Westview, 1991), p. 113. Citing William M. Arkin and Joshua Handler, "Naval Accidents 1945-1988," *Neptune Papers*, no 3 (Washington, DC: Greenpeace and the Institute for Policy Studies, 1989), p. 7, they note that five nuclear-powered submarines have been lost at sea by the Soviet Union and United States. Porter and Brown observe that submarines carry 340 of the extant 745 nuclear power plants and "remain totally secret from the public."

10. *The Guardian*, 16 September 1992. *Newsbrief*, summarizing reports of Britain's agreement to the ban, wrote that the decision

    "is said to have come as a surprise to environmentalists who point out that (Britain) will now be faced with the question where to store its low-level waste as well as its obsolete submarines, which it had earlier hoped to bury at sea. Reportedly, there are seven redundant nuclear submarines waiting for disposal, of which at least the reactor compartments were destined to be sunk in the ocean. For the time being, these boats are expected to be stored afloat. London has said that it still considered that there were good arguments for disposal at sea, but it recognised the weight of international opinion in the matter; however, it would re-open negotiations if opinion changes in favour of dumping at sea." Programme for Promoting Nuclear Non-Proliferation. *Newsbrief*, no. 25, 1st Quarter 1994, p. 13.

    On 8 September *The Guardian* reported Greenpeace charges that Britain was racing to dump (conventional) munitions at sea before an Oslo Convention prohibition on such dumping took effect. Three vessels were dumping a total of 8405 tonnes of munitions, more than in previous years.

11. Reuters, 21 February 1994.

Britain relied on that disposal method. A 1991 IAEA report attributes to Britain more than 75 percent of reported low-level ocean dumping (by radioactive content, but excluding Soviet dumping, which has been extensive, and Chinese dumping).[12] Military nuclear waste appears to be included in the totals.[13] Surveys of some sites are said to show no levels higher than weapons fallout would cause, except that "on certain occasions when caesium and plutonium were detected at higher levels in samples taken close to packages at the disposal site." Since most of the plutonium dumped is British, this may be an allusion to leakage from British containers.[14] Waste with radioactivity exceeding 30 PBq, almost nine-tenths of British dumping including much of its dumped alpha-emitting isotopes, was sunk from 1971 to 1982 at two sites in the Atlantic at depths exceeding 3200 m.[15] The weight of all reported British dumping was 74,000 tonnes.

What of storage on land? Bearing in mind that there is radioactive waste from both the military and civil (power) sectors, and that it is both "low- and intermediate-level waste" and "high-level waste," Britain has a proposed solution for "low- and intermediate-level

---

12. International Atomic Energy Agency. *Inventory of Radioactive Material Entering the Marine Environment: Sea Disposal of Radioactive Waste*. March 1991. IAEA-TECDOC-588. The first such dumping occurred in 1946 about 80 km off the California coast; the last, in the Atlantic, in 1982. The report covers the period 1946-1982, but is limited to *reported* dumping. It states that tritium data is available "since 1975," but does not explicitly say there was unreported tritium dumping before 1975, or that pre-1975 tritium is included in aggregated beta/gamma figures.

    Radioactivity is reported in PBq, where 1 PBq = 10^{15} Becquerel.

    Of a total radioactivity of 45.8 PBq, the United Kingdom deposited 35 PBq and France 0.3 PBq. Almost a third of UK waste in this category was tritium. Most of the radiation—more than 98 percent—is in the form of beta/gamma emission. Of the total 0.6 PBq of alpha emissions, isotopes of plutonium and americium contribute 96 percent, most of that in UK waste. Thus the United Kingdom was a major source.

13. The report omits, however, radionuclides from testing: "The availability of information on the inputs of radionuclides due to atmospheric and underwater nuclear weapon testing is limited due to the confidentiality of the data. This source of radionuclides is not included in the data base." *Ibid.*, p. 12.

14. *Ibid.*, p. 14.

15. *Ibid.*, pp. 30-31, including a figure showing amounts and sites. The two sites are at 46°15' N 17°25' W and 46°00' N 16°45' W.

waste" and a policy of deliberate temporizing—storage for at least fifty years before disposal—on "high-level waste." Or so it appeared until a commissioned Royal Society study group report on the geology of the site proposed for disposal of "low- and intermediate-level waste" introduced the issue of "high-level waste" into its report. Assessing a site at Sellafield at which the waste-disposal entity UK NIREX proposes to lodge waste at a depth of 650 meters, the study group disputed the process of site selection, and added that a site some two miles away would be better for high-level waste. Commentators asked if there were not a "deception" to place high level waste in this repository, a charge which UK NIREX flatly rejected.[16]

No mention of radioactivity, however, leaks into the discussion of "Defence and the Environment" in *The Statement on the Defence Estimates 1994*. Britain will comply with environmental law

> except where Crown or defence exemptions need to be invoked for essential national security or operational reasons.

And

> it is our policy to minimise and, if possible, eliminate the use of substances such as heavy metals, certain pesticides and solvents which are particularly persistent, toxic and bioaccumulative.[17]

Radiation also falls on crews and workers while submarines are in service. The British fleet includes four SSBNs and a dozen SSNs.

---

16. *The Independent*, 16 November 1994. Commentator Tom Wilkie, *The Independent*, 22 November 1994. On site selection, the study group concluded that BNFL's control of the land, rather than geological considerations, had led to the site choice:

    "the optimal siting of a repository should be determined through highly iterative interaction between the scientists and the design engineers. The study group has seen no evidence of such a close relationship."

17. Cm 2550. *Statement on the Defence Estimates 1994*, April 1994, ¶s 578-585, p. 86. "It is Departmental policy to comply with national environmental protection legislations, and relevant European Community directives and international agreements which have been ratified by the United Kingdom, except where Crown or defence exemptions need to be invoked for essential national security or operational reasons." An Under Secretary of State for Defence, Lord Cranborne, is charged with "ensuring that environmental considerations are taken into account at all levels of Departmental decision-making." He is called the "Green Minister" and is said to "act in liaison with other Green Ministers."

All are nuclear-powered. In 1989 the Ministry of Defence set the maximum radiation permissible in one year to 30mSv (milliSieverts). (The International Commission on Radiological Protection regulations fix the maximum at 50mSv.) In 1990 six radiation workers received more than 15mSv but none more than 20mSv.[18]

France

In 1991 France created a National Agency for the Management of Radioactive Waste (ANDRA), to be independent of the CEA. It was instructed by law to inventory "the status and location of all of the radioactive waste in existence on the national territory," a measure prompted by discovery of unauthorized dumping of waste at Bouchet and Saint-Aubin in 1990. It published its first report on 27 April 1993, played down by *Le Figaro*, which quoted ANDRA head Henri Wallard as saying that the report "provides no great surprises"—not in itself surprising since lists provided by the institutions themselves are the principal source.[19]

Nuclear waste produced by the French military program has also been catalogued, to the extent published information permits, by Bruno Barrillot and Mary Davis in an extensive, site-by-site survey.[20] They conclude that "many French sites are contaminated," some as a result of accidents, some because "the military Centers knowingly used 'practices' considered as dangerous and forbidden in civil [nuclear] industry."[21]

Arguing by analogy from US experience and their count of reactor cores, Barrillot and Davis estimate that by the end of the century 4.3 tonnes of uranium enriched to "military quality" will have been

---

18. House of Commons. Session 1990-91. Defence Committee. Sixth Report. *Royal Navy Submarines*. 12 June 1991, p. 45.

19. *Le Figaro*, 28 April 1993, in JPRS-TND-93-015 p. 28. *Figaro* states that lists by the institutions were "supplemented by the critical opinions of the few credible 'antinuclear lobbying' associations (the CRIIRAD and the GSIEN)."

20. Bruno Barrillot and Mary Davis, *Les déchets nuléaires militaires français* (Lyon: Centre de Documentation et de Recherche sur la Paix et les Conflits, 1994).

21. *Ibid.*, p. 17.

used in naval propulsion reactors.[22] All cores will, in due course, become waste requiring disposition.

China

China's program is the least accessible to public inspection. Unlike Britain and France, China does not publish studies of environmental episodes, nor is Greenpeace operating in China.

Revelations of radiation releases in US and Soviet (Russian) weapons programs suggest it would be surprising if no such incidents had taken place in the Chinese program. Nursultan Nazarbayev, leader of neighboring Kazakhstan, charged publicly in January 1993 that China's nuclear tests threatened health and the environment and insisted they should be stopped, but offered no particulars.[23] Just three weeks later Nazarbayev's government announced that it had closed the former Soviet nuclear test site at Semipalatinsk mainly for environmental and health reasons, suggesting that Nazarbayev's criticism of testing at Lop Nor may have been grounded in knowledge of the effects at Semipalatinsk.[24]

Other evidence is anecdotal. A volume of reminiscences of early days of the program recounts primitive uranium extraction, death due to a mining shaft accident, and other details of work under severe hardship.[25] On 9 May 1966 nine Chinese airmen were ordered to fly through the cloud of China's third nuclear test to obtain test data: the

---

22. *Ibid.*, pp. 326-327. They estimate 29 submarine reactor cores and 10 prototype reactor cores at 100 kg each, plus 400 kg for an aircraft carrier and submarine to come into service by the end of the century. How highly enriched? It is a military secret, the authors write, but seems that at the outset it was 90 percent U^{235}. Later CEA reports hint at more lightly enriched uranium. *Ibid.*, pp. 323-324.

23. *The Guardian*, 31 August 1993, an AP despatch reporting Nazarbayev's statement of 30 August 1993.

24. *Nucleonics Week*, 25 February 1993, reporting remarks of Kazakhstan's representative to a meeting of the Economic Cooperation Organization in Quetta, Pakistan.

25. *A Secret Journey: The Story of the Birth of China's First Atomic Bomb.* Compiled by the Shenjian Chapter of the Ministry of Nuclear Industry. (Beijing: Atomic Energy Press, October 1985).

survivors attribute subsequent health problems to their exposure on that day.[26] Fallout from that test was detected in Japan.[27] Lewis and Xue report claims that crews of the first Chinese nuclear-powered submarine suffered radiation exposure.[28]

Until 1980 China tested nuclear weapons in the atmosphere, a practice given up by Britain, the United States and Soviet Union in 1963. However, the number of tests—27 to the cutoff—was only a fraction of Soviet and US tests in the atmosphere.

It was reported, in the context of China's agreeing to the February 1994 ban on ocean dumping of low-level radioactive waste, that China had used 38 off-shore dumpsites for various types of waste, but has said it will phase out their use.[29]

Budgetary Costs

Britain

The object of this section is to provide a rough measure of the cost of Britain's nuclear forces. In the early 1990s Britain's defense budget has run about £24 billion a year, declining from 4.0% of GDP in 1990/91 to a projected 3.2% of GDP in 1995/96. In 1993 Britain estimated a drop in the defense budget in real terms of about 11% between 1990/91 and 1995/96.[30] The 1994 *Statement on the Defence Estimates* offered projected figures for anticipated defense budgets in the years 1994 through 1997, which are shown in table 8.1.

---

26. Reuters, 18 February 1994, citing *Jianxi Daily.*
27. Norris et al., p. 420.
28. Lewis and Xue, *China's Strategic Seapower*, p. 109.
29. *Newsbrief.* Programme for Promoting Nuclear Non-Proliferation. no. 25, 1st Quarter 1994, p. 13.
30. Cm 2201. Ministry of Defence. *The Government's Expenditure Plans 1993/94 to 1995/96.* February 1993. Tables 1 and 2, and p. 5.

TABLE 8.1
Britain: Defence Budget 1993-1997

Defence Budget £ 10^6	Estimated Outturn 1993-94	Cash Plan 1994-95	Cash Plan 1995-96	Cash Plan 1996-97
"Cash plan" projected in 1993		23,490	22,700	22,790
April 1994 Figures	23,450	22,890	22,130	22,230

Source: Statement on the Defence Estimates 1994, ¶s 501-502, p. 67.
Note: The plans projected in the 1994-95 Financial Statement and Budget Report were revised downward "to take into account the transfer to a new Cabinet Office Vote from 1 April 1994 of provision for the security and intelligence services and other minor transfers of provision between the Ministry of Defence and other Government Departments." This change has the effect of shifting about 2 percent of defense costs to other budgets.

They also say that if those changes are excluded, "the new plans represent reductions of £260 million and £520 million in 1994-95 and 1995-96 on the provision agreed in the 1992 Public Expenditure Survey. The budget set for 1996-97 is £420 million less than the previous plan for 1995-96." ¶ 503.

In comparison to the military expenditure of some of Britain's allies, UK per capita defense expenditure exceeded that of Germany, but was less than that of France, and 53 percent of that of the United States (see table 8.2).

TABLE 8.2
Military Spending: UK, France, Germany, and the United States

1993	UK	FRANCE	GERMANY	US
Percent of GDP	3.7	3.4	2.0	4.7
Total (US$ Billions)	35.2	42.6	38.6	293.7
Per Capita (US$)	608	738	481	1142

Source: *Statement on the Defence Estimates 1994*, p. 68.
Notes: Percent of GDP: Defence expenditure as a percentage of GDP (market price). Total: Total defense expenditure in US$ billions. Per Capita: Per capita defense expenditure (US$). They note that calculations use 1993 average market exchange rates and are therefore "only a guide to comparative resource allocation."

As new Trident boats enter service, they will carry three-fourths of British warheads and its prompt distant strategic strike capability. The Ministry of Defence estimated in January 1993 that "the proportion of the Defence budget which the Trident programme takes over its 20 year procurement period remains at less than two-and-a-half per cent on average," a total cost (in 1992-93 prices) of £10.67 billion.[31] (In 1994 the Ministry of Defence estimated the Trident program's cost at £11,631 million.[32]) The Defence Committee of the House of Commons, noting the 2.5 percent figure, points out (italics emphasized in the original) that

> The cost of the Trident programme will of course not end on delivery of the fourth submarine and purchase of the last missile. There will be running costs over the lifetime of the submarines, as there have been for Polaris. MoD has previously stated that the running costs of Trident will be similar to those of Polaris: the Polaris force currently costs around £175 million a year to run. *In response to our query, MoD has estimated that the lifetime operating costs of Trident "are likely to be in the order of £5.5 billion,"* meaning around £185 million a year over 30 years. This estimate, regarded as reasonably robust, comprises £1 billion for manpower, £1.35 billion for refits, £1 billion for stores and transport, £1.2 billion for Clyde submarine base, £1 billion for AWE (Atomic Weapons Establishment) and in-service support costs, and £150 million for decommissioning and disposal: a total of £5.7 billion. *There are evident uncertainties, not least over disposal, for which there is still no long-term strategy.* The figures assume that each boat will have two refits, rather than the three refits planned for each Polaris boat at a comparable cost of around £170 million each, and, despite the greater size of the Trident boat, of comparable duration.[33]

The *Statement on the Defence Estimates 1993* values the "gross costs"—not budget costs—of the nuclear deterrent at £3.9 billion for

---

31. Memorandum submitted by the Ministry of Defence on the Trident programme, 21 January 1993. Reproduced in: House of Commons. Session 1992-93. Defence Committee. Sixth Report. *The Progress of the Trident Programme*. 16 June 1993. Pp 21-22, p. 22. The £10.67 billion figure includes the submarines, weapon systems, missiles, shore construction, and "warhead, miscellaneous, unallocated contingency etc." It does not appear to include operations, administration, or disposal.

32. Cm 2550. *Statement on the Defence Estimates 1994*. Presented to Parliament by the Secretary of State for Defence. April 1994, p. 54.

33. House of Commons. Session 1992-93. Defence Committee. Sixth Report. *The Progress of the Trident Programme*. 16 June 1993, pp. vii-viii.

1993/94 (and £3.8 billion for 1994/95 and 1995/96). This figure assumes some units perform more than one "task." It has the virtue that it allocates non-nuclear units required for protection of nuclear forces, including three escort craft and twelve regular infantry battalions, to the category "nuclear deterrent."

France

The French defense budget for 1994 was to be 3.6% larger than that of 1993 (in current francs), or slightly larger than 1993 (after inflation). In introducing the budget, Defence Minister François Léotard explained the increase as a result of France's policy of maintaining arms independence. Major budget items include a nuclear-powered aircraft carrier, which will be a platform for aircraft carrying nuclear weapons, and new combat aircraft.[34]

In recent years, the annual expenditures for defense have been just under 200 billion francs. In 1992, for example, "crédits de paiement"—the actual budget limit for the year—for defense were 195.268 billion francs. Of this the cost of the *forces nucléaire* was 40.446 billion francs.[35]

As is in the case of Britain, we can also estimate nuclear costs by examining those of the principal strategic nuclear program, the new *Triomphant*-class SSBN (SNLE), the SNLE-NG (*sous-marins nucléaires lanceurs d'engins de nouvelle génération*), and its nuclear-armed missile load. Bruno Barrillot has undertaken a study of comprehensive costs, on the hypotheses that France will arm the four planned SNLE-NG with the M45 missile, or proceed to build and deploy the more capable and expensive M5 missile. The total announced cost (in constant 1990 francs) of the SNLE-NG—boats alone without missiles—has ranged from 70 billion francs (1983) to 81.5 billion (1993).[36] The cost of a set of 16 M45 missiles is 9 billion

34. Reuters, 7 October 1993.

35. *Armées d'aujourd'hui*, Supplément au n° 187, February 1992. *La défense en chiffres 1992.*

36. Bruno Barrillot, *Rapport relatif aux coûts cachés du programme Triomphant depuis 1982* (Lyon and Paris: Centre de Documentation et de Recherche sur la Paix et les Conflits and Greenpeace—France, 25 May 1994), pp. 16 and 18, citing (1993) the *Projet de Loi Programmation* 1995-2000.

francs: three sets—sufficient for four boats—would therefore cost 27 billion francs. The total cost of 4 SNLE-NG plus 48 (3 sets of 16) missiles would then be roughly 108 billion francs.[37]

TABLE 8.3

France: Estimated Costs of the *Triomphant*-class SNLE and Missile Systems (French Francs)

(IN 10^9 1993 FRANCS)	WITH M45	WITH M5	COSTS NOT INCURRED IF M5 ABANDONED
Official costs (SNLE + missiles)	108	186	78
Additional costs	85.17	94.12	8.95
M5 costs already spent			-1.7
Total = Real cost	**193.17**	**280.12**	**85.25**
SNLE-NG Cost Per Boat	48.29	70.03	
TOTAL = REAL COST (US $\$10^9$) [a]	**37.15**	**53.87**	**16.39**
SNLE-NG Cost Per Boat	9.29	13.47	

a At a nominal exchange rate of FFr 5.2 = US$ 1.

"Equipping four SNLE-NG with the M45 would leave the door open to ending the M5 programme."[38] A decision on the M5 has been postponed to 1997. But if it were not halted, what would it cost? Adding a refit requirement for three SNLE-NG totaling 14 billion francs and a cost of 73 billion francs for three sets of M5 missiles to the original 81 billion franc cost of the submarines themselves, Barrillot generates a program cost of 168 billion francs.[39] Add 18 billion francs for two sets of M45 missiles—required by the first three boats, before M5 could be ready on the assumption of a 1997 deci-

37. Barrillot, *Rapport*, pp. 19-20.
38. *Ibid.*, p. 21.
39. *Ibid.*, pp. 21-22.

sion—and the total is 186 billion. Barrillot designates these alternative estimates—108 billion (with M45 alone) and 186 billion (with M45 and then M5)—as "official costs" of the systems, because they are based on cost estimates by government and parliamentary figures.

Barrillot then proceeds to estimate "additional costs." These include infrastructure, communications with the strategic fleet, nuclear tests (anticipated for the T100 warhead of an M5 missile), and other costs. (Dismantlement and disposal costs are not included.) He puts "additional costs" at 85.17 billion (if M45 alone) and 94.12 billion (for the M45, then M5), giving the result shown in table 8.3.[40]

Estimated lifespan costs are compared with annual budget costs of the present submarine fleet and other components of French nuclear forces (Table 8.4). Title III is personnel and operations. Title V is weapons research, development and procurement.

TABLE 8.4

France: Cost Allocation of Selected Components of the Nuclear Weapons System

(French Francs)

1991 Projet de Loi de Finances: Costs (*crédits de paiement*) (10^9 francs)	TITLE III	TITLE V	TOTAL
Strategic air force	1.663	1.395	3.059
Strategic ocean forces	.788	8.894	9.682
R+D &c. for nuclear and space programs	1.042	18.717	19.760
"Prestrategic" nuclear arms	1.713	8.320	10.033
Total	5.206	37.326	42.532

Source: Ministère de la Défense. *Projet de Loi de Finances Pour 1991*. Paris, 1990. (Related ground forces support is omitted.)

In short, nuclear forces (including work on space programs) cost about a fifth of the French defense budget in 1991.

French costs differ from those of Britain in several respects:

40. *Ibid.*, pp. 35-37. Of these sums, 107.87 billion was already committed by 1994.

1. If France chose the less expensive M45 for all four SNLE-NG boats, the "official cost" of three sets of 16 would be 27 billion francs (US$ 5.2 billion). The British Trident II (D5) missiles—the number is not known, but it is probably three sets of 16 plus tests and spares—are said to cost £965 million(US$1.556 billion).[41] France will pay three times as much for its missiles as Britain. (British savings are due in part to US serial production of the missile.)

2. Britain is to spend about £6 billion for the four submarines (including the boats, strategic weapons system equipment, and their tactical weapons system, but excluding the missiles, warhead and shore costs): £6.055 billion (US$ 9.766 billion). The French cost—reported without specifics about what is included—is 81.5 billion francs (US$ 15.67 billion).

3. The French costs for "nuclear dissuasion" include costs of an ambitious satellite reconnaissance program which Britain has not imitated. Britain has limited itself to intercepting communi-cations. France, in addition, plans a range of imaging satellites.

Increased Risk of Nuclear Attack

A nuclear weapon state expects to be targeted by one or more of the other nuclear weapon states. It might, of course, be targeted even if it had no nuclear weapons. It could be targeted but never attacked. The crucial point is that the state which deploys nuclear weapons at the ready compels other nuclear weapon states to consider scripts of threat, preemption and revenge.

When French, British, and Chinese officials publicly discuss their nuclear programs they stress their deterrent or dissuasive role, not their capacity to attract attack. In putting nuclear weapons to sea, they stress that a sea-borne deterrent can hide more effectively, not that it

---

41. House of Commons. Session 1992-93. Defence Committee. Sixth Report. *The Progress of the Trident Programme*. 16 June 1993, p. xiv. (Our conversion at £ 0.62 = US$ 1.) However, since the missiles "owned" by Britain will rotate through the regular US stock, when removed for maintenance and replaced by others, it is not clear that there will be any designated UK "spares."

reduces the number of land-based targets. Of course, SSBNs at quayside and support facilities may still be targets.

Danger of Accidental Detonation or Plutonium Release

Nuclear weapon states do not foster public speculation that a nuclear weapon might explode, for example while in storage near a town or being trucked along an expressway. Nonetheless, there is danger of accidental nuclear detonation or a release of toxic plutonium.[42] Nuclear system designers appreciate the need for prudence. What constitutes a "sufficiently prudent" design, however, is a matter of judgment. Although we have only a limited window into this issue, recent documents set out a number of specific details, some concerning the British Trident program and British procedures. Moreover, these documents are themselves the source and subject of a limited but pointed British debate about the safety of Britain's Trident system. These documents, in chronological order, are:

---

42. US ground-carried nuclear weapon movements were said in 1990 to be roughly "more than one thousand vehicle trips and one million miles per year." If the HE (High Explosive) chemical explosive jacket surrounding a nuclear pit were to explode—the chemical explosive, not the nuclear device—roughly 100 square kilometers downwind would be contaminated. "The number of latent cancer fatalities would be sensitive to the wind direction and the population distribution in the vicinity of such an accident." A fire involving a nuclear warhead would contaminate about 1 square kilometer. Drell Report. Drell also observes that

    "Since the U.S. terminated air-borne alert by nuclear loaded SAC bombers in 1968, there have been no damaging accidents or otherwise unintended incidents leading to a nuclear yield or to dispersal of plutonium by any of our nuclear weapons. There have never been any accidents leading to a nuclear yield."

    This comment is well-fashioned to avoid mentioning that a US aircraft lost a nuclear weapon over rural Spain (and another offshore), with contamination of soil by the first bomb.

    BASIC Report 94.2 volunteers that in Britain "Nuclear weapons convoys travel on all roads and in all weather conditions, between AWE Burghfield and the various operational and storage sites. The journey can be up to 500 miles long." These convoys are many vehicles long, centered on 20-ton trucks with nuclear weapons in the bed. BASIC quotes an unidentified source that on 16 July 1991 a convoy broke down outside Castelside Primary School, Consett, County Durham; and that on 5 June 1991 a convoy in Corbridge, Northumberland, became "lost in one-way system in a small market town" leading to "damage reported to parked cars."

1. December 1990. (Hereafter cited as: the Drell Report.)

US Congress. House Armed Services Committee. *Report of the Panel on Nuclear Weapons Safety.* (Sidney D. Drell, Chairman, John S. Foster Jr., and Charles H. Townes.)

A review of US nuclear weapons safety by three physicists, with full cooperation of the Department of Defense and the Department of Energy. Classified portions are omitted from the public report.

2. 19 June 1991.

House of Commons. Session 1990-91. Defence Committee. Eighth Report. *The Progress of the Trident Programme*.

The Committee's report addresses warhead and safety questions, invoking the Drell Report explicitly. (The Drell Report remains a subject of successive Defence Committee reports cited below). An executive summary of the Drell Report is attached.

3. 11 March 1992.

House of Commons. Session 1991-92. Defence Committee. Fifth Report. *The Progress of the Trident Programme*.

The Committee awaited receipt of the Oxburgh Report.

4. July 1992. (Hereafter: the Oxburgh Report.)

United Kingdom. Ministry of Defence. *The Safety of UK Nuclear Weapons*. Report of the review conducted by a working group led by the MoD's Chief Scientific Adviser. (Text of 12 February 1992 "Report on the Safety of UK Nuclear Weapons," prepared by the Safety Review Group (Chair, Professor Sir E. R. Oxburgh), less deleted classified sections.)[43]

---

43. Reproduced in BASIC Report 92.4. The British American Security Information Council. *Second Report on British Nuclear Weapons Safety: A Response to the*

On 15 October 1991 the Minister of State for Defence Procurement told the House of Commons that Professor Oxburgh had been invited to lead a working group on UK nuclear weapon safety. Its terms of reference sprang from the Drell Report: "To review, in the light of any relevant aspects of the report of the Drell Panel in the United States the safety of the present and prospective UK nuclear armoury."[44]

5. 1992. (Hereafter: BASIC Report 92.4.)

The British American Security Information Council. BASIC Report 92.4. *Second Report on British Nuclear Weapons Safety. A Response to the Oxburgh Report.*

BASIC identifies itself as "an independent research organisation that analyses international security policy in Europe and North America." This text includes the Oxburgh Report, with critical notations by BASIC, and the Drell Report.

6. 16 June 1993.

House of Commons. Session 1992-93. Defence Committee. Sixth Report. *The Progress of the Trident Programme.*

Includes a concise review of the issues as posed by the Defence Committee, the Ministry of Defence's responses, and the Committee's judgment concerning those responses. (This review is reproduced in Appendix 8.1.)

7. 4 May 1994.

House of Commons. Session 1993-94. Defence Committee. Second Report. *Progress of the Trident Programme.*

Oxburgh Report. London, 1992.

44. Defence Committee 1992, ¶ 23, citing a 25 October 1991 MoD response to the Defence Committee, para. 6.

Further queries.

These documents mark successive steps over a four year period by agencies of the US Congress and British Parliament to obtain a clear picture of the safety of the respective nuclear inventories. Because Britain was buying both the Trident missile and the Reentry Vehicle from the United States (although placing its own warheads in the Reentry Vehicle), the Defence Committee could learn about the safety of UK systems from US documents. When it asked to see classified sections of the Oxburgh Report, however, it was refused.

The issues are set out in detail in the section of the report we reproduce here. The main questions, and the probable answers, are these:

- Do British Trident warheads incorporate ENDS?[45]

---

45. The Drell Report explains ENDS as follows:

"In order to enhance electrical safety of nuclear weapons against premature detonation, the concept of a modern enhanced nuclear detonation system (ENDS) was developed at the Sandia National Laboratory in 1972 and introduced into the stockpile starting with the Air Force B61-5 bomb in 1977. The basic evaluation idea is to introduce into the firing system two strong links and one weak link that are located in the same environment within a so-called exclusion region. Both strong links have to be closed electrically—one by specific operator-coded information input and one by environmental input corresponding to a trajectory or spin motion appropriate to its flight profile—for the weapon to arm. The weak link on the other hand would be opened, or broken, thereby preventing arming if there were a temperature excursion, for example, due to fire . . .

"The basic idea of ENDS is the isolation of electrical elements critical to detonation of the warhead into an exclusion region which is physically defined by structural cases and barriers that isolate the region from all sources of unintended energy. The only access point into the exclusion region for normal arming and firing electrical power is through special devices called strong links that cover small openings in the exclusions barrier. The strong links are designed so that there is an acceptably small probability that they will be activated by stimuli from an abnormal environment. Detailed analyses and tests give confidence over a very broad range of abnormal environments that a single strong link can provide isolation for the warhead to better than one part in a thousand. Therefore, the stated safety requirement of a probability of less than one in a million . . . requires two independent strong links in the arming set, and that is the way the ENDS system is designed. . .

"ENDS includes a weak link in addition to two independent strong links in or-

This device is designed to inhibit unintended arming of the weapon and to disable it in case of a fire and some other severe trauma. The United States began installing ENDS in nuclear weapons in 1977. The UK will not say whether it uses ENDS, but it probably does.

- Do British Trident warheads incorporate Insensitive High Explosive (IHE)?

  If IHE, rather than High Explosive (HE), is used to form the chemical shell which causes implosion, the likelihood of an unwanted chemical explosion is much reduced. The British Government will not say whether its Trident warheads use IHE. Possibly not.[46]

- Do British Trident warheads incorporate Fire Resistant Pits (FRPs)?

  FRPs "are designed to provide molten plutonium containment against the (~1000° C) temperatures of an aircraft fuel fire that lasts for several hours. They may fail to provide containment, however, against the much higher temperatures created by burning

---

der to maintain assured electrical isolation at extreme levels of certain accident environments, such as very high temperatures and crush. Safety weak links are functional elements (e.g. capacitors) that are also critical to the normal detonation process. They are designed to fail, or become irreversibly inoperable, in less stressing environments (e.g. lower temperatures) than those that might bypass and cause failure of the strong links.

"... ENDS was ... introduced into the stockpile starting in 1977. At the beginning of this year slightly more than one-half of the weapons in the stockpile (52%) will be equipped with ENDS. The remaining ones await scheduled retirement or modernization under the stockpile improvement program."

46. The Drell Report makes it quite clear that as of December 1990 the US Trident warhead used neither IHE or FRPs. He also notes the opportunity to redesign the warhead to incorporate IHE and FRP, and that if warhead numbers were reduced "a safety-optimized version of the D5, equipped with IHE, non-detonable 1.3 class propellant and a fire-resistant pit, could fly to even longer ranges than at present." The question then is whether the United Kingdom originally followed US design and, if it did, whether it has taken advantage of the intervening period to adopt IHE and FRPs.

missile propellant."[47] The British Government declines to say whether its Trident warheads incorporate FRPs. Possibly not.[48]

- Are UK Trident warheads "one point safe"?

  The MoD has given a "categorical assurance" that they are.[49]

- Do British Trident missiles employ the 1.3 class propellant—described as "practically impossible to detonate"—or the high-energy propellant termed 1.1 class?

  As of June 1993, the United States was supplying Trident missiles designed for the 1.1 class propellant. The MoD was resisting a move to 1.3 class, saying a change would require "major redesign work" and would not be "practicable."[50]

- Are Trident missiles put aboard British submarines with the warheads attached, or are the warheads attached after the missile is aboard?

  The Drell Report voices concern about loading as a time of special danger. If the two steps are taken separately, the missile with its high-energy propellant is already firmly fixed before the warhead is introduced. This is the UK procedure.

A close reading of the attached section of the Defence Committee's

---

47. Drell Report.

48. See note above on IHE and FRPs.

49. Defence Committee 1993, ¶ 11. "One point safe" was defined in 1968 as follows:

    "<u>One Point Safety Criteria:</u>

    "In the event of a detonation initiated at any one point in the high explosive system, the probability of achieving a nuclear yield greater than four (4) pounds TNT equivalent shall not exceed one in one million (1×10^6).

    "One point safety shall be inherent in the nuclear design; that is, it shall be obtained without the use of a nuclear safing device."

    Drell Report, Figure 1.

50. Defence Committee 1993, ¶ 12.

1993 report will make it clear why each of these questions is significant.

Finally, there is one point in the Oxburgh Report which merits emphasis: that assessment of system safety will be inadequate unless the system is considered as a whole.

> A major concern over present arrangements for nuclear weapon safety is that although they are good for the evaluation of individual system elements, they are less good for viewing the safety of the system as a whole. System elements that are separately safe may interact in ways not easily foreseen (e.g. in the case of Trident the whole system comprises warhead, missile, submarine reactor, torpedoes, shore facilities, etc). Overview of the whole system is difficult but essential and is made more difficult if staff are inexperienced or spend too short a time in post. An overview must be maintained by individuals with appropriate technical understanding rather than by briefed officials, whether they be administrators, scientists or from the Services.[51]

This survey confirms that those who believe security lies in nuclear weapons register their strong incentive to prevent accidental detonation. Still, nuclear weapons must be designed to detonate. Small likelihood, possibly horrendous effects, and a risk not zero.

The more likely, though less serious, danger in "accident" is that fire or a chemical explosion would cause nuclear materials—especially plutonium—to be scattered, with severe effects on those nearby and diffuse effects further away.

Danger of Unauthorized Diversion or Detonation

Much less amenable to good will and technical approaches is the problem of deliberate unauthorized appropriation of a nuclear weapon. This has become a subject of open discussion since the Soviet Union collapsed in December 1991.

This speculation posits a willful agent, who may know what is required to use the weapon. Modern systems incorporate means to prevent an unauthorized person from making away with a usable weapon, and above all from doing so without raising the alarm. Once

---

51. House of Commons. Session 1992-93. Defence Committee. Sixth Report. *The Progress of the Trident Programme*. 16 June 1993. P. 30. Quotation from "Extract from 'The Safety of UK Nuclear Weapons'—Report of the review conducted by a working group led by the MoD's Scientific Adviser (July 1992)."

again, however, it is important to stress that nuclear weapons are made to detonate.

We know very little about the measures France and China have taken specifically to address theft and unauthorized use, and only a little more about Britain. The Oxburgh Report spells out security provisions in the most general terms, citing tamper-proofing disablers, impediments to removal from transport vehicles, guarding procedures and nuclear release procedures. "Policy advice" on security of nuclear weapons is the task of the Assistant Chief of the Defence Staff (Policy and Nuclear).[52] British policy that it will not discuss warhead design publicly precludes knowing whether tamper-proofing features which *can* be installed actually *are* installed. US practice is quite different, and revelations in the Drell Report, though it largely concerns "safety," also speak to unauthorised use. ENDS—the safety device of one weak and two strong links we described above—includes one link which requires a code to be entered; the Drell Report recommends that ENDS be installed in all nuclear weapons in the US stockpile. What ENDS means for unauthorized use is that the user must have the "coded information" to input and must transmit it. Since the United States has been installing ENDS since 1977, it seems highly probable that Britain will have installed ENDS in its Trident warheads.

The Drell Report is more disturbing, however, with respect to who has the "coded information" in the US Trident system. While congratulating the US Navy for its "tight system of use controls on its Trident missiles at sea" Drell continues, ominously, that

> However, the Navy's fleet ballistic missile system differs [from US Air Force systems] in that, whereas launch authority comes from outside the submarine, there is no requirement for external information to be provided in order physically to enable a launch. It is also important to evaluate the suitability of continuing this procedure into the future.

This means that—in December 1990, at least—everything needed to launch a US Trident missile was aboard the SSBN when it slipped from the quay. We can speculate that when an order to launch is received (probably) two officers—say, the captain and his executive officer—retrieve codes from locked safes and, in the presence of others,

52. Oxburgh Report, ¶ 2.6.1.

enter their codes according to a countdown protocol. These procedures, like those in missile silos, probably make it impossible for one person, acting alone, to achieve a launch even if he has the other party's codes. What they cannot prevent—and this is the force of Drell's observation—is unauthorized use by a group of confederates including those who have access to safe-held codes. The probability of mutiny aboard an SSBN, or unauthorised commandeering of the ship by a captain and exec, must be very small but is not zero.[53]

We do not know whether the Three follow the United States in sending boats to sea as self-contained nuclear arsenals. The technical reasons to do so are two: the SSBN (SNLE) should not reveal itself to receive a radio message, and the broadcasting facilities might be destroyed. (The "authorisation" message is transmitted at a painfully slow rate, using means designed to be audible at depth. Destruction of those means would become known to the submarine.)

There remains a very serious issue, rarely acknowledged, of unauthorized use writ large.

Danger of Unauthorized Use in Civil War

Where one is not dealing with a lone "madman" or a small criminal cabal, but with important elements of the political and military structure of the state, the measures taken to prevent unauthorized use may no longer be sufficient. In a divided state each side may have specialists with access to the authorization schemes of weapons in their possession. They may include senior military officers and even some of those who designed and built control devices.

Is this far-fetched? A scenario something like this is what concerns those who observe former Soviet nuclear-armed missiles on Ukrainian soil and speculate that Ukraine could figure out required launch codes. The point here is only that part of the judgment of a state about the relative utility and disutility of a nuclear weapons capability must be whether those weapons could be turned against the state itself and the people it serves. The customary "deterrence" ar-

53. Material gathered by journalists at the time of the John Walker spy case, which involved two men associated with US attack submarines, revealed that several members of the crew of one attack submarine were members of a Ku Klux Klan cell.

gument about inter-state stability does not necessarily apply within a single state, for there might be no clear-cut "enemy capital" against which deterrent revenge could be taken. Moreover, civil wars have, in country after country, been unusually brutal.

There is no evidence that British, French, or Chinese nuclear weapons have ever escaped from central control or been targets of a cabal. However, John Lewis and Xue Litai recount Mao Zedong's nephew, Mao Yuanxin, having led a group of "revolutionary youths" to the Chinese test site in 1967 to "exchange experiences," at the height of the Great Proletarian Cultural Revolution; they were arrested, but not without a sharp clash between Nie Rongzhen, head of the Defense Science and Technology Commission, and Chen Boda, head of the Cultural Revolution Small Group.[54]

Comparative Costs

Advocates of nuclear weapons argue that the costs are less than those which a non-nuclear defense would require. In other words, if Britain, France, or China did not have nuclear weapons they might choose to spend more on other military means of defense. That this claim is not self-evidently persuasive can, however, be established by comparing expenditure (Table 8.5).

Table 8.5 shows that in the early 1990s Britain and France spent more than the average of NATO Europe and more per capita even than Germany, despite their nuclear weapons. Their costs were "high." (Japan's markedly smaller *per capita* expenditure is customarily attributed to her accepting US nuclear and conventional "protection," but it may simply follow from her declining to undertake defense

54. Lewis and Xue, *China Builds the Bomb*, pp. 203-204. Mao Yuanxin was himself a recent graduate of the Harbin Military Engineering Institute, which supplied many personnel to the test base. More generally, nuclear weapons work and work on delivery systems was widely disrupted. See Lewis and Xue, *China's Strategic Seapower*, pp. 40-42, and *China Builds the Bomb*, pp. 201-205.

In this context, note also the controversy about whether Gorbachev lost control of the Soviet force for three days during the coup of August 1991. See Roland Lomme, "Contrôle et Prolifération des Armes Nucléaires en URSS," in Pascal Boniface (ed), *L'Année Stratégique 1992* (Paris: Dunod-IRIS, 1992).

programs which were well within her grasp.)

By another reading, Britain and France spent much less than the United States: their costs were "low." The riposte is that the United States over-armed. British defense expenditure in the 1990s as a percentage of GDP is declining, but appears likely to remain above the NATO Europe average. At least the figures show that nuclear weapons did not guarantee cheap defense.

TABLE 8.5

Selected Comparisons: Military Expenditure (1993)

STATE OR GROUP	ME/GNP[a] AS %	PER CAPITA (1993 US$)
Britain	3.6	$587
France	3.4	740
China	2.7	48
NATO	3.6	689
NATO Europe	2.7	419
East Asia	1.9	75
World	3.3	157
Japan	1.0	335
Germany (West)	2.2	454

[a] ME = Military Expenditure. GNP = Gross National Product.

Source: *World Military Expenditures and Arms Transfers 1993-1994.* US Arms Control and Disarmament Agency.

Appendix 8.1

United Kingdom. House of Commons. Session 1992-93. Defence Committee. Sixth Report. (Excerpts). Pp. viii-x, ¶s 10-15. Text in bold is bold in the original.

The Progress of the Trident Programme

II. Safety

Drell and Oxburgh

10. In December 1990, an American expert panel chaired by Dr Sidney Drell, and convened by the House of Representatives Armed Services Committee, issued its report on nuclear weapons safety, concentrating in particular on the D5 missile and its warhead. Several issues were raised of direct relevance to the UK, in particular the positioning of the warheads in the missile's third stage around the motor, the choice of missile propellant and warhead explosive, and the handling of the missile and warhead. Our predecessors examined MoD on these matters in 1991 and criticised MoD's bland and evasive responses in its 1991 Report.[a] In October 1991 the then Minister of State for Defence Procurement announced that the Chief Scientific Adviser, Professor Oxburgh, had been invited to lead a small working group "to review, in the light of any relevant aspects of the report of the Drell Panel in the United States the safety of the present and prospective UK nuclear armoury."[b] The report was received by Ministers in early 1992, and a declassified version placed in the Library of the House of Commons in July 1992.[c] We sought the full version of the Report; in refusing our request, MoD referred to the material withheld for reasons of national security having been kept to a bare minimum, and assured us that they "do not interfere with a proper understanding of the report and its conclusions."[d] While we cannot in principle accept the Government's refusal to provide information to us at whatever level of classification it may be, we accept the assurances that the excised passages of the report are not of critical significance.

Trident

11. In the context of this Report, our principal concern must be the safety of the Trident system, covered in paragraphs 4.4.1-5 of the Oxburgh Report. Oxburgh records that, because of the absence of an alternative team in the UK to provide a back-up validation of the studies at AWE, "the Group can offer no definitive view on Trident one-point safety."[e] In evidence to us submitted in February 1993 however, the MoD stated that—

> "The Committee can be assured that our Trident warheads have now been definitively assessed to be one-point safe."[f]

In oral evidence, MoD witnesses confirmed this, and confirmed "categorically" that the Trident warhead was one-point safe, as a result of further work since the Oxburgh report.[g] **We welcome the categorical assurances given to us that the Trident warhead is one-point safe.**

Propellant

12. One of the principal concerns raised in the Drell Report was over the design of the D5 missile, in that the warheads are grouped around the third-stage motor in relatively close proximity to the propellant, rather than above it.[h] The unusually close proximity of inflammable and potentially explosive propellant and nuclear warheads is naturally a matter of concern. It is self-evident that the UK cannot change the fundamental design of a missile it is buying off-the-shelf. It might however be thought possible to select a propellant which would reduce the possibility of an explosion, and to introduce safety features into the warhead which would minimise the dangers of release of plutonium should such an explosion take place. The propellant proposed to be used in Trident D5 is dubbed 1.1 class, a high energy propellant, which has a 4 per cent longer specific impulse, propelling a rocket to greater velocity and therefore longer range. In the case of Trident D5 missiles, the additional range is of the order of 150 to 200 nautical miles.[i] The alternative propellant is dubbed 1.3 class, a composite propellant, which it is practically impossible to detonate.[j]

The Oxburgh Report observed, somewhat cryptically, that—

> "We are buying the Trident missile off the shelf from the US and unless the US decide to modify their system our only choices are to use it as it is, or not to let it enter service."[k]

MoD confirmed that these constraints applied to the choice of propellant as well as to missile design, and that—

> "the missile would require major redesign work to accommodate a different propellant, and it would not be practicable for the UK to seek to change the design unilaterally for UK missiles."[l]

In oral evidence, MoD confirmed that, not only would a unilateral change of propellant be very expensive, but that even a bilateral decision to change at this stage would increase costs.[m] Nevertheless, we re-assert the overriding importance of safety, and we would welcome further consideration of an alternative fuel even at the cost of a marginal reduction in range.

Handling

13. The issue of propellant safety arises almost entirely in the context of occasions where the warhead and missile are handled together, primarily on loading or unloading of a submarine. Drell expressed concern at the intended US practice of transporting complete missile/warhead assemblies, compared to the UK practice of mounting warheads onto missiles already in submarines. Oxburgh however felt that "one practice may not be significantly preferable to the other" and recommended continuing studies into Trident missile loading and unloading.[n] MoD's written evidence referred only to all aspects of Trident nuclear weapon safety being examined.[o] In oral evidence, the Director General Strategic Weapon Systems told us that whichever method was adopted would be chosen "to minimise the perceived risk."[p] **We commend MoD's willingness to reconsider its hitherto preferred method of missile loading and unloading in the light of safety factors, and we look to the Department for continuing openness on the method eventually adopted.**

Safety features

14. The UK has designed its Trident warhead independently of the US, constrained only by the need for its weight and shape to conform to the requirements of the missile design. There is therefore no reason why the UK warhead should not have different safety features from those on the designated US warhead.[q] The Oxburgh Report stated that the Trident warhead system incorporated "state-of-the-art safety technology for the time it was designed," although "a weapon system safer than Trident could be designed today."[r] It also described it as "comparable to, and in some ways safer than, Chevaline."[s] MoD has confirmed that the UK Trident warhead had "more advanced safety features" than Chevaline.[t]

15. Because of the long-standing practice not to reveal "details of warhead design," MoD have refused to reveal in public whether the design incorporates the three principal modern safety elements—Insensitive High Explosive (IHE), Fire Resistant Pits (FRPs) or Enhanced Nuclear Detonation Safety (ENDS) systems. The Oxburgh Report did not recommend particular safety technologies, but proposed that any safety justification or evaluation should be required to show that the use of IHE, FRPs and ENDS had been *considered*, "along with other technologies that might become available within the timescale of the project."[u] **We consider however that the public are entitled to know whether specific and well-publicised safety features are or are not incorporated within nuclear weapons, as is the case in the United States.** IHE has a much lower probability of detonation as a result of a violent accident than conventional high explosive, but more of it is required to initiate a nuclear detonation, meaning greater weight and volume of explosive. The US Trident warhead uses HE, to avoid having to accept reductions in either the number, yield or range of warheads to compensate for the additional volume of IHE required. The scale of the reduction which would be required is of the order of carrying seven rather than eight warheads.[v] The ENDS system, introduced in the US in 1977, is designed to prevent the electrical system conveying a false firing signal, through the insertion of two "strong links," and one "weak link" designed to fail in

abnormal environments. FRPs are shields designed to protect the plutonium cores in the event of fierce fire, including burning of the explosive. **The probability is that some or all of these are incorporated in the UK Trident warhead: the onus is on the Government to explain why they, unlike our American allies, are unwilling to reveal the facts.**

Notes:

[a] 1991 Report, paras 10-10.

[b] 1992 Report, paras 23-24.

[c] HC Deb, 13 July 1992, col 521w.

[d] Evidence, p 27, A10a.

[e] (Quotes Drell on one-point safety.)

[f] Evidence, p 27, A10b.

[g] Qq 1525-6, 1531.

[h] Drell Report, p 29: 1991 Report, para 12.

[i] Q1597: Evidence, p 34, A17.

[j] Drell, pp 28-29.

[k] para 4.4.3.

[l] Evidence, p 27, A10c.

[m] Qq 1596-99.

[n] para 4.4.3.

[o] Evidence, p 27, A10b.

[p] Q1590.

[q] Qq 1600-1602.

[r] 4.4.5, 6.4.

[s] 6.4.

[t] Evidence, p 27, A10c.

[u] 4.5.3.

[v] Drell Report, page 28.

9

Threats and Fears

In chapter 7 we located the institutions and political parties which strive to determine national nuclear policy. If a nuclear weapons program has "momentum" it can be found among the men and women in these groups and the populace which supports them. Their continued commitment to nuclear weapons is a political fact which advocates of disengagement and abolition must confront.

Chapter 8 approached nuclear weapons from an altogether different direction, asking what costs and harms nuclear weapons entailed.

In the dialectic between the "need" for nuclear weapons and reasons to be rid of them, everything hinges on whether nuclear weapons enhance or diminish security. But "security" and "insecurity" are psychological states, not material conditions. Moreover, capacity to inflict harm matters to the observer only as a "perceived threat." This means that we need to know something about how people in Britain, France, and China see their surroundings. Do they anticipate harm? Of what are they afraid? By whom do they expect to be threatened? The case for nuclear weapons—the reason why the "momentum" of nuclear weapons receives sustaining official and public support—is that there are or *may be* actual threats for which nuclear weapons could be used to deter or destroy the threatener. In this chapter we will canvass some salient perceptions of threat, though certainly not all.

A Schematic Table of Perceived Threats

Whom do the Three fear? The states shown in table 9.1 are those which have nuclear capabilities, or are believed to be acquiring them, plus those non-nuclear states which are "historic rivals." Nuclear policy rises from concern about these states above all. (In addition, as we have observed many times, states explain their nuclear forces as a precaution against future threats from sources not now identifiable.)

TABLE 9.1
Sources of Fear: Nuclear States and Historic Rivals

STATES BY TYPE		BRITAIN	CHINA	FRANCE
(i)	Nuclear weapon states but not allies.	Russia China	Russia United States Britain France	Russia China
(ii)	Historical rivals	Germany	Japan	Germany
(iii)	*En route* to nuclear weapons able to reach national territory.		(India)	
(iv)	Nuclear weapon states, but allies.	United States France (Israel)	(Pakistan)	United States Britain (Israel)
(v)	Other nuclear weapon states	(Pakistan) (India)	(Israel)	(Pakistan) (India)
(vi)	Other states of concern	Ukraine• Iran Libya	Kazakhstan• Ukraine• (Korea)	Ukraine• Iran Libya

Notes: [•] signifies that concerns about Ukraine and Kazakhstan will be largely satisfied upon their completion of obligations under the Lisbon Protocol.

Perceived Threats

Britain, France, and China—like the two superpowers—say they need nuclear weapons for national security. Why they do but others do not is a very interesting issue—at the heart of the NPT—but we will set it aside here. Here we start with the claim that a national security requirement exists and ask what threats give rise to it.

In each of the Three, people focus their fears and uncertainties about the future on a short list of states. Some threaten today; some have threatened in the past; some are *en route* to a nuclear capacity; and some could acquire the capacity to threaten in the future. These imply some states—today the talk is about "new nuclear weapon states"—which cannot be named but are hypothetical possibilities sufficiently strong that military planners take them into account. In addition, we must consider nuclear-armed states which are traditional allies, but which nonetheless have the capacity to destroy.

As it happens, the lists of "concerns" for each of the Three overlap. It is most convenient to take up the respective sources of threat one by one, differentiating—where possible—in how they are perceived by the three second-tier nuclear powers.

Russia

In a nuclear world, states are at best "conditionally viable,"[1] and Russia and the United States are principally responsible for that fact. By recent estimates (May 1994) Russia deploys 7005 warheads on 765 land-based strategic missiles, 520 submarine-based missiles, and 69 bombers. The SSBN fleet consists of 31 submarines. In addition, a further 2658 warheads are deployed on 302 land-based missiles and 40 bombers located in Ukraine, Kazakhstan, and Belarus, under the shared command of the Commonwealth of Independent States.[2]

This force is being reduced in size, and units deployed in Ukraine, Kazakhstan, and Belarus are being moved to Russia. START II envisions a Russian strategic force of perhaps 3200 warheads, fewer than half the number now deployed, by the year 2003 (or 2000 with US assistance). Russia has announced detargeting and removal of weapons from alert.[3] Despite these measures no target on earth is immune from attack.

The Russian force was built to threaten military and civilian targets. Planners in Britain, China, and France have doubtless assumed that their principal cities, bases, military-industrial capabilities and strategic forces have been targeted—and whatever detargeting may

1. Kenneth Boulding, *Conflict and Defense: A General Theory* (New York: Harper, 1963).

2. Estimates of *Arms Control Today*, May 1994, p. 26, on the assumption that several older systems are deactivated (SS-11s, SS-13s, SS-17s, and Yankee and Delta-I class SSBNs). Planners in other countries would also note attentively that the SS-25 (of which 405 single-warhead missiles are deployed) remains in production and that a follow-on missile is reported. *Ibid.*, citing unspecified US intelligence. A flight test of the new missile is expected soon, and deployment later in the 1990s.

3. Russia has signed detargeting agreements with three of the four declared nuclear states, the United States, Britain, and China.

mean, planners who failed to anticipate a Russian strike on their positions would be judged derelict.

On the other hand, Britain, France, and China gain by other Russian steps. The INF Treaty (1987) mandated destruction of intermediate nuclear forces, including missiles along the Chinese border; China in particular welcomed the final terms of the treaty, having feared that missiles from Europe would be transplanted to Asia. Russian withdrawal of tactical nuclear weapons to its own territory reduces the likelihood of tactical nuclear confrontation with Britain or France. China may judge it marginally useful that 40 Bear-H bombers armed with nuclear-tipped cruise missiles have been removed from Kazakhstan, which adjoins China's Xinjiang Province, to Russia.[4]

More difficult to gauge, but ultimately more significant, is the extent of political and technical cooperation between Russia and the Three. Some cooperation—such as Russian military sales to China—would have been unthinkable twenty-five years ago, and Russia is struggling to create political relations with western Europe which shut the door on Cold War confrontation. With time, Russia might become more like a nuclear-armed ally: contingently dangerous, but not a foreground threat. That is not how defense planners speak today. The French *Livre Blanc 1994*, for example, is very clear in portraying Russia as a militarily powerful state whose future is not settled.

The United States

In October 1994 China and the United States resumed military contacts at the highest level, suspended in 1989 in the wake of Tiananmen. The fact remains, however, that the United States maintains a massive nuclear capability which could be directed at China if it chose to do so. We have noted US nuclear threats against China in the 1950s. If such threats seem unthinkable today, military planners must consider actual vulnerabilities.

Certainly the United States and China are not allies, but they have become capable of extensive consultation. The two leaderships are well aware of common interests. When China prepared to go to war against Vietnam in 1979, Deng Xiaoping walked the halls of

---

4. *Arms Control Today*, May 1994, above.

Congress, looking for support, in a calculated approach to caution Moscow against a retaliatory move. But China is also wary. Ronald Reagan's "Star Wars" seemed to threaten the Chinese deterrent. US fascination with "theater BMD" in the mid-1990s has the same effect. So this is not a simple relationship.

Germany

Although defeated and in ruins in 1945, Germany had burned itself into the minds of those in Britain and France concerned with national security. They could well imagine that World War II might have ended differently had Germany achieved nuclear weapons in an otherwise non-nuclear world. Germany had fought two wars against them. At the beginning, therefore, British and French nuclear programs sprang in part from fear of Germany. But post-World War II Germany is their ally; and in achieving alliance Germany promised not to acquire nuclear weapons. A French government of the 1950s set in motion Franco-German-Italian cooperation in a project which Bertrand Goldschmidt terms "close to the military nuclear field," but when de Gaulle returned to lead France in 1957 he blocked the plan. "The general never overcame his concern at the possibility of German nuclear armament," writes Goldschmidt, "and he questioned me at length on this issue every time I had the honor of meeting him during the 1960s."[5]

The German issue became concealed behind the establishment of a coalition to counter Soviet capabilities in central and western Europe.[6]

---

5. Bertrand Goldschmidt, *The Atomic Complex: A Worldwide Political History of Nuclear Energy* (La Grange Park, Illinois: American Nuclear Society, 1982), p. 186.

6. Anton W. DePorte has written of the 1947 Anglo-French Treaty of Dunkirk that it "reflected the growing French conviction that De Gaulle's policy of Franco-Soviet collaboration on Germany was born dead and that France had to cover itself as best it could against a new German state whose emergence it could not prevent, and whose partnership, in some form, it would have to seek." In this treaty—and at the founding of NATO a year later—France "entered into ostensibly anti-German arrangements to be able to accept German revival as part of an anti-Soviet policy." Anton W. DePorte, *Europe Between the Superpowers: The Enduring Balance* (New Haven: Yale University Press, 1979), p. 138.

Could Germany "go nuclear"? In 1958 the United States, resisting calls for denuclearization of East and West Germany, agreed to lodge "dual key" systems with West Germany. The Multilateral Force (MLF) proposed in late 1962 would have put Polaris A-3 nuclear missiles on ships with mixed-nationality crews, including German naval personnel. Andrew J. Pierre writes of this episode that British Foreign Office officials "tended to believe that by pushing the proposal so hard the United States had to some extent created a German appetite for nuclear weapons, but whatever its origins they came to agree that pressures for greater participation in nuclear strategy were building up in Germany."[7] Moreover, the Labour Party

> was even more strongly opposed to the MLF than the Tories or the defence establishment. . . . Distaste for Germany and of any German nuclear role was at the heart of Labour's opposition to the MLF.[8]

The MLF failed. Though Chancellor Ludwig Erhard broached a bilateral "MLF" with the United States, the nuclear option was not on his agenda, nor that of his successors. By the late 1960s "German security concerns about nuclear weapons were adequately satisfied by the consultative arrangement provided by the NATO Nuclear Planning Group in lieu of the abandoned MLF."[9]

Do memories of World War I and World War II still mark French relations with Germany? In 1990 the Civilian Affairs Committee of the North American Assembly noted creation of the Franco-German Brigade but cautioned that "the French are still reluctant to deepen this co-operation, which could for instance include training and provisional basing of German forces in France. Memories from past conflicts being still too vivid, this is something that is not likely to happen within at least the next 10 to 15 years."[10] When the German Eurocorps contingent joined other units in

---

7. Andrew J. Pierre, *Nuclear Politics: The British Experience with an Independent Strategic Force 1939-1970* (London: Oxford University Press, 1972), p. 247.

8. *Ibid.*, pp. 249-250.

9. DePorte, *Europe Between the Superpowers*, above, p. 184. See also Catherine Kelleher, *Germany and the Politics of Nuclear Weapons* (New York: Columbia University Press, 1975).

10. AH 238 CC(90)6, November 1990.

marching down the Champs-Elysées on Bastille Day 1994, the first German troops to parade the avenue in fifty years, former President Giscard d'Estaing wept on television that it was "too soon": "In 1944 every morning I heard the sound of boots, of Nazi songs. If one has such memories, it's difficult to contain one's emotions."[11] Pierre Gallois' views on French defence (reviewed at the end of this chapter) show the intense passion with which French nuclear autonomy and concern about German intentions merge in his interpretation of France's security future.

Nor is World War II forgotten in Britain. On 23 November 1994 a vice-chairman of the Conservative Party, a former cabinet minister, was forced to resign his party post for flailing against Germany and France, one as the source of two world wars, the other as a "nation of collaborators."[12]

• • •

The German question of the 1950s and 1960s turned on the tradeoff between resisting Soviet threats (through Western alliance) and achieving reunification (by conciliating the Soviets). The choice was for alliance. Patience brought reunification. Ironically, the end of the Cold War created a new opportunity for nuclearism. With sharpening awareness of nuclear programs in Pakistan, India, Iraq, South Africa, and North Korea, and the German and Japanese claims for political status through permanent seats on the UN Security Council, the question arose again whether Germany might move to acquire nuclear weapons. Even the absence of serious German proposals for nuclear weapons could not prevent analysts in other states from wondering whether German economic and political surgence might not be

---

11. *International Herald Tribune*, 15 July 1994.

12. *The Independent*, 24 November 1994. Patrick Nicholl's remarks were published at a moment when the Tories were embroiled in internecine struggle over Europe. "I have no great liking for a continent dominated by two countries, the unique contribution of one of which has been to plunge Europe into two world wars in living memory. . . . Too many of my compatriots have died to the strains of *Deutschland über Alles.*" And France "had the nerve to represent itself as a nation of resistance fighters in World War II when in fact it was a nation of collaborators . . ." Also see *Le Monde* 25 November 1994, where a Pancho cartoon has Nicholls saying "Perhaps I ought not to have spoken of Fritz and the Frogs."

followed, in due course, by the rise of nuclearism.

Nonetheless, a Germany which distances itself from a weapons project—by urging non-proliferation, accepting IAEA safeguards, and declining to stockpile plutonium—is simply like other industrial states which command skill and maintain complex and varied research and development capabilities.

Japan

Just as European states have centered concern on Germany for a century and more, China and Korea—and Russia as it looks to its Far East—have fixed on Japan. Like Germany, Japan boasts scientific and engineering capabilities of the highest level. Unlike Germany, Japan has made nuclear power generation a national priority; and—unlike Germany in a second important respect—Japan is stockpiling plutonium. Nothing warns of a possible capacity for prompt nuclearization more clearly than an available plutonium supply, since once the plutonium is in store the nuclear component of an atomic weapon can be fabricated, we are told, "in days."

Japan-China relations have long been plagued by distrust. China lost the Sino-Japanese War of 1894-95 and, as a consequence, surrendered Taiwan and other lands and rights. Japan, which declared war on Germany in 1914, put troops into Shandong, captured Qingdao, and in January 1915 issued the "Twenty-One Demands" to dictator Yuan Shikai's government, demands for extensive economic and administrative powers which Yuan, despite widespread protests, largely conceded.[13] Chinese modernizers still pay tribute to the 4 May 1919 student demonstrators who challenged Japan's efforts to win Chinese territorial concessions from the Versailles Peace Conference. Then Japan invaded China's northeast in 1931, and its northern and coastal provinces in 1937, launching a war symbolized in brutality by the Rape of Nanjing, a war which ended only with Japan's defeat in 1945.[14]

---

13. See Jonathan D. Spence, *The Search for Modern China* (New York: Norton, 1990), pp. 285-286.

14. John Fairbank, Edwin O. Reischauer and Albert Craig, *East Asia: The Modern Transformation* (Boston: Houghton Mifflin, 1965), pp. 382-384, 648, 665-666, 706-717.

Japan's adventure in China ended in nuclear war at Hiroshima and Nagasaki. Japan remained seared by its encounter with nuclearism, even as it emerged in the 1960s and 1970s as a great manufacturing and commercial center. Japan rearmed at US urging from the late 1940s, signed a Mutual Security Treaty with the United States, and took on the mission of patrolling its own seas and those stretching south toward Taiwan. We now understand that its governing Liberal Democratic Party was funded by the US Central Intelligence Agency. Still, Japan was constrained by the political and social reality of its nuclear experience. Civil society cultivated a "nuclear allergy," Japan declared the three non-nuclear principles of "no possession, no manufacturing, and no introduction of nuclear weapons into Japan," and Article 9 of the Japanese constitution—drafted under US auspices—renounced war, banned "war potential," and negated the right of belligerency. A 1980 Japanese Defense Agency White Paper described the limitations on Japan in this way:

> The specific limit of self-defense capability permissible under such constitutional limitation has to be judged in accordance with the prevailing international situation, the standards of military technology and other conditions. But Japan evidently cannot own those weapons which are so powerful that they are used exclusively for the complete destruction of foreign lands. ICBMs and long-range bombers are usually cited as examples of such weapons. . .
>
> Even when some nuclear weapons are considered to be permissible under the Japanese Constitution, Japan has decided never to possess them. Furthermore, Japan also declared internationally in June 1976 that it would not possess nuclear weapons by acceding to the Nuclear Non-Proliferation Treaty.[15]

These principles form the terms of debate around which the Japanese necessarily conduct any decision to prepare for operations abroad or achieve a nuclear capability. At the same time, there has been an ambivalence in Japan's policy, a contradiction between public declarations and private conduct. Some twenty years ago attention was called to the LDP's studied avoidance of the issue of US nuclear-armed ships berthing at US naval bases in Japan. These contradictions broke forth dramatically in 1994 when the *Mainichi Shimbun* revealed a 1969 Japanese Foreign Ministry report which said, in part,

---

15. Japan. Defense Agency. *Defense of Japan 1980*. Sixth White Paper on Defense, pp. 86-87.

> For the time being, we will adopt a policy of not possessing nuclear arms. But we will maintain the economic and technical potential of producing nuclear weapons. . . . At the same time, we must protect this from foreign intervention.[16]

Japan's delay in ratifying the NPT[17] doubtless met with approval from those Japanese who sought to hedge against the non-nuclear principles, or deny that the constitution barred Japan from nuclear weapons, but Japan's ostensible concern with the NPT was of quite the opposite order: that it appeared to ratify the *status quo* and recognize the legitimacy of states' holding nuclear weapons. These issues resurfaced in mid-1993, when the United States sought to obtain support of the G7 for an indefinite extension of the NPT at the NPT Review and Extension Conference of 1995. Japan at first declined to commit to indefinite extension, but then agreed.[18] Japan and the United States have also agreed to work closely on the problem of North Korea's resistance to IAEA inspections.[19]

China's analysts and planners doubtless take a special interest in any signs of a Japanese flirtation with nuclear weapons and long-range delivery systems. For example, they must follow with care the Japanese H-II rocket program, its first rocket test-launched in February 1994 by the National Space Development Agency of Japan. Intended to lift a 2000 kg payload into geostationary orbit, the H-II was designed and built without reliance on US technology, freeing Japan from US restrictions on use of the missile, and is of an advanced design.[20] The H-II is not reported to be configured for weapons

---

16. *International Herald Tribune*, 2 August 1994, citing *Mainichi Shimbun*,1 August 1994.

17. Japan signed on 3 February 1970, before the treaty went into effect, but did not deposit its ratification until 8 June 1976. US ACDA. *Arms Control and Disarmament Agreements*, 1982, p. 97.

18. A sense of the internal debate is suggested by the proposal of Kumao Kaneko, former head of the Department of Nuclear Energy in the Japanese Ministry of External Affairs, that the NPT be prolonged conditionally for ten to fifteen years, subject to the nuclear weapons states committing to a timetable for denuclearization. Cited in Selig Harrison, "Surenchères nucléaires entre Tokyo et Séoul," *Le Monde Diplomatique*, September 1993.

19. *International Herald Tribune*, 15 September 1993, citing an AFP despatch.

20. Dieter Brand, deputy manager of the Tokyo office of Arianespace, characterized the H-II as "not only more sophisticated than Ariane 4 but also more than Ariane 5," now under development with a planned first flight in 1995. *The New York*

purposes, nor does its liquid fueled first-stage LE-7 rocket meet military criteria for prompt launch, but it is a measure of an active missile research and engineering program.

Chinese analysts have also no doubt paid alert attention to a newspaper report that the British Ministry of Defense warned Prime Minister John Major in December 1993 that Japan "has key bomb-making components, including plutonium and electronic triggers, and has the expertise to 'go nuclear' very quickly."[21] The MoD report said that the North Korean nuclear and missile programs threatened to force Japan to give up its non-nuclear stance. Japan promptly denied any "nuclear option."[22] Speculation that a North Korean program would be followed by Japan's seeking a nuclear deterrent was recurrent in comment after North Korea gave notice in March 1993 of its intention to leave the NPT, and has been one argument in the internal US debates whether to take a compellant or accommodationist position toward North Korea's nuclear program.[23]

Some Japanese, however, remain tuned to nuclear possibilities. In May 1994 Yamasaki Taku—opposition Diet member and former defense minister—asked whether Japan should support unlimited NPT extension if North Korea were shown to be making nuclear weapons. His comment prompted Foreign Minister Kakizawa Koji to say that Japan, to clear itself of suspicions whether it would arm with nuclear weapons to counter a North Korean threat, "must make clear that we will continue to support an unlimited extension of NPT."[24]

Against this backdrop, Japan's deliberate plutonium stockpiling necessarily prompts speculation about nuclear weapons intentions.[25]

Times, 25 January 1994.

21. London *Sunday Times*, 30 January 1994, as quoted in Reuters 30 January 1994. It quotes an unidentified expert who had read the report that Japan "could have acquired all the expertise for imploding a weapon without breaking safeguards. All they would need to do is select adequate amounts of plutonium for the core."
22. *The New York Times*, 2 February 1994.
23. Interviews, June 1993.
24. Reuters, 22 May 1994.
25. For example, in the following exchange between Mr. David Sumberg, member of the House of Commons Foreign Affairs Committee, and Douglas Hogg, Minister of State in the Foreign Office, on 6 July 1994:

    (Mr. Sumberg) Can you assure this Committee that plutonium from the

The fact that Japan's leadership has viewed Japan as vulnerable to isolation and rupture of energy supply from abroad is not well-appreciated outside Japan; and so Tokyo's policy of energy independence is not well understood. Specialists on nuclear weapons say that an atomic bomb can be fabricated from plutonium holdings "in a matter of days" by a technically-advanced state.[26] One of the prime design problems a non-nuclear regime must address, therefore, is how Japan can give effect to its non-nuclear assurances.

Korea

There is certainly concern in Japan and the United States that Korea—either North Korea, or a unified Korea—might acquire nuclear weapons. US policy has sought, successively, to win North Korean signature of the NPT, a North Korean safeguards agreement with IAEA, and—after March 1993—reversal of North Korea's suspension of its NPT adherence. It has striven vigorously to persuade North Korea that unsafeguarded plutonium production should be abandoned.

China, too, would of necessity be concerned with a significant Korean nuclear weapons capacity. In the negotiations of 1993-95,

---

THORP reprocessing plant will not be used either by this country or indeed anyone else in the manufacture of nuclear weapons?

(Mr. Hogg) You are concentrating, I suspect, primarily on Japan because that is the most important of our contracts. That is our judgment. Japan, like any other sophisticated industrial country, would no doubt have a capacity to develop in fairly short order a weapon so the question is whether the safeguards are effective and whether we are satisfied with the policy of the Japanese Government? The answer is to both of those latter questions, yes. We believe the safeguards are effective and will be adhered to and we are satisfied by the policy of the Japanese Government.

(Mr. Sumberg) And in turn you are satisfied that the material will not be used from THORP for nuclear weapons?

(Mr. Hogg) That is correct. That is what I tried to say in my answer.

House of Commons. Session 1993-94. Foreign Affairs Committee. *UK Policy on Weapons Proliferation and Control in the Post-Cold War Era.* Minutes of Evidence. 6 July 1994. P. 39.

26. This would be a fission weapon (A-bomb), not a fusion (thermonuclear) weapon (H-bomb); and it requires some assumptions about the isotopic composition of the plutonium.

however, Beijing has urged patience and forbearance. The *New York Times'* Beijing correspondent observed in November 1993 that it was "implicit in China's strategy that it might tolerate the development of a nuclear bomb until it could persuade a successor regime to return to non-nuclear status."[27] A Chinese official with experience in strategic systems told this author in June 1993 that "even if North Korea had a nuclear bomb it would not be militarily useful." Since that time Kim Il Sung has died and there have been more signs of accommodation, though—as US officials closest to the negotiations hasten to point out—nothing is sure.

Belarus, Kazakhstan, and Ukraine

Under negotiated arrangements former Soviet systems in Belarus, Kazakhstan, and Ukraine are held by a command of the "Commonwealth of Independent States" and are its principal *raison d'etre.*

Five questions confronted each of the three new states. Would they transfer *tactical* nuclear weapons to Russia? Would they accept an obligation to perform relevant Soviet obligations under START I (which include dismantling some systems on their territory)? Would they cooperate in their own denuclearization by completing the relevant START steps, and then by sending other strategic systems to Russia? Then, would they join IAEA, with the full safeguards required, as non-nuclear states? And, finally, would they sign and ratify the Non-Proliferation Treaty?

We have reviewed the current status of these forces in chapter 4. It must be underscored, however, that the nuclear weapons in Ukraine are not a Ukrainian striking force: they are under CIS control, implemented by troops and firing procedures said to include a requirement for codes to target and fire. Analysts assume Ukraine sought to obtain the codes. At this writing (June 1995), however, there is no report that Ukraine has the codes or is able to fire the missiles. On the contrary, the force is said to be being gradually destroyed.

Should that change, the objective "threat environment" of Britain, France and China would be further complicated.

---

27. Patrick E. Tyler, *The New York Times*, 28 November 1993.

India and Pakistan

Pakistan and India are identified as "threshold" states. India exploded a nuclear device in 1974. Analysts say—and neither Pakistan nor India convincingly denies—that each could readily assemble several nuclear weapons and deliver them to targets, if they do not already have assembled weapons at the ready. With Israel, they form the set of states which has remained outside the NPT and built—or nearly built—nuclear weapons. They pose an implicit challenge to the nonproliferation regime. China warred with India in 1962 and China's nuclear program was certainly one impetus for India's.

The "fact" of Indian and Pakistani nuclear weapons, even if only roughly correct, poses a set of interlocked questions for policy-makers elsewhere. First, can outsiders do anything to help Pakistan and India avoid nuclear carnage? Second, do Pakistani or Indian capabilities, now or for the medium-term future, encourage others to deploy a nuclear deterrent against India or Pakistan? Third, how can the contradiction between Indian and Pakistani capabilities and the NPT be best addressed? Fourth, can outsiders do anything to draw India and Pakistan into a denuclearized regime?

The United States has tried to steer Pakistan and India away from nuclear confrontation, but without visible success. There is no evidence that Pakistan or India will respond to inducements to set nuclear weapons aside. The October 1994 US agreement with North Korea begins to make a market in nuclear restraint, however, in which near-deployment should command a much higher price than unsafeguarded reactors.

Absent an effective *disengagement regime*, Pakistani and Indian nuclear forces will certainly be cited in internal defense debates as reasons to sustain, extend, or initially develop a nuclear capability. They may also be adduced on behalf of air defense and missile defense programs.[28] The logic of British and French choices since the mid-

---

28. India has tested the Agni, with a reported range of 2500 km and payload of 900 kg. A space launch vehicle (PSLV) with an expected range of 8000 km and payload of 1000 kg is also being tested. Arms Control Association. "The Proliferation of Ballistic Missiles." Factsheet. 10 August 1993. Pakistan also has missiles under development, but of shorter range and smaller payload.

1980s, however, is that deterrence is achieved not by vast numbers, but by the credible capability to strike at all. The main first-order effects, then, would be Chinese and Israeli measures to ensure survival of credible forces, demonstrably able to reach the source of nuclear attack from the subcontinent.

The third question is much tougher. Indian and Pakistani programs pose a problem not only for the NPT, strictly speaking, but for the entire non-proliferation regime of which it is the core. Oddly enough, it is here that Britain, France, and China have special opportunities, though opportunities they are unlikely to seize. In designing prospective disengagement regimes, weighing how their own weapons could be disengaged, they could consider as well how weapons "manufactured but not assembled" could be brought into such a system. The mutual reassurances necessarily part of any such disengagement could be extended to Pakistan and India as well. China and India could explore even more specifically how their asymmetric capabilities could be so configured that they gave the least impetus to "racing." Ultimately mutual reassurance between Pakistan and India is required, something they can only achieve with a simultaneous act of will.

There is reason to believe India received some form of assurances thirty years ago, in 1964, after China's first nuclear test, which came only two years after the Sino-Indian Border War,[29] Britain had already, in October 1956, dropped a British atomic bomb at Maralinga, South Australia, as part of a test series.[30] Some sources claim that Britain then deployed nuclear-armed aircraft in Singapore, though for other reasons, in the 1960s.[31]

---

29. Andrew Pierre, without concluding explicitly that assurances were offered or accepted, treats assurances as a subject of government consideration in the United Kingdom in 1964. While noting senior Indian officials having spoken "with considerable scorn of uninvited proposals for guarantees," Pierre notes that the *Statement on the Defence Estimates: 1965*, Cmnd. 2592, p. 7, after citing the Chinese test, goes on to state that "our nuclear policy must help to provide some reassurance to non-nuclear powers." *Nuclear Politics: The British Experience with an Independent Strategic Force, 1939-1970* (London: Oxford University Press, 1972), pp. 285-288, p. 286.

30. Norris et al., *Nuclear Weapons Databook*, Volume V, p. 86.

31. *Nuclear Weapons Databook*, Volume V, p. 90. "From December 1963 until August 1966, regular detachments of Bomber Command Victors and Vulcans

In any case, the third and fourth questions are deeply intertwined. India proposed in 1988, and repeated in 1994, that India favored a "global" agreement, one which would reduce all nuclear holdings, or eliminate nuclear weapons altogether.[32]

Washington has encouraged India and Pakistan to engage the nuclear issue in a broader context, including China. The United States proposed that nine states (US, Russia, Britain, France, and China; Germany and Japan; and Pakistan and India) meet to consult on an India-Pakistan nuclear freeze.[33] The thrust of these initiatives is to accept that only India and Pakistan can resolve the issues between them, but to offer a broader range of economic and political measures in which an Indian-Pakistani settlement could be located.

During a January 1995 visit to Pakistan and India, US Secretary of Defense William Perry encouraged talks between the parties and urged them not to deploy ballistic missiles. Perry also challenged the view that China poses a threat to India: China "does not represent, in my judgment, a significant threat, either on a global scale or on a regional scale—nor do I believe the Chinese Government has aggressive or offensive intention."[34]

---

were sent to reinforce units in the Far East Air Force (FEAF) during the Indonesian 'confrontation.' Facilities were built in Tengah, Singapore, for the 'Moonflower' and 'Sunflower' V-bomber detachments. According to two sources, these V-bombers were nuclear-armed while in Singapore. [Citation: Freedman, *Britain and Nuclear Weapons*, p. 29; Duncan Campbell, 'Dangers of the Nuclear Convoys,' *New Statesman*, 10 April 1981, p. 7.] According to Campbell, during the 1960s British nuclear weapons were stored not only in Singapore but also Malaysia (then Malaya), Aden, and Cyprus. . ."

32. *The New York Times*, 26 March 1994. Correspondent John F. Burns comments that India insists it not be treated as "strategic 'equal'" to Pakistan, a seventh as populous, and has been "reluctant to accept limits on its nuclear weapons programs while China, a long-standing rival, maintains a wide lead in all aspects of nuclear weapons development."

33. As of May 1994, there were diminishing prospects that India would take part in this scheme. John F. Burns, *The New York Times*, 15 May 1994. Burns reports that India had argued that any such forum should include Asian and Middle Eastern states with nuclear weapons programs, or the capacity to undertake nuclear programs. India has long contended that nuclear control schemes should be on a global basis, and that India should not accept constraints based on Pakistani capabilities.

34. *The New York Times*, 14 January 1995.

Conclusion

The common thread running through these accounts is *fear*. In these cases it is fear of attack or subjugation by others—especially, but not only—wielding nuclear weapons. World War II continues to be a force shaping our sense of horrors. There is a secondary undercurrent of fear which must also be considered: fear of exclusion from office. Political leaders expose themselves to partisan attack if they fail to meet the "standard expectations" for defence in the 1990s. In each of the cases we have cited others either possess or *could possess* nuclear weapons. The possess or *could possess* destructive "conventional" arms. That simple fact requires that defence planners, budgeters, and political leaders show that they have considered the threat and made prudent and at least sufficient preparations.

We should not be surprised by the centrality of fear in the complex of problems we are considering. Thucydides warned us of the ever-present effects of "fear, honour and interest" in the coming of war. In urging in the next chapter systematic and imaginative canvass of alternatives to nuclearism, we propose to address fear directly.

Appendix 9.1

General Pierre M. Gallois: Report and Review of His Judgments on French Nuclear Policy

Among the most outspoken French exponents of nuclear strategy, General Pierre M. Gallois has made a mark on French nuclear policy for more than forty years. As an air force colonel and French member of NATO's New Approach Group, Gallois was asked to brief Charles de Gaulle in May 1956—two years before de Gaulle's return to lead French politics—on NATO's nuclear planning. Duval and Le Baut observe that it is "undoubtedly" to Gallois that French military and political circles owe their understanding of nuclear "dissuasion."[35] In retirement he remains a vigorous controversialist.

In 1994 Gallois joined the fray on France's defense future, in the form of a critique of the *Livre Blanc sur la Défense* put forward by the government after broad consultations.[36] The heart of Gallois' attack on the *Livre Blanc* is that it diverts French resources to "peacekeeping" operations others will not undertake—to France's detriment in what matters—and fails to grasp the requirements for continued security through nuclear readiness. Beyond that, the *Livre noir* is apposite to this study in Gallois' characterization of German intentions, and his citing China as an exemplar of a state foregrounding its true interests.

Gallois rejects proposals that France tailor its nuclear forces to counter "madmen," a theme of those locating new nuclear missions for France.[37] He acknowledges the prospect of new nuclear states, but

---

35. Marcel Duval and Yves Le Baut, *L'arme nucléaire française: Pourquoi et comment?* (Paris: S.P.M., 1992), p. 30. The request that Gallois brief de Gaulle was made by General Lauris Norstad, American deputy to NATO commander General Gruenther. Norstad himself was later to command NATO forces.

36. *Livre Blanc sur la Défense*. (Paris: La documentation Française, March 1994). Pierre M. Gallois, *Livre noir sur la Défense* (Paris: Payot, 1994).

37. French policy had been described as "dissuasion du faible au fort," dissuasion by the weak of the strong. In the early 1990s some proposed as a mission for French nuclear forces countering "madmen"—in conversation Muhamar Qaddafi and Sadaam Hussein were typically cited—which invited the phrase "dissuasion du fort au fou," dissuasion by the strong of the crazy.

argues—citing both the Soviet Union and China—that nuclear weapons impose prudence. If acquisition of nuclear weapons is consequential it is through the possibility of coercing non-nuclear states.

But Gallois does encourage the line that the rise of Islamic fundamentalism poses a threat to France. By the year 2020 Muslims will number 2 billion, and in ten years or so 250 million will border the Mediterranean. "Islamic fundamentalism will be able to place the entire Mediterranean basin under the threat of its long-range weapons" or incite revolutionary movements within countries—such as France—to which they have immigrated.[38]

Gallois' suspicion of Germany is intense. Perhaps it need be said that he is of a vanishing generation, marked by the war. Nonetheless, he puts into political discourse a sketch of a German project, a project of dominance, and leaves no question that French survival requires that Paris recognize that threat and keep France capable and vigilant.

Reunified Germany, "the strongest power of Europe," has opened the door to a realignment of peoples, as Slovenia, Croatia, and the breakup of Czechoslovakia testify. Perhaps sometime in the distant future there could even be a claim for German rights on East Prussia. Germany financed reunification by maintaining high interest rates and forcing unemployment and economic loss on its partners. "What is more natural than that a nation of more than 80 million, very powerful industrially and commercially, sometimes the first and sometimes the second world exporter, have a strong policy, conform to its interests and practice a corresponding diplomacy? But this power itself strikes a blow at the European myth to which France has already sacrificed a great deal."[39] Indirectly at the origin of the

---

38. Gallois, p. 40. Fundamentalism was strengthened by the Gulf War against Iraq, which France had the "unfortunate idea" to join. Western support for Bosnia-Herzegovina is another folly. Pp. 40-42.

To grasp the context of Gallois' nationalism, however, one should appreciate that it is not only Muslim immigrants whom he sees as a threat to France. Inveighing against the Treaty of Maastricht, and citing the *Livre Blanc* on "national cohesion," he writes: "how to maintain national cohesion with the mixing of populations allowed in by the Treaty and, more generally, with the aims of European union? The influx of migrants seeking work—often reduced to unemployment, with the frustrations that follow—and social services doesn't add to 'national cohesion.'"

39. *Ibid.*, pp. 43-45.

"dislocation" of Czechoslovakia, directly at that of Yugoslavia, Germany has wiped away the remnants of the treaties which ended the Allied victories over William II and Adolf Hitler and has punished Serbia for twice having taken the side of the democracies. "The day of 16 December 1991 and the night which followed mark in History the date of the first *Diktat* of the new Germany, imposing its will—the premature recognition of Slovenia and Croatia—on its European partners."[40]

What does this mean for French nuclear policy? "Having inflicted on France the crushing defeat of 1940, the Germans, still today, admit with difficulty the military predominance which the atom confers on the defeated power of yesterday." Gallois attributes Mitterrand's decision to halt nuclear tests in part to a wish to "appease" that German hostility, for that halt will mean "the end, in due course, of French superiority in arms and assurance with respect to the inviolability of its territory."[41] It is clear, he goes on, that Bonn's objective is "to obtain, progressively, the 'denuclearisation' of France to put an end to an unbearable French presence on the continent."[42]

What does Gallois propose? The military plan would take account of the "European construction" in a category termed "conditional," the result of negotiating content and cost. But nuclear weapons would rest in the "unconditional" category, concerned with personnel and materiel "indispensable to the defense of the vital interests of the nation," which are

> integrity and inviolability of the national territory, free exercise of the French people's sovereignty over themselves and in independence.

And he continues:

> No one can perform this sovereign mission for France. It falls on France to furnish all the means and assure them in perpetuity. It is the permanent assurance against unforeseeable supreme danger. Implying considerable risks if the threat is nuclear, it does not permit France to beg for any help at all. This last hypothetical, admittedly extreme, excludes recourse to alliance. Defensive concept, doctrine of even-

40. *Ibid.*, p. 46.
41. *Ibid.*, p. 50.
42. *Ibid.*, p. 51.

> tual use, financing of studies and production, deployment and training, upkeep and modernization of materials concern only France. It is in fact a permanent project and condition, and purely national.[43]

Discussing France's response to the Chinese test of 5 October 1993 and its declared intention to solicit the views of the United States, Britain, and Russia, Gallois insists there is no connection between their nuclear arms and those of China, or of France. While attributing the Chinese program more to its wish to stand among the Powers politically than ensure security, he observes that Beijing discouraged any attempt at intimidation whether emanating from the Soviet Union or India or, at some future time, from Japan. "Not having subscribed to any moratorium, it would probably not bother with suggestions from another country, but would provide itself with the nuclear panoply it judged necessary for its security and its role on the international scene."[44] France, he implies, should act accordingly.

---

43. *Ibid.*, p. 112.
44. *Ibid.*, p. 91.

10

Conclusions

In the preceding chapters we have reviewed the origins and status of the British, French, and Chinese nuclear forces, their institutional complexes, costs and harms, and have identified perceived threats to which they are responses. This review compels us to these conclusions:

1. A strong, articulate constituency in each of the Three advocates the vital necessity of maintaining nuclear forces.

2. In each case, decisions to maintain the nuclearist *status quo* at whatever level, to disengage nuclear forces, or to wholly relinquish nuclear weapons will be *domestic* decisions. Who decides, and what they consider, will be located in internal politics.

3. Any one of the Three (and the Five, the Eight) can veto radical disengagement or abolition. In other words, if the case for nuclear weapons succeeds in any one state then the others will be constrained domestically to reductions, stability measures, and moderate but incomplete disengagement. Critics of nuclearism believe that will not be enough.

4. Analysts who believe that security lies elsewhere than in the nuclearist status quo must take seriously and address the claims and fears voiced by the nuclearist constituency. This does not mean they must convince today's nuclear advocates that they are wrong, or satisfy all their fears, but that they must show there is a non-nuclearist script which is more secure than the present script of reliance on nuclear weapons.

   Such a script must address all the hard questions: what must be verified? how can fears be met by "active reassurance"? what constitutes "adequate transparency"? what risks are tolerable? what capacities must be in place when collective coercion is required?

5. Citizens should be aware that some of the most thoughtful voices questioning nuclearism are those of officials, scientists and military planners who work inside nuclear programs or have responsibility to supervise them. Stereotypic dismissal of nuclear-concerned institutions would be a tragic error, denying the quest for non-nuclear alternatives their understandings and judgments, without which it will face very heavy weather.

6. To show that there is a secure non-nuclearist path, non-nuclearist scripts—including verification and reassurance measures—must be simulated, practiced, tested, assessed, and thoroughly debated. In principle, the Three have a compelling obligation to undertake active, open modeling and assessment, and to use their persuasive powers to enlist other nuclear weapon states and aspirants to do the same. Governments, polities, and societies today do not know how to guarantee themselves against weapons of mass destruction. They must either design, refine, learn and practice the political and social means to achieve such guarantees or accept that nuclearism—possibly regulated, probably as the policy of more states—will continue to shape and to shadow over all endeavor.

Several other conclusions also follow from the cases we have explored:

7. Although our study has centered on Britain, France, and China, the broader conclusion about the prerequisites for denuclearization apply as well to Russia and the United States, and to Israel, Pakistan, India, and any aspirant state.

8. One special characteristic of Britain, France, and China lies in the fact that they would not have the massive "conventional" capabilities of Russia and the United States if they relinquished nuclear weapons. In that sense—even if "nuclear weapons cannot be

used"—nuclear weapons are proportionately more important to their sense of military capacity. Denuclearization will be correspondingly resisted.

9. Britain, France and China are powerful models for nuclear proliferation.

In framing this study as a description of choices, we have concluded that the British, French, and Chinese polities face a series of decisive choices. They must respond to the proposed Comprehensive Test Ban and recurrent NPT reviews. Further choices will confront them until nuclearism is abandoned or the practical barriers to disengagement and abolition prove insurmountable.

Nuclearism, Disengagement, and Abolition

The Three do not carry on open domestic debate about their nuclear futures. We have told of some public discussion, but it is virtually unknown in China, and hardly a prime issue in France or Britain. One effect of 1989-91, however, has been to encourage *partial disengagement measures* by Russia and the United States, with France and Britain participating as well in some respects.

Still, "disengagement" is not a term current in discussion. "Minimum deterrence," as we have shown, is a current phrase, with all Three contending that their forces embody only a "minimum deterrent." Nonetheless, the very mention of nuclear weapons implies the issue of their "control"—as in "arms control"—and their abolition. Even when the possibility is denied, the denial seems to spring from a sense that the emotional and rational appeal of abolition is strong.

This carries us, then, to the question "why are nuclear weapons built and deployed"? The short answer: out of greed, and out of fear.

In my view, one must be sympathetic to the arguments from fear. Fear is not always irrational. The argument that nuclear weapons prevent a recurrence of World War II is a serious one. It stems from a vivid awareness how much cruelty and devastation could be wrought by mass armies with "conventional" weapons.

I see no reason to be sympathetic to nuclearists who imagine that their states gain by holding nuclear weapons—gain in prestige, or "influence," or economic access, or deference. This study does not attempt any "cost-benefit" analysis in which such gains are "benefits" because I believe that holding people at risk of incineration to achieve "prestige" or satisfy greed cannot possibly be consistent with a secure global future.

The issue of nuclear weapons is certainly a *security* issue. It should be framed as one. Are the risks of tolerating nuclear weapons acceptable? are they unavoidable? Can they be adequately mitigated? And if not, then by what alternative path can "security" be achieved, especially given the fact that any transition must take account of nuclear weapons' existence?

There is a very strong case that the nuclearist status quo, however scrupulously managed, is unacceptably dangerous, whether at present levels or at reduced warhead levels. Existence of the weapons invites plausible State cases for their use and the opportunity for private diversion to schemes. Nor is the case solved by reducing numbers: "minimum deterrence" is not an alternative to nuclearism, but one form of nuclearism. The Three define "minimum" as "hundreds."

To the objection that nuclear weapons cannot be "disinvented" I find the following line of reasoning persuasive. The ingenuity which has achieved nuclear weapons and subjected them to social organization and control can also achieve the verification and reassurance required to maintain an abolition regime. At least, under an abolition regime, you begin *without* nuclear weapons and must at worst deal with non-compliance; under a nuclearist regime, you begin *with* nuclear weapons and possession of nuclear weapons is compliance itself. Moreover, an abolition regime would be profoundly simpler to sustain than a regime which permitted some nuclear weapons and prohibited others.

Experience

Abandoning nuclearism would require technical and political preparation. We have suggested experiments and simulations. Their object would be to explore uncertainties and hazards, and give people experience in designing persuasive reassurance measures. This proposal does not issue from a vacuum, for concerns like those posed by radical disengagement and abandonment of nuclear weapons have been encountered in other contexts. A repertoire of verification and reassurance practices has been built into the principal arms control treaties of the last ten years. In addition, experience was forced on the IAEA and United Nations, and their member states, as they improvised to respond to revelations of the Iraqi nuclear weapons program. There have been training exercises. For the most part, however, these practices have not been undertaken for the purpose of training or "simulation and experiment," but they have had exactly that effect. They provide experience in design and actual use of ingenious and complex systems to achieve practical objectives.

Selected steps already taken or in place suggest models which could be adapted to an expansive and imaginative program of "experiment and simulation."

1. Negotiation of a CTB has included work by an Ad Hoc Group of Scientific Experts to design and assess technical means to verify a test ban. In August 1994 the group met to conclude planning of a third "Technical Test" called GSETT-3, "a joint effort to develop, test and evaluate new concepts for an experimental International Seismic Monitoring System."[1]

2. In the years preceding completion of the Chemical Weapons Convention, seminars and exercises were conducted to familiarize national officials with issues which would be raised by treaty implementation.

3. The INF Treaty provided for monitoring of production facilities by teams from the other party. To this end, Soviet personnel resided in Utah and maintained "portal monitoring" at the US cruise missile plant.

4. The British government seeks "greater transparency in military planning to reduce risks of conflict arising out of misunderstanding or design." The British military arms control activity is organized through a 124-member Joint Arms Control Implementation

1. Conference on Disarmament. CD/PV.691. 691st Plenary Meeting. 6 September 1994, p. 4. Intervention of Mr. Dahlman (Sweden).

Group, in which a premium is placed on training.[2]

5. The creation and work of the UN Special Commission on Iraq (UNSCOM) in implementing UNSC Resolution 687 provides a case study in location and rooting out of weapons of mass destruction and systems to produce them. By February 1993 IAEA teams had carried out seventeen inspections, in cooperation with UNSCOM. UNSCOM head Rolf Ekéus reported that "the conclusion arrived at is that the nuclear programme was intended to produce enriched uranium and to develop a nuclear weapon capability."[3] Fifty-seven inspection teams—concerned with nuclear, chemical, biological, ballistic missile and other activities—had been to Iraq by the end of 1992.

6. In preparing to implement the Treaty on Open Skies, many trial overflights were conducted in 1992. These included tests and calibration of sensors. One exercise "tested procedures which included ensuring that sensors were sealed while overflying countries other than those slated for inspection." An analyst concludes that the Open Skies Consultative Commission "was able to show that it could function in an efficient and constructive manner by resolving key issues on which it focused attention."[4]

---

2. Cm 2270. *Defending Our Future. Statement on the Defence Estimates 1993.* (London: HMSO, July 1993), p. 53.:

   "(The) Joint Arms Control Implementation Group (JACIG) . . . is a tri-Service organization comprising 124 Service and civilian personnel, including interpreters in the Russian and German languages. All JACIG personnel, including interpreters, are trained as both inspectors for outgoing inspections and escorts for incoming inspections, and must possess a wide range of professional skills, including recognition of CFE Treaty Limited Equipment (TLE), a good knowledge of the relevant treaties, and language ability. The tasks of JACIG personnel are broadly similar for each of the different treaties. Under the Vienna Document and the CFE Treaty, JACIG provides inspectors and monitors for outgoing inspections and evaluations, as well as escorts for any incoming inspections to the United Kingdom."

3. Rolf Ekéus, "The United Nations Special Commission on Iraq: Activities in 1992," in *SIPRI Yearbook 1993* (Oxford: Oxford University Press, 1993), pp. 691-703.

4. Richard Kokosi, "The Treaty on Open Skies," in *SIPRI Yearbook 1993* (Oxford: Oxford University Press, 1993), pp. 632-634.

The preparation we envisage would include technical assessments, but be broader and more participatory than the cases cited. For example, the issue of "intrusiveness" and "proprietary rights" could be anticipated by simulated on-site inspections of industrial facilities. The movement of nuclear scientists and engineers among laboratories in other countries, envisaged in the 1946 Acheson-Lilienthal Report, takes place in many research facilities, but could be initiated where not previously practiced. More general "societal verification," including cultivated norms calling for exposure of prohibited activity, require thoughtful design for each society and—for example—guarantees for whistleblowers. Specific disengagement measures, such as joint observation of stored weapons systems, are obvious candidates for trials.

Fear

The histories traversed in this study confirm the profound role of fear underlying nuclearism and the tenacity with which nuclearists believe that the future security of their peoples requires nuclear weapons. When expressed as expert judgment, when repeated as justification for partisan conservatives, this conviction gains ready support among the people, who visualize their and their progeny's being threatened with annihilation and nuclear weapons alone serving to safeguard them.

Though much of that fear can and should be addressed by the design and undertaking of "reassurance" measures, a residuum will remain. For that, each person must weigh comparative risks. With respect to another aspect of nuclearism—the insistence that future uncertainties must be hedged against—I do not know any logical answer. I believe a sufficient answer lies in cultivating a deeply woven and decent global community in which collective response to adversity is practiced, but that does not quite respond to the wish for "insurance."

This is the context in which I conclude that a *disengagement regime*, while not having the virtues of abolition, would be distinctly better than any form of continued nuclearism. It is not the point of this study to elaborate disengagement scripts, but their distinguishing mark is that nuclear weapon states would retain nuclear weapons *without prompt access*. Mutual surveillance, technical time-locks, and other possible combinations of social guarantees and technical hindrances would ensure that nuclear weapons not be introduced suddenly, or even in a short time, into ready arsenals. Disengagement responds to the fear that the future might bring some deadly challenge to which nuclear weapons alone would be the sufficient response. Disengagement permits "hedging" but not "brandishing," and incorporates additional multilateral safeguards against unauthorized use. A disengagement regime would satisfy some, but not all, of the intense commitment to maintaining nuclear weapons which is evident in all of the nuclear weapon states.

Having set out these conclusions, we should examine more closely the core argument made for retaining nuclear weapons.

The Core Argument for Maintaining Nuclear Programs

The question implicit in any canvass of nuclear policy is "why should a government want to deploy such capacity to destroy?" The most commonly encountered answer is that they are deployed to deter. But what if the other nuclear weapon states also agreed to give them up? Why then continue to deploy?

Some responses to this question take the form of stories about each country's specific position, its shaping historical experiences. Such stories are needed to understand why some states have developed nuclear weapons and others have not. We find accounts stressing historical experience persuasive for Britain, France, and China, each an imperial power fallen on hard times and then savagely attacked—Britain from the air—in World War II.

Other responses subordinate national experience to the compelling threat of the bomb. A schematic of such responses could have something of the following form:

1. The bomb is a net good
   a. it prevents terrible "conventional" war[5]
   b. it guarantees continued existence of the state and society against unknowable future threats
      • which by definition could overwhelm capabilities.

5. For example, the 1994 French White Book cites the previous White Book of 1972: nuclear arms have the virtue of preventing general war, of "rendering inconceivable resort to total war as a means of policy." *Livre Blanc sur la Défense 1994* (Paris: La Documentation Française, 1994), p. 82.

c. it enables the holder to act more freely, and speak with greater effect, to shape the political surroundings

and therefore should be retained even if abolition were possible.

2. Even if it were *not* a net good, the requirements for abolition are strict and logically unachievable:
   a. existing nuclear weapon states must hold none back
      • but there is no way to prove they have not.
   b. aspirants must be prevented from making the bomb
      • but there is no way to identify them with certainty.
   c. . . . or other weapons of mass destruction
      • including systems not yet imagined.

Evidently, the force of these arguments rests in the massive destructive capability of even a few nuclear weapons, delivered to their targets, and in the impossibility—in a complex landscape—of establishing a negative. (These positions, as sketched, ignore practical arguments from program "momentum" and the difficulty of reconstituting expertise after a program is suspended.)

The leadership concerned can believe *simultaneously* that interest requires nuclear deployment and that the deployed weapons will never be used. If deterrence "works" that should be exactly what happens. By this logic, the deploying Government will never commit the destructive act of which the nuclear weapons are capable. It is therefore immune from any insistence that it consider the consequences of their being used. (But this logic requires, of course, that it blind itself to the "credibility" requirement that others believe it capable of unleashing, and *willing* to unleash, a nuclear attack in revenge.) Something of a self-protective logic, then, underlies China's insistence that it will "never be the first to use nuclear weapons" and that other nuclear weapon states should give "no first use" guarantees, and France's description of its strategic nuclear posture as one of "dissuasion, rejecting all confusion between dissuasion and use."[6]

We believe the arguments cited to justify nuclear forces are made in each of the Three states we have studied.

6. *Ibid.*, p. 79.

Counterarguments—again put schematically—have the following form:

3. Claims that the bomb is a net good
    a. turn on future harms averted, and so cannot be proven;
    b. exaggerate the "voice" attributable to holding nuclear weapons; and
    c. place too little weight on the danger that nuclear weapons, if held, will be used.
4. Claims that even if the bomb is *not* a net good, the requirements of abolition cannot be met
    a. turn on the unnecessarily strict requirement of *certainty* that bombs have not been held back or secretly made
    b. . . . and so fail to compare the *risk* of non-compliance with the *risk* of continued reliance on inventories; and
    c. understate the overwhelming military capacity of collective conventional forces against a common threat.

One summary claim receiving increased currency is that "the only legitimate purpose of nuclear weapons is to deter the use of nuclear weapons." Our purpose here is not to judge that claim, but to point out that *some* of the arguments for the Three retaining nuclear weapons are *nuclear deterrent* arguments. In the schematic arrays of arguments we have just sketched, only claims 2a and 2b are unambiguously *nuclear deterrent* arguments. Others are *utility* arguments. Some utility arguments assign nuclear weapons the mission of deterring conventional war (1a), or war in any form (1b), or war wrought with weapons of mass destruction other than nuclear weapons (1b and 2c); other missions, such an ensuring "a place at the table," are more mundane. It is evident from public statements by officials of Britain and France that they claim a wider repertoire of missions for their nuclear forces than deterrence of nuclear attack. Some missions require the mere possession—neither threat nor use—of those forces. Still, to argue that nuclear weapons mean one is listened to in Europe, or can guarantee the "national sanctuary" against whatever external threat, is not consistent with the norm that "the only legitimate purpose of nuclear weapons is nuclear deterrence."

The relationship of a nuclear program to global security objectives is more intricate, and much more vexed, *if utility arguments are current and persuasive in the internal debate.* In one sense, this states the obvious: if a people believes that having nuclear weapons is a net plus then they are unlikely to abandon them. But this obvious point is necessary: it underscores the urgence of approaching utility claims critically, and of assessing coutervailing risks and costs unflinchingly.

This point is so important that it merits being made again, in a somewhat different way. *If it is accepted that the only legitimate purpose of nuclear weapons is to deter nuclear attack, then the issue of nuclear weapons is transformed into the issue of adequate assurance of denuclearization.* That too is not a simple issue, but it is much simpler than addressing a felt need to retain effective nuclear forces for use against unspecified future contingencies at some uncertain future time. Schematically, the problem of items 1 and 2 of our list has been reduced to addressing non-compliance (2a and 2b) by technical and social means to achieve verification that is *pragmatically adequate*, and by collective force should strictures against non-compliance fail.

Debates about nuclear futures will not go easy. It is a fair prediction that specialists who are convinced that pragmatically adequate verification is unattainable—and that therefore the state would endanger itself to give up its nuclear program—will contest the *deterrence only* norm. And this need not be in any way devious. If one believes that verification of denuclearization is hard, one can easily believe that novel weapons of mass destruction may be secretly developed, or that a "sneak attack" using known "conventional" weapons alone could succeed against the state, or that the state could be "blackmailed" by threats short of attack against which it had no effective response. It is neither here nor there whether nuclear weapons would be, in any of these scenarios, an effective response or the response of choice. The point is just that nuclear weapons do offer the state more options, including terrible and destructive options, should it be threatened. To some that is a capacity of incalculable value which should not be sacrificed.

Moreover, for each of the Three it will make a difference whether nuclear weapons are the *only* means to achieve a secure future, respite from conventional war, and an attentive and respectful hearing. In principle, these should be achievable by other means. Historical understanding, such as an appreciation of China's long-standing vulnerability to Japanese technological superiority, suggests the need for mutual respect and reassurance in an ongoing bilateral relationship. Here "reassurance" is not a bland term, but shorthand for a panel of active mutual practices and initiatives which sustain assurance and make bilateral war "unthinkable."

Emphasis on active reassurance adopts the primacy of politics. In a political relationship, people are recurrently interpreting their situation, querying others' intentions, and negotiating projects some of which, subject in turn to interpretation, are actively undertaken. Primacy of politics implies subordination of technology. Nonetheless, politics is in part *about* technology, and political projects can *incorporate* technology into the practices undertaken. To return to the observation, with which this section began, that the Three in their nuclear programs achieved extraordinary social constructions, we would suggest that issues of verification and reassurance—which are also both technical and political—are appropriate subjects of focused, sustained, imaginative, and effective social construction. Like nuclear weapons programs undertaken by the Three, reassurance of members of another society requires exceptional facility of governance, with respect to one's internal support, as well as the practice of an agile and temperate external politics.

At this moment, however, there is no evidence that any of the Three is committed to create the conditions to achieve "zero nuclear weapons." In the remainder of this chapter we will assay intentions of each of the Three, consider how our methods illuminate their relationship to arms control, and the conclusions we draw.

On British Intentions

If the future were like the past—in this case, like the past since the 1940s—Britain would persist in deploying a strategic nuclear force much like the present one: sufficient SSBNs to have one at sea and some additional air-deliverable capability. It would continue to depend on the United States for missile systems and—maintaining compatibility—warhead design and reentry vehicles. Coordinating closely with the United States, Britain would nonetheless retain a capacity for independent command should it judge that necessary: It could withhold nuclear weapons although the United States chose to use them, or use them when the United States was unwilling, or—the most likely case of disagreement—part from the United States concerning whether or not to *threaten* use.

What are the Next Important Force Decisions Facing Britain?

Having resolved to build four *Vanguard*-class SSBNs carrying Trident II (D-5) missiles, Britain's principal nuclear capability will be set until—say—the year 2020. Of course, just as some fifteen years or more preceded an operational capability for the *Vanguard*, by the same measure a follow-on class would have to be committed about 2005 to be ready in 2020. This schedule could be stretched a few years, but is ultimately forced by the effects of wear and tear due to service at sea.

Britain has postponed withdrawal of the WE 177 free-fall bomb, now to be retired by the end of 1998. On 18 October 1993 the Secretary of State for Defence announced that TASM (Tactical Air-Surface Missile)—a modern stand-off nuclear missile capability akin to that deployed by France—had been canceled. At some juncture a British government must choose whether to modernize or abandon the second leg of its nuclear dyad.

Could Britain Adopt a Nuclear-Armed Cruise Missile?

In the early 1980s the United States deployed nuclear-armed cruise missiles on land (GLCM) and at sea (SLCM). These have been withdrawn.[7] The United Kingdom has shown interest in acquiring the Tomahawk cruise missile—vividly aware how it was used in the Gulf War—but insists it has no interest in a nuclear armed version.[8]

---

7. GLCMs were renounced in the December 1987 INF Treaty, and SLCMs in the September-October 1991 exchange of unilateral agreements between Bush and Gorbachev, in which Bush announced withdrawal of nuclear weapons from surface ships and attack submarines.

8. On 16 March 1994 Winston Churchill asked Rear Admiral Richard Irwin, in discussing a Trident sub-strategic capability, "is consideration being given to the possibility that it might be more cost effective to make a limited buy of

What Would be the Effects of a Change of Party Control?

A Conservative Party defeat in—say—1996 would not in itself assure any change in British posture. We have explained in chapter 7 the Conservative Party's belief that it can beat Labour with the charge it is "soft on defence." Any departure from Britain's maintaining an "independent" nuclear deterrent, in the present sense, would require not only that it be part of a multilateral move undertaken jointly by all nuclear weapon states but also that the domestic position be thoroughly prepared and the move have durable domestic support.

On the other hand, it is difficult to envision today any Conservative government accepting limits on its core SSBN force and weapons design and production capabilities for any purpose other than tactical defense of the nuclear program itself. That does not mean that Britain under Conservative Party governance will resist further steps to tidy up from the profligate production and deployments of the past. It has made important choices—in keeping with those of the United States—to withdraw nuclear weapons from surface ships and set aside obsolete systems. Such measures aside, the Conservative Party is deeply and publicly committed to the maintenance of an independent British nuclear deterrent force.

Tomahawk cruise missiles for deployment either on the Trident submarines or on any other Royal Naval submarines with a tactical nuclear warhead?" Admiral Irwin replied "The Navy are certainly interested in Tomahawk but nothing to do with nuclear weapons. . . The Government has decided to use Trident as the sole sub-strategic weapon after the retirement of the WE 177." House of Commons. Session 1993-94. Defence Committee. Second Report. *Progress of the Trident Programme*. Minutes of Evidence, ¶s 1147-1148.

The US-Soviet undertakings of September-October 1991 would pose a political obstacle to any French or UK plan for nuclear-armed SLCMs. On the other hand, their defence establishments declare continued interest in conventionally-armed cruise missiles. The nuclear possibility cannot have escaped them. The French military chief, Admiral Jacques Lanxade, has urged French acquisition of a cruise missile somewhat similar to Tomahawk, an APTGD (Arme de Précision Tirée à Grande Distance), with a conventional warhead. *Le Monde* 2 November 1994, citing Lanxade in *Défense nationale*. A private US analyst claims there is evidence that Israel is testing a SLCM, with the intention it will have a nuclear warhead. Howard Hough, quoted by David Horovitz, citing Hough's article in *Jane's Intelligence Review*. *Irish Times*, 19 November 1994.

What About Europe?

Similar arguments apply. Strong sentiment in the Conservative Party suspicious of European union would be stirred and given voice by any move to "denationalize" the British deterrent. We have noted that in putting its nuclear force at the disposal of NATO Britain reserved the right to resume sole control at any time.

Will British Nuclear Forces Remain Secure and Credible?

Since SSBNs put to sea in the 1950s it has been understood that they provide the least discoverable platform for nuclear weapons, but that "enemies" will try hard to pursue SSBNs from port and to locate them by technical means. The "technical means" have included vast sea-based phased-array sonars, as laboratories sought to push satellite-borne detection exploiting any sign of an underwater submarine (heat, ocean movement, magnetic anomaly, active laser reflection). Intense secrecy surrounds anti-submarine warfare (ASW) capability and its counter-measures, in part because SSBN credibility *in principle* and survivability *in fact* depends upon a plausible belief that boats can with high probability escape detection. On this subject what one can say is that there are men and women working to devise means to unmask the location of underwater British and other SSBNs (SNLEs), who might succeed. For the most part, however, British SSBNs will not be at sea at all, but in port, only one or two at sea, and one of the four unavailable to sortie. In port they are sitting ducks to precision-guided conventional attack (even if to strike them could be a nuclear *casus belli*). Under these circumstances accident, chance encounter, and betrayal become serious threats to the force, its numbers being so small.[9] The conclusion is that the force may be secure but that there is an important possibility it will not remain so.

---

9. To accomplish needed repair of one of its aging boats Britain has been obliged to keep another, intended for decommissioning, on patrol. Having chosen to build each class of SSBNs in a relatively short time, it risks the effects of their aging simultaneously.

On French Intentions

The French consensus runs so deep that it is difficult to imagine circumstances in which France would be prepared to negotiate away the core of its nuclear forces.

Like Britain, France is building a new class of SSBNs (SNLEs), the *Triomphant*-class. Similarly, the new class sets a clock running which anticipates replacement beginning about 2020 and a decision to replace soon after 2005.

Future uncertainty weighs heavily in the French calculus. In interviews officials specialized in procurement made out a strenuous case for maintaining production capabilities to meet whatever threat might come. This inclination reinforces, and is reinforced by, France's declared commitment to an *autonomous* capacity. As France is not buying its crucial systems abroad, this means that the DGA must be alert to the conditions required to maintain each skill and engineering capability or, at the least, assure it could be reconstituted if required.

What Effects of a New President in 1995?

French politics after the March 1993 victory of the center-right in parliamentary elections has turned on speculation about what measures the new president would endorse.

Certainly, advocates of resumed French testing hoped a new president would endorse that position. They were correct. Even if the new president were drawn to the arguments for a moratorium on tests, as appears to be the case, he might still resist a CTB, or insist on such severe terms (verification, inclusiveness) or escape clauses (limited duration, exclusion of low-yield tests, provision for occasional tests) that an effective CTB could not be negotiated.

Security of the Force

France, like Britain, relies on a small number of SNLEs (SSBNs), and must have similar concerns about ASW. ASW is one field cited for possible Franco-British cooperation.

In placing airborne warheads on a stand-off missile France

achieves a secondary nuclear capability which does not require that its aircraft actually fly to the target, which could be heavily defended. Aircraft may not have the destructive capacity of an SNLE, and are themselves vulnerable to air defence, but they provide (in addition to a "tactical" capacity) a complement to seaborne forces, complicating the case for any attacker who imagined it had the key to destroying SNLEs before they could fire. The logic of this is to commit to a longer-range stand-off missile.

On Chinese Intentions

How is China likely to resolve strategic weapons policy and arms control objectives in the years ahead? The answer is necessarily speculative. It relies on inference from what China has said and done and from interpretation of existing programs. Like the United Kingdom, however, China remains close-mouthed on issues of nuclear policy which have become subjects of public debate in the United States and France. There is little textual evidence to go on. Even the strategic forces—perhaps because of their vulnerabilities—are rarely seen by outsiders.

Still, we can draw a plausible picture of China's likely choices. On the arms control side, several facts hint at China's plans. China signed—in fact, helped bring to closure—the Chemical Weapons Convention, concluded in 1993. Public statements and private comments by Chinese officials say China will sign a Comprehensive Test Ban in 1996 if a CTB is ready for signing, but in other statements China broaches an escape clause ("peaceful" nuclear explosions). China supports NPT extension. China quite naturally welcomes the US and Russian intention to dismantle large numbers of nuclear weapons, but also insists China's nuclear arms will not be ready for bargaining away while Moscow and Washington retain large inventories.

On the side of forces—composition and technical capabilities—China maintains a force of thermonuclear warheads not yet mated to "advanced" delivery systems. Reportedly only four missiles of China's sole true ICBM design are deployed. China's two ballistic-missile submarines (SSBNs) rarely stray far from home port. Although the SSBN-carried missiles and an 1800-km range mobile land-based missile are solid-fuel, China's remaining land-based missiles are clumsier, earlier liquid-fuel designs. Development programs are underway, but China's programs have always proceeded slowly, and are subject to severe technical and budgetary constraints. On the other hand, Chinese involved in the program are said to have told their US counterparts that they intend no warhead modernization, but will rely on warheads already proven. On this hypothesis, the 1994-96 test series is attributed to a program to substitute Insensitive High Explosive for the less stable chemical explosive now relied upon to initiate fission, while leaving other elements of the warhead design unchanged. The more usual understanding is that China is miniaturizing warheads.

What medium-term future—ten to twenty years ahead—would be consistent with this understanding of China's situation? This is what we might expect:

New and Improved Nuclear Weapons Systems

As long as China is committed to deterrence she will address shortcomings of her best systems: the SSBN/SLBM combination, and the DF-5 ICBM.

Norris et al. conclude that "it appears that the Chinese plan to build a small fleet of SSBN's (perhaps four to six) while improving their submarine and missile technology." They report China plans a new SSBN class (the "09-4" class) and a JL-2 SLBM.[10]

Lewis and Hua report that China envisages two mobile missiles. The DF-31, a mobile land-based solid-fuel missile, would fire a 700-kg payload some 8000 km. (The JL-2 is a sea-borne variant of the DF-31.) It is this missile which was reportedly first test-fired on 30 May 1995.[11] The DF-41, also to be mobile and solid-fuel, would be an ICBM with a range of 12,000 km, and would replace the DF-5 liquid-

10. Robert S. Norris, Andrew S. Burrows and Richard W. Fieldhouse, *Nuclear Weapons Databook* (Volume V): *British, French and Chinese Nuclear Weapons* (Boulder: Westview, 1994), pp. 372-373.

11. An AP despatch on 31 May 1995, citing Kyodo, described the tested missile as a solid-fuel missile with a range of 4960 miles. Agence France Presse reported on 4 June 1995 that the Taiwanese military said the missile had been tested only over a 2000 km track, although it was thought capable of an 8000 km range.

fueled ICBM.[12]

Will these Come Forward Quickly and in Large Numbers?

China's practice—reflecting both technical and budget constraints—has been to bring systems forward very slowly. Numbers have been small. There is no evidence this pattern will be changed.

Will China be Ready to Negotiate these Systems Away?

There is no evidence at all that China will abandon nuclear systems except as part of a general, multilateral nuclear disarmament. The practical precondition is prior Russian and US reduction to bring their forces into rough equivalence with that of China.

Does China Consider Interim Nuclear Arms Control Measures Useful?

China's adherence to the NPT, commitment to NPT extension, and readiness to take part in the CTB negotiations all suggest that China sees her interest served by some forms of arms control. Of course, a nuclear weapon state has an evident interest to discourage proliferation, both as a measure of protection against attack and to prevent dilution of the influence associated with its own nuclear capabilities. But that alone cannot explain China's seeming readiness to sign a CTB in 1996. As discussed above, the period 1994-96 would provide China time to perform several nuclear tests, but—if a test ban remained indefinitely in place—she would still forego types of modernization and exploration of blast effects and warhead physics which have been important to other nuclear states' militaries and weapons laboratories. Her commitment to a CTB is more plausible if one weighs the opportunity cost of achieving any nuclear capability beyond a minimally persuasive confidently deliverable deterrent. China remains a society of scarcity, despite recent economic reforms, and pressures on the central budget are intense.

12. John Wilson Lewis and Hua Di, "China's Ballistic Missile Programs: Technologies, Strategies, Goals," in *International Security* vol. 17 no. 2, Fall 1992, pp. 3-40, pp. 28-30.

How Does This Disposition Fare Given China's Chafing at Export Controls?

China continues to insist that it acts in accordance with the terms of the Missile Technology Control Regime and the Non-Proliferation Treaty. Chinese dismiss US charges that transfer of Chinese M-11 missile components to Pakistan, for example, violate MTCR terms. The M-11 could function just below or just above the threshold at which the MTCR prohibition applies. In fact, there must be opposing voices in Beijing, some arguing the utility of the MTCR and NPT and collateral gains in cooperating with the industrial states, others reluctantly accepting export controls provided that China's export rights permitted under the control regime are not further chivvied and constrained. Demand for hard currency by Chinese institutions, especially those in the industrial structure of the People's Liberation Army, will continue to test the limit of commitments made elsewhere in the central government.[13]

Can China Be Confident That Her Nuclear Forces are Safe?

Lewis and Xue believe that China committed to submarine-based and mobile land-based systems in 1967 after deciding that fixed land-based systems were too vulnerable to satellite detection and destruction.[14] There is no reason to imagine, therefore, that Chinese planners are not acutely aware of others' imaging capabilities and missile accuracy.

Conclusion

This speculation suggests that the medium-term future will be much like the recent past. More capable systems will appear and be deployed, but slowly and in small numbers. This suggests an hypoth-

---

13. Cf. John W. Lewis, Hua Di, and Xue Litai, "Beijing's Defense Establishment: Solving the Arms-Export Enigma," in *International Security* vol. 15 no. 4, Spring 1991, pp. 87-109.

14. Lewis and Xue, *China's Strategic Seapower*, p. 143. In 1978 concern about vulnerability was again voiced; Lewis and Xue attribute constraints on the DF-5 ICBM, of which only four have been deployed, to this concern. *Ibid.*, p. 182.

esis, or a hunch, that China's leadership could have taken an important decision about China's nuclear future. It *may be* that Chinese defense planners and budgeters have set a *ceiling on major systems* to cap China's nuclear programs, a ceiling which would remain in place *barring significant new "dangers" in China's international situation.* One way to visualize this hypothesis is to suggest that China will aim *to approach, but not to exceed, the capabilities now deployed by Britain and France*. Moreover, there is no evidence that they feel pressed to reach that point quickly, though there must be concern about the apparent shortcomings of the best systems on which their deterrent relies and a wish to *begin* to deploy more stable, accurate, and longer-range systems within the next few years.

If the 1993-96 test series is directed at miniaturization and MIRVing, one purpose would be to place a multiple-warhead system aboard Chinese missile-launching submarines, as Britain and France have done.

China's future systems would be unlike those of Britain or France in one important respect, if John Lewis' and Hua Di's account of the planned DF-31 and DF-41 is correct and the two land-mobile missiles are not set aside, in that China would place weight on land-mobile solid-fuel ICBMs. France and Britain deploy no comparable weapon. China deploys 36 land-mobile solid-fuel DF-21 missiles with an 1800 km range. Land-mobile systems had a certain vogue in the United States and Soviet Union in the early 1980s; the United States did not go forward with a mobile system, and the 36 Soviet rail-mobile SS-24s are scheduled to be withdrawn under terms of START II, but Moscow continues to deploy additional SS-25 single-warhead mobile missiles. Whether mobile missiles will be as attractive to China in 2000 or 2005 will depend heavily on the dialectic between concealment and detection.

Approaches

Early in this text we identified *capabilities analysis*, *scriptic analysis*, and *focused comparison* as deliberate methods to complement our basic reliance on interpretation customary in narrative historical and political studies. The reader will have observed that these methods have been at some points implicit, not explicit, but that we have turned to them recurrently. Here we wish to call attention to differences among the methods and the differing view of our topic which they foster.

Capabilities Analysis

We noted at the outset that "a state cannot perform acts for which it does not have the means." The stories of the British, French and Chinese nuclear programs all center on the acquisition of means, including those to deliver nuclear weapons and those to watch what other states do.

If the crucial question *within the deterrence paradigm* is whether the Three have each achieved a "secure second-strike capability"—the capacity to take revenge after having been attacked—then the answer is that Britain and France have done so and that China has a sufficient capability that its capacity to retaliate *cannot be dismissed*, certainly not by Russia.

If the question is whether the Three can make modern weapons of the most sophisticated kind, the answer is again qualified. Britain does not make large missiles; she has relied on the United States in other respects, such as mounting a test site, but could reconstitute capabilities with time. China has achieved high technical standards, but it seems unlikely her productive capabilities are as deep as those of Britain and France, as they are unsupported by diverse competitive high-technology civil sectors.

Scriptic Analysis

The scriptic analyst asks what models, examples, strategic practices and stories the practical politician relies upon in interpreting a novel situation. When a story is general and categorical—for example, that unexpected threats arise as if from nowhere and threaten the very survival of the state, requiring the Government of the time to look to the preparations it has made—we can speak of a *script*. When the story is specific we speak of examples, of argument by analogy, of avoiding past mistakes.

We are struck by the power of *fear* among the Three, fear of future threats and attacks. US officials did threaten China with nuclear attack in the mid-1950s, and the Soviet Union brandished nuclear weapons against China in 1969, and targeted China for decades. There was a Cold War marked by deterrent nuclear forces targeted on each other: Russia targeted Britain and almost certainly France, and in turn Russia was itself a target. Fear has been real and has had a real basis. The response has been scriptic—adopting the script of nuclear deterrence—while alternative security scripts—centering on disengagement or abolition, for example—have been kept to one side, lest adopting them as *possibilities* would undermine the deterrence script itself. Only after the Gorbachev speech of 15 January 1986 and the European revolutions of 1989-91 was the pragmatic virtue of alternative scripts a politically admissible subject.

We are also struck by the convergence of British, French and Chinese forces around—roughly—300-500 warheads each and by their common description of these as "minimum deterrent" forces. There does appear to be a script of "minimum deterrence." Reader is doubtless alert to the fact that arsenals of this size and destructiveness, deliverable in principle to any point on the Earth's surface, are "minimum" only according to a strictly conventionalized way of speaking. And yet they do remain different from the strategic inventories deployed by the United States and Russia, even after the mutual unilateral cuts agreed by the US and Soviet presidents in 1991. They appear to be deliberate answers to the question "in a world in which my forces could be attacked first, what is the smallest force that guarantees deterrence?" All Three have come to place their reliance on the model pioneered by Hyman Rickover using the sea as a means of concealment of submarine-borne solid-fuel nuclear missiles, to which they add some aircraft-deliverable capability. China then has some land-based missiles, and France has 18. But the main lines of the forces have converged.

In our parlance, "minimum deterrence" is one form of the "nuclearist" script.

Focused Comparison

This study is not organized around the method of focused comparison, nor does the number of our cases—despite the "shadow cases" of the United States, Soviet Union, Israel and others to which we refer—even approach the eleven episodes which George and Smoke examined.[15] On the other hand, each of the three programs is offered as an initiative to deter nuclear attack; values—"vital interests"—are at stake; and the "opponents" are all others who have the capacity to attack it with nuclear weapons or other means.[16]

Instead, we have addressed the Three nuclear programs and the reasons advanced for maintaining them. We have brought the same questions to all three programs. Among the important questions we have asked are

- How was this program undertaken? By whom? For what declared purpose?
- Who in the state favor, and who oppose, nuclear forces?
- How much does this program cost? What are its environmental consequences?
- What have successive Governments said about arms control?
- To what extent have their programs aided, or been aided by, other nuclear weapon states?
- What expressions of fear or concern about external attack figure prominently in explanations for maintaining the program?
- How does the internal contest to govern affect positions which political figures take on nuclear forces?

We have found many similarities, but also differences, in the results. Cooperative relations with a nuclear ally—Britain's relations with the United States—explain British readiness to forego the autonomy which China and France prize. Having multiple threatening "neighbors"—China's perceiving Russia, the United States, Japan and India as states which could target China—increases the number of conditions to be met before nuclear weapons could be relinquished. And although secrecy continues to mark nuclear weapons practices of

---

15. Alexander George and Richard Smoke, *Deterrence in American Foreign Policy: Theory and Practice* (New York: Columbia University Press, 1974).

16. If we were following George and Smoke even more closely we would have identified the dyadic deterrent relationships among the Five and with others (including China-India, for example), and then brought systematic questions to the historical and relational material of chapter 9 "Threats and Fears."

all Three, China's state obsession with secrecy poses an obstacle to her adopting reassurance practices which could enhance her security. But important differences such as these are overwhelmed by the common presence of resistant nuclearist constituencies, whose existence is clear but whose arguments and initiatives remain partially concealed behind the shield of military secrecy. The practical effect of these constituencies is evidenced by their arguments for continued nuclear testing.

Conclusion

A main conclusion of this study is that nuclear weapon states have a special obligation to consider non-nuclearist options. This obligation is not one author's fancy, but a necessary implication of the special status of the Five as permanent members of the UN Security Council, charged by the Charter with responsibility to meet threats to international peace and security. I propose that they do so by systematic, thorough, imaginative, open and extensive design and simulation of non-nuclearist paths, putting special emphasis on transparence, mutual reassurance, and collective measures against non-compliance.

Any nuclear weapons program encourages imitation. If "nuclear proliferation" is a problem the first reason for it is that several states appear to believe that nuclear weapons are worth enormous sacrifice. If their actions confirm that judgment, they can only expect that states which can will either build nuclear weapons or create capabilities to do so. The 1994 revelation that Japanese leaders twenty-five years earlier contemplated keeping such capabilities in place confirms the proliferation risk dramatically.

China, France, and Britain could choose to bring their weight to bear on Russia and the United States, either toward fuller disengagement, or to abolition itself. Whether they will do so is a domestic choice available to those with a voice in each state. This study accepts that the United States and Russia are likely to prove to be the most tenacious adherents to nuclearism, but in both countries nuclearism is subject to criticism and—which may prove more important—no longer "automatically" confirmed by the Cold War. The first step, if this study is correct, should to be to design, display, and thoroughly study non-nuclear scripts.

A second conclusion is that the Three all display restraint. True, some stems from abandoning old weapons, some from difficulties building new systems and getting them to work, and some from tight budgets. Nonetheless, these acts of restraint also coincide with an interest in slowing the tempo of nuclear arms, creating a chance to talk and to make them governable. The case for continued restraint, and broader restraint, is compelling.

The Three are talking more about their nuclear programs than they did before the Cold War ended. They are showing more to each other. This suggests an hypothesis—if not a conclusion—that their leaderships have come to appreciate more than before how much their own security lies in giving others adequate assurance. We see signs of a closer relation among verification, assurance, and security. A third conclusion, certainly, is that whatever posture the Three adopt toward further arms control and disarmament initiatives will rest heavily on the case which can be made for persuasive verification.

Finally, we would stress one more time the centrality of perceived interest and internal political judgment. Whatever similarities have led us to compare Britain, France, and China, each conducts its domestic political debate around terms of "interest" which are nationally defined. This is acutely the case when the subject is a "decisive" weapon and the stakes are long-term national security. Only by weaving a fabric of assurance which respects and acknowledges those national concerns and internal debates can the threat of nuclear weapons be contained.

Glossary

ABM	Anti-ballistic missile
ACCHAN	Allied Command Channel
ACE	Allied Command Europe
ACLANT	Allied Command Atlantic
AGEX	Above-ground experiment
AGT	Above Ground Test
ALCM	Air-launched cruise missile
APTGD	*Arme Précise Tirée à Grande Distance*
ASMP	*Air-Sol Moyenne Portée*
ASW	Anti-submarine warfare
AWE	Atomic Weapons Establishment
AWRE	Atomic Weapons Research Establishment
BASIC	British-American Security Information Council
BMD	Ballistic missile defense
BNFL	British Nuclear Fuels, Ltd.
BWC	Biological Weapons Convention
CCP	Chinese Communist Party
CD	Conference on Disarmament
CEA	*Commissariat à l'Energie Atomique*
CFE	Conventional Forces in Europe
CIS	Commonwealth of Independent States
CND	Campaign for Nuclear Disarmament
COGEMA	*Compagnie Générale des Matières Nucléaires*
COSTIND	Committee of Science, Technology and Industry for National Defense
CSCE	Conference on Security and Cooperation in Europe
DAM	*Direction des Applications Militaires*
DCN	*Direction des Constructions Navales*
DGA	*Délégation Générale pour l'Armement*
DSTC	Defense Science and Technology Commission
ENDS	Enhanced Nuclear Detonation Safety
EPC(N)	Equipment Policy Committee (NUCLEAR)
ERW	Enhanced radiation weapon
FCO	Foreign and Commonwealth Office
FN	Front National

FRP	Fire resistant pit
GLCM	Ground-launched cruise missile
GSD	Ground sample distance
HE	High explosive
HEU	Highly-enriched uranium
HLG	High Level Group
HMG	Her Majesty's Government
IAEA	International Atomic Energy Agency
ICBM	Intercontinental Ballistic Missile
IFRI	*Institut Français des Relations Internationales*
IHE	Insensitive high explosive
INF	Intermediate nuclear forces
JACIG	Joint Arms Control Implementation Group
MBB	Messerschmitt-Bolköw-Blum
MIRV	Multiple independently-targeted reentry vehicles
MLF	Multi-Lateral Force
MoD	Ministry of Defence
MORI	Market & Opinion Research International
MSBS	*Mer-Sol Balistique Stratégique*
NADGE	NATO Air Defence Ground Environment
NATO	North Atlantic Treaty Organization
NDIC	National Defense Industrial Commission
NDIO	National Defense Industry Organization
NOP	Nuclear Operations Plan
NPG	Nuclear Planning Group
NPT	Non-Prolifeation Treaty
PAC	Penetration Aid Carrier
PALEN	*Préparation à la Limitation des Essais Nucléaires*
PC	*Parti Communiste*
PLA	People's Liberation Army
PPSM	*Plan Pluriannuel Spatial Militaire*
PS	*Parti Socialiste*
PTBT	Partial Test Ban Treaty
Pu	Plutonium
RPR	*Rassemblement pour la République*
SALT	Strategic Arms Limitation Talks
SIPRI	Stockholm International Peace Research Institute
SLBM	Submarine-launched ballistic missile

SLCM	Sea-launched cruise missile
SNLE	*Sous-marin Nucléaire Lanceur d'Engins*
SNLE-NG	*SNLE de Nouvelle Génération*
SSBN	Ballistic-missile nuclear submarine
SSD I	Special Session on Disarmament [I]
SSN	Nuclear [attack] submarine
START	Strategic Arms Reduction Talks
TBR	Test Ban Readiness
THORP	Thermal Oxide Reprocessing Plant
TLE	Treaty Limited Equipment
U	Uranium
UDF	*Union pour la Démocratie Française*
UN	United Nations
UN AEC	UN Atomic Energy Commission
UNGA	UN General Assembly
UNSC	UN Security Council
UNSCOM	UN Special Commission
US	United States
USSR	Union of Soviet Socialist Republics
VSEL	Vickers Shipbuilding and Engineering Limited
WEU	Western European Union

Selective Bibliography

British, French and Chinese Programs

Authoritative Texts

Convention on the Prohibition of the Development, Production and Stockpiling of Bacteriological (Biological) and Toxin Weapons and on Their Destruction. (Signed 10 April 1972. Entered into force 26 March 1975.)

Convention on the Prohibition of the Development, Production, Stockpiling and Use of Chemical Weapons and on Their Destruction. (Signed 13 January 1993.)

Treaty on the Non-Proliferation of Nuclear Weapons. (Signed 1 July 1968. Entered into force 5 March 1970.)

Analyses and Discussions

Arbatov, Alexei G. "Multilateral Nuclear Weapons Reductions and Limitations," in John C. Hopkins an Weixing Hu (eds), *Strategic Views from the Second Tier* (below, 1994), pp. 211-235.

Boyer, Yves. "French and British Nuclear Forces in an Era of Uncertainty," Patrick J. Garrity and Steven A. Maaranen (eds), *Nuclear Weapons in the Changing World*, pp. 111-126.

Dillon, G. M. *Defence Policy Making: A Comparative Analysis* (Leicester University Press, 1988).

Drell, Sidney D. "Reducing Nuclear Danger: Reflections on the Roles of France, China, and Britain, and on a Test Ban," in John C. Hopkins an Weixing Hu (eds), *Strategic Views from the Second Tier* (below, 1994), pp. 239-248.

Goldschmidt, Bertrand (Geroges M. Temmer trans.). *Atomic Rivals* (New Brunswick, NJ: Rutgers University Press, 1990).

Larkin, Bruce D. "Second-Tier Nuclear States and Prospects for Deep Cuts in Nuclear Weapons," in Klaus Gottstein (ed), *Aspects of Security Policy in a New Europe* (Munich: Forschungsstelle Gottstein in der Max-Planck-Gesellschaft, 1994), pp. 46-67.

McLean, Scilla (ed). *How Nuclear Weapons Decisions Are Made* (London: Macmillan, with the Oxford Research Group, 1986).

Miall, Hugh. *Nuclear Weapons: Who's in Charge?* (London: Macmillan, with the Oxford Resarch Group, 1987).

Norris, Robert S., Andrew S. Burrows and Richard W. Fieldhouse. *Nuclear Weapons Databook. Volume V. British, French, and Chinese Nuclear Weapons* (San Francisco: Westview Press, 1994). Natural Resources Defense Council.

Quester, Geroge H. "British, French, and Chinese Nuclear Forces: Old Issues and New," in John C. Hopkins and Weixing Hu (eds), *Strategic Views from the Second Tier* (below, 1994), pp. 249-268.

Yost, David. *Western Europe and Nuclear Weapons* (Livermore, California: Center for Security and Technology Studies, 1993).

COLLECTIONS (SELECTED COUNTRY STUDIES FROM THESE VOLUMES ARE CITED SEPARATELY)

Ball, Desmond and Jeffrey Richelson. *Strategic Nuclear Targeting* (Ithaca: Cornell University Press, 1986).

Boyer, Yves, Pierre Lellouche and John Roper (eds). *Franco-British Defence Cooperation: A New Entente Cordiale?* (London and Paris: Routledge for the Royal Institute of Inteernational Affairs and L'Institut Français des Relations Internationales, 1989).

Garrity, Patrick and Steven Maaranen. *Nuclear Weapons in the Changing World* (New York: Plenum Press, 1992).

Heuser, Beatrice (ed). *Nuclear Weapons and the Future of European Security* (London: Brassey's, for the Centre for Defence Studies, King's College, University of London, October 1991). London Defence Studies 8.

Hopkins, John C. and Weixing Hu (eds). *Strategic Views from the Second Tier: The Nulear Weapons Policies of France, Britain, and China* (San Diego, California: University of California Institute on Global Conflict and Cooperation, 1994).

Karp, Regina Cowen. *Security with Nuclear Weapons? Different Perspectives on National Security* (New York: Oxford University Press, 1991).

Britain

AUTHORITATIVE TEXTS

United Kingdom. Central Office of Information. Reference Pamphlet No 329/89. *Britain and Arms Control: A Chronology.* August 1989.

United Kingdom. DOGD 80/23, July 1980. "The Future United Kingdom Strategic Nuclear Deterrent Force." Paragraphs 9-12 are appended to Michael Quinlan, "British Nuclear Weapons Policy: Past, Present, and Future," *below*.

United Kingdom. House of Commons. Session 1992-93. Defence Committee. Sixth Report. *The Progress of the Trident Programme*. 16 June 1993.

United Kingdom. House of Commons. Session 1993-94. Defence Committee. Second Report. *Progress of the Trident Programme*. 4 May 1994.

United Kingdom. Ministry of Defence. Cm 2201. Departmental Report by the Ministry of Defence. *The Government's Expenditure Plans 1993/94 to 1995/96*. HMSO, February 1993.

United Kingdom. Ministry of Defence. Cm 2270. Statement to Parliament by the Secretary of State for Defence. *Defending Our Future. Statement on the Defence Estimates 1993*. HMSO, July 1993.

United Kingdom. Ministry of Defence. *The Safety of UK Nuclear Weapons.* Report of the review conducted by a working group led by the MoD's Chief Scientific Adviser. July 1992.

ANALYSES AND DISCUSSIONS

Croft, Stuart and Phil Williams. "The United Kingdom," in Regina Cowen Karp (ed), *Security with Nuclear Weapons?*, pp. 145-161.

Freedman, Lawrence. *Britain and Nuclear Weapons* (London: Macmillan, for the Royal Institute of International Affairs, 1980).

Freedman, Lawrence. "British Nuclear Targeting," in Desmond Ball and Jeffrey Richelson (eds), *Strategic Nuclear Targeting*, pp. 109-126.

Gowing, Margaret. *Britain and Atomic Energy, 1939-1945* (New York: St. Martin's Press, 1964).

Gowing, Margaret, assisted by Lorna Arnold. *Independence and Deterrence. Britain and Atmoic Energy, 1945-1952* (New York: St. Martin's Press, 1974). Two volumes.

Gregory, Shaun. *The Hidden Cost of Deterrence: Nuclear Weapons Accidents* (London: Brassey's, 1990)

Hoffman, Mark. *United Kingdom Arms Control in the 1990s* (New York: Manchester University Press, 1990).

Keohane, Dan. *Labour Party Defence Policy Since 1945* (Leicester: Leicester University Press, 1993).

Marsh, Catherine and Colin Fraser (eds). *ublic Opinion and Nuclear Weapons* (London: Macmillan, 1989).

Pierre, Andrew J. *Nuclear Politics: The British Experience with an Independent Strategic Force, 1939-1970* (London: Oxford University Press, 1972).

Quinlan, Michael. "British Nuclear Weapons Policy: Past, Present, and Future," in John C. Hopkins and Weixing Hu (eds), *Strategic Views from the Second Tier* (*above*, 1994), pp. 126-140.

Scott, Len. "Spirit of the Age or Ghost from the Past? Labour and Nuclear Disarmament in the 1990s," *Political Quarterly* (London), v 62 n 2, pp. 193-203.

Simpson, John. *The Independent Nuclear State: the United States, Britain, and the Military Atom* (London: Macmillan, 1986).

Stevenson, John. Third Party Politics since 1945: Liberals, Alliance and Liberal Democrats (Oxford: Blackwell, 1993). Institute of Contemporary British History.

Tugendhat, Christopher and William Wallace. *Options for British Foreign Policy in the 1990s* (London: Routledge, for the Royal Institute of International Affairs, 1988).

France

AUTHORITATIVE TEXTS

France. Commissariat à l'Energie Atomique. Rapport annuel. [Annual]

David, Dominique. *La Politique de Défense de la France: Textes et Documents* (Paris: FEDN (Fondation pour les Études de Défense Natinale), 1989.

France. Assemblée Nationale. N° 2877. Projet de Loi de Programmation relatif à l'équipement militaire et aux effectifs de la défense pour les années 1992-1994. 3 July 1992.

France. Assemblée Nationale. Commission de la défense. Rapport d'information n° 847. *La simulation des essais nucléaires*. René Galy-Dejean, Jacques Baumel, Jean-Michel Boucheron, Daniel Colin, Pierre Favre, and Pierre Lellouche. 15 December 1993.

France. Office of the President. "Texte intégral du plan français de désarmement." 3 June 1991. *Le Monde*, 3 June 1991.

France. *Livre blanc sur la défense*. 1994.

ANALYSES AND DISCUSSIONS

Barrillot, Bruno. "French Finesse Nuclear Future," in *The Bulletin of the Atomic Scientists*, v 48 n 7, September 1992, pp. 23-26.

Barrillot, Bruno. *Rapport relatif aux coûts cachés du programme Triomphant depuis 1982*. (Lyon and Paris: Centre de Documentation et de Recherche sur la Paix et les Conflits and Greenpeace—France, 25 May 1994).

Barrillot, Bruno and M. Davis. *Les déchets nucléaires militaires français*. (Lyon: CDRPC, 1994).

Boniface, Pascal. "La dissuasion nucléaire dans la relation franco-allemande," *Relations internationales et stratégiques* N° 10, Été 1993, pp. 19-25.

Boniface, Pascal. *Vive la Bombe : Éloge de la dissuasion nucléaire* (Paris: Edition•1, 1992).

Boyer, Yves. "French and British Nuclear Forces in an Era of Uncertainty," Patrick J. Garrity and Steven A. Maaranen (eds), *Nuclear Weapons in the Changing World*, pp. 111-126.

Chilton, Patricia. ""French Nuclear Weapons," in Jolyon Howorth and Patricia Chilton (eds), *Defence and Dissent in Contemporary France* (London: Croom Helm, 1984), pp. 135-169.

David, Dominique. *La politique de défense de la France* (Paris: FEDN, 1989).

Duval, Marcel and Yves Le Baut. *L'arme nucléaire française; Pourquoi et comment?* (Paris: SPM, 1992).

Gallois, Pierre M. *Livre noir sur la Défense* (Paris: Payot, 1994).

GREFHAN (Groupe d'Etudes Français d'Histoire de l'Armement Nucléaire), Institut de France. *Les Expérimentations Nucléaires Françaises*. Paris, 1993.

Hébert, Jean-Paul. *Stratégie Française & Industrie d'Armement* (Paris: Fondation pour les études de défense nationale, 1991).

IFRI (Institut français des relations internationales). *La guerre des satellites: enjeux pour la communauté internationale* (Paris: IFRI, 1987.

Laird, Robbin. *France, the Soviet Union, and the Nuclear Weapons Issue* (Boulder, Colorado: Westview Press, Inc., 1985).

Morel, Benoit. "French Nuclear Weapons and the New World Order," in John C. Hopkins and Weixing Hu (eds), *Strategic Views from the Second Tier* (*above*, 1994), pp. 105-118).

Schubert, Klaus. "France," in Regina Cowen Karp (ed), *Security with Nuclear Weapons?*, pp. 162-188.

Ullman, Richard H. "The Covert French Connection," in *Foreign Policy* no. 75, summer 1989, pp. 3-33.

Yost, David S. "French Nuclear Targeting," Desmond Ball and Jeffrey Richelson (eds), *Strategic Nuclear Targeting* (*above*, 1986), pp. 127-156.

Yost, David S. "Nuclear Weapons Issues in France," in John C. Hopkins and Weixing Hu (eds), *Strategic Views from the Second Tier* (*above*, 1994), pp. 19-104.

China

Authoritative Texts

China. Shenjian Chapter of the Ministry of Nuclear Industry. *A Secret Journey: The Story of the Birth of China's First Atomic Bomb* (Beijing: Atomic Energy Press, 1985).

China. *Break the Nuclear Monopoly, Eliminate Nuclear Weapons* (Beijing: Foreign Languages Press, 1965). Contains:

- Statement of the Government of the People's Republi of China (October 16, 1964)
- Press Communique on the Explosion of the First Atom Bomb (October 16, 1964)
- Press Communique on the Explosion of the Second Atom Bomb (May 14, 1965)
- Premier Chou En-lai (Zhou Enlai) Cables Government Heads of the World (October 17, 1964)
- Break the Nuclear Monopoly, Eliminate Nuclear Weapons (*Renmin Ribao* Editorial, October 22, 1964)
- New Starting Point for Efforts to Ban Nuclear Weapons Completely (*Renmin Ribao* Editorial, November 22, 1964)

China. Statement of the Chinese Government. Advocating the Complete . . . Prohibition of Nuclear Weapons . . . 31 July 1963. *Peking Review*, n 31 1963, 2 August 1963, pp. 7-8.

China. Statement of Vice-Premier and Foreign Minister Qian Qichen to the 49th Session of the UN General Assembly, 28 September 1994. *Beijing Review*, v 37 n 41, 10-16 October 1994.

Analyses and Discussions

Lewis, John Wilson and Hua Di. "China's Ballistic Missile Programs: Technologies, Strategies, Goals," in *International Security* vol. 17 no. 2, Fall 1992, pp. 3-40.

Lewis, John Wilson and Xue Litai. *China Builds the Bomb* (Stanford, California: Stanford University Press, 1988).

Lewis, John Wilson and Xue Litai. *China's Strategic Seapower: The Politics of Force Modernization in the Nuclear Age* (Stanford: Stanford University Press, 1994).

Lewis, John Wilson, Hua Di, and Xue Litai. "Beijing's Defense Establishment: Solving the Arms-Export Enigma," in *International Security* vol. 15 no. 4,

Spring 1991, pp. 87-109.

Naughton, Barry. "The Third Front: Defence Industrialization in the Chinese Interior," in *The China Quarterly* n 115, September 1988, pp. 351-386.

Shambaugh, David L. "China's National Security Research Bureaucracy," in *The China Quarterly* n 110, June 1987, pp. 276-304.

Xue Litai, "Evolution of China's Nuclear Strategy," in John C. Hopkins and Weixing Hu (eds), *Strategic Views from the Second Tier* (*above*, 1994), pp. 167-189. Based on Chapters 9 and 10 of Lewis and Xue, *China's Strategic Seapower*, above.

Other Useful Materials

Bundy, McGeorge, William J. Crowe, Jr., and Sidney D. Drell, *Reducing Nuclear Danger: The Road Away From the Brink* (New York: Council on Foreign Relations, 1993).

Forsberg, Randall. "Confining the Military to Defense as a Route to Disarmament," in *World Policy* v 1 n 2, Winter 1984, pp. 285-318.

Goldblat, Josef and David Cox (eds). *Nuclear Weapon Tests: Prohibition or Limitation?* (Oxford: Oxford University Press, 1988). A study of the Stockhom International Peace Research Institute and the Canadian Institute for Peace and Security.

Goldschmidt, Bertrand. *The Atomic Complex: A Worldwide Political History of Nuclear Energy* (La Grange Park, Illinois: American Nuclear Society, 1982).

Gorbachev, Mikahil. "Nuclear Disarmament by the Year 2000." 15 January 1986.

Joeck, Neil and Herbert York. *Countdown on the Comprehensive Test Ban.* Institute on Global Conflict and Cooperation, University of California, and the Ploughshares Fund, Inc.

Kohl, Wilfrid. *French Nuclear Diplomacy* (Princeton: Princeton University Press, 1971).

Lakoff, Sanford (ed). *Beyond Start?* Institute on Global Conflict and Cooperation, University of California. IGCC Policy Paper No. 7. 1988. Incorporates the study *Strategic Stability Under the Conditions of Radical Nuclear Arms Reduction* by a working group of the Committee of Soviet Scientsts for Peace, Against the Nuclear Threat, and comment on the study.

Newhouse, John. *De Gaulle and the Anglo-Saxons* (New York: Viking, 1970).

Quester, George. "Conceptions of Nuclear Threshold Status," Regina Cowen Karp (ed), *Security with Nuclear Weapons?*, pp. 209-228.

Sagan, Scott D. *The Limits of Safety: Organizations, Accidents, and Nuclear Weapons* (Princeton: Princeton University Press, 1993).

SIPRI Yearbook. (Annually since 1968/69). Stockholm International Peace Research Institute.

United States. The Library of Congress. Congressional Research Service. *Non-Proliferation: A Compiliation of Basic Documents on the International, U.S. Statutory, and U.S. Executive Branch Components of Non-Proliferation Policy.* Zachary S. Davis and Warren H. Donnelly (compilers). 18 December 1990.

Index

WIDENER UNIVERSITY
WOLFGRAM
LIBRARY
CHESTER, PA.